Cannabis in Costa Rica

A Study of
Chronic Marihuana Use

Cannabis in Costa Rica

A Study of Chronic Marihuana Use

Edited by
William E. Carter

 ISHI A Publication of the
Institute for the Study of Human Issues
Philadelphia

Library of Congress Cataloging in Publication Data:

Main entry under title:

Cannabis in Costa Rica.

    Bibliography: p.
    Includes index.
    1. Marihuana—Psychological aspects. 2. Marihuana—Physiological aspects.
3. Drug Abuse—Costa Rica. I. Carter, William E.
BF209.C3C36   615'.7827   80–14726
ISBN 0–89727–008–8

For information, write: **90254**

Director of Publications
ISHI
3401 Science Center
Philadelphia, Pennsylvania 19104
U.S.A.

To the memory of Eleanor Carroll,
tireless champion of the human factor in drug research

Contents

Contributors

Linda Phillips Arizmendi is a nutritionist at Colorado State University in Fort Collins.

William E. Carter, Ph.D. is Chief of the Hispanic Division at the Library of Congress.

Wilmer Coggins, M.D. is Professor of Community Health and Medicine at the University of Florida in Gainesville.

William Dawson, Ph.D. is Professor of Ophthalmology and Physiology at the University of Florida in Gainesville.

Claudine G. De Frenkel, M.A. is Instructor in Anthropology at the Universidad de Costa Rica in San José.

Paul L. Doughty, Ph.D. is Professor of Anthropology at the University of Florida in Gainesville.

Alvaro Fernandez, M.D. is with Hospital México in San José, Costa Rica.

Jack M. Fletcher, Ph.D. is involved in child development research at the Texas Research Institute of Mental Sciences in Houston.

Juan Hernandez G., M.D. is with Hospital Calderón Guardia in San José, Costa Rica.

Mary Anna Hovey is a sociologist in Gainesville, Florida.

Carlos Francisco Jimenez A., M.D. is with Hospital México in San José, Costa Rica.

Ismet Karacan, M.D. is Professor of Psychiatry at Baylor College of Medicine in Houston.

Dina Krauskopf, Lic. is a psychologist in San José, Costa Rica.

John Bryan Page, Ph.D. is Research Instructor of Psychiatry at the University of Miami.

Ian Rawson, Ph.D. is Assistant Professor of Anthropology at the University of Pittsburgh.

Paul Satz, Ph.D. is Professor of Clinical Psychology at the University of Florida in Gainesville.

Joaquin Roberto Solano C., Lic. is Director of Laboratories at Hospital México in San José, Costa Rica.

Edward Swenson, M.D. is with Syntex Research in Palo Alto.

William R. True, Ph.D. is Specialist in Public Health at Veterans Hospital in Saint Louis.

Foreword

The easy generalizations so often made about marihuana use tend not to reflect reality. Research increasingly indicates that the reasons for and results of such use are not the same for all groups and are not the same through time; a full understanding of the impact of the drug on human life can come only through knowledge from a wide range of social and cultural settings.

Costa Rica is one such setting. Many nuances of traditional use in that country vary markedly from patterns of use as we know them in the United States and western Europe. Yet, Costa Rica has long maintained close ties with the United States and Europe and experienced heavy cultural influences from these quarters. For this reason, in spite of some difference in use patterns, the experience of Costa Rican urban marihuana users, especially of those who live in San José, is of direct relevance for societies such as our own.

Up to the time the Costa Rican research began, no intensive investigations of the effects of chronic cannabis use had been carried out on a noninstitutionalized Latin American population (unless one includes Jamaica in Latin America). This partly explains why Costa Rican authorities in the Ministry of Health were anxious that such research be done in their country and why they offered their full support from the very beginning. Official Costa Rican concern about the effects of marihuana was and is great, in some degree mirroring concern in the United States.

The support of the Ministry of Health held a significance far and above what it would in most countries. The legal code of Costa Rica specifies that all research on drugs be coordinated through the Ministry of Health and that police and other law-enforcement authorities offer their full cooperation for such research (Ministerio de Salubridad 1974: art. 114). Such legal sanction was of great importance for the full and proper execution of the research.

Dr. Socorro Rodriguez, as subdirector of mental health, was the first strong sponsor of the research in the Ministry. By the time the project got underway, however, Dr. Rodriguez had left for postdoctoral training in Chile and had asked that Licenciada Virginia Ramírez de Barquero, director of the Departamento de Drogas Estupefacientes, coordinate our efforts. From that time forward, Lic. Barquero played a significant role in the conduct of the research. She saw to it that we obtained proper legal guarantees from the Ministry of Security and that these guarantees were extended to our subjects. This was no mean feat. That we were conducting a scientific study and needed legal safeguards for ourselves and our subjects was seen by some narcotics officials as a threat to their legitimate operations. They felt, quite properly, that, having been given the mission to enforce laws regarding the sale, production, and possession of cannabis, they could not close down their operation. Their hesitancy led to a lengthy round of interviews and explanations with various authorities and eventually involved even the wife of the then Costa Rican President, José Figueres. It was fortunate, in all these negotiations, that we were able to count on the strong support of the United States Embassy.

In addition to these formal relationships, essential for the conduct of the sociocultural phase of the research, others were needed for the medical phase. For this purpose, through Ministry of Health officials, we were introduced to Dr. Federico Faerrón, director of the Hospital Mexico, Costa Rica's principal social security hospital. It was then with Dr. Faerrón's assistance and support that Costa Rican medical research personnel were recruited to codirect and execute specialized parts of the study.

Once this groundwork was laid, it became possible to finalize the research design in consultation with our Costa Rican colleagues. Overall, the research design had thus represented two years of planning, consultation, and study and had involved several dozen persons in both the United States and Costa Rica.

Most essential of all, of course, were the many working-class Costa Ricans who participated enthusiastically in the study, often at the cost of personal discomfort, inconvenience, and even jeopardy. Their unflagging interest in scientific inquiry was a constant encouragement to those of us charged with collecting and analyzing the materials.

As is evident from the extensive list of authors, the project was in every way a coordinated team effort. Funding came from the National Institute on Drug Abuse (NIDA), through contract no. NO1-MH3-0233 (ND). General project development and coordination were handled by William Carter. Wilmer Coggins planned, coordinated, and supervised all biomedical and psychological studies. Paul Doughty shared with Carter supervision of the anthropological studies. William True and Bryan Page carried the brunt of the very difficult fieldwork.

Most of the remaining individuals who made major contributions to the research are included in the list of Contributors. A few who are not listed there, however, deserve special mention. In Costa Rica, Zulema Villalta de Brenes proved to be an outstanding stenographer, and she and her husband superb logistics coordinators. Walter Serrano also assisted in these efforts. At the University of Florida, Richard Chiofolo played an indispensable role in statistical processing and computer analysis, Steny Guilarte served as project secretary, and Tulia Allen typed the original final report in both Spanish and English. Subsequently, in La Paz, Bolivia, Ann Robison Carttar patiently prepared the revised manuscript for publication.

The person on the University of Florida campus who originally brought together researchers from NIDA and the university was Dr. Elizabeth Eddy, then director of the university's Urban Studies Bureau. Once this contact was made, the sincere interest and continuous support of two NIDA project officers,

Ms. Eleanor Carroll and Dr. Stephen Szara, were of key importance. Without their firm belief in the need for studying marihuana use cross-culturally and in the fullest possible context, the project would never have come to fruition.

William E. Carter, Editor
Washington, D.C.

1/ The Problem

Until the 1960s, "traditional" marihuana users in the United States tended to be lower-class members of ethnic or racial minority groups, or artists such as musicians and movie actors. By the latter part of that decade, however, marihuana use had greatly expanded and had become associated with generational conflicts, protest movements, and antiestablishment currents of all types. Few of the individuals who turned to marihuana during those years could have been called heavy users. Because of cost, risk, and lack of any great popular experience or history of use, only 9 percent smoked more than four or five marihuana cigarettes a week (Shafer et al. 1972: 40–64). By international standards, this could hardly have been called chronic use. Yet the large numbers of people turning to the drug heightened public concern over its potential effects, effects that could be fully understood only through the study of populations who had used the drug for a longer period, with greater intensity, and who, except for the nearly universal drugs of alcohol and tobacco, had not become poly-drug users.

In other areas of the world, marihuana use has been more widespread, heavier, and of greater duration. In parts of Africa, India, and Central and South America, many individuals have traditionally smoked marihuana in quantities equaling daily tobacco smoking in the United States. This being the case, and with a growing demand for scientific knowledge about the long-range effects of the drug, it is logical to turn to other countries and peoples for answers we cannot find at home.

The study of marihuana use in other cultures can broaden our knowledge in a number of ways. As in the case of other drugs, the perceived effects of marihuana have varied substantially from culture to culture and from setting to setting. While such variations may complicate research, they also provide a richness and a dimension of considerable importance to the understanding of human behavior. In looking at marihuana in the United States alone, we run the risk of becoming entrapped in the narrow confines of our own cultural viewpoints, and we may generalize too amply from samples restricted to only one cultural experience. During its long history, marihuana has been widely diffused, used in many environments, and, until recently, subjected to virtually no regulation. It has been considered divine and sacred, a multipurpose medicine, a stimulant, a depressant, an aphrodisiac, a stupefier, and a giver of euphoria.

Heavy use in a society like Costa Rica can help us answer many remaining questions regarding its chronic effects. Unlike most chronic users in the United States and Europe, those in Costa Rica have not been heavily involved with more potent substances such as heroin, morphine, and cocaine. Except for their simultaneous use of tobacco and alcohol, for which adequate controls can be developed, they have not been poly-drug users. Their primary recreational drug has been and is marihuana, and thus they are a nearly ideal population from which to learn about chronic effects of that much debated substance.

Although traditional marihuana users in Costa Rica differ in these important respects from traditional users in the United States and Europe, the country as such is very much a part of the Western world. Costa Rica has long maintained close ties with the United States and Europe and has received heavy cultural impact from these areas. The changing role of marihuana itself stands as a case in point. Until a few years ago, its use was confined to a minority of the adult working class, mainly males. During the late 1960s and early 1970s, however, coinciding with similar developments in the United States and Europe, marihuana use rapidly diffused into the middle and upper classes, particularly among the country's youth. Conservative estimates are that at least 25 percent of all university students have tried the drug and that its use has also spread to secondary schools. This diffusion of what was formerly a lower-class trait to more privileged groups has produced an enormous interest and concern among government officials, who are as anxious to learn about the drug and its implications for human behavior and health as are their counterparts in the United States and western Europe.

Clear differences in use patterns separate traditional Costa Rican lower-class users from those newer ones who have attained university and high school levels of education. While both groups also use tobacco and alcohol, only a few of the former have had experience with other drugs, and this has tended to be sporadic. By contrast, high school and university student users have tended toward poly-drug use, mixing barbiturates and amphetamines (but rarely heroin or cocaine) freely with marihuana.

At first we had hoped to work with both traditional users and new users. But the fact that few of this newer type had smoked marihuana long enough to be considered chronic users (by our definition, ten years or more) discouraged us from the outset. We also found that users with a high level of education and/or a privileged social status were reluctant to become involved. They had too much to lose. By simply being identified with research on the effects of chronic marihuana use they could jeopardize their futures. Another problem was the fact that they had indulged, often heavily, in other drugs. Thus, even if we could have located among their group individuals who had smoked marihuana for ten years or longer, we would have had no way of knowing whether observed abnormalities would have been due to marihuana use or to the use of barbiturates, amphetamines, or even LSD. Reluctantly, then, we concluded that we would have to limit our focus to Costa Rica's traditional users, that is, to members of the working class who followed patterns of use that had been common in the country for at least two generations.

In assessing the impact of any drug on the human organism, one of the first tasks is to separate out a large number of basic social and biological factors that in themselves could account for problems of social, psychological, or physical health. To accomplish this, we decided to search for a baseline population of approximately eighty users and to balance this population with approximately twice as many nonusers of the same ages, economic and educational levels, marital status, and occupational categories. Because practically all Costa Rica's marihuana users simultaneously use alcohol and tobacco, we also had to balance the population for levels of use of these two drugs. The responsibility of developing this baseline sample of users and controls rested with three young anthropologists. Since we planned to use the same sample for all phases of the research, everything depended on their initial success.

The confrontation with a large metropolitan area such as San José, the capital of Costa Rica, was a matter of concern. The city contained 437,000 persons. How could one go about finding marihuana users in such a mass of people, particularly when the drug was prohibited and marihuana smokers were actively pursued by the narcotics police? How could such individuals be sampled? What controls could be employed? Where would the users live and work? Would they, and their respective controls, agree to cooperate with the demands we would have to make of them? We were not dealing with institutional settings such as prisons or universities wherein one can find willing or coercible subjects for almost any purpose. By design and necessity our subjects had to come voluntarily from the open ranks of society. They would have to be free to retire from the project when they wished. The dilemma haunted us from the outset of the study, for we ran the risk of losing our subjects at critical moments and after considerable investment. On finishing the study, however, much to our surprise and pleasure, we realized we had been overly apprehensive; we had lost only one subject.

In searching for their baseline sample, the anthropologists employed a basic technique of their profession: participant observation. They went into neighborhoods and talked and interacted with the people who lived and worked there, renewing contacts day after day. Bars, street corners, stores, places of work, and homes were frequented until, slowly, acquaintanceships were built up and confidences established. The anthropologists found, just as their colleagues had experienced elsewhere, that once they had achieved a modicum of friendship with a subject and developed mutual confidence, they had great freedom and opportunity for inquiry. Eventually they discovered that no topic was out of bounds.

The intimacy of the research, the topic, and the interpersonal confidences established created a complicated situation. With freedom of inquiry came a heavy responsibility. A subject would give confidential information about himself, and by doing so would make himself vulnerable. How could the researcher protect such confidence and repay it? Such a question, in these circumstances, was especially poignant because, relative to the economically poor subject population, we were affluent and influential individuals representing highly endowed and powerful institutions.

There were heavy responsibilities and moral and legal dilemmas on every hand. If the researchers were to be effective, association with the project by any subject could not result in his suffering gratuitous and involuntary punishments.

Yet a cooperating individual might, simply because of his association with the project, be accused—rightly or wrongly—of drug-law violations.

Protection extended by the Costa Rican Ministry of Health and Ministry of Security was a step in helping us out of this problem, but it by no means solved it entirely. During the two and a half years that the project lasted, the field staff often appeared as character witnesses on behalf of subjects and other persons in the general study population.

In carrying out an initial medical screening, various illnesses and health problems came to light. Where possible, the project actively aided all subjects who had some problems finding effective assistance. In most cases, this meant referring them to the appropriate section of public health institutions and hospitals run by the national social security system. In some, eyeglasses were purchased by the project for people who had never had the opportunity to acquire them or who never realized they needed them. Thus there were a number of real, practical rewards for those who participated in the research as subjects.

During the course of the research, we discovered that many subjects understood the scientific dimension of their participation. For a number of them, participation in the study was a matter of considerable personal pride, and several subjects, both users and controls, indicated that it was the most important thing they had ever done.

RESEARCH DESIGN AND METHOD

In all, the research lasted some thirty months. During the first twelve months, a base sample of 84 users and 156 nonusers was selected and screened. From this population, we then developed a carefully matched subsample of 41 users and 41 nonusers for detailed research during the second year of the study. All users in both the base and the matched-pair samples smoked marihuana regularly (most on a daily basis) and had smoked the drug for more than ten years prior to our meeting them.

We do not pretend that our samples were representative of all Costa Ricans or of all Costa Rican marihuana smokers. Because of the secrecy and controversy of marihuana use in general, no representative sample of users has been made in any study to date. Our base sample of 240 subjects was stratified and purposive. It was male, urban, and representative of the stratum of society that could be termed "working class." We can only guess at possible results had the sample focused on females, rural dwellers, or other social groups or classes.

The fact that the sample represents various occupations, standards of living, residences, and lifestyles allows us to ascertain whether the use of marihuana is associated with certain occupations. Yet the sample cannot be taken as statistically representative, nor can sample norms be generalized to all of Costa Rican society.

This is not to say that our statistical analyses lack validity. The control procedure of matching users and nonusers on the variables of age, economic and educational levels, marital status, occupational categories, and alcohol and tobacco consumption ensures that any differences found between the users and nonusers are not due to differences in these basic control variables. Thus, valid comparisons between subgroups of the sample are possible.

Random selection of the sample was impossible; such selection can be made only when records for the entire population exist. In a nation where there is one large central city and many small hamlets, taking a random sample of locations can easily lead to results that do not reflect reality; the inclusion of the one city would inflate the sample, and the exclusion of that city would deflate it. Thus our subject population should be seen as skewed to this extent.

No one knows precisely the overall distribution of users and nonusers in Costa Rica. On the basis of over two years of interviewing and participant observation, however, we have reason to believe that marihuana use is not randomly found or represented in all strata of society. Until recently, use was limited to particular sections of the country, and to date its use is still more widespread among males than among females.

In recruiting the sample, to qualify as a marihuana consumer, a subject had to have used the drug for at least ten years at a minimum rate of three cigarettes per week. As it turned out, our users smoked much more, averaging almost ten cigarettes per day (2.0 gm of material or 24–70 mg of THC) for the previous decade.

Each individual selected had to agree to cooperate in the many interviews and observations of a medical and social nature over an eighteen- to twenty-four-month period. As each was selected, he was administered a general questionnaire and interviewed concerning family, social relations, and economic status. Each had to be free of any disease that would impair his performance in the study. To determine this, all subjects were screened through a standard medical, mental, and physical examination during the first twelve months of the research. An upper age limit of fifty years was imposed in order to restrict, to some extent, the effects of aging. Finally, all subjects were given a series of clinical and laboratory tests:

> *Blood count:*   Hemoglobin, hematocrit, white-blood-cell count, white-blood-cell differential and erythrocyte sedimentation rate
>
> *Blood chemistry:*   Fasting blood sugar, blood sugar two hours after a 100 gm glucose load serum glutamic-pyruvic transaminase, urea nitrogen, prothrombin time, alkaline phosphatase and serum protein electrophoresis
>
> *Urinalysis:*   Standard urinalysis for pH, specific gravity, protein, sugar, and microscopic examination
>
> *Stool examination:*   Single specimen for ova, parasites, and occult blood
>
> *Serological test for syphilis:*   Venereal Disease Research Laboratories test
>
> *Chest X-ray:*   Standard 14″ x 17″ posteroanterior and lateral views
>
> *Electrocardiogram:*   Standard 12 lead, resting ECG
>
> *Visual-function screening test:*   Snellen acuity, refraction, slit lamp examination, applanation tonometry, fundus inspection by ophthalmoscope, color vision using Ishihara test plates

All screening tests were performed single-blind, so that the examiner would have no prior knowledge as to whether the subject was a user or a nonuser.

Physicians and all laboratory and technical personnel understood the need for subject anonymity and for objectivity in evaluating the results of the screening tests. Each subject was assigned a number that was subsequently used as the *only* identification for *all* interviews, tests, and screening procedures.

Although we recognized the potential effect on the outcome of the study of screening out from the study group individuals with certain illnesses, we felt that the benefits in doing so far outweighed potential problems:

1. Subjects with illnesses of chronic relapsing nature, such as tuberculosis, or of a highly recidivistic nature, such as syphilis, might have alterations in their physiologic status during the course of the study, caused either by the disease process itself or by the drug therapy.

2. The research design, consisting of detailed studies of carefully matched pairs, would be impaired by matching one individual with a serious illness with another who did not have that illness; it would have been impossible to match subjects for illness as well as for the six basic variables for which we did control.

3. The initial method of subject selection was based on social networks. This preempted any conclusions that might have been drawn about disease incidence in the study sample.

Because of such considerations, we made a sharp distinction between potential subjects with a diagnosable disease and those who simply had abnormalities. Subjects in whom problems were found during the physical examinations or in laboratory, chest X-ray, electrocardiogram, or eye examinations were excluded only if our findings led to the diagnosis of a specific disease state. Further exclusions were made only if an impaired function directly threatened participation in the special test batteries designed for the matched-pair study.

Once all preliminary screening had been completed, forty-one pairs of subjects were matched for more exhaustive and careful studies. The criteria for matching were the following:

1. *Age:* We defined a range of plus or minus four years as the acceptable tolerance between subject and control. The vast majority of matches were within two years.

2. *Marital status:* This was difficult to define, given the unstable nature of many of the pairings. Stable free-union and stable marriage were equated. Serial involvement with women was distinguished from lack of experience with women. Martial status changed with some of the subjects as we were working with them. Therefore we had to be quite flexible with this criterion.

3. *Education:* We defined education as none, primary incomplete, primary complete, secondary incomplete, and secondary complete. In calculating years of formal instruction, we took into account institutional socialization such as time in the reformatory or seminary. Generally we accepted subjects within one "step" of their match. Thus, a user with four years of primary might be matched with a nonuser who had completed all six years of primary.

4. *Occupation:* To match on occupation, we decided that it was not necessary to demand the identical job in the match. We equated all artisan crafts and trades such as construction, shoemaking, and tailoring and matched them interchangeably. We decided to do this after observing that the subjects often knew several of these trades and orbited among them depending on the market for services. We did not match between white-collar occupations and the trades and crafts.

5. *Alcohol consumption:* We designed a question sequence, modified from an instrument of the Costa Rican Center for Studies on Alcoholism, which scaled alcohol consumption on a 0 to 17 scale. We accepted matches between subjects scoring within four points of each other, eliminating those whose consumption was at the top of the scale.

6. *Tobacco consumption:* We determined the number of pack years the subject smoked, and we matched the control within a range of plus or minus two pack-years.

Matching was done by finding a nonuser with characteristics very close to those of a user. On the six matching variables, both the group results and the results for each individual pair had to be similar. The fact that we had obtained for the base sample approximately twice as many nonusers as users aided greatly in obtaining close matches. Our logistical sequence was to settle first on the user and then to search for a nonuser. To assure objectivity, the final selection was made by members of the research staff who were not personally acquainted with the subjects. All matching was done on the basis of identification numbers rather than names.

The major purpose for matching each user with a nonuser was to eliminate the six basic matching variables as possible causal factors. Thus, for example, were our results to indicate that marihuana users had significantly lower nutritional levels than nonusers, this difference could not be attributed to alcohol or tobacco consumption or to basic socioeconomic differences between the two groups, as might have happened had the variables not been controlled. To further sharpen our controls, persons who regularly or extensively used other drugs such as barbiturates, amphetamines, or paint thinner were excluded. Also excluded were users of all opiates, cocaine, and similar drugs. Such exclusion created no real problems. As has already been stated, use of these substances is rare in Costa Rica.

Once the matched-pair population had been selected (see Table 1), research on both the sociocultural and biomedical levels intensified. The anthropologists visited the subjects and observed and interviewed them at length, following up on the initial data gathered during the preceding year. Extensive life histories were obtained from the matched pairs, and all users were given in-depth interviews covering their drug-use history and experience. Family characteristics, socialization, institutional and peer-group influences, and personal and social problems were explored in detail. The resulting data were then systematically organized and interfaced with all materials gathered during the first year of the study, as well as with the psychological and medical data that were being collected simultaneously.

Biomedical studies of the matched-pair population were directed at a number of unanswered questions. They included physically noninvasive tests to discriminate subtle evidence of central and peripheral nervous system impairment, because of the repeated assertions that chronic marihuana use leads to brain damage; an evaluation of pulmonary function, because of contradictory evidence on the effects of short-term marihuana smoking; and a measure of testosterone levels, because of the report of Kolodny et al. (1974: 872–874), relating these levels to sexual function in chronic users. Early in the course of the research, improvements of technology for measurement of Delta 9 THC and other cannabinoids in human blood led us to add this measurement as well to the test battery, in conjunction with sleep electroencephalogram observations.

For a time we considered conducting a study of the effects of marihuana upon the chromosomes, in order to test some of the recent hypotheses advanced in this area (Stenchever et al. 1974; C. and R. Leuchtenberger and Ritter 1973; NIDA 1974: 113–114). After considerable thought, however, this portion of the study was dropped because of the lack of a proven method for ascertaining the causes of chromosome damage or change.

Numerous studies of neuropsychological function had preceded the research. Dose-related effects of marihuana on short-term memory and reaction time had been well documented. There was also evidence suggesting that color discrimination was impaired by marihuana use. Whether such effects persisted in long-term users of the drug when they were tested in a drug-free state was, however, unknown.

In tackling the matter of nervous-system function, the problem of selecting tests commonly used in the United States which would be valid when applied to a different cultural group (i.e., Costa Ricans) was given serious consideration. In the end, eleven neuropsychological tests and one personality test were chosen to assess a variety of functions relating to memory, intelligence, neuromuscular function, and motivation. All were standardized in Costa Rica on a pilot sample of eighty-six subjects before being included in the final test battery:

1. Wechsler Adult Intelligence Scale (Wechsler 1965; 1968)
2. Digit Span (M. Williams 1968)
3. Rey-Davis (Nonverbal Learning) Test (M. Williams 1968)
4. Word Learning Test (M. Williams 1968)
5. Delayed Recall (M. Williams 1968)
6. Verbal Memory Task (Wechsler 1965)
7. Facial Recognition Memory Test (University of Florida modified version 1971)
8. Benton Visual Retention Test (Benton 1963)
9. Finger Oscillation Test (Reitan 1964)
10. Halstead Tactual Performance (Reitan 1964)
11. Finger Localization Test (Benton 1956)
12. Cattell 16 PF Test (Cattell 1970)
13. Sentence Completion Test (developed by project staff)

Additional insights as to the possible effect of chronic marihuana use on the central nervous system may come through tests of visual function. Changes in pupillary responses, ocular tension, and subjective appreciation of colors have been repeatedly attributed to the use of marihuana and hashish and have been frequently documented. The possibility of subtle change in eye function through long-term use has, however, been relatively neglected. It is generally accepted that the neural retina of the eye is central nervous system tissue in its embryology. We felt, therefore, that careful evaluation of visual function, using more discriminating tests than those ordinarily employed, could offer an elegant method of assessing nervous system functions using noninvasive techniques.

In consulation with the Visual Committee of the National Academy of Sciences, we designed a special series of tests to delineate subtle changes in visual function under conditions of changing illumination and with stationary and moving test objects. Dark adaptation, measured by the Goldman apparatus, was used as an indication of peripheral retinal function. Following dark adaptation, with the pupils naturally dilated, pupillary response to light was recorded by cine-photo (16 frames/sec.) for 100 seconds, as an indicator of autonomic nervous system function. The rate as well as the magnitude of the pupillary response was measured. Applanation tonometry before and after a one-quart water load was done to define any differences in ocular tension which could be attributed to marihuana use. The Shirmer Test was used to measure lacrimal fluid production. Finally, a sensitive quantitative method of measuring variations in color perception in the red-green group was followed by using the Hecht-Schlaer anomaloscope.

Our final set of measures for evaluating the effect of chronic marihuana smoking on the central nervous system consisted of a series of electroencephalograms taken during sleep for each individual in the matched-pair subsample for eight consecutive nights. The sleep electroencephalogram-electro-oculogram (EEG-EOG) is recognized as a particularly sensitive method of evaluating the effects of drugs, especially the effects of drugs that affect the central nervous system. It is one of the few reasonably nonintrusive methods of monitoring central nervous system activity in the human brain, and in drug evaluation it has several advantages over the waking EEG. First, since there are at least two, and possibly more, distinctly different states of consciousness during sleep, in a sleeping subject one can assess drug effects under a greater variety of natural "conditions" than in a waking one. Second, the sleep EEG-EOG is more clearly organized than the waking EEG, and the brain-wave patterns can be easily categorized as belonging to one of the five distinct stages of sleep. In the normal waking EEG, there is only one recognizable overall pattern. Third, the sleep EEG-EOG is characterized by the periodic occurrence of a number of discrete waveforms, such as sleep spindles, K-complexes, eye movements, and alpha, beta, and delta waves. These waveforms can be analyzed and described in detail by automated methods. There is growing evidence that these waveforms may be the most sensitive aspect of the sleep EEG-EOG with respect to drugs.

In addition to this general reason for employing the sleep EEG-EOG in the study of a drug, there is a more specific reason for using it to study marihuana. One of the frequently reported effects of marihuana is drowsiness or sleepiness. This suggests that the drug may have hypnotic qualities. In fact, some habitual smokers who are insomniacs have reported that they use the drug precisely because it helps them sleep at night. The sleep EEG-EOG is the logical tool for studying the hypnotic effects of a drug. Some investigators have used the sleep EEG-EOG in evaluating the effects of marihuana. The number of subjects has usually been small, however, and methodological defects have often character-ized the studies. Consequently, these studies have not yet provided a clear picture of the acute or the chronic effects of the drug.

The question of the effect of chronic marihuana smoking on pulmonary function is an important one, particularly in light of our growing knowlege of the damage that tobacco can cause to the respiratory system. In approaching this problem, one of our basic tasks was to differentiate the effects of marihuana smoking from those of tobacco smoking. Matching users and nonusers by level of tobacco use gave us considerable control. This we then refined by administer-ing an adapted version of the Chronic Bronchitis Questionnaire that had origi-nally been developed by the British Medical Research Council and was subse-quently employed by the European Coal and Steel Community. This instrument provided us with a detailed history of exposure not only to tobacco smoke but also to fumes, dust, and fungi in occupational settings. It also recorded in detail such pulmonary symptoms as cough, shortness of breath, bloody sputum, and chest pain.

For each member of the forty-one matched pairs we recorded a forced spirogram before and after the inhalation of a bronchodilator (metaproterenol), using a Krogh-type spirometer (Vitalograph). Vital capacity was measured as an estimate of restrictive ventilatory disease. Forced expiratory volume was mea-sured at one second as an indication of large-airways obstruction. Volumes at 25 percent to 75 percent, and 75 percent to 85 percent, of the forced expiratory volume (FEF $_{25-75}$ and FEF $_{75-85}$) were measured as indications of small-airways obstruction. Pulmonary diffusing capacity using the carbon monoxide rebreath-ing technique was then measured as an indication of pulmonary emphysema or pulmonary fibrosis.

The effect of marihuana on sexual function had received little attention from the scientific community until the report of Kolodny et al. in 1974. This study of twenty men showed significantly lower testosterone levels in a user group than in a matched, nonusing control group. When three of the twenty users discontinued marihuana use for two weeks, their plasma testosterone re-turned to higher normal levels. The conclusions, however, were immediately called into question. A separate but almost simultaneous study of plasma testos-terone levels conducted in a closed-ward setting by Mendelson et al. (1974) on a group of twenty-seven young men yielded no evidence of testosterone diminu-tion. The subjects in the Mendelson et al. study were smoking marihuana at levels considerably higher than those reported by Kolodny, but for only twenty-one days. A third study has given still different results. This measured the effects, in a closed-ward setting, of the oral administration of Delta 9 THC. It reported that there were transient decrements in testosterone levels which re-turned to baseline levels when the THC was discontinued (R. Jones, personal communication).

Such conflicting reports on the acute effect of cannabis on plasma testoster-one levels led us to question possible chronic effects. To assess these effects, we collected venous blood samples with subjects in the fasting state at 7:00 A.M. to 8:00 A.M. In thirty-eight of the forty-one matched pairs, the collection was satisfactory and was shipped to laboratories in the United States for analysis. The majority of samples were analyzed by the Reproductive Biology Research Foundation Laboratory in Saint Louis; samples for six subjects—two users and four controls—were analyzed by Bioscience Laboratories in Van Nuys, California.

For drug research in general, the study of chronic effects in natural settings is relatively new. In terms of marihuana, the vast majority of previous research has either focused on acute effects and/or been confined exclusively to laboratory settings. Exceptions have been those studies carried out in Egypt, Jamaica, and Greece. We find it encouraging that the results of the studies in Jamaica and Greece generally corroborate what we learned in Costa Rica. We feel that the somewhat different Egyptian results are easily explainable, and we shall discuss that matter in Chapter 9.

We cannot guarantee that the results of our efforts will be responsibly used by those who read them either in the United States or in Costa Rica. In view of this uncertainty, insofar as participating individuals are concerned we have taken the precaution of substituting pseudonyms for real names and places. For anyone interested in San José as such, reading our work may prove to be a frustrating experience, since familiar *barrio* names and places are disguised. Despite this fact, the thrust and meaning of the research remain.

The pages that follow will not put to rest the many questions surrounding all marihuana use, nor will they settle any moral issues. They will, however, illustrate, illuminate, and broaden our descriptive and analytical views and produce some more refined and sharpened hypotheses. They will not please those whose partisanship on one side or the other of the issue is already defined. What they will describe and analyze are the social, cultural, psychological, and biomedical effects manifested in a population which has chronically smoked an average of nearly ten marihuana cigarettes (2.0 gm of material or exposure to 24–70 mg of THC) per day for a minimum of ten years (mean 16.9 years) prior to the beginning of our two and a half years of intensive research.

2/Marihuana in Costa Rica

HISTORY

When users are asked whether they know anything about the origin of marihuana in Costa Rica, most answer that it was a substance used by the Indians long before the white man discovered the land. Such claims of antiquity are significant, for they reflect the feeling on the part of users that their habit is old and well entrenched in the traditions of their country. From what we know about the worldwide diffusion of cannabis, however, they must be looked upon as false. No historic reference can be found for cannabis or its products during the pre-Columbian period in Costa Rica. Instead, the most comprehensive agricultural history of the country implies that cannabis must have come into Costa Rica through the Spaniards, by including it in a list of important agricultural products introduced to Spain by the Arabs during the Middle Ages (Sáenz Maroto 1970: 55).

The Spanish Crown directly fomented the diffusion of cannabis into the New World. In 1554, officials of the Seville Company advised the Council of the Indies that flax and hemp seeds would be sent in the next embarkation, although nothing is known of their fate (Ayala 1930: II, 384; Haring 1939: 156). Nine years later, in 1563, Philip II openly ordered hemp sown in various parts of the American empire.

This appears to have been the first of many attempts to establish a hemp fiber industry in the Americas. Most were directed at South America, particularly Peru and Chile, but few succeeded (Cappa 1890: VI, 132–133, 134). So it is that in 1607 the Audiencia de Panamá could state categorically that neither hemp nor flax was being harvested within its jurisdiction (Serrano y Sanz 1908: 170). The crop had no better luck in the kingdom of New Granada (Colombia). A description of Tunja, dated 1610, contains the following statement: "Neither is hemp harvested, nor can it be found in the land" (Simón 1953: iii, 315). Even in Peru, hemp production was very limited. Rope for needs such as shipping had to come from Spain (Cobo 1891: II, 418–419; Vázquez de Espinosa 1948: 422, 677; Ruiz 1952: I, 257, 269).

Toward the end of the colonial period, hemp production was again stimulated by the Crown through the offering of free land and tax benefits to those who would initiate it, and a pamphlet was distributed recommending the use of a new mechanical device for separating the fiber. Yet these efforts met with little success. As in previous periods, only Chile maintained or developed the capacity to export the fiber (Patiño 1969: 395; Partridge 1974: 39). For items such as sandals, rope, cordage, sacks, harnesses, and fishnets, other parts of Latin America either imported hemp or used cabuya; cotton took the place of hemp for candlewicks (Patiño 1969: 109; Partridge 1974: 40).

As Partridge has recently noted, the use of cannabis as a psychotropic is a different question from its use for fiber. The cultivation of hemp does not always give rise to cannabis smoking; as an example, cannabis has been exported to Spain from Chile since 1545, but until recently the use of the plant as a psychotropic has not been reported for that country (Partridge 1974: 41; Ardila Rodríguez 1965: 49).

One of the earliest psychotropic uses of cannabis in Latin America seems to have occurred in Brazil. There is considerable linguistic evidence that West African slaves introduced cannabis smoking to that country (Patiño 1969: 405; Walton 1938: 24; Aranugo 1959: 313; Partridge 1974: 40). The ritual use by some Brazilian indigenous groups would seem to indicate an early diffusion (Partridge 1974: 40, referring to Wagley and Galvão 1949: 41), however, to other ethnic enclaves.

With regard to Hispanic America, we know that cannabis was cultivated in Mexico immediately after the first trip of Cortés and that its introduction has been attributed to Pedro Cuadrado, one of the conquistadores. We also know that by 1550 an ordinance had been passed in Mexico prohibiting the cultivation of cannabis, thus indicating its possible use as a psychotropic (Ardila Rodríguez 1965: 48; Partridge 1974: 40).

Even if cannabis had been used psychotropically at such an early date in Mexico, there is little indication that such use diffused widely throughout Central America. For Costa Rica, the earliest printed reference is an 1864 import-tax exemption for hemp cloth used in packing cotton; this would seem to indicate that the fiber (i.e., cannabis) was not locally available (Sáenz Maroto 1970: 146). In 1886 mention is made of the fact that since hemp sandals are widely used by poor people they will be taxed at only $0.65 per kilogram.[1] But nothing precedes it or follows it. Understandably, when in 1908 Henri Pittier published a listing of commonly used plants of Costa Rica, he included neither cannabis nor *cáñamo*, the Spanish term for hemp.

Pittier's disregard for the substance came one year after Marcial Peralta and Henry Bryal had been given permission to form a company for its growing and manufacture on the Costa Rican Central Plateau. Their license authorized them to plant at least one-half million cannabis plants in the Paraíso canton of Cartago and to establish a factory to produce rope sandals (*alpargatas*), hats, cloth, and gunnysacks (Sáenz Maroto 1970: 147).

Pittier was a careful, comprehensive researcher. It is surprising, then, that he disregarded a direct encounter with cannabis on the part of his right-hand man, Adolph Tonduz. When at the close of the nineteenth century Pittier had been at the service of the United Fruit Company, he had asked Tonduz to make as complete a collection as possible of the plants that were growing along the right-of-way of the Limón–San José railroad. Close to the Atlantic coast, Tonduz found a number of cannabis fields planted by "coolies" who had been imported to work for the company and who were using the female cannabis plant for smoking. In relating this experience to the Costa Rican pharmacologist, Otón Jiménez, Tonduz spoke of what was perhaps the first Costa Rican campaign against marihuana smoking. He had observed fighting and disorder among the immigrant labor groups, and he attributed this to the "coolies' " use of marihuana. He therefore advised Minor Keith, head of United Fruit, to have the fields destroyed immediately and totally (Jiménez 1971: 7–8).

Tonduz worked in Costa Rica from 1889 to 1908. His observations make it clear that marihuana was being smoked for its psychotropic effects by the turn of the century (unfortunately his encounter with the "coolies" is undated). The laconic way in which his observations have been reported leave a number of important questions unanswered, however. The word "coolie" today refers to an individual of mixed Chinese, Indian, and/or African descent. It is pejorative, and it implies the lowest possible social status. During the nineteenth century, the word appears to have been used exclusively for Orientals.

The "coolies" observed by Tonduz had probably been brought into Costa Rica to work on the Limón–San José railroad. The contract for building that railroad was approved in August 1871, and shortly afterward laborers, mainly Chinese and Jamaican, were recruited for the venture. Work on the railroad suffered from a scarcity of laborers until 1888, when de Lesseps abandoned his Panama Canal project and the many immigrants who had been brought in to work on that project became available. In 1887, Minor Keith, who had taken over the task of completing the Limón–San José railroad, persuaded the Costa Rican government to agree to the importation of two thousand Chinese laborers. There was considerable objection in Costa Rica to this move, and it was finally justified only on the basis that the Chinese were "the people most able to resist the influence of warm and humid climates." Throughout the same years, sizable numbers of Jamaicans were hired for the same reasons (Stewart 1964: 64–68).

Marihuana smoking could have been brought in by any of these labor groups; Ardila Rodríguez says simply that the diffusion of cannabis smoking to this part of the world dates from the building of the Panama Canal and from the "intense human interchange which resulted" (Ardila Rodríguez 1965: 82; Partridge 1974: 42). If it were the Jamaicans who first brought the custom into the country, however, several factors could be difficult to explain. Cannabis was not introduced into Jamaica until 1840, through indentured laborers from India. The first Jamaican laborers were brought in to work on the Limón railroad only thirty years later, in 1871. It would seem doubtful that thirty years would have been sufficient for the use of cannabis to diffuse throughout the Jamaican population to the extent that impoverished migrants would bring both the seed and the habit with them. Furthermore, the pattern of cannabis use in San José today is exceedingly simple when compared with that of Jamaica. If it was the Jamaican blacks who introduced cannabis to Costa Rica, one must then explain why most of the Jamaican complex has been lost today on Costa Rica's Central Plateau.

Until the last decade, the heaviest use of cannabis in Costa Rica has been reported first for the area of Limón and second for the Pacific banana-producing zones. The following account is illustrative:

I am an exemplary case of marihuana use. From the time I was very young, I had to work, and in this way I took the road for the banana zone. Those were hard times. The zone was true hell; one lived there in deplorable conditions. At times liquor was so expensive that one could not drink, and so of course, to kill time, many smoked marihuana. That way, little by little, I became careless until one day I found myself with a joint in my mouth, and I kept on smoking with pleasure.

In the banana zone it was common for us to smoke marihuana, and it was sold in enormous quantities. Later I came to the Meseta Central, and here the situation was the reverse. One could hardly find marihuana, and when he did it was in the slums, in Barrio Keith and others to the south of the City, where the criminals hung out. There I would go with my friends to purchase the drug.

The years have flown by, and it has become easier to buy [marihuana]. The custom has become diffused until we have reached the situation we find ourselves in today, whereby it is smoked everyplace in San José, while in the banana zone use is disappearing. That really is strange. [*Prensa Libre*, June 22, 1971]

Otón Jiménez, the man who has given us our earliest scientific report of the psychotropic use of cannabis in Costa Rica, doubts that the drug diffused from either "coolies" or the Jamaicans. Rather, he sees it as coming into Costa Rica from contacts with Mexico and from volunteer soldiers who learned to use the drug when serving in Europe during World War I. Be that as it may, we do know that by the 1920s marihuana smoking had become a formal concern of the Costa Rican government. That concern had its origin in 1913, when Costa Rica sent a delegate to the Second International Conference on Opium and signed its first international drug treaty. Substances discussed by the conferees were crude opium, prepared opium, morphine, heroin, and cocaine. No mention was made of cannabis (Secretaría de Salubridad Pública y Protección Social 1930b: 40). Momentum from the conference did eventually lead to marihuana control, however. In 1923 the first laws regulating drugs were passed, and in 1927 the first drug board was created. On March 15, 1927, a decree was issued regulating the import, export, and sale of opium, and on October 24, 1928, decrees were issued controlling both heroin and marihuana, in the latter case covering all aspects: production, sale, possession, and use (see Table 2). In 1929 a new law was proposed which would make fines and prison terms even stiffer. Growers would face three to six months in prison, and dealers and users would be subject either to fines of 50 to 5,000 colones or to confinement for one to two months (ibid. 49). In 1930 this new law was formally adopted by the Congress (Secretaría de Salubridad Pública y Protección Social 1930a: 4).

Undoubtedly, this sudden interest in marihuana was related to its growing use in San José itself. During the closing months of 1929, the Secretariat of Public Health and Social Protection had begun a campaign to "combat the vice of narcotic drugs that is beginning to develop among young craftsmen and prostitutes in a certain sector of the capital city" (Secretaría de Salubridad Pública y Protección Social 1930b: 3). In June 1929 the campaign had uncovered a number of drug users and dealers. Its stated purpose had been to establish general control, to give treatment to users, and to imprison dealers. An account of these activities anticipates the type of reports that became common in subsequent years:

It is a pity that photographs were not taken of those who were found in those centers of drug use, because of the pitiful state they were in, destroyed physically and morally by the enervating drugs. They had the appearance of true human rags. . . . Many of these subjects confessed that due to the repulsion they felt toward work and to the desperate need to sniff heroin or to smoke marihuana, they had been forced to sell their clothing, their family possessions, and even to steal, in order to purchase the drug which the dealers sold to them at fabulous prices. [Ibid.: 4]

According to the report, heaviest use was in San José itself, especially in the district surrounding the San Juan de Dios hospital. Most users were said to be workers in cottage industry, such as shoemakers and bakers. During the course of the campaign, sixty-eight arrests were made. Forty-two of these led to sentencing. Twenty-four men and three women were accused of heroin use; one man was arrested for morphine use, and seven men and two women for marihuana use. Eleven were accused of dealing in heroin, nine of dealing in marihuana.

The marihuana users tended to be quite young, ranging in age from ten to twenty-five. Their occupations were those of shoemaker, baker, and prostitute. None reported using more than one or two cigarettes per day, and the only ill effects they claimed to have felt were occasional dizziness and headaches. All were classified as poor. (Ibid.: 13–14)

Shortly after this campaign was carried out, there seems to have developed a growing appreciation of the possible medical uses of cannabis. In a 1938 publication, *Synopsis of Vegetable Medicine* (Pérez-Cabrera 1938), we find a long paragraph on marihuana that begins by saying that continued use leads to idiocy and lethargy, but then proceeds to discuss the drug's constructive medical uses. Maladies considered treatable with cannabis include epilepsy, obsession, tetanus, rheumatism, cholera, madness, spasms, intestinal disorders, cancer pain, neuralgia, asthma, whooping cough, hydrophobia, delirium tremens, retention of urine, and excessive menstrual bleeding. The drug is also said to aid in hypnosis. Only very brief suggestions are given as to the type and amount of dosage for each of these purposes, however, and wide-ranging medicinal use of the drug by Costa Ricans seems never to have developed (ibid.: 87).

The new Sanitary Code issued in 1949 continued to make no distinction between marihuana and "hard" drugs such as opium, heroin, and cocaine. Growing, importing, exporting, sale, and purchase were prohibited. Growers were made subject to imprisonment for from six months to one year, while workers in cannabis fields could be imprisoned for from 25 to 180 days or subjected to fines of from 50 to 360 colones. Habitual users, in lieu of being imprisoned, could be sent to the National Hospital for the Mentally Ill for detoxification. Possession was practically equated with sale, and both could be punished with noncommutable sentences of from six months to three years of prison (the latter being harsher punishment than that imposed upon the growers) (Ministerio de Salubridad y Protección Social 1950: 20, 22–23).

In 1972, the Costa Rican government approved the Single Convention on Drugs and Narcotics, which had been issued by the United Nations on March 30, 1961, and which had been operationalized by the Costa Rican Ministry of Health as early as 1965. By this act, Costa Rica accepted international responsibility for the control of production, processing, and trade of a number of psychotropic substances, of which marihuana was one. Formal approval of the Convention closely followed the establishment, for the first time in Costa Rican history, of a special police force, the sole mission of which was the pursuit of illegal drugs and drug users. By the time our study began, in July 1973, there were thirty-eight full-time narcotics agents. The main thrust of their activity was to suppress marihuana growing, trade, possession, and use.

Partly in response to these changes, a new Sanitary Code was approved in 1974. With it the penalties for growing and selling marihuana were increased, while those for possession were lightened. Marihuana continues to be treated as completely equal, before the law, to all other psychotropic drugs listed in the U.N. Single Convention. But Costa Rica's special situation is implicitly recognized in that the only substances other than marihuana mentioned in the code are coca and poppies, both of which can also be easily grown in the country's tropical setting. With this new law, growers, exporters, importers, processors, transport middlemen, wholesalers, retailers, and runners are all subject to the same sanctions: from five to ten years of imprisonment. Users are to be given medical treatment rather than prison sentences and fines (Ministerio de Salubridad y Protección Social 1974: arts. 371–372, 126, 127).

The law has been difficult to execute. Production tends to be scattered and small-scale, and large- and even moderate-scale vendors are skillful enough either to avoid the law or to know how to manipulate it if caught. The result is that users, particularly in the poorer neighborhoods of San José, tend to be harassed, their sometimes very modest supply of cigarettes being taken as evidence that they are dealers. The idea of rehabilitating users has yet to be put into practice, for there is neither agreement on rehabilitation techniques nor resources to apply them.

What little is known, then, of the history of cannabis in Costa Rica indicates that, while the plant has been used less widely than in some other Latin American countries (e.g., Mexico, Colombia, and Brazil), it has nevertheless been around long enough to give rise to a definite tradition. Cannabis never was the basis for a well-developed fiber industry in the country. However, it clearly has been used for its psychotropic qualities for at least seventy-five years and perhaps for more than one hundred years. Marihuana smokers associate its use with the very foundations of their country. But they are probably wrong. Forms of use are surprisingly simple, and time depth of more than a century seems exceedingly doubtful.

PREPARATION

Cannabis use among the long-term users in the Costa Rican laboring class sample is relatively devoid of variety. The staple for use is the *picadura*, the chopped-up tops and flowers of the female *Cannabis sativa* plant. This is consumed most commonly in the form of a wheat-paper cigarette, which contains not less than 175 and not more than 300 milligrams of marihuana, according to repeated weighings of net contents of street-sold cigarettes. Occasionally the contents of several of these cigarettes will be combined to form cigars. Smoking is the almost exclusive method of consumption. Preparations other than picadura are extremely rare.

Field-workers' reports, however, include references to three other preparations. The first of these is a black liquid, called *caldito*, which is claimed by users to be the result of prolonged boiling of picadura. Although the process does not resemble the preparation of Indian *bhang* (Chopra and Chopra 1957), the end product could have psychotropic effects, for it often contains diffused particles of the picadura.

A second special preparation known to some users is *pambelé*.² It bears a close resemblance to the Indian *ganja*, as described by Chopra and Chopra (1957: 19), and is imported from Colombia in the form of flat leaf-shaped blocks composed of compressed resin and plant material. Costa Rican users consider it a delicacy. A small amount of the substance may be scraped from the edge of the block into a cigarette paper and then rolled and smoked in the same way as picadura. Users claim that a pambelé cigarette is worth ten of any Costa Rican–grown marihuana.

The third special preparation in use in Costa Rica is known as *hachís*, a generic term applied to any concentrated form of cannabis. Most descriptions of hachís use come from older users, that is, those with twenty-five or more years of experience. One of them claimed to be able to manufacture two of three basic varieties. The first is a solid block of resin. For its manufacture, the dried plant is pounded with a Coca-Cola bottle, a residue collected and compressed into a rectangular box, and the whole then buried and allowed to harden. When the block has aged sufficiently (a period of four weeks or longer) it is removed from the ground. Shavings from the block can then be smoked.

Another cannabis preparation given the name hachís employs psilocibin mushrooms. Its process of manufacture is as follows:

Ingredients:

4 oz. marihuana in picadura
6 oz. 95% alcohol
1 oz. honey
1 oz. psilocibin mushrooms

Place marihuana, alcohol, and honey in a 16-oz. mayonnaise jar, mix ingredients thoroughly. Bury the jar in a safe, shady spot and allow ingredients to steep for a week. Open and add mushrooms. Allow materials to steep an additional week, then remove from the ground. Strain the liquid from the marihuana and place in a distillation retort. The distillation apparatus should have two collection chambers placed along the vapor-carrying tube. The first will collect the condensed *esencia* (essence) of marihuana (what is known in the United States as "hash oil"). The yield will be 1–2 grams, depending on the quality of the marihuana used. Preferred mode of use is to add one or two drops to a shot of brandy.

The final form of hachís is that of a powder. We were unable to obtain the recipe, but we did obtain a description of its nature and use:

. . . They said that it was hachis . . . they gave my brother five packets and three to me . . . I took one in a half a glass of water . . . afterward a whole blessed day . . . and the following day I was high . . . but it was very strange . . . I don't know, but I wasn't hungry . . . It was a very white powder . . . and I couldn't figure out how they got it . . . It must be a process.

The powder may be drunk, as described above, or it may be combined with tobacco and smoked in a pipe.

Such special, strong preparations represent but a tiny percentage of cannabis use by our sample. For daily use, even in the cases of those who are familiar with the stronger preparations, picadura rolled into cigarettes is the overwhelming preference.

PRODUCTION

Because it would have exposed our informants to risk of arrest, the anthropological field team did not visit a professionally run marihuana plantation. One amateur operation was visited, but it was so poorly cared for that its potential yield was doubtful. We were, however, able to elicit two excellent detailed descriptions of cultivation, which appear to be accurate and which corroborate each other. The two informants who supplied these descriptions did not know each other, yet they agreed on all the details of marihuana planting except the time needed for maturation before the plant can be cut and dried.

Costa Rica has many zones where cannabis can be easily cultivated. Users generally cite Limón, on the Atlantic coast, and Buenos Aires, south of and within the Talamanca mountain range, as the areas where the best domestic cannabis is grown. For cannabis that is high in THC, they claim that one must search for a hot climate with sufficient but not overabundant rainfall. They do not describe exact water tolerances of the plant, but, given the high temperatures of areas such as Limón and Buenos Aires, the water needs must be great. The first step in planting is preparation of the plot. For this, standard slash–and–burn is used, that is, the vegetation is cut and dried and the area burned, the burn taking place just before the beginning of the rainy season. One corner of the plot is set aside as a seedling nursery. There the seeds are planted two by two, six inches apart. They must be carefully tended during the first six weeks of growth, because during this period they are quite vulnerable to insects and competition from other plants. When the seedlings have reached a height of six to eight inches, they may be transplanted to the larger plot. In the transplanting process, female plants are preferred. Furrows must be made in the larger plot, and the seedlings set one *vara* (33 inches) apart along the furrows. Thereafter, plants may be left to fend for themselves, except for occasional irrigation and application of insecticides.

Harvesting is begun by peeling the bottom of the plant stalk near the root, after which the plant is left a week to dry before breaking it off at the bottom for stripping. In stripping, the lower, thicker leaves and branches are ignored, but the upper leaves, flowers, and seed heads are carefully cut off with a curved pruning knife. These parts are then placed in the shade for drying, which takes fifteen to twenty days. Once the material has dried sufficiently, it is chopped into very fine particles by either the harvester or the vendor, who uses a very sharp knife and a cutting board or scissors. Seeds may be saved for replanting, or they may be left in the picadura to increase its weight and volume. Sometimes the thick stems are also finely chopped and included in the picadura to increase weight and volume.

Such procedures do not suggest sophistication in terms of resin production. Costa Rican users and growers are limited in their perceptions of the capabilities of the cannabis plant. Growers know that the plants must be cared for intensively during the first six weeks of life, but they do little or nothing to stimulate resin production or to extract the natural high-potency substances that occur during the plant's natural growth. They are aware of cannabis' dioecious nature, recognizing basic morphological differences and the great suitability of the female for marihuana production, but their preference for the female seems based on greater leaf production rather than on greater resin production. Users are vaguely aware of the existence of more potent cannabis preparations, but except for a few individuals they do not really know what they are or how they are made. Cannabis planting and extraction technology in places like India, Egypt, and Mexico has developed over the centuries into an exact art of resin stimulation and careful manufacture of specialized potent forms. Costa Rican cannabis production rarely goes beyond cutting and chopping of the dried plant material.

Evidence of the lack of concentrated preparations in Costa Rica is abundant in newspaper reports of police confiscations of cannabis. In clipping files that date from 1970 to 1975, there are only a handful of references to high-potency cannabis preparations, and these have usually been in the possession of foreigners. The overwhelming majority of reported police confiscations range in size from a few ounces to shipments of one hundred pounds, usually in the form of picadura, although occasionally in the form of whole, uncut plants.

The relative crudity of cannabis production in Costa Rica may be due in part to the constant efforts of police to capture quantities of the drug and to arrest shippers and growers. Plantations must be relatively isolated and inaccessible in order to be safe from the narcotics agents' periodic sorties into the growing areas. Under such conditions, intensive cultivation of the plants, with careful resin production and collection, would be very difficult. And since large-scale cultivation would multiply the number of people who know the location of the planted field, plots are purposely kept small and left untended from just after transplanting until harvesttime.

FORMS OF USE

By far the predominant smoking vehicle for marihuana is the cigarette rolled in wheat paper, the mildest-tasting paper available at a low price. The paper is bought by individual marihuana vendors in 8½″ by 11½″ sheets at ₡0.50 per sheet (US$0.06). Since eighty-two cigarettes can be made from one sheet, to convert one pound of picadura into roughly 1,800 cigarettes a vendor will buy sixty sheets.

The wheat paper used to roll the street cigarette is characteristically yellow in color. This color stains the hands of both users and rollers, and it may be removed only by hard rubbing on whetstone or rough brick. Even though many people still smoke tobacco cigarettes that are also home-rolled with this paper, yellow stains on the thumb and forefinger of the right hand are considered identifying signs of marihuana users, both by their fellow users and by the police. The oldest users in the sample often achieve an almost mahoganylike hue on their fingers as a result of years of use.

The rolling process is quick and unceremonious, with an emphasis on rapidity and efficiency. Often especially skilled rollers are employed. Practically anyone can roll five hundred to six hundred cigarettes in a day; skilled workers, of whom there are relatively few, can roll twice that amount. Such people are paid ₡150 to ₡200 per week (US$17 to US$23). Most rolling is done on an informal basis, where two or three trusted friends help in the rolling of small amounts ranging from four ounces to half a pound. In return for such services, the participants sometimes receive marihuana for their own use, but the relationship between the vendor and his rolling party can also involve complex reciprocity that may go beyond both monetary compensation and payment in kind.

Once rolled into cigarettes, the marihuana is packaged into "rolls" of twenty-five cigarettes, and it reaches the consumers either in this form or as individual cigarettes. The "roll" is tightly packed and can be easily concealed in a sock or pocket. Users may also wad loose cigarettes into a ball and wrap them in plastic or cellophane so they can be hidden in the mouth and even swallowed during police search and questioning.

According to the users with whom we worked, the eating of cannabis never brings about a psychotropic reaction. They cite instances of having to swallow quantities of the drug when arrest seemed certain and of feeling no cerebral alteration as a result. Marihuana has not yet invaded Costa Rican pastries. Some cooking with cannabis was noted in our brief exposure to university-related "Age of Aquarius" ethos groups, but it has not penetrated the older tradition of marihuana use as it exists in Costa Rica.

Because the cigarette has much more paper than normally would be needed to hold such a small amount of picadura for immediate smoking purposes, it can take a lot of rough handling. The cigarettes are long and thin with a double or triple lateral overlap and closure at both ends. They are made to take punishment in the street.

When a user is about to smoke his cigarette, he never simply lights up. The cigarette must first be opened and the tightly packed contents loosened. The material is often carefully examined for color, smell, twig content, and seeds. Twigs are discarded and seeds are either crushed or discarded because they do not burn evenly. Even so, most regular users have tiny burn holes in their shirts, caused by hot seeds that have dropped out of the cigarette while smoking. If the picadura has no smell it is considered too old to be very potent. Color is used as a rough guide to the source of the material, a system of classification which will be described in more detail later.

Vendors will often keep a quantity of marihuana hidden in the ground before it is sold. Users have a special test to discover whether this has occurred. If marihuana remains in the ground for more than a few days, the picadura can be infested with insects that spin webs in the material. When the user passes a pencil tip through material that has been subjected to these conditions, the picadura "beards" on the end of the pencil and hangs there. Good picadura always falls away from the pencil tip.

Costa Rican marihuana smokers do not pass the lighted cigarettes from one smoking companion to another. Individual users smoke their own cigarette from beginning to end, without offering a single puff to those around them. Exceptions occasionally occur among the youngest of consumers, who sometimes pass around the last cigarette of the "roll," possibly in imitation of scenes in movies made in the United States. The general pattern, however, is of nonsharing and seems to be a function of the volume of use. It simply would not be practical for users to share individual cigarettes when each user smokes several joints in a single session. Individual consumption, as seen through field observation, can range up to forty cigarettes[3] in a single smoking session.

In order to minimize paper consumption, Costa Rican users often combine the contents of several street-size cigarettes, which, as explained above, have an excess of paper. The resulting *puro* (literally, "cigar") may contain the picadura of as many as six or seven street-size cigarettes.[4] Other smoking styles include the following (see Figure A):

> *Pipa de paz* (peace pipe):   A wooden tube two to three inches long which is closed at one end and has a hole in the side for insertion of the *bicho* ("joint"). This is used by younger consumers, who often hang it around their necks on a long leather thong. The peace pipe enables the smoker to finish the joint without touching it.
>
> *Cachimba* (name given to any tobacco pipe used to smoke cannabis):   Sometimes cigarettes are inserted into the bowl of the pipe, and sometimes loose picadura is placed in the bowl, either by itself or mixed with tobacco. The mixture is made in this order: one layer of tobacco, one layer of marihuana, and one layer of tobacco. Compared to cigarette smoking, pipe use is relatively rare. Users claim that it is practical to use pipes for smoking marihuana only when the material is available in abundance, because more waste accompanies pipe-smoking than cigarette smoking. The advantage of pipe use is the elimination of paper from the smoking process.
>
> *Coco seco* (dried coconut):   This is a rare style said to be used in Limón by the blacks to test batches of freshly cured marihuana for potency. A coconut is perforated at one end and the meat cleaned out through the hole. It is then dried, and when the drying is completed another hole is made in the other end. Dried marihuana tops and flowers (not yet chopped) are inserted in the first hole. Hot charcoal is then also inserted through the first hole, and the smoker inhales through the second hole in the coconut.
>
> *Pipa de agua* (water pipe):   Another rare form of smoking. The only two designs observed by field-workers were a composite wine-bottle–straw–bowl design and a one-piece bamboo pipe. The smoke is drawn through the water and thereby cooled, reducing harshness.
>
> *Caja de fósforos* (matchbox):   The user perforates the top of a wooden

matchbox, making a hole just big enough to insert a single cigarette. He then tears out one end of the tray section. The cigarette is lit and inserted in the hole, and the user inhales through the open end of the box. The wide opening and the mixing of air and smoke that result are said to give a more powerful initial "rush."

The above descriptions assume an abundance of marihuana, but most users consume very sparingly and carefully smoke even the dregs. In this regard, they are very similar to North American marihuana users. The following are Costa Rican methods to *matar la tocola* ("kill the roach"):

Taco: By far the most frequently used method, the taco is made by emptying the tobacco from the end of a regular tobacco cigarette and placing, in the space that is opened up, the final piece of the marihuana cigarette. This end is twisted and moistened, so that the roach will remain secure. The cigar is then lighted, and the entire tandem cigarette is smoked.

Muleta (literally, "crutch"): Costa Rican users make muletas out of the handiest material available. This can be any kind of twig, a broomstraw, matchsticks (either wooden or cardboard), a bobby pin, or a paper clip. Twigs and wooden matchsticks are broken, and the roach is placed in the broken notch. The two ends are then pressed against each other so that the roach is held in between. Broomstraws and cardboard matchsticks are split, and the roach is pressed between the two split ends. Bobby pins and paper clips are used in the same way as cardboard matchsticks.

La bandera (the flag): Because most street cigarettes have an excess of paper, the user may reroll the cigarette using only one third of the paper. The excess is used as a handle for the marihuana cigarette, enabling the user to hold the cigarette without having to resort to a taco or a muleta. (It might be noted here that excess paper, if not smoked, is never thrown away carelessly. It is either burned, chewed into a little gray ball, or saved for future use. Narcotics police identify this paper with marihuana use and become suspicious of the places where it is seen lying around.)

TYPES

There is little consensus among users regarding local typologies or taxonomies of marihuana. Color and place of origin appear to be the principal identifying factors. Place of origin usually refers to the place from which the material was brought directly to San José, usually Limón or San Isidro del General. Thus, marihuana that is produced in Talamanca and shipped through Limón becomes Limonese marihuana. If shipped through San Isidro, it becomes San Isidran. Limón is said to produce two varieties. One is almost black in color, with an earthy aroma and a harsh taste that irritates the throat. Its effects are strong, and they are felt very quickly after smoking is begun. The other, *la rubia*, or "the blonde," is almost yellow in color and is less fusty in aroma and much less harsh in taste. It is also strong, but the effects are delayed until ten to fifteen minutes after smoking begins.

San Miguelito, a variety that comes from Panama, is one of the more controversial marihuanas recognized by Costa Rican users. The dried leaves have been described as yellow and curly, brown and straight, and many variations in between. It usually has many more seeds than the other varieties, and it is recognized unanimously as one of the strongest marihuanas available to the Costa Rican consumer.

According to cannabis users in our sample, San Isidro del General produces a marihuana that is passable but that does not receive overall ratings as high as *la negra* from Limón and San Miguelito from Panama. Table 3 lists the characteristics attributed to the varieties named most often by Costa Rican users.

Medicinal Preparations

As compared to reports by Rubin and Comitas (1975) for Jamaica, cannabis in Costa Rica does not have a wide variety of medicinal applications. We learned of only three medicinal preparations, and all were specifically used for alleviating either coughing or asthma. Possibly the focus on asthma remedies is related to the high frequency of acute asthma attacks in San José. The city has an extremely damp climate, and asthma is a common malady.

The user who first gave us details as to how hachis could be manufactured also supplied us with a cough medicine recipe. First marihuana must be steeped in pure cane alcohol. The resulting liquid is then mixed with honey and a sugar-base soft drink syrup. Two tablespoons of the end product are guaranteed to clear up the most stubborn, persistent cough.

The most commonly mentioned asthma remedy, however, is a tea made from the boiled root of the cannabis plant. This preparation is known to people outside the marihuana-smoking social networks and is even used frequently by people of respectable social position. Less frequently mentioned is another boiled preparation, using the seeds of the plant. Cannabis seeds are first placed in a thin cloth and crushed by beating the cloth with a heavy object. The cloth is then placed in water and boiled with the seeds inside. Both remedies may be consumed as hot infusions by the asthma sufferer.

Belief in the efficacy of marihuana for treating asthma can be strong. One man told us of the way in which he and his three brothers all suffered from asthma from the time they were small children, occasionally experiencing acute attacks. Along with the older of his two younger brothers, he began smoking marihuana at an early age. Except for occasional wheezing, neither has suffered from asthma since they began regular use of the drug. The youngest of the three never took up marihuana smoking and died at the age of twenty in an acute asthma attack. His older brothers attribute the death to the fact that he refused to use marihuana.

The simple smoking of marihuana is claimed by users to have a number of additional medical benefits. It is said to cure headaches, hangovers, loss of appetite, impotence, depression, and general malaise.

MARKETING AND DISTRIBUTION

To reach the consumer, cut and dried plant material must travel from sixty to two hundred miles. The mode of shipment depends mainly on the order of magnitude of the load that is to be delivered. Since a healthy female plant can produce up to four ounces of material, by growing one plant every two square meters, a single hectare may produce over one thousand pounds of dried marihuana. Because narcotics police use helicopters and light planes to spot plantings from the air, marihuana growers seldom plant fields as large as one hectare. Rather, they prefer to set out only three or four plants, interspersing them with other crops. This procedure involves very little risk of discovery.

The high level of profit makes small-scale planting enticing (see Table 4). As one user put it: "For a farmer to earn ¢400 with maize, he has to work hard. But one can earn that much with only a few plants of marihuana." If the farmer who has grown two pounds of marihuana is willing to take an extra risk and transport his crop directly to a wholesaler in San José, he can realize close to ¢2,000 (US$234) for his trouble. Otherwise, he may contact a transport middleman, who will pay 400 to 600 colones (US$47 to US$70) for a pound of the dried material. Use of such a middleman eliminates most of the risk involved for the small-scale marihuana grower because he has to carry his product only to the nearest node of transportation networks.

The small-scale marihuana grower can arrive in the central metropolitan area by several means, with his merchandise concealed on his person, in suitcases, or in bags of produce. Regular air and train service arrives from Limón daily, and bus service, with the improvement of the roads to Limón, is now regularizing. San Isidro del General lies along the Pan American Highway, so the opportunities for transport from that area abound.

Large-scale shipments of marihuana are more difficult to conceal, but they still find their way into San José. Trucks of all sizes and descriptions pour into the metropolitan area constantly, carrying produce, grain, coffee, lumber, and livestock into the city. It is relatively easy to conceal a large load of marihuana in such shipments, while carrying other cargo which is also profitable to the transporter. Once in the central urban area, the marihuana can be delivered directly to a wholesaler. Because the field team did not consider it prudent to follow the links of the marihuana distribution system to its most central points of connection, we know relatively little about this process. Wholesalers have entirely too much to lose by discovery, and they are likely to be evasive. According to what we have gathered from users, however, the unloading point of large marihuana shipments is seldom the storage site used by the wholesalers. Marihuana is stored at the unloading point only temporarily; then it is transferred to the place from which it is redistributed. This transfer is executed by employees of the wholesaler called *galetas*, a slang term for "runner" or "messenger." Large caches of marihuana are stored in ordinary houses or small businesses and are sometimes buried. Except for the small quantities they may desire for personal use, truly large-scale wholesalers seldom have marihuana in their possession. Most handling of the material is done by the runners.

There are, however, medium-scale wholesalers who rarely have more than thirty or forty pounds of material. It was impossible to determine whether these buy from the larger-scale wholesalers or whether they receive marihuana directly from growers or transport middlemen. We do know, however, that some wholesalers on this level have their own plantations of cannabis. They are usually more directly involved in their trade than are the larger wholesalers, and they depend less on runners for carrying out individual transactions. These medium-scale operators are the ones who appear most frequently in the police arrest reports. Newspaper accounts of their captured stores represent them as major drug confiscations, but they are really minor. Large-scale wholesalers seldom expose themselves to the risk of capture; their runners, who are sometimes caught, seldom have more than a small fraction of the wholesaler's total cache in their possession.

Both kinds of wholesalers sell marihuana to retailers, who deal directly with consumers. A retailer seldom buys more than one or two pounds of marihuana at a time, and he may buy as little as one-half or one-quarter pound. It is he who makes cigarettes for sale on the streets, often with the help of his family or friends. In the rolling process, foreign matter is often added to increase the earning power of a given quantity of marihuana. The substances most often mixed in are native plants that, when dried, have an appearance similar to that of marihuana: *borraja* leaves (*Borago officinalis* L.), *dormilona* leaves (*Mimosa invisa Mar.*), *chayote* leaves (*Sechium edule Sw.*), and even ordinary lawn cuttings. Sometimes even the dangerous but very abundant *reina de la noche* (*Datura arborea* L. and *Datura sanguinea* R. et P.) is added to increase weight and volume. Outright falsification also occurs. This is usually done by impregnating one of the dried adulterant plants mentioned above, generally *dormilona*, with turpentine or kerosene.

The urban network of marihuana distribution is schematized in Figure B. Solid lines connecting the nodal points represent the usual and safest way to move marihuana through the network; dotted lines represent alternative and more risky routings. Boxes represent sources of production or centers of redistribution; circles represent agencies of transport. Most consumers deal with people no higher in the network than the runners. Large-scale wholesalers (wholesaler I in the figure) are almost never in direct contact with their merchandise or their customers. Although the most experienced and astute consumers try to buy as often as possible from medium-scale wholesalers (wholesaler II in the figure), ordinary consumers usually have to buy from retailers. Many retailers would prefer to employ runners, for it is the safest way to do business. Few, however, can afford the luxury. Some retailers solve the problem by offering board and room to adolescent street boys. In general, the retailer is the only marihuana vendor in direct contact with individual consumers and is so well known that he is often given a nickname.[5]

If a retailer is very astute and keeps clean of the law, he may graduate to a larger-scale operation and become a medium-scale wholesaler. In exceptional cases, retailers can even develop into producers. Part B in Figure B illustrates the most successful of all, a vendor who deals in all phases of production and marketing, including the growing process, transportation, bulk distribution, and retail sales.

Prices constantly fluctuate. Between July 1973 and August 1975, a roll of marihuana cost from ¢20 (Fall 1973) to ¢50 (Summer 1975). The most frequent price was ¢35 (US$4.09). Since a retailer may expect to make 1,800 to 2,000 cigarettes from a pound, which costs him between ¢600 (US$70) and ¢1,000 (US$117), and must include in his costs the price of rolling paper (¢0.50 per sheet, 60–70 sheets per pound), his gross profit per pound will range from ¢1,600 (US$187) to ¢2,000 (US$234).

It seems clear that the consumer is paying for the illegality of marihuana. Retailers, with 150 to 200 percent gross profit, charge heavily for the constant threat of arrest and imprisonment. In the case of many, operating costs include bribes and other payoffs to law enforcement officials. Total gross per pound profit can range from ¢2,400 (US$281) to ¢3,000 (US$351), and this for only about twenty-four man-hours of labor, including production, packaging, and transport (see Table 4).

Although small-scale marihuana vendors have many *modi operandi*, they always focus on centers of assemblage. Sometimes they use already-existing interactional nodes such as bars, dance halls, busy corners, an artisan shop, or a school playground. At other times they create their own node, with buying and selling of marihuana as the principal focus of activity. Sites chosen for such purposes may be the vendor's home, a street corner, or a coffee field.

Stylistic variations for actual sales are numerous, but all can be classified into one of two types: the direct secretive and the disassociative. The first is used for quantities no larger than a roll and may be employed in public places, where quickness and unobtrusiveness are most important. The second is characterized by the vendor who goes to a nearby cache of marihuana (also called a *galeta*) to retrieve the amount of material desired by the client and then returns to make the sale.

Direct secretive sales can be carried out in a variety of contexts. On a *barrio* street corner, the client approaches a known vendor with a package or newspaper in his arms. This package contains money to pay for the marihuana. The vendor receives the package, removes the money and replaces it with a roll of marihuana often with the same motion of the hand. Another common approach is for a vendor to pose as a shoeshine boy. In the course of shining a client's shoes, he receives money from him and slips a roll or other desired amount into his sock. One master of the direct secretive method of sale functions in a crowded dance hall. He manages to supply up to twenty individuals with marihuana in the space of an hour and a half without attracting attention or giving the impression that he is doing anything other than enjoying the dance.

Disassociative tactics in marihuana sales are often employed when the transaction must take place fairly close to the vendor's cache and when he feels the need to disassociate the sale from the hiding place. The disassociation may be either simply spatial or both spatial and temporal in nature. If spatially disassociative, the buyer may be taken to a neutral spot to deliver the money and wait for the vendor to retrieve the marihuana from his cache. This procedure allows the vendor to ascertain that the buyer is not being followed, thereby lessening the likelihood of arrest. This tactic is common in neighborhood settings outside the business center.

A variation on spatial disassociation is the situation in which the vendor and client make contact on the street and the client gives money to the vendor for his purchase. The vendor calls a runner-assistant forward and instructs him on the amount of marihuana to be removed from the cache. Then the vendor tells the client to meet the runner immediately afterward to take delivery at a point no more than a block away from the place of the encounter. The vendor thus avoids handling the marihuana and having it associated with his street position.

A colorful example of this basic approach was observed in a deserted coffee plantation. The vendor sold marihuana only at night, and his cache was buried somewhere in the coffee grove. When a client came who was not one of his known clientele, he was made to wait in the darkness while the vendor disappeared into the mist to hide the money he had just received and to retrieve the desired amount of merchandise from the buried cache.

For transactions in the business center of San José, spatial-temporal disassociative tactics are both necessary and elaborate. The vendor receives money from the client, usually so that it looks like part of another kind of money transaction. The client is then instructed to meet the vendor (or a known runner) at a place several blocks away at a given hour. This serves to separate the delivery of money from the delivery of marihuana both spatially and temporally and minimizes the possibility of incriminating the vendor.

Although there are a few contexts in which vendors sell marihuana openly, chance meetings on the street between a vendor and a well-known and trusted client can lead to an immediate direct sale. Certain bars cater to smoking. One bar has inconspicuous mirrors mounted on the walls angled so patrons in booths with their backs to the door can surveil the entrance. Convenient open windows permit tossing away the evidence should lawmen enter the bar. Finally, isolated parts of the country where marihuana is grown also feature open sale.

Special techniques for marihuana delivery into carefully guarded institutions, such as prisons, reformatories, and even a seminary are described by consumers. Prison delivery is by far the most difficult and elaborate, in spite of the fact that inmates claim it is easier and safer to obtain marihuana within the prison than outside it. Visitors and prison guards are apparently the intermediaries. Socks and shoes, some with hidden chambers under the heel or sole, are preferred as hiding places. Picadura placed there may shift and fill concave spaces. Prison officials are now so familiar with the woman's trick of inserting a roll in the vagina that a policewoman examines female visitors as a matter of course. Homosexuals are known to use the rectum in a similar manner. Several users tell the story of a *mejenga*, or impromptu soccer game, that started inside the penitentiary and ended suddenly when the ball was kicked over the wall. It was returned quickly, but the players disappeared immediately after catching the ball to divide up the marihuana that had been stuffed into it during its brief visit on the other side of the wall. The permeability of the penitentiary is such that a user-inmate is said to be able to send an "order" to his outside vendor with fair assurance of delivery.

As with any sales enterprise, the successful vendor of marihuana must have a certain modicum of social graces. Among his clientele he should be known as *buena gente* (the Costa Rican equivalent of "good old boy"). He can develop this reputation by occasionally giving away small amounts of marihuana to his customers and by affability and sociability with the people in his neighborhood. He often has some sort of avowed skill as an artisan, which he uses as a front for marihuana-selling operations. If successful, he will become the linchpin of a viable and long-lasting social network.[6]

Consumers themselves do some redistributing of marihuana, either making a slight profit, or reselling at cost. More than one user claimed never to have to pay for marihuana because it was always freely supplied him, either as payment for work or as an outright gift. Since smoking is often a social act, a user with money frequently invites those without. Young users may pool their funds into a *puesto*, or "bank," with which they buy a roll. Were they to make the purchases individually, such a quantity would not be within their reach, for loose cigarettes are 25 to 50 percent more expensive than those bought in quantities of twenty-five or fifty. Such a group of users tends to ask an older and more experienced user to do the buying. Once the purchase is made, they meet at a prearranged place to smoke, and they finish the roll in a single sitting. The organizer of the effort usually ends up with more cigarettes than his monetary contribution alone would merit.

PHARMACOLOGICAL CONTENT

One difficulty in evaluating the effects of long-term use of any given drug is the problem of relating dosage to measured effect. With regard to marihuana we have made the simple assumption that heavy use over a long period of time would be more likely to cause measurable effects than would light use over a short period of time. We have furthermore assumed that irreversible changes in body function, if present at all, could be more readily identified in long-term, relatively heavy users than in casual or short-term users.

The problem of assessing effects of long-term use is compounded when the drug is a naturally occurring one such as marihuana rather than a single chemical agent that can be specifically identified. It has long been recognized, for example, that severe liver damage is associated with chronic heavy alcohol use, whether in the form of wine, beer, or distilled liquor. But it is also known that many very heavy drinkers have no demonstrable liver damage, even after decades of alcohol abuse. Dietary and genetic factors have been suggested as important intervening factors. But even after centuries of observations, the exact relationships remain unclear.

Marihuana contains a number of pharmacologic active compounds, all of which are considerably more complex in their molecular structure than alcohol (ethanol). Technical capabilities for identification of these compounds are relatively new. It is clear that Delta 9 Tetrahydrocannabinol (Delta 9 THC) is a principal active ingredient and that administration of Delta 9 THC will produce most of the subjective effects consistently reported by experienced marihuana smokers. Likewise, there is consistency between the pharmacologic effects of small oral doses of Delta 9 THC and the effects of inhaling marihuana smoke.

We do not assume that the marihuana samples collected over our two-year period of research are completely representative of the marihuana smoked by the users in our sample; their experience of up to thirty years makes such an assumption difficult. Nevertheless, samples were collected at different times of year, so that at least the two-year period covered by the research was well represented.

In all, thirteen separate samples were obtained in the form in which the drug is sold to consumers—dried and chopped into picadura and/or rolled into cigarettes. Through repeated weighings of confiscated street rolls of twenty-five cigarettes each, we found that each roll consistently weighed close to five grams. Thus, a ten-gram sample would usually consist of two rolls. We found the cigarette to be so uniform that it came to serve as a basic unit of reference for determining the individual dosage levels among the users in the study sample.

Analyses were done in triplicate using thin-layer chromatography and gas chromatography, in laboratories designated by the National Institute on Drug Abuse. The results are presented in Table 5. Noteworthy is the presence of cannabidiol (CBD), since there is evidence that it interferes with the effects of Delta 9 THC (Karniol et al. 1974).

DAILY LEVELS OF MARIHUANA USE

Use-level data were obtained in two different ways. First, subjects were asked to report on their daily use patterns by twenty-four-hour recall, giving information as exact as possible and including precise numbers of cigarettes smoked and the times at which the smoking occurred. Second, subjects were asked to estimate their average level of use over time. All the twenty-four-hour recall data for each user was averaged, and then the mean marihuana consumption per day was computed for the entire sample of forty-one users. This turned out to be 9.6 marihuana cigarettes per day, with a median of 7 and a range of 2.5 to 40.

Intensive use-history interviews in which the subjects were asked to estimate their daily average consumption rates comprised the second method of use-level elicitation. The consistency between the general self-estimate in the life-history interviews and twenty-four-hour recall data was very close. Estimates of average use ranged from 2.5 to 25 cigarettes per day, with a mean of 11.8 and a median of 10. Though higher than the twenty-four-hour recall reports, the difference is not great.

Level of marihuana consumption is, of course, dependent on access to the drug; some users who have high smoking capacities are limited by their financial situation. We observed individuals smoking up to eighty marihuana cigarettes in a single day when they could afford to do so.

In order to compare the impact of such use with data found in other cultural traditions, we computed the mean Delta 9 THC content for all samples analyzed during two years in the field and found it to be 2.1 percent by weight. This we multiplied by the amount of material consumed in milligrams. We found the results comparable to results of other studies of chronic cannabis users.

The light Costa Rican user in our sample who smoked 2.5 cigarettes per day would be exposed to about 10 milligrams of Delta 9 THC. This would be comparable to the exposure of the typical chronic user in the United States, as reported by Rubin and Comitas (1975: 192). The average Costa Rican user, who smokes about ten cigarettes per day, would be exposed to somewhat less Delta 9 THC (about 40 mg) than his Moroccan, Indian, or Egyptian counterparts (60 to 90 mg). The heaviest user in our sample, a man who smokes an average of forty cigarettes per day, would be exposed to 160 milligrams of Delta 9 THC and thus would be on a par with heavy hashish smokers in Morocco and India and with heavy users in the United States armed forces in Germany. Figures for the heavy Egyptian hashish smoker are somewhat higher: 200 milligrams per day (Rubin and Comitas 1975: 192). Yet, the Costa Rican user who occasionally consumes eighty to one hundred cigarettes in a single day is probably exposed to over 350 milligrams of Delta 9 THC. The users in our Costa Rican sample thus represent a range of cannabis consumption quite comparable to that reported in other studies. Considering the absence of concentrated cannabis preparations in the country, Costa Rican users are actually doing much more smoking than their hashish-using Indian or Moroccan counterparts to achieve similar dosage levels.

The standard Costa Rican marihuana cigarette sold on the street contains approximately 200 milligrams of picadura. Assuming that approximately 50 percent of the THC content is lost to the air or destroyed in burning (Manno et al. 1970), the average daily dose of Delta 9 THC would range from 3.18 milligrams (2.5 cigarettes with a THC potency of 1.27 percent) to 149 milligrams (40 cigarettes with a THC potency of 3.7 percent). The mean daily consumption of our user subjects (9.6 cigarettes) would provide a range of Delta 9 THC of 12.1 milligrams per day for the least potent samples to 35.3 milligrams per day for the most potent.* In the scheme of comparative usage levels presented by Rubin and Comitas (1975: App. VI), they would be "typical users."

PUBLIC PERCEPTION OF USE

Heightened public concern about marihuana developed when, in the late 1960s, many students in Costa Rica's better schools and universities began using the drug. The *Prensa Libre*, a San José newspaper, contributed to this concern when it launched a massive campaign in 1972 against marihuana use.

> Until a few years ago, marihuana was considered a product used only by persons living in low-class *barrios*, people without much culture and generally of very few resources.
> Nevertheless, over the years, with the invasion of new "currents" of the hippie type, marihuana jumped the barrier that society had imposed and now it is consumed permanently and, even more seriously, increasingly among young people of the cream of society . . . whether these be students or professionals.

With the realization that marihuana use was jumping class barriers came a sharp rise in drug-related arrests. During 1974–75, 2,299 persons were apprehended by the narcotics police for drug offenses, and an additional 514 dealers and 360 "vagrants" were reported and presumably investigated. The vast majority of the arrests (98 percent) were for marihuana use or trade, indicating that concern over illicit drug use was limited almost exclusively to that substance.

In addition to its regular police force, which itself accounted for many drug-related arrests, the Department of Narcotics of the Ministry of Public Security fielded an average of twenty-one agents between 1973 and 1976. Super-

---

*For exposure figures, see Table 6. The figures in that table should be multiplied by 0.50 to obtain estimated dosage levels.

vising their work were some fourteen administrative officials—40 percent of the drug-enforcement body. Supplementing the efforts of this group were a number of "honorary" police, who worked for no pay as informers and contact persons and who were given the privilege of carrying badges. Presumably, their activity helped to account for the increased numbers of "vagrants" and traffickers reported to police.

Based upon our detailed field knowledge, we very conservatively estimate that no less than 10 percent (11,400) of the San José male population over fifteen years of age uses marihuana on a regular basis. Given the number of arrests (over 95 percent of whom are males) for marihuana possession or dealing, this would mean that about 26 percent of male users were detained between 1973 and 1975. In our sample population of users, 57 percent reported that they had been arrested more than two or more times.

The hundreds of kilograms of picadura and thousands of cigarettes confiscated by various authorities between 1973 and 1975 (see Table 7) may seem impressive to anyone unfamiliar with marihuana use in Costa Rica, for the 342.9 kilograms of picadura confiscated could have made 1,371,600 cigarettes, and this, combined with the cigarettes captured, yields an average of 58,479 cigarettes per month that were denied to Costa Rican marihuana users. Upon closer examination, however, these amounts are not so convincing. The average user in our sample population smoked about ten cigarettes daily. The amount reported captured by all sources between 1973 and 1975 would supply only 230 persons smoking at that rate. Thus, officials seem to have been confiscating less than 2 percent of the estimated marihuana supply (10,260 kg per year) of the city. Per arrest, the average number of cigarettes confiscated was forty. The range, however, was great. While most arrests were for possession of only one or two cigarettes, some were for as many as one thousand.

In view of such activity, one would expect to find direct effects on supply, that is, as confiscations grew, one would presume that marihuana would become increasingly scarce. Yet such was not reported by our subjects; 88 percent said they had no difficulty in obtaining cigarettes when desired.

Where confiscations do seem to have impact is in terms of cost. When confiscations rise and are highly publicized, dealers respond by raising prices arbitrarily. In a matter of only three days, the cost of a roll can rise from ¢20 to ¢35, and in another two days to ¢50.

Over the years, marihuana supplies seem to have remained relatively stable. Looking back at the data available for the 1950s (see Table 8) we find that in 1950 the amount of picadura confiscated was only slightly smaller than in 1973 and 1974 combined. This would seem to indicate that marihuana consumption in the early 1950s was just as highly developed as it is today. Yet during the early 1950s there were neither special police units working on the problem nor great public concern about it.

Examination of the confiscation and arrest records in the Ministry of Health archives reveals that the distribution of marihuana across the country is wide. While the greatest number of arrests were made in San José and its suburbs such as Alajuela, Heredia, and Desamparados, large numbers were also recorded for Limón on the Caribbean coast and in a number of smaller towns in the hinterland, especially in areas of production (see map on facing page).

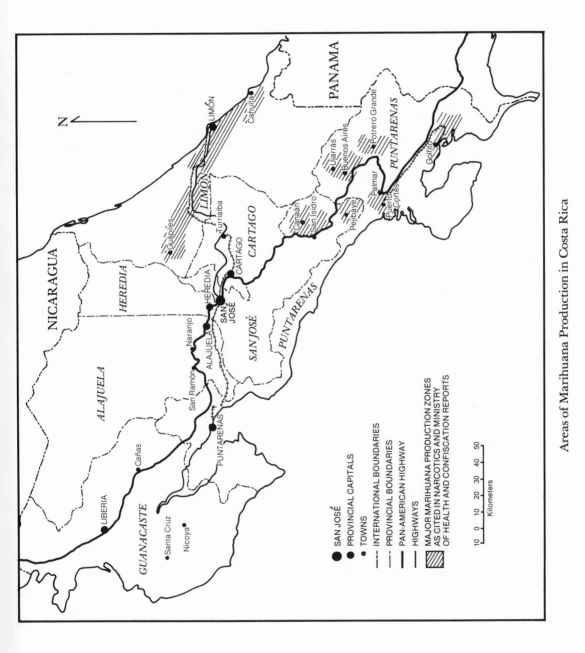

Areas of Marihuana Production in Costa Rica

The effects of sharply increased police activity and news media publicity during the past several years appear to be considerable. Between 1973 and 1975 the narcotics police gave some twenty-five lectures on the subject and assisted 533 students with information for school projects. This represents an interesting contrast with the situation that existed prior to the late 1960s. A sampling of San José newspapers back to 1905 reveals, for example, that the subject of drugs, with the notable exception of alcohol, has been covered only sporadically in the press. Although we know that morphine, cocaine, opium, and possibly marihuana were all in use at the turn of the century in San José, the winning presidential candidate in 1905, Don Cleto Gonzalez Víquez, ran on a platform advocating sharp curbs only on alcohol consumption (*Prensa Libre*, July 22, 1905: 2) and noting that many states in the United States had "blue laws" for such a purpose. Alcoholism was such a problem in San José that patent medicines were advertised as "cures" for the affliction (*Prensa Libre*, September 12, 1905: 2). In 1906, a congressional debate focused on abuses of alcohol but also considered opium, morphine, and cocaine, all of which reportedly were widely used in upper-class social clubs of the time (*La Nación*, March 22, 1957: 20). Marihuana, however, was not mentioned. As a regular news item, use of the substance remained until recently only an occasional topic, competing for space on "public news" pages. There it came out rather sparsely, compared to the coverage given robberies, automobile accidents, contraband television and watches, and alcohol problems.

Perception of marihuana as a serious social problem grew slowly. After the publication of the Inspección General de Hacienda marihuana report in 1957, a reader who responded revealed that he had organized a concerned group of parents in Barrio México upon discovering that his twelve-year-old son smoked regularly. His alarm was further piqued by the fact that his son's "pusher" was only eleven (*La Nación*, March 22, 1957: 24). Despite such revelations, marihuana enjoyed little notoriety among the literate public. In 1961, for example, one newspaper, for its "man in the street" question, asked three middle-class readers what should be done about clandestine drugs in Costa Rica. All said that the drug problem was serious, but the only drugs mentioned were barbiturates (*Diario de Costa Rica*, February 24, 1961). So low was the level of concern regarding marihuana that not a single Costa Rican magazine or journal indexed in the National Library had published an article on the subject, and, for the period prior to 1970, fewer than fifty newspaper articles had appeared.

After 1967, interest rose quickly. In that year, marihuana articles ranked a distant second to articles reporting police raids on illegal alcohol stills. During the six months sampled in *La Nación* for that year, clandestine alcohol manufacture was the subject of eighty-seven articles, and marihuana use, confiscations, and arrests the subject of only thirty-seven. Neither subject was featured in an editorial or other special column.

Late in 1968, however, marihuana suddenly moved off the police, accident, and contraband pages and became the subject of wide-ranging debate and controversy. The change was triggered in part by publication of a short article by Dr. Lascaris, a philosophy professor at the University of Costa Rica (*La Nación*, November 6, 1968: 15). With a humorous touch he noted that, compared to the effects of alcohol, which is sold by the government monopoly, the effects of marihuana did not appear to amount to much and that, unlike other drugs, marihuana did not seem to be habit-forming and did not appear to be the problem many thought it was. The result was a quick reaction from several readers, the Patronato Nacional de la Infancia (a government dependency), and the newspaper's editor, all attacking the professor's position. He was accused of promoting the hedonistic destruction of national morals, ethics, and personality, and the marihuana issue itself was given notoriety.

By 1969 the papers were full of lengthy pieces dealing with the topic from many angles. *La República* ran four very long review articles reporting and commenting on the results of research done largely in the United States. *La Nación* featured a series of reports on the local marihuana situation with several editorials calling for action against the drug and for stiff penalties for those involved. In one article, the director of admissions of the penitentiary was quoted as saying that most crime in Costa Rica was probably committed under the influence of the drug (*La Nación*, July 7, 1969: 12) (an assertion which appears not to have been borne out in the police reports). The reputed relationship between marihuana and crime soon became widely accepted. The minister of education attributed the increase in vice and immorality to a rise in marihuana use. The Costa Rican representative to the U.N.'s World Health Organization proclaimed, using U.S. Bureau of Narcotics sources, that the marihuana habit leads to delinquency, crime, and violence. And one year after the Lascaris article had been published, a minister of government called for serious study and the informed opinions of "psychologists, sociologists, and educators" because "many users are people of high esteem" (*La Nación*, October 27, 1969: 14).

The social chemistry of marihuana thus clearly emerged. Throughout most of its rather covert history in Costa Rica, marihuana use had been a cultural trait of insignificant persons. Once the drug moved from the police-blotter reports to editorial treatment, and was undeniably consumed by persons other than those labeled *malvivientes* and *antisociales*, it became a national concern. By 1975, the narcotics police were stating that 90 percent of all drug users in San José belonged to the upper strata of the community (*Excelsior*, May 23, 1975: 8). Given the fact that the vast majority of arrests for dealing and possession are made in the poorest neighborhoods of San José, such a statement would seem hard to justify. Yet it does reflect the enormous changes that were occurring in public opinion.

Newspaper articles attributed the greatly increased use among middle- and upper-class youth to a diffusion of the hippie culture of the United States. The interpretation was probably accurate. Not only does it seem unlikely that these young people would consciously imitate the habits of individuals at the bottom of their society, but their pattern of use conformed to that of middle-class Americans far more than it did to lower-class Costa Rican norms. Until the sudden explosion of use among middle- and upper-class youth, the marihuana user had been thought of as the dregs of society. As the term *marihuano* had been used by Costa Rica's middle and upper sectors, it connoted not only drug use but thievery, violence, filth, and depravity. It would hardly be a model to be emulated.

The extent of the diffusion process was, at times, unduly exaggerated, however. In 1972 the official student newspaper of the University of Costa Rica published a manifesto declaring that a "foreign Central Intelligence Agency" was plotting to destroy student autonomy and activism by introducing marihuana into the university. The manifesto is so extraordinary that it bears quoting in full:

> Some extrauniversity elements with dubious connections have been painting the walls surrounding the University City with slogans such as "Students, smoke pot," etc. These same elements are those that are determined to introduce marihuana into the university campus. They are well-known by Costa Rican authorities, who appear to lack interest in controlling them.
>
> The end sought by these traffickers (as everyone knows, linked to a foreign Central Intelligence Agency) is very clear: to destroy the prestige and fighting power of the student movement in order to, in this manner, finish it off when it is deemed convenient, together with university autonomy itself. The apparent use of drugs among the university population (which they, through their agents masked as students and through a few "cultural colonizers," try to make appear as massive) will be no more than a pretext to carry out a whole series of machinations that they plan against the university and its students.
>
> We are interested, above all, in emphasizing the foreign origin of the vice and the wicked ends toward which certain individuals are being used from abroad and with the support of some Costa Rican groups themselves. Marihuana, a few years ago, was the vice of "shoeshine boys and people of low life," and today we see that it is being made to appear as a symbol of prestige, given the fact that it is consumed by masses of people in North America. This is an indication of the way that they culturally colonize our youth.
>
> "Students, wake up!" Defend the prestige of the university and of university students.
>
> Denounce the traffickers to the Federation of Costa Rican University Students (FEURC) and realize the danger that this habit means (because of the wicked designs and the known provenience of the same) for the university community and for our country in general.
>
> *Signed:* FAENA. FAU (Frente de Acción Universitaria), FEP (Frente Estudiantil del Pueblo), FESC (Frente Estudiantil Social Cristiano), JUS (Juventud Universitaria Socialista), LAU (Liga de Acción Universitaria), MIJ (Movimiento Iglesia Joven), MUSDE (Movimiento Universitario Social Demócrata), TRABAJO UNEI (Unidad Estudiantil de la Izquierda), FEUCR (Federación de Estudiantes Universitarios de Costa Rica).

By no means all elements of the university were in accord with the manifesto. In fact, the University Committee for the Free Costa Rica Movement (Comité Universitario del Movimiento Costa Rica Libre) soon published a rejoinder (*Prensa Libre*, June 1, 1972). But the manifesto represented the thinking of dominant university-student political groups, and the spin-off it created made it difficult for us to build constructive professional relations within the university community.

If two words could be used to describe recent handling of the marihuana issue on the part of the Costa Rican press they would be "alarmist" and "sensationalist." From January 1970 through June 1975, four of the major San José newspapers (*La Nación, La República, Excelsior, La Prensa Libre*) carried a total of 1,753 articles on drug abuse (see Table 10). Of these, 49.8 percent (873) dealt with marihuana. Fewer than half as many articles (365) appeared on all other drugs put together and dealt mostly with the arrest and trial of foreigners—Colombians, Panamanians, North Americans, and Ecuadorians—who were caught passing through Costa Rica with shipments of cocaine. Articles about legal charges affecting narcotics officials and a judge numbered 192, and 175 articles dealt with the general drug campaign, always including and often focusing principally on marihuana. Finally, 50 articles dealt with the need to alter the country's drug laws. It is particularly significant that in a country with one of the highest rates of alcoholism in the world[7] less than 1 drug-related article in 16 spoke of alcohol as a problem (98 out of a total of 1,753).

These articles not only reflected public opinion; they helped create it. The largest number of articles dealing with marihuana were published in 1971 and seem directly related to the diffusion of the hippie-drug complex of the late 1960s. It was becoming increasingly clear that marihuana was perceived as *the* Costa Rican drug problem. The largest category of articles on the subject reported on the arrest and trial of marihuana vendors, while the largest corpus of articles on hard drugs dealt with their use in other countries. Almost all hard-drug-related arrests were of foreigners rather than Costa Ricans. Marihuana had become a Costa Rican phenomenon, while hard drugs such as cocaine, heroin, opium, and LSD were perceived as foreign. So permeating was this perception that many articles began by speaking of "the drug" and "the drug addict" and only later clarified that they were really referring to marihuana.

Costa Rican professionals brought onto our research team expressed surprise from time to time that our subjects appeared normal. Because we had designed a single-blind procedure, our physicians and psychologists could rarely say for sure whether the subject being examined was a user or a nonuser. The news media of the country had led them to expect the worst kind of behavior and abnormalities. An example is the following, paraphrased from a *Prensa Libre* article titled "Marihuana: Poison for Youth" (June 17, 1971): "Salient characteristics of the marihuana smoker are irregularity in school attendance, poor discipline, poor grades, reddening of the eyes, bad temper, poor physical appearance, mendicancy, theft, and solitariness. When a student is under the influence of the drug, he becomes animated and hysterical, talks rapidly in a loud voice, laughs uncontrollably, at times appears like a sleepwalker or fool, has a distorted perception of time, and is difficult to manage."

Other newspaper accounts assert not only that marihuana leads to sexual impotency, through lowered male-hormone secretion, but also that it is responsible for abnormal births. "While under the effect of the drug, the *'marihuano'* is, at times, passive, although highly suggestive. Because of this suggestivity, he can easily be convinced to commit criminal acts. On occasion he becomes aggressive, loses his self-control, and attacks, injures, and even kills when crossed." As a result, the addict "is soon a useless and dangerous member of society. He may beat his parents, attack his younger siblings, and kill those whom he loves. He never works, but rather gives himself over to theft, by which he lives and obtains his cigarettes" (*Excelsior*, April 27, 1975). Young people from "distinguished" families who turned to marihuana have developed red eyes, yellowed and dry skin, cracked lips, nervous tics, and stupor" (*La Nación*, May 26, 1971); marihuana users have also engaged in group sex orgies while under the influence of the drug (*Prensa Libre*, April 1, 1971; *La Nación*, October 8, 1973), have become mentally ill (*La Nación*, October 19, 1974), have made knife attacks on the narcotics police (*La República*, October 31, 1974), have engaged in bribery (*La Nación*, November 8, 1973), have practiced homosexuality and sex aberrations, have lost their power of concentration, have suffered anguish, terror, and nervous tension, and have turned to suicide (*La Nación*, December 1, 1973).

Considering the many scientific reports that have been published about marihuana over the last decade, an occasional balanced accounting of the pros and cons of the issue might be expected in the media coverage. But such is rarely the case. Scientists are interviewed, and scientific reports are quoted, but very selectively. A local psychiatrist, when interviewed, is quoted as saying that while marihuana habituation is less strong than that of other drugs, it unleashes schizophrenic and demented mental processes, in addition to causing lesions in the organism, and that all this has been confirmed by studies on brain damage carried out in Canada, the United States, and England. Use of the drug is also reputed to cause genetic damage and damage to the sex glands (*Excelsior*, March 27, 1975).

Of the sixteen newspaper accounts of foreign marihuana research published between 1970 and 1975, only two refer to any positive or questionable effect of the drug. One speaks of its possible use in treating arthritis and the other of its possible use as an analgesic for terminal cancer patients (*La Nación*, February 1, 1971). The remaining uniformly direct themselves to the description of disastrous effects.

To initiate the *Prensa Libre*'s antimarihuana campaign in 1971, a group of Costa Rican physicians reported, "on the basis of scientific research and their long experience both in Costa Rica and abroad, [that marihuana] (1) is a depressant; (2) inevitably establishes the need for continual use; (3) leads to the use of harder drugs such as heroin, LSD, and others; (4) interferes with mental processes (poor performance in studies, etc.); (5) leads to permanent nervous tension; prevents physical and mental rest; leads to a constant state of desperation; (6) leads to the loss of sensitivity, love, and affection; a large percentage of marihuana users give signs of madness over time; (7) disturbs the brain cells and leads to acts of violence" (*Prensa Libre*, May 24, 1971).

Other reports on "scientific research," published at about the same time, claim on the one hand that marihuana is carcinogenic and on the other that its use can lead to serious psychoses. Raymond Mague and Louis Harris of the College of Medicine of the University of North Carolina are quoted as stating, on the basis of experimentation with rats, that the tar of marihuana smoke produces the same destructive changes in the skin as does tar of tobacco smoke. The researchers are fairly reported as requesting that their findings be interpreted with caution and that the reader should realize that, for a human to suffer similar effects, he would have to smoke forty marihuana cigarettes a day (a dosage well within the range of Costa Rican use), but the article is headlined simply "Marihuana Can Produce Cancer" (*La Nación*, May 8, 1971).

With regard to marihuana and psychoses, a report was published based on the work of William T. Moore and Harold Kolansky, in which marihuana was said to interfere with an individual's perception of reality and to lead to the development of a delusional system. Subjects who stopped marihuana use were reported to have moved away from delusions, but their memory lapse and lack of concentration were said to remain. Kolansky is quoted as saying that the adolescent who smokes marihuana is playing chemical Russian roulette because his personality is unstable and changeable by nature. If he has, in addition, a psychological problem, "marihuana can be like dynamite—it can blow up like a bomb" (*Prensa Libre*, May 14, 1971).

Such reports have deep impact on the development of public opinion in Costa Rica. If taken uncritically they can be seen to justify the traditional equation of marihuana with hard drugs and the incessant and zealous campaign against the substance on the part of the police. The list of ills attributed to marihuana by the Costa Rican press, quoting carefully selected scientific studies, is surprisingly long. In addition to those already cited, it includes acceleration of cardiac rhythm, inflammation of the cornea, nausea, vomiting, irritation of the respiratory passages, dryness in the mouth and throat, and lung cancer (*Excelsior*, April 27, 1978; *La Nación*, March 28, 1973).

Of particular interest in the newspaper discussions on the relationship between marihuana and lung cancer is the fact that the author of one study, Wolfgang Voegl, is quoted as saying, "No one smokes 20 cigarettes of marihuana daily (as they do with tobacco), but the smoke of the marihuana cigarette is deeply inhaled and held in the lungs as long as possible, something that does not occur with tobacco." Voegl is then reported to add, "It is almost certain that a person can absorb as much tar with only two marihuana cigarettes as with a [20-cigarette] pack of tobacco cigarettes" (*La Nación*, March 28, 1973). What escapes the news reporter entirely—and probably escapes the Costa Rican public in general—is that there are many traditional marihuana users in their country who smoke as many or more than twenty cigarettes per day and that many tobacco smokers inhale as deeply as do those who smoke marihuana.

Because Costa Ricans esteem freedom of speech, contrary voices are occasionally raised. One group of professionals, interviewed in January 1971, asserted that marihuana does not create physical dependence, although they hastened to add that it could create psychological dependence. Its basic effects, they felt, were to break down internal controls and so to release "primitive impulses." In general, they noted that those "addicted" to the drug suffered social, psychological, and physical deterioration. They cited the case of individuals with artistic sensitivities who used marihuana to increase their creativity. But, they noted, the moment arrived in which these individuals deteriorated to such an extent that they could not reach their goals no matter how much they smoked. Some users, they claimed, reacted euphorically; they fell into an unreal and false world. Others, they noted, felt impelled to commit crimes and suffered suicidal tendencies. Basically, they saw reaction to the drug as tied directly to personality. In some cases they felt that young people turned to it to overcome a basic timidity. In others, they believed it was used to facilitate verbal communication. Generally they felt that users maintained their capacity for judgment and remained more lucid than those who became intoxicated with alcohol (*La Nación*, January 8, 1971).

Increasingly throughout the 1970s, voices in Costa Rica were raised to treat the marihuana user as a victim of disease rather than as a criminal. This attitude was formalized in the 1974 Health Code and seems to be penetrating the judiciary. Narcotics officials have been quoted as complaining that they have arrested many individuals for possession, only to find them released by the courts (*La República*, May 17, 1974). And even narcotics agents themselves have been depicted as feeling pained by their duty to accuse persons of drug violations when some of these individuals live in "absolute misery" (*La Nación*, August 29, 1974).

Indisputably, marihuana remains the major target of illicit drug control. Throughout the first half of this decade, persons apprehended for marihuana violations accounted for 98 percent of all drug-related arrests (see Table 9). Over only a two-year period, 3,107 Costa Ricans were detained (as opposed to reported) either for possession of the drug or for dealing in it, while only 68 (2 percent) were detained for offenses connected with all other drugs put together. The monthly average of marihuana-related arrests of Costa Ricans came to 129; the number of arrests for all other drugs came to only 2.8. Seventy-five percent of all those arrested for marihuana had cigarettes only, while 25 percent were found with picadura.

Marihuana use continues to be an important issue in Costa Rica. It is difficult to find individuals who are neutral on the matter. Longtime users are largely convinced that the drug is harmless and that the laws and public attitudes are grossly unjust. Nonusers, however, tend blindly to accept the most pejorative of news releases. Such polar viewpoints, which exist at all levels of society, make any balanced popular, or even scientific, evaluation difficult.

NOTES

1. En consideración a que el calzado de cáñamo, conocido como el alpargatas, por su gran uso entre las gentes no puede pagar fuertes aforos, se le fija el $0.65 por kilogramo (Sáenz Maroto 1970: 146–147).
2. Pambelé is also the name of a Colombian prizefighter who was holder of the world welterweight title, a fact which suggests the perceived potency of this material.
3. Smoked over a period of about two and a half hours.
4. The precise manner in which *puros* and street cigarettes were smoked will be discussed in Chapter 6.
5. Maintenance of the confidentiality of informants does not permit us to provide illustrations of the colorful, often humorous, complex of nicknames.
6. Only in cases of relative abundance will a vendor on the retail level sell marihuana in forms other than the street cigarette. In Limón, for example, street vendors sell cannabis in "fingers," i.e., ten grams of picadura. One Limonese vendor uses pages of *Watchtower* magazines to package "fingers." Members of the field team have seen a few cases of small-scale vending of picadura in the San José area, but the practice is relatively rare. When sold in picadura, the cannabis comes in small plastic bags of about ten grams called *puchas* (pouches) or in matchboxes that can hold about four grams.
7. The National Survey on Alcohol Use has determined that 7.1 percent of the population between fifteen and fifty-nine years of age has serious problems with alcohol. On the Central Plateau, 14.9 percent of men and 0.62 percent of women between these ages are reported to be alcoholic (Comisión sobre Alcoholismo 1972: 17).

3/The Study Setting: San José

San José is located on a broad intermontane valley, commonly referred to as the Central Plateau, at an altitude of 1,160 meters. Within fifty kilometers are the other three major cities of Costa Rica; as a result, the area completely dominates the rest of the country. Although the plateau is today increasingly urban, it was not always so. From its discovery by conquistador Juan de Cavallón in 1561 until relatively recent times, it held only a rustic farming complex of scattered homesteads and rudimentary villages. Because the Spanish found neither minerals nor exploitable Indians there, the area remained a colonial backwater for centuries. The nearly total absence of colonial buildings dramatically underscores that fact. Although the metropolitan area of San José today holds almost a half-million residents, the visitor is impressed by the city's smallness.

Immediately north and south of the downtown section are sloped ravines and streambeds that provide natural boundaries between the central city and the surrounding ridges. The low land near the streams and ravines, and the areas between the ridges, have provided space for residential neighborhoods as the urban population expands. Most marginal housing is toward the bottom of the ravines. The most prominent ridges are found along the east-west axis of the city and run through the length of the valley ringed by volcanoes and the hills. The government has stimulated growth along this axis by building major highways and widening downtown streets to facilitate traffic flow. The contrast between the east-west axis and the north-south axis is striking. Driving along the former, one is impressed by industry, new housing, "big money" commercial vigor, new highways, new construction, and the kind of chaos associated with rapid change. The north-south route takes one through mixed industrial and working-class neighborhoods, marginal ravine *barrios*, and commercial and industrial development following along main arteries that lead to the suburbs, and ultimately into the coffee groves that ring the city.

Downtown congestion graphically demonstrates the city's magnetism. Used school buses purchased in the United States carry the city's population to and fro and, in some instances, continue to display their signs, for example, "Monroe County Unified School District." Most buses carry colorful names like Cassius Clay, Batman, Jesse James, Lightning Bolt, and The Last Hope.

People are drawn to the urban center for a multitude of reasons. A group of boys carrying cleated shoes and a soccer ball are off to the huge sports field, the *sabana*, some blocks to the west for a game. Stout mothers, arm in arm with nubile young daughters, are doing family shopping. Old men wander to the sidewalk cafés on the Central Park to drink coffee and watch the passersby. Young men make suggestive comments to women about their most intimate attractions, while the latter stoically ignore the compliments.

Driving anywhere in the metropolitan area, one is impressed by the number of bars in nearly every block. Some are rustic, unadorned places selling the cheapest liquor, a cane-based drink called *guaro*, without the snacks, or *bocas*, eaten in other more respectable establishments. Like the buses, these bars sport intriguing and humorous names: The Office, The Fleet, Ringo's, The Big Shot. Their ragged clientele know official Costa Rica only through the law officers who occasionally round them up for drunkenness.

One gets a number of impressions while driving randomly about the city. Notable is the forest of television antennae that fill the sky regardless of economic status. Electric wires assume baroque, spidery patterns of complexity as rewiring and modification of the system create generations of electrical fixtures. Huge gangs of children fill the streets. Axle-breaking chuckholes catch the sightseer by surprise, reminding him of a cartoon that appeared in *La Nación*. Two citizens were standing in the street looking at a smoking crater. The first asked if this were a new volcano. The second replied, "No, it's a bus making a stop at the bottom of a hole."

Driving away from the center of town, passing through the tableland residential zones, the small towns built on low ridges, and the commercial and residential construction rising at the edge of the urban areas, one abruptly comes to rural Costa Rica. Here the contrast is stark, for chiseled green hills and volcanic structures give an Alpine aspect to the country. Tiny villages sustained by a variety of agricultural products seem centuries removed from exhaust-blanketed San José. Ox carts can still be seen; barefoot farmers sporting canvas hats and carrying the omnipresent machete ride their horses for hours to travel from farm to marketing town. Completing their business, they tie up their steeds in front of local saloons and buy a drink at the bar. This is the earlier Costa Rica, agricultural in base, sparse in population, and isolated from the world. From it only recently has modern San José emerged.

THE DEVELOPMENT OF CITY LIFE

According to the Costa Rican Academy of Geography and History, San José was founded in 1737 (Academia de Geografía e Historia 1952). By the end of the eighteenth century, the city had grown to only slightly under 5,000 inhabitants (Rodríguez and Terán 1967: 27). Its isolation was extreme. When independence from Spain was proclaimed in 1821, it took several months for word to arrive from Guatemala, and only then were belated celebrations held.

During the nineteenth century, the internal municipal organization of San José gradually developed, with appropriate administrative units and utility services. The first census of the country in 1864 showed that the city had grown to only slightly less than 9,000 residents. During the second half of the nineteenth century, the opening of the British market for coffee (as symbolized by the growing fleet of merchant vessels of William Le Lachear) brought Costa Rica's first significant participation in world commerce (Stone 1975: 82–87). It also triggered the first significant population growth and eventual urbanization of the San José area during the first half of the twentieth century.

THE EVOLUTION OF MODERN SAN JOSÉ

The recent growth of San José has been rapid and dramatic (see Table 11). It resulted in extensive development of residential areas near the center of the city. These grew in two great surges. The first occurred during the two initial decades of this century and brought about the formation of the "southern *barrios*," from which many of the subject population were drawn. No more than one or two miles from the center of town, these were largely established in their present physical configurations by the early 1920s (Rodríguez and Terán 1967: 74). During that decade (ibid.: 76) the density of housing greatly increased, with some residences falling into impoverishment and the majority being built contiguous to one another. A second surge is reported for the late 1930s and 1940s, when a more distant set of southern *barrios* developed and a complex of neighborhoods east of the center emerged. These neighborhoods also provided a number of subjects for the study.

Housing construction since the 1950s has continued to be intense, the most notable examples being the government housing authority projects south and west of the city's center. The government has been ambitious in providing housing and urban services to the expanding urban population, and although residents' expectations about the quality of services have exceeded actual accomplishments, vital services and transportation arteries have been successfully established. Of particular note is the extensive system of bus routes, which provides convenient, cheap transportation for the entire urban area.

Although rapid growth has dramatically changed the physical configuration of San José, the tradition of anchoring everything to the heart of the city has not changed. All bus routes feed either into Central Park facing the cathedral or to special stops within a few blocks. There is no interneighborhood service, unless the individual's stop happens to be between a given neighborhood and the center of town. All transfers are made on or near Central Park. At rush hour, seemingly endless charges of exhaust-belching buses roar along the edge of the park, unloading and loading. Police frantically blow their whistles, and hundreds of passengers wait for their approaching buses.

Central Park, with its adjacent streets, is the most dramatic interactional node of the entire city. Its confluence of activity practically guarantees meeting an acquaintance. A number of individuals seem to be permanent fixtures: shoe-shine boys, a couple of guards, traffic police, evangelists, lottery vendors, money changers, newspaper vendors, indigent beggars and musicians, car washers, self-appointed car watchmen, loiterers, and, of course, employees of surrounding bars, restaurants, and commercial establishments. Many of these individuals serve as information brokers; messages left in the park will usually be delivered the same day. Nearby businesses assure a constant flow of humanity. Surrounding the park are the city's most popular movie theaters and several crowded all-night restaurants and bars, and within a couple of blocks there are a number of dance halls where contact with prostitutes can be made. Without walking more than two blocks from Central Park, one can experience the extremes of San José life. An example is the way in which the elegant Gran Hotel Costa Rica and National Theater provide stark contrast to cheap bars and brothels only a few hundred yards away. Thus it is that the central area of the city can play a key role in the lives of a wide range of San José residents and can provide a stable point of reference and identification in the midst of constant change.

THE PHYSICAL CONFIGURATION OF RESIDENTIAL NEIGHBORHOODS

While relatively densely populated, the city is small in area and is perceived by its natives in terms of a very rural system of orientation. A series of key landmarks such as a store, a building, even a tree, are used as points of reference from which directions are given in *varas*, technically a measure of 33 inches. Thus a city block is arbitrarily perceived as being 100 varas long, and a house will be located 300 varas south and 50 varas east of a well-known fig tree, or 25 varas south of the Primavera drugstore. Given such directions, any *Josefino* could find the place.

The perception of smallness and intimacy is reinforced by the city's architecture. Construction during the first half of this century was primarily one-level, with only some of the more elegant downtown residences and commercial buildings having two or more floors. In a typical neighborhood, small businesses abound, often occupying the front room of a residence. There are grocery stores (*pulperías*), shoemaker shops, hardware stores, furniture shops, bakeries, automobile repair and body shops, tailors, and other small retail or service establishments. Interspersed among them are narrow-fronted houses, usually of frame construction, which extend to the middle of the block. These are extremely long houses, often with an open patio at the back for laundry and a small garden. While not elegant, they generally contain a number of amenities. Thus, compared to the working class of many Latin American countries, the subjects recruited for our study could be said to be well housed. They enjoyed the full gamut of urban utilities, high levels of cleanliness, modern sanitary facilities, potable running water, and structures which, though crowded, were sound in construction and provided adequate protection from the generally mild climate. Table 12 summarizes their situation.

The peculiar physical configuration of such dwellings has been given much importance by Costa Rican observers. Rodríguez and Terán (1967: 140–141) assign social personality characteristics of independence to the predominance of individual houses with private entrances and point out that residents often emphasize their uniqueness through idiosyncratic decorative arrangements or house color. Part of Costa Rica's historical legend holds that colonial poverty gave birth to rough egalitarianism and permitted each man to become a landholder, assume middle-class behavior, and participate freely in democracy. Although this popular interpretation has been recently attacked (Stone 1975), it certainly seems reinforced in the social idea of a house.

The Urban Setting as a Study Site

A standard approach for studying an urban area is to select a neighborhood or two and conduct an investigation modeled after the kinds of community-study procedures used in a small town or tribal setting. Procedures include mapping, surveying, interviewing, and engaging in participant observation, but always within the context of *barrios*. The restricted zone is treated as if it were a totality in terms of social processes and focuses. We realized at the beginning of the project, however, that marihuana smokers and their nonsmoking counterparts would not be conveniently located in one *barrio* and that they would not form a separate social entity. We were faced with the problem of recruiting and working with a group dispersed throughout the city and probably representing a broad spectrum of social types.

Our most complex initial problem was how to establish contact with a population of lawbreakers (i.e., consumers of an illegal drug). Not only were they dispersed over a metropolitan area of 436,862 people, but their customary behavior included evasion. Social contacts with strangers could be dangerous, for who could tell whether, under their cover as researchers, they were not really masking their real identity as law-enforcement officers?

During our first days in Costa Rica, we were fortunate in locating a few interactional nodes where marihuana users met; there we exchanged news and gossip and bought small quantities of the drug for immediate consumption. Included also were nonusers. The sites for such interaction included a park corner, a bar, a street corner, and an athletic field. We began to habituate these places, make ourselves visible, answer questions, and chat with anyone who happened by. Gradually it became accepted that we were not INTERPOL officers and that we could be talked into buying a round of beers or providing transportation.

We discovered through these experiences that we had originally underestimated the social worlds of our target population. Drives to "run an errand" for a contact sometimes turned into hours-long treks all over the San José metropolitan area as "business" was conducted. In such tours, it became obvious that the individuals with whom we had begun to work were part of interactional networks that defied all geographical and residential boundaries.

We were dealing, then, with a fluid population that roved about using highly sophisticated methods of communication and exchange. One could "send a telegram" by leaving a message with a trusted friend in a particular street corner bar. Transmitted by word of mouth through mutual acquaintances, it would usually be "delivered" the same day. Communication could be maintained even with friends inside the penitentiary. The person inside could scribble a "cable" on a cigarette wrapper and "wire" it out, usually with a guard or a visiting friend, and the scrap of paper would be passed along until it arrived at its destination.

By working through such networks, we conservatively estimate that we came to know in passing at least 1,500 persons. We grew to perceive the city as a series of interactional nodes such as bars, street corners, residences, stores, barbershops, shoemaker shops and the like. Individuals who lived in, worked in, or regularly frequented such places became brokers for street news and points of reference for others in their circle of acquaintances.

This view of a metropolitan area as a field of interrelated social networks contrasts sharply with what is presented as the "official" organization of urban life. Government statistics and census data are organized according to a hierarchy of administrative levels and territories in which a number of neighborhoods or parts of neighborhoods are grouped together in what is called a district. Data in official reports tend to be averaged for these different units. In Costa Rica, several districts form the canton, a larger unit roughly parallel to a county in the United States. Cantons, in turn, are components of provinces, of which there are seven in Costa Rica.

As we became familiar with San José, we noticed that groupings bore little relationship to these formal administrative units. A single district might contain an upper-class neighborhood, a working-class *barrio*, and a shanty settlement. Thus we were forced to conclude that census data, as traditionally presented in terms of mean average of income and social status for districts and cantons, had little utility for an accurate study of urban life in San José. The real social units of San José were based on personal, not anonymous, relationships. Individuals interacted with people they knew. Neither urban pace nor population density forced them to deal with unknown persons and unfamiliar processes. A study of formal institutions such as factories, businesses, the government, or unions could never reveal the real dynamics of such a structure. Individuals found ways to buffer themselves from the full impact of the city by activating personal relationships and by reducing city space to a personal level. They defined their social environment through selection of interactions and constantly reorganized even formal institutions.

In spite of these problems, we are convinced that choosing an urban setting for the study of illegal and stigmatized behavior provides many advantages. Although difficult to locate, once recruited, subjects are within easy access of specialized facilities such as hospitals, diagnostic centers, and laboratories. The way that their illegal behavior relates to general social adaptation is easily studied, for they are more free to define their individual social worlds than are their rural counterparts. Family sanctions tend to be less intense than in rural areas, and thus subjects are usually more willing to take risks. Finally, because their primary reference groups tend to be more than mere family, development of a sample that crosscuts geographical and economic boundaries becomes more feasible.

A TYPOLOGY OF RESIDENTIAL NEIGHBORHOODS

While San José is compact, it does contain a wide range of residential neighborhoods. By using the social-network approach, we eventually dealt with all but the wealthiest and the poorest of these neighborhoods and developed a typology. This was based on systematic visits to the neighborhoods, an assessment of housing and services that were available, geographical relationship to the center of town, transportation, construction, and future plans for change as suggested by road building, new services, housing or other improvements. Our typology began with the residential areas that have remained intact in the center of the city, and moved to the periphery.

I.   Central City Barrios

San José's central *barrios* form the commercial and residential heart of the entire metropolitan area. Occupying the few square blocks around Central Park, they are the locus for a wide range of economic activity and housing types. Historically, they were the first to be developed as residential areas; their streets are shown on the earliest maps available for San José (Rodríguez and Terán 1967: 35, 45). As commerce developed, much of their residential space was converted to other purposes. Today this central area is characterized by a high degree of diversification. Walking through these *barrios,* one encounters congested car, bus, and truck traffic on narrow, two-lane streets. Capricious double-parking clogs the traffic flow, causing a din of honking horns and clouds of diesel and gasoline exhaust fumes. Jammed against the narrow sidewalks are a plethora of shops and businesses. Shoemakers and tailors provide personal services along with barbershops and small soda shops, which serve simple meals, fruit drinks, and coffee. The range of facilities is impressive. In no more than two blocks, one may recap a tire, rebuild a battery, buy shoemaking supplies, order custom-made shoes, have a quick drink, buy a lottery ticket, order a tombstone, bind a book, visit a prostitute, eat a meal, or catch a bus to a wide array of destinations. First- and second-run movie theaters, popular dance halls, bars featuring shows combining vaudeville and topless dancing, restaurants, all night cafés, and rooming houses that service prostitution are also concentrated in the area. At night, activities reach a level almost as high as that during the day.

Police are omnipresent. Unarmed traffic officers (*tránsitos*) are visible day and night. Black-and-white Dodge radio cars tirelessly patrol. Raids are made sporadically on neighborhood bars, with drug traffic, largely marihuana sales, being the target of the generalized searches and interrogations. Inebriated men are picked up daily and taken to the central penitentiary, where a detoxification clinic provides first aid. Yet one still commonly finds comatose individuals on the sidewalks at night and in the early morning.

Housing in the area is quite varied. Expensive apartments are available in new two- to three-story structures that have been built in the last few years. Old frame houses and new business buildings are found in the same block. But these older structures are swiftly disappearing. Many have been torn down to make room for government office buildings and schools. Some lots have been cleared and converted into lucrative parking lots. Space for a few playgrounds has been preserved, including small plazas with well-used fixtures and benches.

Half the central *barrios* take their names from the parish churches. These tend to be stark structures made of concrete, wood, and metal sheeting painted intriguing combinations of blue, orange, yellow, and white. Artistically and architecturally they descend from no tradition of note. In one case, a forbidding barbed-wire fence surrounds the church grounds, barren except for a small cornfield and the massive, stark, faded ochre-painted church building. Yet, in spite of such apparent evidence of disinterest, church attendance is high; Sunday Masses are standing room only throughout the day.

These central *barrios* tend to blend into each other with no definite boundaries. Often the residents themselves are uncertain about the exact limits of their neighborhood. Generally, the outer fringes of the central *barrios* and the adjacent section of the contiguous *barrios* are similar in socioeconomic and housing type.

II.   Stable Residential Barrios—Contiguous to Central City

These neighborhoods are usually separated from the central city by such boundaries as railroad tracks, a stream or small river, or a ravine. Several straddle major thoroughfares and serve as conduits into the city. They developed during a period ranging from the 1920s to the late 1940s and early 1950s. Typically they still contain some open space, and their outer fringes blend into open fields or coffee groves.

The mix of businesses and residences is striking, though less so than in the central *barrios*. A common pattern is for house owners to convert a front room into business and to continue to reside in the remainder. Such space is typically used for shoemaking, barbershops, small vegetable stands, or grocery stores.

The common structure throughout the area is a frame house with a corrugated metal roof. It is generally well made, neatly painted with clean interiors and decorated with a range of religious symbols, plastic flowers, and assorted figures and ceramics. Government services are ubiquitous. All *barrios* regularly receive water, electricity, and garbage collection. Because of heavy traffic and lack of maintenance, roads throughout the area are characterized by chuckholes and roughness. In one of the *barrios* a mild demonstration was held during July and August of 1973 to protest the state of such roads; soon afterward repairs were made.

While the *barrios* are basically residential in character, a few contain some light industry. One *barrio*, for example, has a vegetable oil plant with its attendant warehouses and machine shop, an office machine warehouse, a sausage plant, a clothing factory, and a series of grain and grocery chain warehouses. Workers in these businesses are free to live either in the *barrio* or throughout the city. Yet the presence of the business itself brings a certain stability:

> Now the *barrio* is just a bit changed because now it has a good road and it has more industry, you see? Factories and all that, and a higher level of people is

coming in. Before it was just a slum with a bad road and was popular with people with no resources, who lived in shanties. We are improving now, bit by bit, because better people are coming in.

Each *barrio* typically has a parish church with an undeveloped park adjacent to it. In some of the *barrios*, the church administers small parochial schools. Protestant churches are in evidence, with at least two or three in each *barrio*. Pairs of immaculately attired Mormon missionaries also make regular sorties into the area.

A notable mark of upward mobility in these *barrios* is the "overbuilt house": a modest frame residence to which have been added extra rooms, a porch, a garage, expensive wooden facades, elaborate iron grating over the windows, and metal or wood fencing. Expenditures for such additions may be explained by the individual's attaining a level of income or savings which permits migration to another more prestigious area. When he chooses to remain in the *barrio*, he demonstrates his higher status through conspicuous consumption.

These stable *barrios* contiguous to the central city provide relatively inexpensive housing with easy access to both the business hub and the outlying sections of the city. Within most *barrios*, the poorest housing is located on the steepest slopes and near the bottom of the ravines. These may be no more than shacks pieced together from packing crates. Steep alleys wind down to the stream bottom and are packed on both sides with houses. Yet even here, most have electricity and television antennas.

Space is more abundant than in the central *barrios*. Empty lots are common and are often converted into athletic fields for nearby residents. Since soccer is *the* sport of Costa Rica, it is not surprising that many of these *barrios* have their own athletic teams and clubs. Where these are strong, one finds well-appointed athletic fields at local school sites, some of which even have night lighting.

III. Stable Residential Barrios—Government Housing Projects

A number of housing projects have been constructed by the government in the last decade, largely for middle-class and lower-middle-class residents. These are intended to be "planned" communities with a full range of services. The houses are typically one-level concrete-block structures built in a continuous configuration, like row houses. One resident characterized his home in such a project as follows:

> My *barrio* is for the middle class, and I find that we have all we need and are better off than the majority of the *barrios*. We are progressing—though we need more schools and more sports fields—but we're making giant strides. I think it's better than any other middle-class *barrio*.

Each house has a small grass plot in front and a small utility yard behind. Uniformity is a stated goal; project regulations forbid modification of the house appearance. However, residents overcome the regulations by applying their own color of paint and by building fences, gardens, or a miscellany of structural appendages. A major social security system clinic serves the residents of the largest of these projects, while those of other projects have easy access to ambulances or smaller clinics. Such facilities reflect coordinated central planning.

Most projects of this type have been built in undeveloped coffee groves and other open spaces. Some, however, have been grafted onto existing *barrios*. In these cases, the contrast between preexisting lower-class housing and the new government-sponsored lower-middle-class housing can be stark; it underscores the problems faced by public-housing programs. Because these programs must be self-sufficient, the government has been forced to give priority to housing for middle-class workers, at the expense of housing for the poor. The latter, though a greater need, has been given a relatively low priority.

In design and execution, Costa Rica's housing projects are intended to be low-density and comfortably residential. A pedestrian-mall is designed with the special needs of children in mind, broad walkways and grass plots running through the center of each block. Such untrammeled space is ideal for play and neighborly interaction.

Much like the structures they are replacing, some of these houses have been converted to commercial establishments, largely into tailoring, shoemaking, or electrical-repair shops. Such conversion, however, is much rarer than in the contiguous old-style residential areas (Type II, above). Although there are groceries, meat shops, and small soda shops in these projects, the range of services available is much more limited than in the areas nearer the center of the city. Most residents depend on bus transportation and do their shopping in town.

Lower-class residents in other *barrios* of the city mention the projects as examples of desirable housing to which they themselves aspire. One commented:

> But the poor don't have it—they have to go live far away from the capital. A project is pretty and all, but one like me can't live there—the houses are expensive—people who work in offices, accountants, skilled people, they can live there—I can't pay for one of those houses—only people who have had the luck to study and get good jobs. It can't be like that with me—because the working class has all the problems.

IV. Satellite Towns

Before the recent mushrooming of San José, many small towns surrounded the capital and enjoyed completely independent identities. Today, though retaining to some degree the physical form of provincial towns, they have been swept into the political and economic whirlpool of the nation's capital. At their core, they are Spanish-colonial-type grid towns centered on the plaza-church complex. Their outer boundaries tend to remain distinct, marked by open land or specific breaks in topography. Yet they are being increasingly integrated into metropolitan San José.

Some of the satellite towns lie directly in the path of San José's rapid development. One town has already been engulfed by the city, and others may be absorbed within the next few years. As a whole, the satellite towns provide a wider range of entertainment and economic resources than the contiguous residential *barrios* of the city proper. They have their own cinema, a wide range of restaurants and dance halls, and abundant athletic facilities. Many have their own markets and such diverse businesses that one seldom needs to go to the central city to shop.

Several of these towns have well-known civic fiestas that periodically draw residents out from the central city. They tend to contain a variety of socioeconomic strata, with housing for both ends of the social scale. In many ways they are microcosms of the larger society. They are the site of a wide range of government institutions: civil guard posts, clinics, schools, Red Cross facilities, and *alcaldías*, or seats of municipal government. They have their own cemeteries and branch offices of downtown banks. And at their center is always the plaza, hub of activity for business, government, and simple social interaction.

At least half the satellite towns have developed into bedroom areas for San José's professional and upper classes. The elegant houses built by these groups stand at the fringes of the old towns, however, and their occupants interact only minimally with the traditional residents.

V. Peripheral Transitional Barrios

These are *barrios* in a present state of great flux. Initially they were occupied by impoverished working-class families. Today they are characterized by extensive street-paving, rapidly expanding commercial development, destruction of old housing, new factories, and much open land. The next five years will determine which of several possible development paths each will take. Light industry could predominate, residential housing could take over, or there could be a variety of mixes of the two.

Because they are in such a transitional state, contrasts of residence type are striking, with new upper-middle-class residences being built near streets with strikingly lower-class housing. Land speculation, land-price inflation, and competition for available space has provoked and will continue to provoke tension between new home owners, investors, and old residents.

These areas are notable for their variety. One has a number of large, elegant "motels" especially constructed to serve as discreet trysting places. Only a few yards away there are mundane furniture factories, coffee groves, housing of disparate levels, and a small shopping complex. The presence of much open land and such a variety of alternatives leaves the future of the *barrio* most uncertain.

Made of concrete with simple designs, churches in these transitional neighborhoods are typically new and are adorned even less than the stark structures found throughout the central city. The plainness of these and the equal plainness of plazas and other centers of assemblage suggest that these *barrios* are transient and corporateless. In spite of abundant land, little is being set aside for communal uses. Public spirit and pride would thus appear to be conspicuously low.

VI. Squatter Settlements

While squatter settlements have been described as providing massive housing for many of Latin America's poor urban population, they are relatively rare in San José. The two from which we drew subjects are only three and ten years old. Each has several hundred residents who invaded land belonging to the municipality in a haphazard fashion. They have both grown steadily, although without the kind of planning and coordinated strategies reported for *barriadas* in Lima (Mangin 1970). Both have line village configurations with shacks hugging both sides of very narrow, essentially impassable dirt streets. There is no pavement or sidewalks, although the older of the two settlements does have electricity, water, and a small concrete chapel with a corrugated metal roof. The chapel, built by the residents themselves, doubles for meetings of the sports club and for weekly movies sponsored by a priest from a nearby satellite town that has "adopted" the settlement.

If services and official recognition of land rights are to be obtained, good relationships with the government are vital. One resident summarized the situation:

> I like the people and the atmosphere [*ambiente*] in the *barrio*. It has to change though, put in a road—something the government has to do. When we built there, they told us that we couldn't because it belonged to the government and that at any time some tractor would come and knock down all the houses. They couldn't because there were so many children in the *barrio*, and since then there hasn't been any trouble. It was just a threat. I think that the government can't do anything because we are children of our fatherland and we have a right to the little piece of land that belongs to us.

The government is no longer threatening the existence of these areas. To the contrary, the welfare agency has even begun studies to develop a program to give new low-cost housing to the residents of the newer settlement.

Squatter housing is inevitably ramshackle. Loose boards and pieces of tin roofing gleaned from construction sites are put together to form residences of conglomerate appearance. The older shacks have room divisions elaborately appointed with hardboard walls and are decorated with magazine cutouts, plastic flowers, and religious ornaments. Some of the most makeshift, however, are built of nothing other than cardboard and will probably fail to last a single eight-month rainy season.

Community structure is more apparent in the older settlement than in the newer one. Shortly after the settlement was formed, a local "Committee for Community Progress" campaigned for utilities. Though this group is now dormant, it did accomplish its end. The *barrio* also fields a very good and usually winning soccer team. Its fame is such that several men who live in an adjacent, prestigious residential community have even joined. We have never heard these players refer to the settlement's poverty. Instead, they speak of how proud they are to be members of a winning team. A major *barrio* effort raised money to buy the uniforms that are now worn at all games. Though poor, then, the residents seem to take pride in the place in which they live. Community spirit is far livelier than in the transitional *barrios*.

VII. Rural Communities

Although the rural villages from which we drew 3.5 percent of our subjects are agriculturally based, they are only forty minutes from downtown San José by bus. They enjoy basic government services common to other rural areas: the rural police guard and a school. Other institutions present include community-center buildings, branches of Alcoholics Anonymous, and, in one case, a small library. Every village has a church, though these vary in maintenance and quality. Priests generally visit these rural villages on a monthly basis.

The villages are enveloped by coffee groves. Housing is varied and includes old wattle and daub, adobe, and modern concrete-block structures. The range of commerce in the villages is very limited, with only a small bar or two and a couple of small groceries in evidence. For most shopping, residents travel to San José. Many families have members who commute daily to the city for work.

As is the case all over Costa Rica, soccer is popular. Rustic soccer fields are everywhere, and groups of boys gather daily for informal games. Social life is tranquil. In the evenings, people are frequently seen walking in family or age-mate groups along the narrow paved roadways traversing the settlements.

Despite the fact that San José comprises a metropolitan area of over 400,000 persons, with a diverse array of commercial, industrial, and residential areas, it has an amazingly intimate character. A person can pass quickly from one type of neighborhood to another and constantly meet acquaintances. The unifocal nature of the transportation systems facilitates this and contributes to a "personal" rather than an anonymous style of life. One can easily reach the farthest neighborhood in but a half hour from the center of the city.

SAMPLE REPRESENTATIVITY IN SOCIOECONOMIC TERMS

Table 13 shows that our subjects were drawn from a variety of *barrios* and *barrio* types. Out of the 546 *barrios* that have been identified for the metropolitan area (Fonseca-Tortós et al. 1970: 15), we recruited subjects from 45. We were impressed that such a broad representation could be assembled through the simple pursuit of networks emanating from a limited number of interactional nodes. This suggests that mobility over the metropolitan area is such that networks spread all over the city and that persons often interact without regard to their place of residence.

To assess the representativity of our sample, we related it to a general socioeconomic profile of the metropolitan area. This we based on mean income, as abstracted from the 1973 census. Table 14 presents these data by neighborhood type, albeit with two fundamental limitations:

1. We broke the census down into its district elements—each element being roughly a square block—and defined *barrios* for the neighborhood types in terms of these elements. A difficulty here is the absence of precise *barrio* boundaries, as evidenced by the lack of agreement among *barrio* residents about the boundaries.

2. One census element often spans two or more *barrios*. For example, a squatter settlement located in a sparsely settled section of the metropolitan area may be found in a census element which also includes an upper-middle-class housing development. Thus, *barrio* analysis, based on the census elements, cannot yield a completely accurate socioeconomic profile, given the fact that elements spanning more than one *barrio* have been deleted from the analysis.

Table 14 shows that subjects recruited for our base sample tended to earn salaries somewhat below the average for their *barrios*. In general, however, they fell within normal limits for wage earners in their respective neighborhood type.

In another effort to remedy the lack of social perceptivity in census tract data, Fonseca-Tortós et al. (1970) recognized the homogeneous quality of many of the named *barrios* in the city and attempted to rank them for the whole metropolitan area. Their work is part of a series of studies on social stratification sponsored by the Centro de Estudios Sociales y de Población (CESPO) and financed in part by the Ford Foundation. They began by selecting 285 *barrios* from the urban area. For each of these they then set topographical boundaries—a difficult task, given the imprecision of the *barrio* concept itself. Next they programmed elements from the 1963 census to construct demographic data at the level of each *barrio*. Using mean income calculations for each of these *barrios*, and mean values for housing quality, they then developed an index of socioeconomic level for each *barrio*. This enabled them to rank order the *barrios* and subsequently to make relative comparisons.

By correlating this *barrio* ranking with the residences of our subject population, we have been able to assess the representativity of that population in terms of *barrio* economic ranking (Table 15). A paired *t*-test was run on the percentages of subjects from both the base sample and the matched-pair sample that corresponded to each *barrio* decile rank; the differences were found to be not significant. In other words, our matched-pair sample was as representative of *barrio* heterogeneity as was the base sample. Only the lowest and the highest deciles were not represented.

Our sample, then, represented a wide range of residential *barrio* types and economic levels. It was especially representative of the lower, or laboring, class. By using the network approach, we were able to avoid working with only an insular, unconnected group. Our approach assured us that we would learn of drug use in natural settings of San José where normal social life would not be impeded by institutionalization or clinical environments. Because individuals in our sample were contacted through their participation in social networks in which we ourselves came to participate, they form a socially connected, geographically disperse, economically active group, allowing us to obtain an insider's view of how marihuana has been incorporated into daily living by urban Costa Ricans.

4/ The Subjects as Children

A GENERAL PROFILE

The young age at which many of our subjects began to use marihuana led us to give particular attention to their experiences as young children, especially as these involved family, school, and informal groupings of peers. To set the stage for such inquiry, an initial personal-data questionnaire was administered to the entire 240 subjects recruited for the base sample. Although the questionnaire covered a wide variety of topics, the answers it generated revealed very few differences between users and nonusers. Subjects were questioned about their parents (whether living or dead), the age at which they had left home, with whom they had lived as children, how many brothers and sisters they had had, and whether there had been emotional disturbance in the family. The only significant differences to emerge concerned the persons by whom the individuals had been raised. More users than nonusers had grown up in reformatories or with persons other than their parents or grandparents (see Tables 16 and 17). While it is impossible to say that such experiences would *make* a boy turn to marihuana, in the case of being sent to a reform school, it would probably reflect an unstable childhood and a greater likelihood of being exposed to marihuana users.

When the matched-pair subsample was analyzed independently from the original base sample, only one other difference emerged: more users than nonusers had older sisters. In general, with both the base-line and the matched-pair samples, the similarities between users and nonusers far outweighed the differences. Yet many of these were merely structural in nature. When we probed deeply into the early personal experiences of the eighty-two individuals selected for the matched pairs, we discovered that the content and process of their backgrounds often varied markedly.

The Costa Rican working-class family is a direct product of its rural background of small, independent holdings relatively isolated from one another and exploited by nuclear units. Parental stability, close ties with extended kin, and a reluctance to develop relationships on the basis of mere geographical propinquity—all seem to be features functionally geared to such a way of life.

In many ways, the Costa Rican family reminds one of farm families of the United States Midwest. Families manage to maintain continuous control over their holdings by passing ownership on to a favored one or two offspring in the style of the Irish stem family. Godparentage and fictive kin ties are largely ignored.

Given such a traditional family structure, the Costa Rican is free to choose employment wherever he sees fit. A solid conjugal relationship acts as a stabilizer, and frequent contact with the closest members of his bilateral kindred provides him with insurance against the ravages of unemployment, illness, or other such calamities. His tenuous ties with neighbors leave him latitude for participation in associational and special-interest networks such as music, sports, drug use, and political partisanship. At the same time, the general stability of mother-father and parent–child interactions provides lasting points of reference in the midst of rapid change.

As described by our informants, a typical family of orientation has about five members, including both parents, two or three children, and occasionally a bilateral relative. The range, however, is wide, with some households as small as one and others as large as sixteen, where economic constraints and pressures have forced family clustering. To lower rent for a short time or extended periods, families will graft onto each other, doubling up on space and halving costs. Typically, a sibling of husband or wife will also live "temporarily" until he or she is able to make an independence break. Finally, an aging parent may pass his or her last years as yet another member of the household.

For most of the matched-pair sample, both biological parents were present during at least the early years of childhood. In 20 percent of the cases of users and 5 percent of nonusers, single-parent households were headed by the mother. In fewer cases the households were headed by the father. (See Table 18.)

In cases that did not fit the general pattern, the relational structure of a nuclear family was maintained by the introduction of surrogate parents. Thus grandmothers or aunts and uncles would fill in the breach. There was no clear tendency for such individuals to be either patrilineally or matrilineally related. The overwhelming pattern was one of bilateralism. One man related such an arrangement with a paternal aunt:

> My father never lived at home. Finally things got so bad that my aunt took me home with her. I never saw my father, and I loved my aunt more than my mother. I was happy with her. She gave me food and clothing. My older brothers and sisters sometimes slept with us in the house or went with another aunt. I stayed there until I got married when I was eighteen. My own family had disappeared. They were all over the country.

When men had, as children, been treated decently under such arrangements, they reacted positively to them.

Although, as already noted, the majority of parental bonds were stable, a considerable minority, about 30 percent, were dissolved before the subject reached the age of twelve. Table 19 shows how parental relationships were likely to have ended. Dissolution of the family was usually precipitated by the death of a parent and accompanied by an unsuccessful economic adjustment. Children were often divided up among relatives, but some ran away and no family structure remained whatsoever. Normally, structure could be maintained with surrogates in parental roles or with a single-parent household.

In contrast to the pattern reported for much of Latin America, bonds of fictive kinship, godparents and *compadrazgo*, seem little elaborated (see Table 20). Where contact was maintained with a godparent, little more than a social greeting was exchanged, and none of the customary gift-giving and assistance was bestowed upon the godchild. One subject described the relationship all too typically, as follows:

> I got stuck with a poor godfather. He never helped me. I can't remember a single gift from him. My parents had to baptize me; I was one and almost walking, so this man offered to be the *padrino* [godfather]. They accepted to speed things up, and so I was baptized. But he never did anything for me.

Many could not remember ever having met their godparents and did not even know who they were. Some acknowledged that their relatives in the country were much more active in keeping the ties of ritual kinship alive. In the city, however, neither godparenthood nor *compadrazgo* seems important to the working class either as a religious sacrament or as a set of social relationships.

Interactions within the family of orientation were highly developed for both users and nonusers. Interaction with both sides of the extended kindred was also elaborate, with visits even daily among kinsmen. Propinquity with relatives was a highly valued residential goal that one still sees in the manner in which kinsmen tend to cluster in *barrio* neighborhoods. Thus one subject mentioned that his brother went "away" to live on the other side of town but returned to the neighborhood because it was too difficult to keep in touch with his kin.

In spite of such propinquity, many informants insisted that they were reluctant to depend on relatives for help and in fact claimed never to do so. At the same time, life-history details revealed significant help and exchange among relatives. One man told a story of family hostility and absence of any help whatsoever and yet later explained how an aunt had generously given his family the lifetime free use of a small farm. The ambivalence seemed due to the informant's own insecurity and inability to contribute to the family because of his being perpetually unemployed and an alcoholic.

Moving from house to house was common, although 36 percent of both users and nonusers did not move once in their entire childhoods. Twenty-six of forty-one—63 percent of both users and nonusers—moved less than once every year. These moves were necessary because of job changes, doubling up on housing, or an economic pinch or windfall. Moves were part of the adaptive strategy for maximizing resources.

The customary behavior of these families of orientation centered upon the home. Rented or owned, the house became home base for the workingman who returned for dinner, as well as for children returning from school with their school uniforms soiled from the day's scuffles and games. The home's anchor was seen as a hardworking mother. She lost her attractiveness quickly, giving birth, washing, cleaning, tending babies and aging parents, and dealing with swarms of neighborhood children.

More than for any other member of the family, for the female spouse the residential *barrio* was the main social horizon. Neighborhood shops and services were often within a block of the house, so she did not need to walk far to shop, have shoes mended, or have a school uniform repaired. Although she would sometimes send a young child to run these errands so as not to leave a baby alone, she liked to get out of the house even for simple tasks. An infrequent trip downtown to pay the electric bill was a treat, and even standing in line at the bank for up to an hour was an honorable and proper way of watching people, eavesdropping for news, and breaking the routine. We heard many accounts of these journeys, young boys learning about the shape of the city and an adult world of commerce and responsibility. A special treat of ice cream would seal the impression of high adventure.

Most informants expressed general satisfaction with their childhood homes and life (see Table 21). Usually this was stated in modest terms:

> My life, my childhood, wasn't opulent but it wasn't impoverished either. We stayed on top because my father worked and my mother rented out little houses, and we were able to defend ourselves. Not really comfortably, believe me, but we weren't desperate either.

Although not statistically significant, the higher percentage of users expressing negative feelings about childhood would seem related to their higher rate of home abandonment, to be discussed later.

Families of orientation were usually seen as supportive and rewarding rather than rancorous or frustrating. One subject described how roles were positively defined so as to minimize family discord. His experience was typical:

> We never had fights in the house. No one was mean like that. Yelling and fighting, never. I was the oldest and set the example and corrected my brothers and sisters, and they respected me. They could be playing, and one word from me was an order. My mother told them that they had to respect their older brother and do what I said.

Most subjects knew very little about their parents' courtship and marriage. They seemed surprised at the suggestion that they talk about it, and some responded, "It never occurred to me to ask." In the few cases where answers were forthcoming, it appears that the parents had known each other for several months to a year before becoming engaged and that the engagement had lasted for several months before marriage. In a few cases, engagements had lasted for years. Stable common-law arrangements were accepted as being of equal status with formal church marriages.

Parents generally got along amiably (see Table 22). One user described his parents' relations:

> My parents got along always. There was complete coordination between them. My father never punished me. He gave me advice, said, "Don't do that, do this." He had me say an Our Father when I was bad, nothing more. My mother was another story. She used an electric wire which really stung. But thank God for them, because they were right and if it hadn't been for them I might be like some

of the men in the *barrio* who drink and beat their wives. My father always told me never to spend a lot of time in bars, and I didn't. A father's advice is important because he has a lot more experience and can tell you what to do.

Very few remembered relationships that were predominantly hostile. In these exceptional cases, bitter fights typified normal interactions between parents. Not surprisingly, such relationships usually ended in separation or divorce. When parents argued, it was usually over the father's drinking or a shortage of money, although such arguments did not lead to less drinking or more money. Generally the debates would end in a stalemate. Some subjects referred humorously to a "tie score," one parent scoring a "goal" one time, the other scoring on another occasion. In a few families, arguments led to actual fighting and blows.

Our subjects' general sense of satisfaction with childhood (see Table 23) was based on many experiences. Men who felt that they had been treated fairly as children—had had enough to eat, had related to their parents, siblings, and relatives in a rewarding way, had had opportunities to play with friends, and had enjoyed the opportunity to go to school—expressed contentment when giving us their life histories. Men who were dissatisfied with their childhood tended to come from families that were not economically solvent and that had absent parents, high alcohol use by the father, fights among family members, or inconsistent and capricious treatment meted out to the children.

Mothers were generally seen as sympathetic figures, mediating between stern fathers and obstreperous peers. Costa Rican motherhood is celebrated in an elaborate Mother's Day on August 15, a national holiday coinciding with the popular Latin American celebration of the feast of the Assumption of the Blessed Virgin. Mothers are feted, sung about, and revered, but they work hard for their rewards.

For the families in which our subjects grew up, routines began early. When the sun rose at five in the morning, it was already late in the homes of working-class families. Mothers had to get their spouses to work in buses that started running at 5:00 A.M. and children off to school, which began at 7:00 A.M.

Subjects' fathers felt that good wives and mothers would never stray far from home. They thought that trips downtown should be kept to a minimum and that to be seen loitering in the street was unseemly. A man whose wife and children strayed from home was seen as not exerting enough control or authority.

Fathers tended to work full time in a stable job (see Table 24). Those who did not, often absented themselves from the family altogether. Accounts of the nature, quality, and success of the father's work were good predictors for the quality of living in the home. Not surprisingly, fathers could fulfill their family obligations only if their personal habits and preparation permitted it. The variety of skills they could offer was important in allowing them to take advantage of different job markets. The construction trades were particularly vulnerable during the eight-month rainy season, for workers were laid off at any moment for inclement weather and would lose salary for the lost hours.

Salaried workers were paid on Saturday at midday. Part would inevitably be spent immediately on a few drinks with friends, and the balance would be rationed out over the week. Although some fathers gave a weekly allowance to their wives, the majority simply turned over a daily sum for the family's food and household expenses.

Slightly less than half of the users' and nonusers' fathers tended to drink heavily. One of the first things these subjects mentioned about their fathers was the amount of liquor they consumed. In the words of one:

> All I can remember about my childhood is that my father was an alcoholic. He did incredible things to my mother when he was drunk. That is why I never drink now. I won't give my children this example. He was so different when he didn't drink. He was decent and treated us well. But drunk, just stay out of his way!

When subjects complained of going hungry as children (as they often did), alcohol was often mentioned as the cause.

As a rule, fathers tended to spend their free time with their peers from work or with friends rather than with their families. Through control over the family budget, however, they asserted their role as head of the household in an authoritarian manner. Subjects often found that their mother ran the house until their father came home and that then he would take charge. Superior-male authority patterns seemed solidly entrenched as operating principles in most homes.

More than half the respondents said they were not at all spoiled (*chineados*) as children. They talked about general family poverty as not permitting it. Those who thought they had been spoiled described special trips downtown for something to eat and gifts of money to go to the movies or to buy candy. Gifts at Christmas were also a sign of recognition. Elaborate rewards, such as the one described below were, however, very unusual:

> Once they gave me a bicycle. I had gotten into so much trouble at school that they thought they could get me to behave if they gave me a nice present. . . . I kept up with my studies and passed that year. They gave me a new suit of clothes when I passed.

More common were stories of parental punishment. All subjects were punished from time to time. In general, they perceived such treatment as deserved. When they did not, they felt that mothers were less just than fathers (see Table 25). Some punishments were perceived as so unjust that they led the individual to leave home. When describing such situations, subjects focused on the severity and humiliation of the acts:

> My mother punished me hard. When I was little she put my sister's dresses on me so that I wouldn't leave the house. God! I just hated that! I stripped off all my clothes, and the moment she stopped watching me I grabbed my other clothes and ran away. I liked to wander around the rivers, fishing and things like that.

Relations with siblings apparently were highly variable. Often subjects developed a buddy relationship with a brother of nearly the same age. Yet even in very close families sibling feuds developed. One young man described how such cleavages could occur:

My brother and I had a contradictory relationship. He got along fine with me, but I couldn't stand him. He drank when I was little, and he scared me. I tried to keep out of his way then, and I still don't have anything to do with him. I had two sisters, one older and one younger. I got along fine with them. We understood each other and lived at home together. My other sisters were older and had left home, so I didn't know them very well.

Weekly routines included Sunday Mass, a must for the most pious member of the family. This was nearly always the mother. In the words of one informant:

> My mother was a fanatic about religion, but my father wasn't. He was—how shall I put it—he was one of those who didn't believe in anything or anybody. He didn't even have an idea of God. It was because of the liquor that he never thought about it. She was just the opposite. Exaggerated! The house was full of saints and candles. Every night she was praying to some saint. She'd go to Mass to pray to the saints, then come home and do it again.

As children, subjects tended to go to Mass with their mothers but rarely became sufficiently involved with the church to serve as altar boys. Because Mass attendance was under parental or motherly pressure, they stopped going regularly during adolescence, thus gradually moving into the predominant adult-male pattern for this segment of Costa Rican society.

In speaking of their present perception of the church and the priesthood, few had anything good to say. Several told stories about priests who were capricious in chastising them as children, and some claimed that priests had made homosexual advances to them when they were budding adolescents. In no case was a priest described as an admirable role model.

Religious instruction tended to come exclusively from either the mother or some other female figure. Simple prayers were taught and often recited together. Concepts of God were vague; he was seen as punitive and supportive, both and neither. Sexual guidance was almost nonexistent. Most parents encouraged their children to participate in catechism classes given in school or church; thus most subjects had been baptized and had taken First Communion. More emphasis was placed, however, on decorous behavior in front of neighbors and friends, avoiding scandals, and eschewing gossip.

> My parents and my grandmother talked to me about morals and good behavior. They told me that if I saw an older person in the street I was to say "Good afternoon" or "Good morning" and be very respectful. "Stay out of things that don't concern you," they said. Every night my grandmother and I prayed an Our Father together. They always gave me good advice and were very firm. If I went into the street without permission, they would spank me.

Family ritual cycles are traditionally a way of structuring relationships and reinforcing roles. In Costa Rican working-class homes, however, ritual within the family seems little developed, and the events of Christmas were the only calendrical family ceremonial activity reported. Christmas Eve, *la noche buena*, was fondly remembered as the night when the family gathered to wait for Baby Jesus to arrive with gifts. During the vigil, all ate tamales and drank black coffee.

The women might drink a heavily sweetened eggnog called *ronpope*, but the men would manage to find something stronger. A crèche scene, a *portal*, would be a menagerie of dolls representing wise men, shepherds, firemen, farmers, salesmen, and the like. They would be surrounded by plastic trucks, trees, ornaments, moss, stumps, lights, tinsel, and, for the big night, baskets of grapes and apples—two very expensive imported fruits. The *portal* would remain in place until the end of January or the beginning of February, when the neighbors would be invited in and all would say a rosary and then drink a mildly alcoholic corn brew called *chicha* just before the dismantling.

When asked to talk about family customs, these are the events subjects would describe. Many *noche buenas* were more modestly celebrated, and, lamentably, some households were regularly forgotten by the Baby Jesus altogether. Other kinds of family ritual such as birthday parties, family dinners, reunions, Sunday treks, and the like were not remembered as regular or even sporadic happenings. This paucity in family ritual holds even today. Family mealtimes are austere events, birthdays go by unrecognized, Sundays are marked by independent plans, and, in general, family ritual events are scarce and pale.

Typically, the parents of our subjects did not belong to clubs, sports teams, or community organizations. They might have attended public meetings organized around a problem or project, but they did not tend to affiliate with any organization with a regular schedule of activities, nor did they show any leadership in solving *barrio* problems. They generally did not belong to or participate in church guilds, nor did they help the parish in any tangible or organizational way.

Their political actions were similarly passive. They would vote in the elections every four years (voting is required by law, although the law is rarely enforced) but would rarely help by volunteering their time. (See Table 26.) Only four parents (10 percent) of nonusers and seven (17 percent) of users were reported to have had problems with the law. It is well to note that these difficulties were usually related to public inebriation.

The pattern that emerges is one of a general reluctance to become involved. This continues into the present generation of subjects, for they fear the risk of public exposure or commitment. Even neighbors are looked upon as threatening.

> My family wasn't well thought of in the *barrio*. We were not much involved in things—politics, for example. The neighbors nearest us hated the way my parents voted and made it rough on them. There were arguments, and my parents decided it was better not to have anything to do with them. They didn't like having friendships in the neighborhood. They preferred enemies.

A value emphasized time and again by these parents seems to have been that one should live tranquilly (*vivir tranquilo*), exercising caution with those who might cause "problems."

As children our subjects were constantly tugged between their introverted families of orientation and the natural attractions of peers encountered at school and on the street. Family demands to contribute to their own support came early:

I worked as a kid collecting fares in the buses. I put in half a day in that and went home and played and studied. I was going to school at night, so I did my homework whenever I had some free time. Sometimes I made furniture which I sold. I was about twelve then.

Many remembered working extensively with family members on business deals or jobs. Family economic crises, such as the death of the father, often made the son in large part responsible for the economic fate of his siblings and mother. Less urgent, but common, economic responsibilities involved the selling of tidbits of food cooked by an older sister or the mother, working with a brother gathering coffee or cutting weeds, selling gum or candy, shining shoes, or carrying bundles home for shoppers. Earnings from such work went into the family of orientation throughout childhood.

On reaching adolescence, it was common for our subjects to work and to bring their earnings home. Their jobs were usually ruggedly physical; lack of preparation made it difficult for them to find other types of work. Father-son partnerships in business or a trade were rare. While many subjects learned their father's trade, they refused to be bound by it, and today the two rarely collaborate on a project. Cottage industries such as shoemaking and tailoring are seen to have dropped in profitability because of mechanization, and both fathers and sons have increasingly been forced to broaden their skills in order to make a living.

In general, the childhood families of our subjects enjoyed economic stability and experienced neither upward nor downward mobility. Those who did recall a decline in the family's fortunes attributed it to the father's inability to work, caused in some cases by injury and in others by alcoholism or simple laziness. The decline was usually accompanied by an abundance of children and a restriction in the mother's alternatives.

Marihuana Smoking and Family Dynamics

In analyzing the life histories of our matched pairs, we came across the startling finding that twenty-four of the users and only five of the nonusers had abandoned home before the age of sixteen. This striking contrast suggests that, in spite of a pattern of similarity in general family-of-orientation structure, the content and process must have been quite different. Basic variables relating to the quality of family life—such as adequacy of food, degree of punishment, and favoritism shown to the subject's siblings—correlate with an early abandonment of home and suggest the kinds of incentives that existed to prompt the subject to leave. Once he had left home, the subject came into intense contact with street culture, and there he was often initiated into marihuana use.

Mothers and fathers of both users and nonusers came in equal proportion from rural zones, provincial towns, and the San José area. These origins are significant because they suggest that many respondents had access to a geographically dispersed kinship network which could be a resource in time of need. Migration patterns, however, reveal that in spite of this similarity in family background, users and nonusers of marihuana had different opportunities to be exposed to street culture and peer gangs.

Table 27 shows dramatically that our subjects have been, in many ways, the pawns of Costa Rican urbanization. Three time periods are defined: T1—place of origin of parents; T2—place where subjects spent their childhood; T3—place of respondence. The time of greatest migration to the city for the users' families, 44 percent, turns out to be between T1 and T2, before full entry into childhood; that is, the parents came to the city when the subject was an infant or before he was born, the result being that he passed his early years in the city itself. For nonusers, the time of greatest migration to the city was later, 36 percent between T2 and T3, that is, after their childhoods had passed. The likelihood of their being introduced to street culture at an early age was therefore greatly reduced.

Other differential family dynamics related to early abandonment of home on the part of users and concomitant entry into street life are strongly suggested by seven additional key factors and experiences:

1. Inadequacy of food as a child
2. Inadequacy of housing as a child
3. A mother working full- or part-time outside the home
4. Delegation of financial responsibility by the father to the mother
5. A weak father figure, as seen through a lower tendency to assume leadership roles
6. Preferential treatment of children, especially the subjects' siblings
7. Downward mobility

Inadequacy of food and housing was recorded in the life-history analysis when the subject recalled that he had suffered hunger as a child, that meals were missed (or that there was no money to buy food), or that housing was markedly poor and cramped. While only one of these is significant at the .05 level, taken together the two may be seen as an index of general poverty. (See Tables 28 and 29.) More could have recalled inadequate food because tolerances for conditions of residence are more flexible.

One important variable distinguishing the childhood of users from nonusers is the presence of a working mother more often among users (see Table 30). And in the families of future users, fathers either shared or delegated financial responsibility to their spouses significantly more than in the families of nonusers (see Table 31). In addition, there was a trend, although not significant, for the fathers of users, more than nonusers, to avoid community leadership roles (although in absolute numbers neither group appears to have produced many leaders) (see Table 32). These data suggest a possible pattern of female dominance in the families of users, a pattern which counters the norm in Costa Rican society.

Coupled with these tendencies was preferential treatment within the family. Users reported a much higher level of favoritism on the part of parents during their childhood (see Table 33). Although some of this preferential treatment was directed to themselves, the really significant difference in the pattern is that more of it was perceived as being directed toward their siblings. The families of future users thus appear to have been inconsistent in meting out rewards and punishments, and this in turn could have encouraged sibling rivalry, reflected in adult life by the fact that users perceived their siblings as better off and more favored.

Another statistically significant childhood experience distinguishing future users from future nonusers is downward socioeconomic mobility, adding to the picture of weakly constituted troubled families (see Table 34).

Two other family variables, mothers' use of alcohol and tobacco, seem also to have been important in determining whether the subjects would become marihuana users in later life (see Tables 35 and 36). In both cases, significantly more users than nonusers had mothers who were moralistic to the point of being abstemious. No such correlations were found with regard to tobacco and alcohol use on the part of fathers or with regard to drug use, including marihuana, on the part of either parent. The data on the mothers of users are highly suggestive. They indicate that individuals did not turn to marihuana because of a lack of moral standards in their home but rather that the opposite may have been the case.

The syndrome that preceded marihuana use, then, would appear to be early urban residence, general poverty, a working and moralistic mother, inconsistencies in child-rearing practices leading to sibling rivalry, and downward socioeconomic mobility. Closely associated with this syndrome is the abandonment of the childhood home. Parental punishment may have been a triggering factor. Of the twenty-nine users who left home before age eighteen, twelve reported having received excessive punishment in childhood. Of the thirteen nonusers who abandoned home, three reported such treatment. In some cases, brutal or humiliating punishments were the single reason given for running away.

Disintegration of the household itself appears to have been another important cause. Of the ten users who suffered such a fate, eight began immediately to live on their own; of the twelve nonusers whose childhood homes dissolved, only three went off to live on their own. The others found friends or relatives willing to take them in.

No single early experience, then, seems to have led to marihuana use. Yet many subjects who later became users had truly traumatic childhoods. Because of the death of a key parent, the financial disintegration of the family, or the incapacitation of the father, they were forced to fend for themselves. Some had to pay their own way when they were no more than six years of age. They shined shoes, stole food, begged, and worked as errand boys or package carriers to survive; they were street people in the extreme.

Reactions to the Classroom:
Early Initiation into Formal Institutions

Although education is seen in most countries as a mechanism of social mobility, this belief is especially well embedded in the minds of Costa Ricans. Though not more economically powerful than her neighbors, Costa Rica has made education a point of national pride. A favorite government slogan is that the country has more teachers than soldiers.

Great pressure is placed upon children to respond to such an opportunity. Those who do not respond tend to suffer pangs of guilt. One of our user subjects put it as follows: "I'm one of the few illiterates Costa Rica has. I never attended a day of school." Although he was overestimating Costa Rica's rate of literacy, his shame would have been less acute had he lived in a country with less public attention to formal education.

Given the fact that formal education has been viewed by generations of Costa Rican parents as a primary tool for social mobility, it is not surprising that subjects talked extensively about their experiences in school when discussing their childhood. Although in our base sample there were more illiterate nonusers than users, nonusers were also more heavily represented in the higher educational categories (primary complete, some secondary, and secondary complete) (see Table 37). Since one of the matching criteria was education, in the matched-pair subsample approximately 55 percent of both users and nonusers had completed primary school or more. Yet users were generally less tolerant when speaking of their school experiences, and data on expulsions indicate that, when in school, they had been more rebellious.

The classrooms attended by our subjects had been organized around the development of a copybook and the memorization of its contents. Examinations required attention, discipline, and preciseness—tedious requirements for many a budding adolescent. Prizes were given for excellence in a particular subject, for writing a poem that caught the teacher's eye, or for drawing a pretty picture. Rare was the student, no matter how inattentive, who did not manage to receive at least one prize. Students hardly ever had time to participate in extracurricular activities, though soccer games were ubiquitous.

Parents were often involved in the schooling process, providing assistance in the form of school uniforms and supplies, and, from time to time, help on homework. The latter, however, was sometimes counterproductive. One subject recalled how his mother had "helped" by standing behind him while he was doing his homework and hitting him on the head whenever he made a mistake. Such zealous parental concern may be attributed to the extensive public recognition given education and to pressures created when employers demand and easily find job seekers with at least complete primary schooling.

A significantly higher number of users than nonusers classified their school behavior as mischievous and recalled having had serious problems with school authorities (Table 38). The worst punishment available to the school authorities was expulsion. Fourteen of the users had suffered this fate, compared with only five of the nonusers (Table 39). The expulsions were usually provoked by the commission of an act that was seen as outrageous by the school administrators.

> I was kicked out of school because I was really nasty. I had asked permission from the teacher to go to the bathroom. That was a lie. I ran around and played in the corridors and slid down the banisters. Then I went to the bell which they used for recess. I banged on the bell, and all the kids came running out to play. The director came running out too, but at me. He grabbed me and told me not to come back to school. They were tired of me by then. He was yelling at me and yanking on my ears. Boy, was he boiling!

Although education was an important value in the society, young boys commonly had to drop out of school because of economic constraints. In addition, the attraction of friends, swimming holes, and the street gang provided strong competition for the organized discipline of the classroom. Table 40 shows self-reported attendance history.

Tables 37, 38, 39, and 40 show clearly that, as a group, future marihuana users found less satisfaction in their school experiences than did those who became nonusers. Yet they seldom blamed the institution; instead, they suffered guilt that they had not taken advantage of the opportunities afforded them.

School problems always tend to be extensions of problems encountered at home, and the two usually feed on one another. Both lead to an early disenchantment with one's lot, a desire to escape, and a willingness to engage in rebellious, antisocial, or illegal behavior, of which marihuana use would be a prime example. Understandably, adults reflecting upon such experiences would tend to remember themselves as "bad" boys (see Table 41).

Although some subjects seem to have had only marginal success in school, most appear to have internalized the values implicit in a vast educational investment: that education is good, available, and will provide important rewards to those who perform according to the institution's expectations. Thus many subjects desired that their own offspring take full advantage of educational opportunities and apply themselves conscientiously in school. Nearly all the 35 percent of both users and nonusers who described "plans" for helping their children reach high goals felt that education would be a major factor in enabling them to obtain high-paying jobs, professional status, and other dramatic steps upward.

Adolescence: The Budding of Adult Relationship Networks

During our subjects' adolescent years we see logical continuations of the trends established during childhood. As in childhood, the proportion of future marihuana smokers who left home was significantly greater than that of their non-marihuana-smoking controls. Inadequate food seems to have been a major contributing factor. (See Tables 42 and 43.)

Overall, the most significant persons in the socialization of our subjects were their biological parents. But for those 70 percent of users and 30 percent of nonusers who left home in either childhood or adolescence, groups of age mates must have played extremely important roles. Running with a gang was a major means of accumulating social knowledge, and it formed a base for one's future friends, co-workers, and neighbors. Groups of adolescent boys would gather on street corners, sports fields, or in coffee groves, playing or talking. The older members of such groups would provide role models that were brash and cocky, typified by risqué overtures directed at interesting women who passed. Recreation for these groups would include soccer games, visits to houses of prostitution (usually a first initiation into sex), and many hours *hablando paja* ("shooting the bull"). It was in such contexts that our subjects tended to learn how to use alcohol, tobacco, or marihuana. Drinking with peers and older friends, and taking recreational treks to different parts of the city, to the port city of Puntarenas, or to a country locale or a coffee grove near the city were and are popular pastimes.

The contrast between such groups and the formal relational grouping of the family was striking. The street and the family formed two points on an axis—two extremes where different lessons and different behaviors were learned. The two offered polar attractions: the dull routine of family and the adventurous interaction of peers. Peer groupings tended to be fairly broad and included young men and boys from about ten years of age to the late teens. It was the older boys who often furnished the example and instruction in how to smoke marihuana.

Young men who opted for primary interaction with street groups sometimes migrated to the banana zones of the country, where they met others like themselves, similarly seeking their fortunes in the high-paying, hard-living world of growing and harvesting fruit. This was the street culture of San José transplanted to the industrialized agricultural zones, but a mobile street culture nevertheless. Initiation into such groups involved several shared diagnostic experiences: looking for sex together on arduous jobs, drinking together, sharing a special slang, and often smoking marihuana. Thus, for many, marihuana was first identified with a combination of work, recreation, and friendship. Such associations tended to continue throughout the smoking career.

Much of this adolescent activity would be defined by society, of course, as delinquency. During adolescence, future marihuana users developed a pattern strikingly different from that of nonusers, thus reaping the harvest of the problems of early childhood: weakly constituted families, working and moralistic mothers, disciplinary excess and inconsistency, sibling rivalry, poverty, and downward social mobility. In many cases, they had seen their parental home destroyed through separation, divorce, or death and had had a series of negative experiences in school. It should come as no surprise that many, during adolescence, began to engage in delinquent behavior and were sent to the reformatory (see Table 44).

The fact that 36.6 percent of the chronic users in our matched-pair sample had at some time or other served a reformatory sentence whereas not a single nonuser in the sample had done so would seem to be one of the most significant findings of our study (see Table 45). On the basis of these figures and the content of the life histories themselves, one could argue that the reformatory had served as a school for marihuana smoking as well as for other delinquent behavior. Noteworthy in this regard is that although 17.1 percent of the nonusers spoke of their delinquent acts during adolescence, not a single one had been taken to the reformatory for these acts. By contrast, 83.3 percent of the users who committed delinquent acts were sentenced. A reasonable hypothesis for the difference would seem to be that users were pursued by the authorities. Once designated as "drugees," they became more vulnerable both because of continued marihuana smoking and for other reasons, whether related to marihuana or not.

Two other facets of the life histories of these individuals indicate that when users were adolescents they were as a group already moving along a course different from that of nonusers. The first of these is their work record (see Table 46); the second is their pattern of courtship (for discussion of courtship see Chapter 5). Both indicate less-than-solid involvement in the traditional institutions of society.

Socialization, Marihuana, and Alcohol

In commenting on the relationship of adolescent behavior to marihuana smoking, it would be well to note that similar relationships exist with regard to alcohol. Both users and nonusers who were reported to be heavy drinkers as adults proved to have been significantly ($p = .01$) more delinquent and were more often involved in fights as youths ($p = .02$) than were moderate or light drinkers. (No such relationship between future marihuana use and physical aggression in youth was found.) As with marihuana users, those individuals who are now moderate or heavy drinkers were absent from school significantly ($p = .03$) more often than were light drinkers and abstainers. Moderate and heavy drinkers also came from families that had serious conflicts with the law, church, or school ($p = .05$), and such drinkers are now significantly ($p = .005$) more involved in extralegal economic activity than are light drinkers and abstainers.

Although moderate and heavy drinkers were spoiled and indulged more as children than light drinkers and abstainers ($p = .01$), they tended to consider their overall childhood experiences as being only fair to bad ($p = .05$). Moderate and heavy adult drinkers tended to work more as children than did abstemious and light drinkers. They were also more likely to abandon home as teenagers than were light drinkers.

Just as in the case of marihuana use, it is not possible to say that it was alcohol use that *caused* these events and conditions. Like marihuana, alcohol was an important substance and symptom among the working class, widely available and used to escape the stresses of daily life. How pervasive its use and abuse is in Costa Rica is shown by the fact that the National Commission on Alcoholism (Morales and Chassoul 1972: 2–5) reported that 93 out of every 1,000 deaths in the country were alcohol-related, that 59.7 out of every 1,000 hospitalizations were for alcoholism, and that 53.3 out of every 1,000 hospital admissions were for cases of delirium tremens. The manufacture and use of *chirrite,* or *guaro* (cane alcohol), on a clandestine and illegal basis is a major criminal activity in all areas of the country; over one thousand illegal stills are destroyed every year (Morales and Chassoul 1972: 8–10). Drunkenness and alcohol-related crimes accounted for 66 percent of *all* arrests in Costa Rica in 1971 (Sotela and Morales 1972: 5); in the same year, marihuana arrests accounted for only 2 percent.

Socialization: An Overview

Perhaps the most important feature in the childhoods of users and nonusers is the general overall similarity of socialization structures. In terms of content and process, however, major differences appeared at an early age. The most striking was the decision to leave home. We cannot say that such a decision was triggered by marihuana use. Rather, it tended to lead to it. Of the nine users who left home at age twelve or earlier, eight began smoking after leaving home and one began at the same age. Of those who left home between thirteen and sixteen years of age, six were already smoking, six began at the time they left home, and three began smoking later. The major reason given for leaving home by the fifteen who had begun to fend for themselves between ages thirteen and sixteen was economic opportunity. Not a single subject reported that he left home because of marihuana use.

TEN CASE STUDIES

The meaning of the structures and processes discussed in the preceding section can be better understood when placed in the context of real personal experiences. For this reason, we present here, in abbreviated form, ten life histories drawn from our matched-pair sample. Just as we cannot say that our general subject population is "normal" for working-class San José society, so too we do not make this claim here. It would be impossible to select in any perfect manner the "typical" user or nonuser from our subjects.

The five users and their matched nonusers discussed here present some divergences from the pattern described for the wider study. Yet these are minor. During childhood, the smokers were more downwardly mobile than were the average smokers in the total matched-pair sample of forty-one, and during adulthood they have been more involved in street life. During the same period of life, the nonsmokers suffered more excessive punishment than did the average nonsmokers for their total matched-pair sample. Other than these three exceptions, the five matched pairs discussed here are quite representative of the larger matched-pair sample of eighty-two.

Of the ten subjects discussed here, three users and three nonusers were born and reared in the San José metropolitan area. The others spent their childhood in provincial areas outside the capital. As was the case in the larger matched-pair sample, both groups of individuals were reared largely by their biological parents, and it was common for many other kinsmen to be closely involved with their upbringing.

We are struck by the fact that no statistical differences were found between users and nonusers with regard to punishment and rewards received by their parents. Looking at the ten illustrative cases presented in this chapter, we suggest that, while there may not have been a quantitative difference in punishments and rewards in the families of orientation of users and nonusers in the full sample, there could have been a qualitative difference, especially if we take into consideration the context in which punishments and rewards were administered. The ten life histories reviewed here suggest that the nonusers were treated more consistently by parents and were less subject to capricious acts or events than were the users. Nonusers also were more constantly controlled and placed in responsible roles by their families. With respect to schooling, they were less frequently involved in disruptive behavior, absenteeism, and expulsion.

We have already learned from the full matched-pair sample that more users than nonusers left home before age eighteen, that more users spent some time in the reformatory, and that significantly more nonusers worked full-time during adolescence. There was a trend among users' families of orientation toward downward social mobility during adolescence, as contrasted with a relatively stable or even upward socioeconomic movement for nonuser families during childhood. In this selection of ten individuals, these trends are even more strongly represented than in the full matched-pair sample.

In our analysis, we first present a brief summary of each individual and then go on to review the factors in his life history that tend to differentiate between users and nonusers. Where possible, each subject is allowed to speak for himself. The names used are, of course, fictitious. To aid in interpretation, all users have been given names beginning with *M,* all nonusers names beginning with *J.*

Manuel

Manuel, a user, is twenty-four years old, a short, wiry man who dresses ostentatiously. He is amiable and a lively conversationalist, attributes that contribute positively to his work as a shoeshine man and small-time gambler. He is an expert in executing the "shell and pea" game (*chapas*). His childhood was spent in San José with his parents, although his father's work as a clerk was unstable because of alcoholism. His mother also worked from time to time. Manuel says he was spoiled by his parents and believes that he was the favorite child, even though this meant nothing more than his mother giving him the responsibility of accompanying his father and seeing to it that he did not get drunk. Manuel perceived his father to be unconcerned about his education and imposing only occasional light punishment. Although his mother punished him violently, Manuel considered this to be just and warranted. His father's alcoholism led to brusque social descent, loss of the family's home, and a move by the family to a "fifth rate" hotel in a high-crime neighborhood.

In these circumstances, family discipline was extraordinarily weakened as the children were sent into the street to obtain food and clothing in any way they could. Manuel was about nine or ten years of age at this time. In school he reached only the third grade, and by then he had already tried to run away several times. His mother went to look for him just as she had searched for his drunken father. By the age of ten he permanently abandoned his home.

In his new milieu, Manuel made money by carrying marihuana from one individual to another; he was using the drug himself by the time he was ten years old. He began to steal in order to eat and to smoke; subsequently he was sent to the reformatory several times, eventually finishing his studies there to the sixth grade. Between his tenth and fourteenth birthdays, when not in the reformatory, Manuel slept in doorways protected by pieces of newspaper and cardboard. At fifteen he began to live with a prostitute who acted as a fence for the things he stole. It was she who introduced him to the world of the shoeshine "boys," where Manuel found a type of street life that pleased him. From that time onward, in his words, "I have only gone with whores."

Despite such vicissitudes, Manuel now lives with his parents. His father has given up alcohol, the ambience of the home is now pleasing, and his father has again taken to managing the family budget. Manuel says he has had no children. He smokes marihuana on social occasions and when he works, saying that his favorite experience is to be "high" and that what he desires least is "to be arrested." He feels that he has experienced a change in character since he began smoking, becoming less troublesome and more passive. He considers himself a reformed sinner, not a delinquent. He thinks that he is constantly harassed by the police simply because of his experiences in earlier life.

Jaime

Jaime, a nonuser, is Manuel's match in the subsample. At twenty-three years of age he is tall, thickset, and muscular. He is an artisan and was born in San José. He lives with his parents at the present time and has always lived in the same neighborhood. His parental home was never dissolved, despite various problems. His father, a carpenter, worked only sporadically due to alcoholism, and the family's social status dropped. He was a violent man, and when he was drunk he punished Jaime arbitrarily. Jaime remembers, however, that when his father was sober he was responsible and good. Jaime is pleased that his father stopped drinking seven years ago. He thinks of his mother with great affection and feels that when she punished him she did so justly: "My father beat us and it didn't hurt him at all. My mother, yes. It hurt her more than it did us."

As a child, Jaime suffered from lack of adequate clothing and food. Together with his siblings, he had to assume major adult responsibilities at an early age.

In contrast to Manuel's mother, Jaime's mother did not work outside the home. His formal schooling went up to the eighth grade. During his childhood his parents did not want him to work, so that he would have time to study. Nevertheless, by adolescence, Jaime wanted to earn money and to have serious relationships with girls. At first he continued to study at night while working, but little by little he lost interest in studying, not only because he would come home exhausted from work but also because he saw no connection between his studies and moving ahead in his work. Jaime gave part of his earnings to his father to help in the family's finances, and he would make gifts to his mother. As a result, the family's economic status improved. His father subsequently stopped drinking, obtained a loan, and built a small house for the family.

Jaime was married after a long engagement to a girl from his neighborhood; they live in a house next door to his wife's parents. He is now a father, and he feels very satisfied with his marriage, claiming that his marital responsibilities move him to plan and "get ahead." He does not have extramarital relations. Jaime thinks he is poorly paid, although together with his buddies from the job he has developed a system for building savings. He is an active leader in sports and has taken part in two citizens' organizations in his neighborhood. He thinks punishment should be applied to marihuana traffickers, although not to simple users. If he discovers that one of his friends uses marihuana, he breaks off the relationship with him, for he fears that he might be tempted to use the drug himself. He defends the advantages of alcohol over marihuana, although he does not enjoy being drunk. His favorite pastime is socializing with his friends.

Miguel

Miguel, a marihuana smoker, is thirty-eight, very short, and rather ugly in the opinion of his acquaintances. Although quite thin, he is apparently healthy. He presently works in a small shop as an artisan.

Born outside the capital, Miguel spent his childhood in the provinces. His mother left home when Miguel was four years old, according to his father because she was a whore. He later found out that she had died. Miguel was raised by his father, his paternal grandmother (who assumed the maternal role), and later his stepmother. His vision of his childhood is that of an abundance of money and free movement. He remembers very pleasant involvements in such things as scouts, excursions to the beach, soccer, and the movies.

Miguel enjoyed helping his father in farming. Although his father's punishments were severe, Miguel always counted on the help of his stepmother to avoid them. Similarly, his grandmother not only helped the family by raising and selling animals but also indulged and protected him. Miguel points out that although he helped his grandmother count her money, he never stole from her because she gave him enough for his needs. On reaching school age, he was first taught by tutors at home and later entered regular public school. After the seventh grade, Miguel was sent by his father to study in the latter's homeland, a neighboring Central American country. He had trouble adjusting to the punitive character of the school, and for this reason he returned to Costa Rica, where he finally reached the eighth grade.

During his childhood and adolescence, Miguel thought that money was the key to social success, especially in school and with girls. "I knew how to win the teachers over . . . I took them gifts . . . since I always had money I invited them and I heard them say . . . this 'little black' child is really good." With girls, "as every man, I kissed them; I had many girls . . . because my daddy gave me money, I invited them to the theater and to go around the city. . . ." He was nevertheless treated like a child by his family and spanked until he was an adult. He said his friends dared him to have sex, until Miguel, without letting his father know it, had relations with a prostitute at the age of eighteen. "I was completely dominated [by my father] until I was nineteen." Ever since his adolescence, he has distrusted friends and feels better alone. Miguel says he never had a friend who could advise him or in whom he could confide.

Miguel began using marihuana at age fourteen, when he discovered that one of his friends in town was a vendor. From that time on he used marihuana regularly, hiding his use from his parents and his teachers. He feels that marihuana has helped him overcome his basic timidity.

On leaving school, he learned his trade through his own initiative, although he was supported by his father, who provided him with a teacher. When Miguel was twenty-five, his father died, and he became "independent." At age twenty-seven he began to live with a woman who already had several children. After four years, however, she walked out on him, leaving him to care for their child. At the present time, Miguel lives with his little boy. They have only one bed and regularly eat in restaurants. The family with whom they share a house occasionally helps them out. Miguel says that his favorite experience is sex and that what he desires least is to be without money.

Julián

Julián, a nonuser and match for Miguel, is also thirty-eight years of age and appears short, thin, and somewhat sickly. He presently works in a printing shop. His free time is often spent in heavy drinking.

Julián spent his childhood with his parents and brothers in San José. In recalling his childhood, he emphasized their economic well-being, the military rank held by his father, and the father's violent and sadistic punishments visited on him and his brothers. On occasion his mother joined in these punishments; once she sent Julián to army headquarters with a message for his father in which the boy was denounced for his bad behavior. Julián's father responded by having him arrested and held prisoner in the headquarters jail. At times the blows that his father administered were so violent that Julián had to be treated medically by his mother.

During childhood, Julián was given small domestic tasks and often cleaned his father's guns. He was encouraged by his father to earn extra money for his school. His grandmother gave him a great deal of support, often criticizing his father and giving Julián food.

Julián doubts that he is his mother's real son because he once heard his parents talking while they were having sexual relations, the mother declaring that Julián was not hers. This led him to prefer his father to such an extent that, when he was once seriously ill, his father alone took care of him. His mother, he said, did not want to visit him even when he was hospitalized.

The revolution of 1948 profoundly affected Julián's family. His father spent three years in prison, and the family suffered and fell from a status of prestige to one of defeat and downward social and economic mobility. The experience, however, consolidated the family union. The mother worked washing clothes, and Julián began heavy work while still in school. Although his academic performance was good, his father allowed him to drop out after the eighth grade. He had been so mischievous and shown such great interest in girls (the school was coeducational) that he had at one point been expelled. On leaving school, he started off as an office boy in a print shop, learning the trade with the help of a printer uncle.

Upon marriage, Julián left his parental home, but his wife eventually died, and he found himself a widower with two children, living with his parents-in-law. During the period of his wife's illness, his use of alcohol intensified. Julián was happy with his marital life, and he has not recovered from the loss. He feels extremely guilty that his passion for alcohol impeded his giving support to his wife when she needed him. However, he continues to miss work because of periodic alcoholic crises. While his favorite activity is to be with friends, Julián says that what he likes least is to be drunk.

Marcos

Marcos is thirty-four years of age, of medium height and a robust physique. He has a broad face and a tense expression and seems aggressive. Marcos has smoked marihuana for many years. Today he operates a small business.

Marcos's mother was a single girl, and he never knew his father or had a male surrogate. Shortly after birth, he was left in the care of an aunt while his mother worked. All lived in San José. Marcos remembers this period as one of intense suffering characterized by hunger and maltreatment on the part of the aunt. He is visibly moved when he speaks of his childhood, and it bothers him to recall this painful period. He remembers that the money his mother gave to his aunt was spent on her own children, who were always preferred over him. Unable to stand the situation any longer, Marcos ran away when he was six years old, going to the marketplace, where the owner of a food stall gave him help and protection. Marcos slept in the street underneath automobiles and carts or in the passageways of the surrounding houses. He worked in the market carrying purchases for housewives and maids, until in adolescence he suffered a serious accident. From that time on he dedicated himself to the transport and wholesaling of vegetables, an activity which in his adult life has culminated in his being the owner of a wholesaling business and moving to a rural zone near San José.

When he was ten, Marcos became curious about marihuana and started using it, even though at first he did not like the effects. He continued his use sporadically, however, "to give myself the luxury of saying I am a *marihuano.*" He also began to drink *guaro* (cane alcohol), but he quickly abandoned that habit because he saw that it produced great personal and social deterioration. Under the influence of alcohol, he says, "I found myself going around filthy dirty . . . life didn't matter at all to me . . . I got involved in violent fights."

When he was twenty-seven, Marcos began to use marihuana more regularly. He had a new group of friends—all marihuana users—who shared his commercial and business interests. At the same time, he began to have relations with a woman who worked as a maid. Since their child was born, Marcos has lived permanently with her and her other child. The woman, a primary-school graduate, does not work outside the home. Although she and Marcos never married, Marcos plans to take the plunge sometime in the future, "especially to give my children more courage and to give them more of the support of father and mother." Marcos feels very proud of his business and speaks lovingly of his spouse, his well-furnished and carefully maintained home, and the academic successes of his children.

He selects his friends with caution, taking care that they are "true" and not delinquent or criminal. He enjoys meeting with those who are marihuana users for joint smoking sessions. For other recreation he likes swimming. But he takes care that his wife not be in these friendship groups: "She doesn't merit being in that sort of atmosphere, because the habit has such a bad reputation." His favorite experience is to be working; what he desires least is "to have a boss."

Jorge

Jorge, a nonuser and the match for Marcos, is thirty-seven years of age. He is alert, muscular, and of medium stature. Jorge speaks reluctantly, and to many he appears older than his years.

Jorge is an illegitimate child. He spent his childhood in the countryside helping his mother and studying with the help and stimulus of the daughters of the owner of the farm where his mother worked. His attendance at school was encouraged, he recalls, by the fact that, on the way to school, he could eat in an aunt's house. "I didn't have time to be with friends."

When the owners of the farm sold their property, Jorge was forced to move with his mother and his brother to San José. The former landlords helped his mother keep their possessions and earnings, however, so that he was able to complete the sixth grade. Shortly thereafter, Jorge started to work full-time as a fare collector on a bus, until he could learn to drive through lessons given him by the bus driver himself. He then began to work as a bus driver, a job he continues to hold.

Jorge has always felt very close to his mother, even spoiled by her. She punished him firmly, but without excess and together with well-accepted advice. He slept in his mother's bed until adolescence, and throughout his early life he competed with his older brother and with other relatives for her affection. His mother still lives with him.

Jorge had his first sexual experience at sixteen years of age with a prostitute, and after several courtships he married his present wife, with whom he has had three children. He praises his wife's patience in caring for his seventy-five-year-old senile mother. Jorge has bought a house and is paying off the mortgage. His favorite experience is being with his family, and what he desires least is being unemployed.

Mario

Mario, a marihuana user, is thirty-four years of age. He is of medium stature, thin, and appears sickly. Mario now works as a baker's helper. He spent his childhood in the San José metropolitan area, living with his parents. He was punished violently by his father and mother for his repeated failures in school and for the times he would play hooky to go swimming with friends. Mario perceived his father as indifferent and his mother as loving and concerned about his development. He was used to eating at any time of day, and his mother would hold his food for his arrival. He felt as uncomfortable at home as he did at school; as a result, he tended to flee from both places.

His mother was well-organized and economically active, trying to compensate for the problems created by his father's alcoholism. His father turned over most of the money he earned to his mother, who administered the family's budget. Mario and his wife continue the same arrangement today.

After many absences and expulsions from school, Mario felt so disgusted with the institution that he finally stopped attending. He did not finish the fourth grade. His parents accepted his decision but did not make him take a job immediately. During his adolescence he worked only sporadically: "What I enjoyed doing was wasting time, hiking through coffee groves, going out with girls, going to the theater, dancing, drinking, and playing billiards." He had no plans for his future. It was with a group of friends that he had his first sexual experience at thirteen years of age. His introduction to marihuana use came at about fifteen, encouraged by colleagues in the shoe shop where he worked. He began to smoke the drug regularly at age eighteen.

Mario left home when he was sixteen to earn money in the banana zone of Costa Rica. There he contracted malaria, however, and became so ill that he had to return to his parents' home. The illness, he says, transformed his character from that of a "fighter" to that of a "pacifist." Mario looked upon his mother's death as a turning point in his life. Following her death his activities became less ordered, and he was frequently in jail. Only upon marriage did he begin to pull himself together again.

His amorous adventures in the coffee groves eventually led him to marriage with a woman he had made pregnant. He believes that the negative image his parents-in-law have of him would not have developed if he had married his wife under different circumstances. Today he and his wife live with her parents, and Mario contributes to the support of the house. He seldom sees his children, mainly because of his work hours.

Mario hides his use of marihuana from his children and hopes that they will never take up the habit. He is satisfied with the education his children are receiving and with the relationship he has with his wife. But he feels frustrated in his desire to move ahead, and he sees no way to achieve mobility. He views himself as unlucky and absolutely at the mercy of fate, finding it difficult to be interested in anything, even sex (although he does feel stimulated sexually after he has smoked marihuana). Mario's favorite experience is to feel "high," and what he desires least is to be unemployed. He has gone through short and occasional periods of unemployment.

Juan

Juan is a nonuser and the match for Mario. He is thirty-five years old, tall, thin, athletic, and handsome. He exudes self-confidence and, by trade, is a taxi driver.

Juan spent his childhood in one of Costa Rica's provinces, together with his mother, brothers, and aunts. His mother was divorced when Juan was very small, so that he has worked in heavy labor from the time he was six. His mother married a second time, and they moved to San José, even though this did not help their precarious economic situation. Because of this, Juan's mother worked as a traveling salesperson in the banana zones, and he often went with her. When he recalls this period of his life, Juan feels ashamed; the economic stresses experienced by his family forced him to leave school when he was only in the fourth grade.

His mother dominated their home life, and Juan remembers that his step-father even had to ask her for money to buy cigarettes. Juan's mother punished him when he would go out with gangs of children or when he would neglect his work. During adolescence, Juan earned money for the family to help his mother. His mother controlled his drink, his cigarette smoking, his outings, and his friends. He felt very timid with women and would break into tears if prostitutes accosted him. At sixteen a brother initiated him into sex with a prostitute, and the next year he left home to free himself from his mother's apron strings. During this period he received much support and help from his maternal grandfather.

Juan worked then as a fare collector on buses; he caroused and became acquainted with some marihuana users. He lived with a prostitute, and the two spent all he earned on diversion. Nevertheless, he critically observed the circles in which he was moving: he avoided marihuana because the users "turned out like morons," and he took care not to contract a venereal disease. Eventually he stopped living with the prostitute when he realized he was losing all his money. He believes that from these experiences he learned an important skill: to manage his affairs. He feels that he recovered his lost childhood during his free adolescent years. "At seventeen years of age, I was an old man; I had not had a childhood." Juan then returned to live with his mother, who made him feel she needed his help. At twenty-two he got married and began to build a home. He feels content as a married man and is now concerned with getting ahead: "I've always liked to get ahead, to forget the past and to live for the future." He gets along well with his bosses, he insists on vacations, and often asks them for loans. He had run-ins with his wife about housekeeping, and he insisted that she work harder. At age twenty-nine he began to drink excessively, but then he stopped drinking because of a crisis that occurred in his home. He said that his wife "must be anemic because she wants to sleep the siesta." His wife, however, shares his interests in savings and in obtaining better furnishings for the house. In this sense he acknowledges United States influence, which derives from a visit he made to that country to see his mother after she married her third husband, a North American.

Juan is proud of the scholastic achievement of his children, and he worries about their developing proper ethics. When they disobey he punishes them violently. He likes friendships but avoids letting them develop into intimacies. He is cordial with his neighbors. However, Juan feels old and enjoys going out on dates with young girls who are still virgins. His favorite experience is to be with friends, and what he desires least is to be drunk.

Martín

Martín is a marihuana user. He is thirty-two years of age, of medium height, muscular, and handsome. He has no regular job but earns his living by "hustling" *(camaroneando)* in the street.

Martín comes from a rural zone, where he was raised by both his parents with his several siblings. He tells his story in a complaining way: "I have been a martyr since I have been small." As a child he almost died in a fire but was saved at the last minute by an aunt. Martín saw no sense in attending school because when he returned home he had to "submit to forced labor." His father insisted that Martín help carry out the tasks he had taken on as a farm worker. Martín remembers that no matter how hard he tried to perform, his father was never satisfied and punished him harshly and unjustly. Martín emphasizes that this punishment was not like that given normally to children but much more drastic, as if his father were trying to exterminate him. He describes his father as rude, illiterate, and a man who wanted nothing better for his children. He felt his father was unconcerned about the fact that his children were exposed to serious work hazards. His mother was passive and did not intervene, maintaining a cordial relationship with her husband. Occasionally even she would punish Martín harshly.

At age fifteen Martín felt that he could stand the situation no longer; he left home and found refuge in the house of the aunt who had saved him from the fire. His father sought him out there, however, and offered him a choice between returning home or being sent to the reformatory. When Martín said he would prefer the reformatory, his father promised better treatment at home. However, he was treated no better at home, so Martín ran away again and resolved to look for work and never return. On arriving in San José, he stole and was stolen from. Martín says that his friends were responsible for his growing delinquency. He says his "bad luck" and "problems of alcohol" were what eventually put him into the reformatory and what led him into the penitentiary and the penal farms. The halls of justice and "the police are what mortify me."

Martín began to use marihuana at age seventeen, having become interested when he saw others smoking it. He liked the feeling of being "high" and said, "My problems went away for a little while, but that was the only thing I liked." He smokes the drug when he feels impatient, and he thus obtains a tranquilizing effect to forget his impatience and stop worrying.

Martín has never developed a stable relationship with any woman. He has three children from different relationships but maintains contact with none of them. His first sexual encounter, at age sixteen, was with the mother of a friend, who took the initiative with him. His favorite experience is being alone, and what he finds least pleasant is being arrested and jailed.

José

José is a nonsmoker and the match for Martín. He is a thirty-two-year-old bus driver who appears tall, stout, and tranquil. He is an easy talker. José has always lived in the San José metropolitan area. His parents were separated when he was only a few months old, so his mother was the predominant figure during his childhood. Their economic status was low, and food was inadequate. José had to take on heavy responsibilities during both childhood and adolescence. He was not interested in school and frequently played hooky. His impoverished wardrobe made him feel ridiculous before his schoolmates, this being a major factor in his decision to leave school permanently when he was in the fourth grade.

During his childhood, José's mother married again. His stepfather was affectionate when he was sober, but bellicose and chastising during his frequent bouts with alcohol. Because of his problems with drink, his stepfather did not have steady work. As a result, his mother had to work full-time as a servant in the home of his aunt, who was also his godmother. José's mother gave him an extraordinary sense of rectitude and security. His godmother protected him too and provided him some economic support. José remembers his mother's punishing him for small thefts, for playing hooky to go horseback riding, and for neglecting his duties either at home or at school.

During adolescence, José became very interested in sex, having his first experience at age fourteen with a prostitute. He says this encounter confirmed his physical vigor and gave him a great deal of self-confidence. Subsequently he began to concern himself with making money in order to dress well and impress the girls. When "my clothes or shoes began to wear out, I felt ashamed because I liked the girls. That forced me to work in the country. I spent about four years there between ages thirteen and seventeen. Then I learned mechanics and from there rose to become a bus driver, traveling to other Central American countries with great pride and pleasure. They never imagined that the son of such a poor woman could learn so much." At age twenty José married a woman whose educational and economic status was higher than his own. They have three living children. The first birth was attended by José's mother. One fetus was born deformed, and José's wife's life was in danger. Facing the situation, he found that he would have sacrificed the life of his son for that of his wife. Today that son is mentally retarded, although he is well-accepted by both parents.

The family continues to live with José's parents-in-law, who insist that this arrangement go on, for it assures them of some support. José is unhappy with the situation because he considers some of the other relatives bad examples for his children. For the same reason, he refuses to invite his friends to his home. He feels that he and his wife cannot maintain the type of orderly home they both desire. In his concern to provide his children with a good example, José neither drinks alcohol nor smokes cigarettes in their presence. When angered, he becomes violent. He becomes very upset if more money is spent than earned, although he enjoys sharing his money and spending it with his family as an expression of his affection. His favorite experience is to be working; what he abhors most is to be in debt.

CHILDHOOD

The Users' Mothers

Although a key figure in the early lives of most people is the mother, in the case of these five users such proved to be the exception rather than the rule. Miguel and Marcos were abandoned by their mothers, and Martín had a mother who was only a passive figure. Only Manuel and Mario saw their mothers as playing the major role in their socialization.

MANUEL

"My mother considered me her favorite. Maybe this was because I was her first boy child. She treated me very well; she gave me money when I asked for it. My father did the same. My mother was the only one who punished us, because we did not pay attention to her. Maybe we started to do something and we did not do it well. Then she would beat us. Once I took a little bit of money from her when I was a very small child; you should see what a beating she gave us . . . never unjustly." "I was her favorite. She took me on an outing every day . . . and she sent us out to be with our dad and keep him from drinking so much."

"My mother was good, she was a very decent lady. You can't say that she belonged to 'society,' but she did like to stand out from the masses. She never gave us bad advice and never suggested anything bad. . . . She would say, 'How would it occur to you to take money from a little old lady who needs it herself? If a person works honorably, no matter how badly he's paid, he never dies of hunger.' My mother suspected that I smoked. And she would give me advice: 'Be careful not to smoke, because it could cause you harm; it could damage your lungs.' "

MARIO

"My mother was . . . well, she spoiled me most. She was always telling me how much she loved me, with words and all, that is, when she wasn't angry. When she was angry, it was different. She was the one that punished me the most. My father was somewhat distant. . . . I spent a lot of time as a child in the street, out in the fields and the coffee groves. I didn't like school. That was the reason I was punished the most, only that."

"My mother was very economical . . . she saved because my father drank so much. He would spend as much as fifteen to twenty-two days drinking without going to work. She would then put an end to it by seeing that he had money for only his cigarettes. Because when my father didn't drink, he didn't need any other money. She took care of all the rest of the money in the house. She had the best form of taking care of such matters."

The Nonusers' Mothers

All five nonusers grew up with their mothers. Julian's mother abetted the sadistic treatment given him by his father. Thus, he did not feel close to her, and today he doubts that she was really his mother. The other four nonusers feel that their mothers were figures of strength, strict in the application of justice and demanding with respect to their contribution to the home as children. Here are some of their comments.

JUAN

"This is the way we grew up . . . not surrounded by friends. We were prohibited from going out with gangs of friends. We did play from time to time, but we had to hide this from my mother, because if she realized we were doing it she would beat us. We had to work. There was no time for things like these."

"She always talked to my younger brothers about how I had grown up and become a man by her side, helping her, that I had never abandoned her when she really needed me. . . . She said to me . . . that if I were a fighter, no matter where I would be things would turn out well. . . . I was the type of person who was used to living tied to my mother's apron strings. . . . And even to go to the movies I had to ask permission."

JORGE

"She was good with me because she wouldn't go anywhere unless I was with her." "Since I am an illegitimate son, I had to help my mother. My mother worked cooking on that farm . . . they gave us room to have our own cows, and that's where I learned to take care of such animals."

JOSÉ

"If I behaved well, sometimes my mother would give me money to go to the movies." "My mother would always give me advice. If I were lazy, late, or early she would shame me." "My brother got into trouble and was taken to jail . . . I helped him get out, but my mother resented the fact. She told the commander that her son should not be freed since he had never paid attention to her. Then she punished him." "When she was ironing she would say, 'I want to have an honorable son. I want you to be a hard worker and to go to school and learn something so that people will not humiliate you' . . . and she would keep ironing until midnight while I went to sleep, but I was always happy because I was at the side of my mother."

The Users' Fathers

Of the five users discussed in this chapter, Marcos never knew his father and Mario's father appeared on the scene only rarely. But fathers seem to have taken a relatively important role in the socialization of the remaining three users. Manuel's father spoiled him and occasionally punished him when he did not live up to expectations. The fathers of Miguel and Martín were very strong, protective, and even overdominating. Those of Manuel and Mario had serious problems with alcohol abuse.

MARIO

"Part of the very little education that I have I got from my mother, not my father. I didn't depend as much on him as I did on her . . . he saw me as a distant son." "It was my mother who kept me in line; my father punished me only once."

MIGUEL

"[My father] was a very hard worker . . . he was a businessman." "I never wanted to go with my mother. I liked to live with my father and my grandmother better." "My father was a very rigid man . . . the only thing he did was work." "My father had many friends, important personages." "He would beat me from time to time, when I would get lost in the streets or would play without permission or would come home very late." "My father was a tough fellow who did not like me to get into mischief." "I grew up in an atmosphere where my father had money . . . I didn't do anything because my father had money . . . I was a spoiled brat . . . you should see how spoiled I was. He gave me everything I asked for."

MARTÍN

"I was always what vulgarly would be called a scoundrel in my father's eyes . . . it was very bad luck. . . . I was more active than my other brothers and always tried to get ahead and to be right on top and to get things done as quickly as I possibly could. Well, my father didn't like that sort of behavior. And so he whipped me and beat me excessively." "[On the farm] there were too many animals and too much to do, and my father, in order to ingratiate himself with the boss, always promised all sorts of things that he could deliver only by using us children."

MANUEL

"We had plenty of money; we had everything we needed. When we were very small, our dad took us on outings and bought us everything we wanted, and so we became very self-satisfied . . . but afterward things began to change and he began to be careless about everything." "My father preferred that I drink. Well, I guess that is just the sort of atmosphere he grew up in. You see he was a gambler and still is a gambler, not with games like *chapas* that cheat the passersby but with legal games like the kind you find in fiestas." "My father punished us very little, and this was for the times that we would leave the house without eating and without doing our chores."

The Nonusers' Fathers

Of the five nonusers discussed here, Jorge and Juan never lived with their fathers, and José did so for only a brief period. Both Jaime and Julian's fathers were alcoholics and were violent disciplinarians when under the effects of alcohol. Jaime's father spent a period of years away from the home because of his work. Jaime's father also drank a great deal. Julian's father spent some time in prison as a political prisoner, after which he returned home and established a better relationship with his son.

JAIME

"My father did unbelievable things to my mother when he was drunk. But I don't hate him, even though he did incredible things under the influence of liquor. When he was well and healthy, things were very different." "If we got a bad grade in school, he would beat us as hard as he could. His parents had treated him the same way. I prayed to God that I would not turn out to be like that."

JULIÁN

"My father was a military man. . . . He liked us, but he could also be a severe disciplinarian. . . . He beat us a lot. . . . He would say to me, 'Take off your shirt,' . . . and he would hit me with a whip. . . . He would hit me hard, hard, hard, and afterward I couldn't stand even to put on a shirt. I wasn't given cream or anything else, nothing." "When he was really drunk he used to beat my mother also . . . we would cry a lot." "But he was a good father. . . . When I was sick he would worry about me." "He was quite a character! And then they took him to prison." "He gave us everything. When he was around we didn't need anything."

Users' Surrogate Parents

In the group of five users, the only two who had close relationships with a surrogate parent during their childhood were Miguel and Marcos. Miguel had an indulgent stepmother who acted only to protect him; he also had a protective and loving paternal grandmother who helped him to accept the social norms she thought were important. Marcos had a surrogate mother in his maternal aunt; she was not affectionate, neglected his needs, and was a harsh disciplinarian. When Mario's mother died, no surrogate figure replaced her in his life.

MIGUEL

"[My stepmother] never hit me. Rather she tended to defend me. . . . She hid me until my father left for work. . . . When he would arrive at night he would say, 'Did that bum come home?' Then my stepmother would say to him, 'He came home early and he is sound asleep. How are you going to beat the boy? Wait until tomorrow morning.' And the following day my father would not beat me."

"My grandmother was the one who talked to me about morality and science . . . about being respectful to older people . . . about not taking things that did not belong to me. . . . At night, when we went to bed, my grandmother and I would pray together. My grandmother was very strong-willed. It was she who never wanted me to do anything bad. She would never let me out into the street without my asking permission first. If I asked for permission I think I could even have gone to hell, but without permission, nothing. She would simply beat me." "I lived with my grandmother almost more than I did with my father. . . . She spoiled me more. . . . We lived very close, next door to one another." "I helped count my grandmother's money, and she trusted me. . . . I counted everything for her . . . and I would wrap it all up and say to her, 'Here you have this-and-this amount, Granny,' . . . and I never stole from her, because she gave me whatever I asked for . . . so that I could go out and have a good time. I never suffered real need. And that is the reason I am the man I am. I have never been in jail like a thief."

MARCOS

"My mother was unmarried. We grew up with one of our aunts who did us quite a bit of harm. I know that my brothers were treated better, maybe without even thinking about me." "The way they told it to me, the best things were for my aunt's son, and maybe this was at the expense of the money my mother gave her so that we could be cared for. . . . When I realized what harm her treatment was causing me, I ran away from home. . . . Maybe I stole for hunger or maybe just to steal. Sometimes I would go into her kitchen and simply stuff myself with rice and beans when she was not looking. When she realized what I had done, she really did me in. She would pound my hands, put hot pepper in my eyes, tear my clothing into pieces, throw me out into the street, and that sort of thing."

Three of the users, Manuel, Marcos, and Martín, had critical moments in which other figures intervened. For Manuel the crisis came suddenly when his father lost everything he owned. Manuel's family had to move in a very disorganized way to a neighborhood where he found himself surrounded by criminal activity. Up to that time he had had the occasional help of a godmother in dealing with the alcoholic crises of his father. Marcos had to work with a vegetable salesman when, at the age of six, he left home. Martín remembered an aunt who saved him from a fire when he was small, and he went to her when he decided to leave his paternal home.

MANUEL

"We were going to school. We had had no breakfast, and we arrived after lunch. We hadn't had coffee, nothing. Once in a while we would have a little piece of bread or a little bit of sugar water, but that and nothing more. My sister and I would run off and steal bananas there for three months in all. That could be the reason I began to know that kind of people [criminals] and then I began to like them. I felt that way I could help my mother more. I liked to work, and the first week I had a job I worked barefoot." "I would go to the market when we lived nearby, and that is the way I got to know people. I got acquainted with some characters who would steal a banana here, a papaya there, and take them off to sell. Then I really became a buddy of those fellows. And that's the way I began to get connected with the underworld."

MARCOS

"I went down to the market on foot, and there I met a person I'll never forget. He was a fellow who picked me up when I was still wet, and my clothes were in rags from the treatment my aunt had meted out. He took me off to a store and bought me new clothes. He gave me food and said, 'If you are sleepy, just stay here and take a nap.' And so I stayed and I slept for two or three days. Afterward I began to be his helper and to earn my own bit of money."

MARTÍN

"When I was about one year and three months old, our house caught fire, a little thatched-roof hut. My aunt came and rescued me from the flames just in the nick of time." "When I was fifteen I realized that things were very bad at home and that I could not stand it any more. On my birthday I decided to run away from home. I roamed around without knowing where I was going or anything else. I finally went to my aunt's house, the one who had saved me from the flames. It was the first time I had gone there, and she did not recognize me. I told her all about my problems, and she let me stay . . . until my father finally came to take me back home."

The Nonusers' Surrogate Parents

With the five nonusers, three had significant relationships with parental surrogates.

JOSÉ

"When I was about five years old my mother married my stepfather, and he beat me from that time onward. When I was about eleven he split my back open. He drank a great deal. Since we received no help from him, my mother had to work for us children. The only ones he would give money for were the children that he and my mother had had together." "The fights always came when he was drunk. He realized what he was doing when he was healthy and sober, but when he was drunk it was a horse of a different color."

"It was our godmother. We called her the mother who raised us. We would go to her house if we were hungry. . . . We would go there to eat, because my mother would work there." "Only my sister and my godmother, only they would see to it that I did my homework. My mother was illiterate." "She would give me used clothing, but good clothing, you see."

JUAN

"The person who helped us more was my mother's father. He helped us too much. He was like a second father until he saw that we were grown. Afterward we had to help him, because he had taken care of us for years."

"I was nine years old, and we were returning to San José. We were looking for some way to find work. There was a lady who took me in. There were two teachers who lived in the house, and I would work as their errand boy and clean their house. And I behaved myself well. They gave me clothing and food." "They gave me a gift that year. It was the first Christmas present I had ever had."

JULIÁN

"My grandmother was the person who saved me, because she would say to me, 'Look, old big balls, if that whore [his mother] doesn't give you anything to eat, just come over here and I'll give it to you.' And then my grandmother would give me some *atole* or some cornmeal." "When my father would beat me or discipline me, then I would go to my grandmother's house and sleep with her. She really spoiled me. She would feed me and let me smoke [tobacco]."

ADOLESCENCE

The stress of a lower-class childhood in Costa Rica serves in many respects to prepare the individual for demands made upon him in adolescence. We find that the majority of our select group, both users and nonusers, had already been employed (not always regularly) either by their parents or independently by the time they reached adolescence. Two of the users, Manuel and Marcos, were already on their own in the streets of San José before they were nine years old, and so they early acquired the survival skills required for this tough life. Both became regular smokers of marihuana by the time they were ten.

At puberty, and in the years following, the individual consolidates his experience into adult patterns. Peer-group pressures are intense, and rebellion is common. The teenage struggles of these ten men are typical: identity problems, search for self-confidence, disagreements with parents, conflicts with authority, finding work, developing relationships with women other than their mothers, and, for some, simply surviving.

Adolescence Among Users

MANUEL

In his brief biographical sketch and in excerpts from his life history where he talked about his childhood, we have already seen a few of the conditions Manuel faced as he came into adolescence, and the style of life he began to adopt during this period of his life. It would have been natural for him to assume that the type of support received from his parents during his childhood would continue, but this did not occur. On reaching adolescence, Manuel found himself suddenly deprived of the means of fulfilling some of his basic needs. He describes his situation as follows:

"Maybe if my father would have continued to treat us the way he did during my childhood we would not—that is, I would not—have fallen into the life I have come to live, nor would I have suffered what I have suffered, nor would I have the needs I have today. God, we might have turned out differently; I might have become very serious about my studies. I am not a dummy; I passed every grade and never failed, but, my Lord, I lost those opportunities and had to learn how to get along in the street."

Manuel's situation appears to have been aggravated by the fact that in his childhood those adults responsible for his socialization did not offer him clear goals; his father became an alcoholic and turned to gambling. His mother's behavior was inconsistent: he was either neglected or indulged. His attempts to run away were simply devices to gain attention. Manuel speaks with pride of the way his mother spent entire afternoons looking for him in a way similar to the way he had sought her husband when he was out on his drunken binges. This failed, and by nine years of age he left "home."

It is in the context of these conditions that Manuel found an alternative among peer groups oriented toward immediate gratification. He assimilated their aggressive style of street life, which included occasional employment, floating residence, theft, marihuana smoking, womanizing, and high-risk acts as normal parts of life. His first sexual experience was with a prostitute who lived with one of his accomplices in theft: "I was twelve years old. I did not know anything about women and was just beginning to live. Then I became a friend of this guy, and we stole together. About that time I met the fellow's wife. When he was taken off to jail, I went by his house without knowing what had happened . . . and next thing I knew I was spending the night there with his wife. Can you imagine that? I kept living with her, and after that I got acquainted with other women and left her."

In this context, Manuel's marihuana use helped consolidate his weak affective bonds with both friends and women through sharing the pleasure and the risk of use with them. During his adolescence, work seems to have been only a supplementary activity, resorted to only when it did not interfere with his immediate gratifications. Manuel was in frequent trouble with the law, and his repeated arrests reinforced his negative image of the law and of society.

MIGUEL

In contrast to Manuel, Miguel during his formative years saw no great inconsistency in the behavior of his father and his grandmother. However, their overprotection and dominance helped undermine his self-confidence. He was given things without having to work for them. And so Miguel rarely had to depend on himself. His feelings of insecurity and timidity were accentuated in the sexual sphere. We do not know how his lack of physical attractiveness and his negative image of his mother may have contributed to this insecurity. But we do know that Miguel began using marihuana to cope with it: "The only thing I got out of marihuana was that I was timid in approaching girls, and with the drug I lost that timidity. With pot I lost all fear. Afterward I talked with the girls and did all sorts of things. I was always afraid of talking with them about love . . . but when I was high I lost that fear. In contrast, before knowing pot, I was timid. . . . That's the reason I defend marihuana."

Miguel continued to distrust friends and to seek protection in isolation and in family: "I never was a member of a gang. I had one or two friends I would go out with. . . . But usually I was by myself. . . . Because if one has bad friends, he doesn't know whether he is a thief or not."

Miguel lost interest in his studies, particularly when he faced the possibility that they would take him far from home. Thus he proposed to his father that he be allowed to study tailoring, and he obtained his father's support. He is the only user of this group not to have lived "in the street."

In synthesis, Miguel remained timid, insecure, and dependent, and during adolescence his father continued punishing him as if he were a child. He stayed at home until his father died, when Miguel was twenty-five. As an adult he was briefly married. Now he lives alone with his son. Lacking social and personal satisfactions, Miguel uses marihuana as a compensating instrument.

MARCOS

Marcos's adolescence seems to have been full of experimentation. He left home, then returned, had many women, smoked marihuana, and then went through a crisis with alcohol. "I slept in the street for about five years. Afterward, when I felt that I was a real man, I got myself an apartment. I paid for that apartment until I was about eighteen, when I decided to return home. . . . My aunt wasn't there anymore. . . . Only my mother had stayed." ". . . I have hardly ever had friends. . . . I always went around by myself; I never liked friends . . . all I would do was chat with them for a while. . . . I had something like five sweethearts."

Although Marcos tried marihuana during his adolescence, he did not become a regular user until he was a full adult. "I used to go around with girls in the market and with boys who had already begun to smoke pot. Shit, I would even get pot for them sometimes, but it wasn't something that I liked very much. And so afterward I left it entirely . . . for about ten years. . . . I had begun to smoke pot when I was a boy just so I could say that I was a *marihuano*."

Marcos emerges as an individual of great inner strength who has survived harsh experiences and obtained gratification thanks to his personal characteristics and abilities. He has had a high achievement orientation and realized his first great successes during adolescence. It is worth noting that after using marihuana in his youth, mainly to achieve a sense of importance among his peer group, he stopped using it. His search for pleasure led him to use alcohol in excess. Later, at the age of twenty-seven, he resumed regular use of marihuana. As an adult, he does not establish deep social ties but concentrates his efforts on personal achievements. He feels that his experiences during childhood and adolescence prepared him well to face the demands of life: "I thank the street more than school. Now I understand that I learned more in the street than if I had been studying."

MARIO

For Mario, school generated an image of discipline and unpleasant experiences. His home life placed few demands upon him, and he was not oriented toward work or social responsibility. His peer-group life was oriented toward pleasure-seeking activity: "In that group I was the youngest one. They taught me a number of things . . . all about sexual intercourse, and how to smoke pot."

Speaking of the school, "The only thing that came out was that I was bad, or at least a smart aleck." "Then when I was a little older, I began to like money. That's when I decided to leave school. I went out and got a job, but I did not work long, only about fifteen days. So I began to spend my time out in the fields and coffee groves. It was worse because I had the whole day free, you see? They didn't force me to work, so I became just a bum. Afterward I decided to learn shoemaking, but I never did anything with it. I learned in order to have something to pass time. But not to earn anything from it."

"Since I never had anything to do, I really became a street boy, and I never liked to work during the day. But I had to do something, don't you see, and, shit, that's the reason bread-making appealed to me. I would have the whole day free. I liked to go down to the river and all that sort of thing. That way I could have the whole day free."

"Oh yes, the banana zone! The first time I went there I was only fifteen or sixteen. The second time I was about nineteen or twenty. The last time I went I got malaria. It was a bad experience. I needed all sorts of things; I had no work. Because I was underage, they would not give me any work. Both times I really suffered and had no work, for the same reason. In order to work down there, you have to have a work permit, and I never took one with me. The second time I never really intended to go there . . . but before I knew what was happening, there I was." The bout with malaria, Mario says, changed him a lot, from a "fighter" to a "pacifist."

"I began to smoke pot in the shoeshop when I was about fifteen years old. That's where I saw my first pot smoker. I asked him what that stuff was, and he told me. At first I was really impressed, because pot has such a bad reputation. He offered me some, and I said, 'Why not? Let's see what it does to me.' And I liked it . . . that is to say, I liked the vice . . . and sure I changed a lot. I wasn't the same fellow. At first I felt inhibited when I was around people, but that's the way it affects a person most. That is, you feel like you want to get away from people, and it seems to you that everybody realizes what you are doing and they are spreading rumors about you. That is the principal defect of pot; it isolates people from social life, and you don't want anything else except the joint."

Mario's school experiences were largely negative, and he left after the fourth grade, ostensibly to work. Although his indulgent mother, who never demanded any responsibility on his part, had failed to prepare him for such a role, his immediate needs for money forced him to look for work, but without any long-range goals. Thus his employment as a baker fits his desire for pleasurable experience. And so he launches into a job that will allow him time to continue various pleasurable activities, and he uses marihuana in this context.

MARTÍN

During his childhood, Martín developed a deep sense of neglect, inferiority, and resentment. This finally led to his running away from home at age fifteen to avoid tensions he found to be unbearable. He was poorly prepared for life on his own, however. "My problems were critical at that time. Since I didn't know anybody or anything in the city, shit, everything was very critical for me. Things haven't changed all that much. I have come to understand that few have lived thirty-three years the way I lived. Here, as you see, I never have had anything. I've never had a decent job to see me through life. And so, with that sort of history, what else can I say about my teens?"

"I didn't know San José, I didn't have friends, and I didn't know where to go. And then I met up with this man whom I'd never seen before. He acted as if he knew exactly who I was, and he said, 'Come on, buddy, let's go, let's see what we can feel.' All that for me was new."

"On several occasions I got odd jobs cleaning or sweeping or working as an errand boy. And then one day I said, 'What I am going to do is steal a kit from a shoeshine boy,' and that's what I did, and since that time I've worked as a shoeshine boy." "Usually when I have got into trouble it has been because of my so-called friends. You should see the bad luck I've had, the way I've got into trouble and have even been sent off to the penitentiary."

"I began to be interested in girls when I was very small. I looked for them at all costs, but I really didn't take a mental interest in girls until I was eighteen or nineteen."

"When I was about seventeen, I had a friend who smoked a lot of pot. Since I always liked to try things, I asked him to give me one." "Afterward I felt terribly hungry, dizzy, and sleepy. It was like being a little drunk."

What we see in Martín's adolescence is a search for survival in the street, immediate gratification of needs, and an absence of deep emotional ties. His initiation to marihuana forms part of this orientation. His interests never gave rise to lasting relationships. Martín's sense of identity is weak. He takes what he needs, and he receives what is offered. Yet he feels deprived of everything and consequently feels responsibility toward no one.

Adolescence Among Nonusers

JAIME

During his adolescence, Jaime remained in his parental home, although he actively pursued outside interests. His socialization during childhood was consistent, dominated by his mother, and reinforced by rewards obtained at school. Because of alcoholism, his father was an unstable figure during Jaime's childhood. During adolescence, however, Jaime's father assumed a more powerful family role when he obtained a mortgage and bought a house, thus helping the family to achieve upward socioeconomic mobility.

"We were really very poor until I was fifteen, and then our house was transformed." "Still, in the fifth grade I wanted to be a doctor. But that profession is not the way they would make it appear. When I got into high school, all of my dreams crashed to the ground. It was then that I realized that what I really wanted was to be my own boss, so that no one could order me around. I was generally pretty well behaved. I paid attention to what my mom told me. Where I did get out of control was in high school. You see, all of my grade school had been with only boys. Well, when I got into high school and there were girls around, I sort of lost control. I invited girls over, I courted them, I went out on dates with them, I even stopped going to school. I flunked out. Afterward I enrolled in night school, and things went a little bit better, because I was already working and I had decided to continue my education myself. It wasn't my dad telling me I had to. That's when I began to think more seriously. But I couldn't keep it up. I would start work at six thirty in the morning and would come out at six thirty in the evening without eating or anything." "Now, if my job had required some sort of study, I would have kept it up. But there where I worked you don't need study, all you need is skill. I don't like studies. I have no desire to finish high school or get more education, with all the sacrifice that means. Better just leave it alone."

"When I was fifteen, I met a young fellow who took me to the shop where he worked. And then during his lunch breaks he would supervise my practice. He was the best decorator that there is in Costa Rica, and he is the fellow who taught me. That is the fellow I have to thank that I have a skill today."

Jaime seems to have evaluated adolescence realistically, his possibilities of accomplishments. He pursued his schooling to seek the type of training that would give him the fundamental skills he needed to make a living, but this was primarily provided by a colleague at work. His parents did not overprotect him, and he continued to live at home throughout adolescence, often helping his parents. He did not leave home until he married, when he took up residence next door to his wife's family.

JULIÁN

By the time Julián reached his teens, he had already worked at a variety of jobs, some of which were fairly demanding. When his alcoholic father was taken off to jail, his family became more closely knit and more egalitarian. Despite this, Julián's father continued his directive and protective role, and when at home he maintained a severe disciplinary regime. In discussing this period of his life, Julián cites a full range of activity.

"I would go to work at four o'clock in the morning and come home at six in the afternoon, stuck up in the brush pile that we call *montaña*. There are so many snakes there that they make one dance. Afterward I worked in a salt mill. And my father worked as watchman. That was about the time of the 1948 revolution. Afterward I decided to try my hand as a painter. We were hungry, many times hungry. When I was about eleven, they put my father in jail for two years and ten months. That was a time of great suffering, because we did not have a father. Each one of us tried to earn the little bit he could, and my mother took in washing. That was all we had to live on, can you imagine? We always tried to take my dad a little bit of food."

"My high school was coeducational. I got acquainted with a girl there, and after we talked for a while we both ran off to the park. We stole a pair of bicycles and began to cycle around town. Later they caught both of us and expelled us from school. That is to say, they called my father and explained the whole matter to him, and they were going to give us another chance, you see? But I told my dad that I did not want to study any more, that what I wanted to do was work. That was certainly a foolish thing to do, that business of not wanting to study." "My dad took it in his stride. 'You don't want to study,' he said, 'then you better not. In that case, go to work and give me some help.' "

"When I was more or less fourteen or fifteen, I got an apprenticeship with my uncle and learned how to manage machines. My aunt would give me food, that is, I learned a skill . . . I learned how to do just about everything to run a print shop." "And then I began . . . living a different kind of life, more normal, more correct. I even got a little girlfriend, for I was now working and had more money to spend. And, good God, I left those gangs. Sometimes I would go and rent bicycles with a friend or play billiards, go to the theater, eat, or just walk around peacefully." "And then my father changed as I was growing, at least in his attitude toward me. In spite of that, even when I was seventeen or eighteen I could not come home later than ten o'clock at night."

Even though Julián suffered from brusque downward socioeconomic mobility during one period of adolescence, the family managed the situation well and emerged stronger, despite the hardship. Julián was given recognition for his contributions to the family, and some of the arbitrariness to which he had formerly been subjected by his father was softened. Thus Julian's decision to leave school was accepted positively, and he was encouraged to find a trade through a kinsman. The disciplinary control of his family gradually diminished rather than being broken abruptly, and he left home only upon marriage, to live with his in-laws. One could say that his passage into independent adulthood was facilitated by these relatively protected conditions. However, as in the case of his father, Julián has had sporadic problems with alcohol abuse.

JORGE

Jorge shows a strong sense of continuity from his childhood experiences in his fatherless family. His move from the country to the city was not an abrupt and demanding change but instead productive and adjusted to smoothly. His relationship with his mother was very close, and they were interdependent.

"When I was only twelve we lived in that house I've talked about, and my mother, the only work she did was to iron some. I had to take care of my little brothers and sisters." "It was as if I were used to those sorts of jobs; I didn't think of any other sort of job that could be better."

"Shit, when I was about fifteen I really wanted to learn to drive. Yes, that's what I liked, I don't know why, but dangerous things always appealed to me."

"I was a fare collector [on a bus]. And then I met that family that had a girl. And after two years, when I was working as a taxi driver, we began our courtship."

From childhood on, Jorge had been building his sense of identity and self-importance while fulfilling family responsibilities, which he always accepted. He had steady employment and was not driven to achieve higher goals. Although married, his mother continues to live with him.

JUAN

In his teens, Juan was able to maintain the drive for achievement that he had developed during his childhood. His needs for independence in matters of friendship and sexual relations, however, were controlled by his mother, who dominated the family. When he left home for two years, at age seventeen, he developed his adult role, and when he returned to his mother's home for a short time before his marriage, he and his mother had a more egalitarian relationship.

"What I dreamed about from the time I was small was having money and not suffering so much in life. I would say, 'Someday I'll have money. I'm not anybody and I don't know anything, but I think I can get there if I try hard enough.' "

"I had problems with my mom because I came home sometimes with a few drinks under my belt or because I had a package of cigarettes in my pockets. Then she would try to keep me like a spoiled child at home. That's when I decided it was better for me to get away, and I went to the banana zone to find whatever work I could run across. I was seventeen, I was old, and I had never had a childhood. I had never known what it was to be young, and that was the way things were even when I came back from the banana zone and returned home. My mom tried to keep me at home; she would get sick because she said I was far away and that I was the one who helped her a lot."

"As a kid I wasn't involved in gangs. I played, yes, but not very much. . . . But then when I saw that life out there was better, when I began to reason for myself, then I began to go out with friends. Yes, we would go to dances, movies, and out to drink. I would go out with my stock to sell, and I even had problems with one of my friends. He wanted to steal my customers. He would go and sell where I was supposed to sell, so that I couldn't sell anything. And so we had a fight. There was no other way."

"It seems to me that I lived better when I was young, because at least I felt free. I was more than seventeen before I knew what life was all about, and I really got a late start."

"If I had a lot of money, I would like to spend a lot too. I was nineteen years old and a poor man when I decided to shack up with a prostitute, and after six months I saw that that was not getting me anyplace but rather was corrupting me . . . and when I saw everything was turning out so badly, I got out of there. I went back home, and then I came back here to San José and got a job as a taxi driver."

Once Juan had lived through his independent experiences and had a firmer sense of himself, he adopted a style of life that was productive and acquisitive. Throughout his adolescent experiences he was able to evaluate events critically, and now he constantly seeks to improve his socioeconomic status. He continues to be influenced by his mother, who through a new marriage has become upwardly mobile.

JOSÉ

José acquired self-confidence in childhood, and this continued through his adolescent years, when he received strong support from his mother and stepfather. He had worked regularly from childhood and continued to do so as a teenager, although he engaged in various adventures as well.

"The first woman I had was when I was about thirteen or fourteen. My brother said to me, 'Let's go, let's go out with the men.' And they went out with the whores, and then one day a friend of mine said to me, 'Let's see for ourselves. Why not?' And then he came and told the others that we wanted to go too, and they paid, and he paid, and the woman was with me; that was the first time. Two years later I brought my first woman home . . . a young thing . . . I was about sixteen years old, and my family didn't say anything."

"There were always four of us that got together . . . because there was one s.o.b. whose father and grandfather had lots of money. He liked to go out with me because I was decisive, that is, in the group I was the most daring. If some bully tried to beat us up, and if we could not get back at him through brute force, then I figured some other way so that we would always come out on top . . . that's the reason the guys liked to go around with me, right? And I liked to go out with them because they had plenty of money."

"When I was about twelve I left school and began to work in the post office." "And then later I had to go out and find a job in the country because my mother wouldn't give me any money . . . then afterward I got a job in a mechanic shop because my mother didn't want me to go out into the country any more."

As José worked out his self-identity, he experimented with several jobs and involved himself in ventures that gave him confidence and satisfaction. School did not contribute to his adolescent needs. Instead, he held many jobs, even traveling about Costa Rica and later to Central America. His mother, godmother, and stepfather remained important figures throughout adolescence, and he lived intermittently with his mother until he was married at the age of twenty. José's family showed an unusual capability for dealing with his emerging sense of independence, even on the sexual plane.

SOCIALIZATION AND MARIHUANA USE

There are literally hundreds of events that contribute to any individual's character and pattern of behavior. This group of ten persons shows a wide range of personal experience and response. When reviewed as individuals, each man emerges with his own problems and personality. Yet if we place their experience in a standard contextual setting, some patterns emerge that distinguish the users of marihuana from the nonusers.

In Tables 47 and 47A, a series of life events and situations are systematically reviewed for each person in childhood and adolescence. By doing this, some striking differences and similarities can be seen. As small children, the two groups have remarkably similar patterns of socialization. Indeed, the only significant areas of discrepancy in this group of ten occur with respect to the fact that more of the nonusers were raised primarily by their mothers and were subject to heavier discipline. Significant characteristics of the user group that contrast with those of nonusers are the early abandonment of the home (two cases) and heavy involvement in street life outside the family's control (three cases). None of the nonusers left home as a child, and only one of them was seriously engaged in street life as a child under twelve years of age.

Thus, while the sum of overall "positive" and "negative" experience for the two groups was virtually identical, the two persons—Manuel and Marcos—who began using marihuana as children uniquely did so after accumulating a common series of experiences. Both had working mothers, both felt that they had lived deprived and neglected childhoods, both abandoned home at a very early age (six and nine years) to live by their wits in the street, and both were from downwardly mobile families. Taken individually, none of these events necessarily leads to marihuana smoking; indeed, many of the nonusers as well as the other users had passed through one or another of these experiences. In the cases of Manuel and Marcos, however, the association of all these things together, and at an early age, is clearly related to their interest in marihuana. For both Manuel and Marcos, the drug was part of street lifestyle and contributed to their adjustment in it.

Of the remaining eight who did not take up marihuana smoking at this time, each in some way remained subject to adult controls and discipline, however imperfect these may have been. Thus Juan and José, whose negative profiles most closely approximate those of the two childhood users, never left home and were "tied to their mothers' apron strings." Although Juan tried, he was not allowed to run with street gangs and was continually reminded of his responsibilities as the oldest boy in a fatherless household. José was also given heavy responsibilities and remained much attached to his mother, despite downward social mobility and other problems.

Among this group, then, it is difficult to attribute early marihuana smoking to any single event as such, but it can attributed to a powerful combination of negative factors and extrafamilial situations, of which Manuel's and Marcos's experiences are an example. We view the absence of any stable family life or figures, and the need to succeed among one's street companions, as the principal factors in their early acceptance of marihuana use.

During the adolescent years, however, the user and nonuser groups diverge more sharply. An accumulation of negative experiences on the part of users contrasts with increasingly positive events in the lives of nonusers. The sum of the differences is striking. The childhood problems of Manuel and Marcos continue. Both Mario and Martín become enmeshed in street life independent of their families or parental figures. Both leave home by sixteen years of age, are not regularly employed, and accept responsibilities for only themselves. Both try marihuana after entering street life and become regular users by their mid-teens. Martín becomes involved in criminal activity and has an alcohol-abuse problem, two further traits associated with street life at this period.

Miguel, in view of his socialization experiences, is an atypical user. Although he generally escapes the cumulative effect of a series of negative experiences, closely paralleling nonusers in this regard, he nevertheless develops into an extremely insecure, isolated individual with weak family ties, despite his dependency upon his father. Miguel's father continues to treat him as a teenager. Timid, dominated, and the subject of ridicule, Miguel is the last of his group to engage in sexual relations, being goaded to do so by his peers. For him, marihuana use is not an element that binds him to street companions and their colorful lifestyle; instead, it is a device that helps him psychologically to overcome his sense of insecurity with women and to escape from a domineering father. Thus, his use of the drug is prompted by his self-considered personal shortcomings rather than by his involvement in a demanding social environment.

Among the nonusers, the distinguishing features of adolescence are several. Most important are their continuing relationships with their parents and families. Not only did all the men in this group maintain strong relations with one or both parents throughout adolescence, but only one—Juan—left home even as a teenager, and the move was only temporary. After working outside San José for two years, he eventually returned, at age nineteen, to live again with his mother until he married a couple of years later. While none of the users was married as a teenager, three of the nonusers were, and the others followed shortly thereafter. All the nonusers were regularly employed in their teens, whereas among the users only Miguel and Marcos were thus involved.

In general terms, we see that the socialization pattern for users involves a constant erosion of effective and affective family ties and a simultaneous increase in personal need. By the end of their adolescent life, all the users, except Miguel, had cut their family ties and were living essentially for themselves. In all but one case, regular marihuana use followed within a year or so of this break. Nonusers, on the other hand, retained family ties and responsibilities, however unpleasant they were at times. Family life and associated values remained preferable to the vicissitudes and risks of street life, of which marihuana use was one.

In Chapter 5 we will explore the dimensions of our subjects' adult lives, seen as a product of their early lives and experiences. Our five users were, in essence, all "on their own" as they entered adulthood. All the nonusers were still dependent on their families in important ways. This contrast in developmental patterns not only characterizes the set of ten individuals reviewed in detail here but also typifies the course of maturation and experience of the larger matched-pair and base-sample groups.

5/Marihuana
and User Lifestyles

Our base sample of 240 individuals gave us our first real insights into the similarities and contrasts between the adult world of users and that of nonusers. Primarily, these insights came from responses to the initial personal-data questionnaire (see p. 55 above). They were extremely valuable in helping us identify variables to be explored in greater detail with the matched pairs, in providing us with a basis for the matching process itself, and, even when statistically nonsignificant, in helping us to interpret the context and meaning of marihuana use among working-class residents of greater San José.

The questionnaire was administered during the time of the Costa Rican national elections, when general political interest was high. Not surprisingly, given that context, many subjects reported involvement in one of the seven political parties. Forty-seven (30 percent) of the nonusers and sixteen (19 percent) of the users professed for the National Liberation Party, the party currently in power. In this and other aspects of political activity, there were no statistically significant differences.

Both groups were overwhelmingly Catholic: 57 (85 percent of the 67 who reported) of the users and 125 (91 percent of the 137 who reported) of the nonusers. The remainder listed Protestant or no preference. Although the differences between users and nonusers were not statistically significant, it should be pointed out that 29 (19 percent) of the nonusers and 40 (48 percent) of the users did not respond to the question on religion.

An additional index of the relative lack of involvement on the part of users in institutionalized religion was their low level of church attendance. Over 50 percent either had never attended or did not attend at the time they were interviewed. The majority of nonusers did attend at least occasionally. (See Table 48.)

A variety of questions were asked concerning occupation and income. Many subjects in both groups reported that they first had begun to work at a very early age. By the time they were twelve years old, seventy-nine (50.6 percent) of the nonusers and forty-two (50.6 percent) of the users said they had been employed. Such experiences are typical. It is common in Costa Rica to see relatively young boys in a variety of street and hustling occupations: shining shoes, acting as messengers, and selling fruit, newspapers, gum, candy, and other products.

A few subjects said they were currently unemployed, a temporary condition frequently encountered in the working–class population: eleven (7 percent) of the nonusers and fourteen (17 percent) of the users. The most frequently mentioned occupation was that of artisan (e.g., shoemaker, carpenter, mechanic, construction worker), followed by transportation workers, service workers, and sellers. (See Table 49.)

Although no strong differences emerged between the two groups for type of occupation, a statistically significant difference was found for monthly wage (see Table 50). Nonusers reported significantly higher earnings. Reasons for this difference are found in the distinctive lifestyle of some of the users, a lifestyle that will be discussed in greater detail later.

An additional group of variables probed through the initial questionnaire concerned the amount and kind of contact subjects had had with law–enforcement agencies. To some degree, because of the illegality of their marihuana use, users had been arrested and jailed more frequently than nonusers (see Tables 51 and 52). The differences that emerged reflected divergent lifestyles but also simply the fact that marihuana use is illegal and actively suppressed in Costa Rica.

When looking at the types of offenses for which subjects had been arrested and jailed, the greatest contrast between the two groups was found with regard to rather serious crimes (see Table 53). Users had been arrested more frequently not only for narcotic offenses but also for property and other offenses. Nonusers had been arrested more frequently for misdemeanors. Considerably more users than nonusers had been jailed for felonies; few in either group had been jailed for misdemeanors. Yet, as we shall see in subsequent discussions, these differences in level of criminal activity were not necessarily caused by marihuana use. Instead, they seem to be related to a host of factors going back to the earliest childhood experiences. As we came to know intimately the participants in our matched–pair studies, we discovered that there were many heavy users of marihuana who had never been arrested and who, except for their marihuana use, were indistinguishable from the nonusers.

By definition, users confessed to more narcotics crimes than did nonusers. What could not be determined at this initial juncture was whether their self–reported *non*narcotics crimes were in any way triggered by their use of marihuana. Users were also more subject to arrest and convictions for any kind of crime, possibly because their known marihuana use led to greater surveillance by the police.

One of the more interesting findings to emerge from this initial questionnaire concerned marital status. At the time the questionnaire was administered, there tended to be a higher percentage of married nonusers than married users. Eighty-four percent of the users reported previous involvement in consensual unions, whereas only 47 percent of the nonusers did so. However, at the same time that nonusers reported a higher incidence of marriage, they also reported more instances of remarriage. Thus, for both groups, the state of marriage was far more stable. The data suggest that marihuana users tended to remain single or to become involved in consensual unions, whereas nonusers were more likely to be involved in conventional marriage and remarriage. (See Tables 54, 55, and 56.)

The number of children reported by each group was not significantly different. For both groups the average number of children was relatively low: 1.8 for users and 2.2 for nonusers. Users reported smaller households, but the differences were not statistically significant. Mean household size for users was 4.4; for nonusers it was 6.0.

Nonusers owned their own homes a little more frequently than did users, but the differences again were not statistically significant. Nor were there any significant differences in the type of housing or household attributes the two groups had.

In summary, for the base sample of 240 individuals, relatively few differences were uncovered through the administration of an initial questionnaire. Of the fifty-four variables probed through the questionnaire, only ten clearly differentiated between the background and current adult status of users and nonusers. If there were a general trend, it would be that, compared with nonusers, users were less stable individuals and had more tenuous ties with family.

A PARADIGM OF USERS

The results of this initial questionnaire, combined with our first contacts with users, led us to develop an early stereotype, which we later discovered was inadequate if not actually incorrect. Our initial user contacts were with individuals who, by comparison with nonusers, seemed to be vagrants and hustlers. When asked how we could locate them for follow-up interviews, the users would often indicate a certain street corner or house, whereas the nonusers would usually name a worksite for working hours and their home for later in the day.

There seemed no doubt that many users followed the street-hustler style of life. But, as the research advanced, we discovered that although these were the most conspicuous, they were not the most numerous. By the time we developed our matched sample of forty-one pairs, we had learned that the majority of users were stable, "solid" citizens, resembling nonusers much more than street-hustler-style users.

The way marihuana itself was employed gave us a basis for typologizing our user population. Those with control over their immediate social environment had a wide variety of available settings in which they could smoke the drug; those with little or no control over that environment had a more limited range. All were forced to hide their practice from the authorities, but the latter were forced to hide it from their families, neighbors, fellow workers, and supervisors as well.

We chose to employ the term *stable worker* for users who had access to smoking environments that were safe from the law and insulated by the complicity of their families or fellow workers. For those who, because of the lack of such complicity and protection, were forced to do their smoking in vulnerable places such as street corners, we employed the term *street movers*. Finally, we employed the term *pastoralist-escapists* for those users who dared not smoke at home or on the job but who, because of their unwillingness to risk open street smoking, retreated to rural settings for their smoking sessions.

We found that the paradigm was a surprisingly powerful one. Typically, the stable smoker either was the ruling head of his household or had made enough peace with other adults in the household to be able to smoke at home. With his home as a basic refuge, the stable smoker had little need to expose himself to the risks of community sanction and possible arrest in pursuing his habit. He often succeeded in finding work in situations where fellow workers also smoked marihuana, especially in occupations such as shoemaking, baking, tailoring, trucking, or taxi driving. We found that shoemakers had a particularly marked reputation for marihuana use on the job.

Other adults in the homes of stable users (wives, in-laws, parents, etc.) tended to be tolerant but disapproving. Only in rare cases did they actively share the user's habit. The stable smoker generally eschewed social contexts for smoking outside his controlled environments. He considered running with a *barra* (crowd) to be risky and so, on those rare occasions when he smoked on the street, he was likely to smoke alone. This did not mean he was antisocial in his behavior. There were bars in San José where certain people could smoke with relative impunity, because sufficient vigilance and precautions were maintained by the management to ensure the security of their clientele. The cigarettes smoked in these places were usually brought to the bar by the user himself; if the bartender knew him well, however, the bar itself would provide him with material.

Street movers were constantly active in the sidewalk life of San José and highly skilled in the language and bustling activity found there. Usually they entered street networks during early or middle childhood, propelled by unstable home situations. Although street movers might live in a family household, they seldom smoked there. Many stayed alone in cheap rented rooms in the boardinghouses that surrounded the central market area and red-light district. There they might make a precarious peace with management willing to tolerate smoking in their rooms, but only so long as the rent was paid. When landlords did not approve of such behavior, these users were forced to limit their smoking to the streets of the city or the coffee groves surrounding it.

Street movers tended to be younger than stable smokers, with a mean age—in our sample—of 28.1 and a range of twenty to forty-three years. Their style of life contrasted sharply with that of stable smokers. Home and family life were at best spotty, and often nonexistent. The typical street mover lacked a steady job, although he might work sporadically on an *ad hoc* basis (a pattern which is called *camaronear,* or "to shrimp," in the local street argot). His diet reflected his general lifestyle; it tended to be sporadic and uneven. In many cases, lacking a household to which to resort for steady meals, he took what he could get in the streets, and this was often neither nutritious nor satisfying.

The third user type, the pastoralist-escapist, represented the desire on the part of a growing number of younger lower-class users to embrace certain parts of the "Age of Aquarius" ethos of North America. Most users of this type, known to the research team, were too young to qualify for the user sample. Those who were old enough had begun smoking before the arrival of stylish drug use in Costa Rica but had taken some of the superficial characteristics of the "Age of Aquarius" pattern once it appeared on the scene. Being younger on the whole than the other two user types, the pastoralist-escapists usually still lived with their family of orientation. Otherwise, they were similiar to the street movers in the general mercurial quality of their lifestyles. They tended not to hold steady jobs or at best to change jobs frequently. Although they had spent time participating in street culture, often being exposed at a very early age, they did not demonstrate the same skill in street survival as did their street-mover counterparts.

These three categories within our paradigm are, of course, not hermetically sealed. Stable smokers may become street movers if their families break up, and pastoralist-escapists may very likely mutate into stable smokers as they become older and more experienced. Yet such transformations are far from inevitable. Many street movers continue their lifestyle well into middle age.

Of the forty-one marihuana users chosen for the matched-pair studies, twenty-three were stable smokers, sixteen were street movers, and two were pastoralist-escapists. Classification into these three basic categories was based on two years of familiarity with the smoking habits and life history of each subject; it greatly clarified distorted impressions obtained through the initial questionnaire.

ADULT SOCIAL WORLDS: THE MATCHED-PAIR SAMPLE

Since one of the matching criteria for the final sample of forty-one pairs was marital status, no significant differences could or did emerge in this regard. Seventy-five percent of both users and nonusers were either married or lived in stable free-unions; the remaining 25 percent lived either alone or in serial liaisons.

For those subjects who stayed with their parents through adolescence, the time of marriage or the initiation of a free union was usually also a time of breaking away from the childhood home. The range of ages at which marriages or free unions took place for the entire matched-pair sample spanned from the mid-teens to the late twenties. At the time of the interviews, the average duration of these liaisons was nearly the same for users and nonusers: eight years for the former and six years for the latter.

Subjects in the matched-pair sample had generally met and married women who were much like themselves. About 64 percent of the spouses tended to be of the same socioeconomic status as the subject, while 15 percent had been of higher status and 21 percent of lower status, with no significant differences emerging between users and nonusers. In terms of education, about one third of the spouses were better educated than the subjects, one third the same, and one third lower. A quarter of both groups' spouses had come from the same *barrio* as the subject himself. Most subjects had met their wives in their own neighborhoods, through work contacts, or in a dance hall.

More users than nonusers had married after a relatively short period of courtship. Twenty-two percent of the former and only 4.9 percent of the latter reported courtships of three months or less (see Table 57). This difference could be explained partly by the fact that nonusers tended to come from rural areas of the country, where lengthy courtship patterns are customary. An example is the following:

> I knew my wife for about eight years. We were known as a couple forever it seems. Finally it got to the point that people were saying that I was taking advantage of her by not marrying her. Her parents were getting chilly to me and my parents were wondering if I was going to be a man about it. So we got married, and I'm glad about it.

For users and nonusers alike, courtship generally involved a period of free union lasting from a few months to the entire courtship period. When asked about their marital status, many who were living in free union claimed they were "single"; their real relationships were ascertained only after considerable discussion and observation. They preferred free union to marriage because they perceived it as helping them avoid problems and preserving independence. In most cases, however, such relationships approximated the marital status in form and responsibility.

In two relational networks with which we worked, every man was formally married. This seems to have been related to the fact that these men and their spouses were both reared in the same geographical vicinity in which they presently live. In their interviews, these men stressed the functional utility of their spouses' families and how they looked to them as readily available and important resources.

In at least two cases, it was church rather than family that precipitated formal marriage ties. The individuals involved had converted to a Protestant sect during their courtship and were strongly urged by fellow parishioners to seal their relationship with the bonds of religion.

Once involved in either marriage or free union, the couple clearly divided responsibilities for household management. The exact nature of this division, however, differed significantly between users and nonusers. The former tended to help more frequently with household matters, reflecting in part that a larger percentage of users had spouses who worked outside the home. All subjects claimed that they "ran things" at home. Such views are suspect, however, given the fact that the general tendency in Costa Rican households is to let the women take charge of domestic issues.

Although subjects were almost always in constant contact with extended kindred networks, their households were largely restricted to the immediate nuclear family. Approximately 75 percent of both users and nonusers lived with only spouse and/or children, and, in an additional 10 percent, only one other relative was present. Users tended to change residence more frequently than did nonusers, and users had a higher rate of job turnover.

Domestic relations tended to mimic the family situations in which the subjects had been reared. In general, subjects reported that their relationships with their spouses were "tranquil," punctuated only by occasional verbal arguments about liquor and money. When fights were reported as continuous, these usually led to separation, with the male taking a mistress and reducing his contact with the family to a minimum. In such cases, he often continued to contribute to the financial support of the family. No differences were reported between users and nonusers with regard to the quality of the marital relationship. However, when the subject population was viewed in terms of level of alcohol consumption, abstainers and light drinkers appeared to maintain better relations with their wives than did moderate and heavy drinkers.

As a group, the users seemed to continue their adolescent peer-group ties into adulthood. To a significant degree ($p = .01$), users said that they preferred to spend their free time with friends rather than with families. In spite of this difference, users tended to have longer-lasting unions with their spouses.

Punishment of children was left primarily in the hands of the mothers. Although fathers reported that they occasionally took disciplinary action, further probing revealed that they deferred to their spouses in this regard. Reinforcement of good behavior through gift-giving was not well-developed. What constituted "good behavior" was largely defined by the mother and instilled by her. Religious and ethical teaching was primarily her job.

A third or less of the men of either group were active in community affairs, church, or politics and in this sense provided weak role models for their children. Only 12 percent accepted leadership of any sort. Despite this general pattern of weak participation in public life, significant differences did emerge between users and nonusers; the latter were more likely to become leaders ($p = .01$). Given the users' long histories of problems with authorities and organizations, this finding suggests another striking continuation of early patterns and is congruent with users' continuation of peer-group relationships established during adolescence.

In general, the men's primary zones of interaction and those of their spouses were discretely segregated, with the household constituting the *only* overlapping domain. The male world rarely impinged upon family circles. Friends were seldom brought home, and interaction between family and peer groups was minimal.

Except in cases where the spouses had a job or an independent income, the men tended to control the household's financial affairs. They generally kept the other members of the family on a strict allowance, which they doled out on a weekly or even daily basis. Because the amount of money set aside for household management was usually limited, supplies tended to be purchased in very small quantities and trips to the local store were frequent.

Mealtimes in the homes of the subjects were simple affairs. They were prepared first and foremost for the man of the house and left in the kitchen. Other members of the family would help themselves when they were hungry. Customarily, the man would eat upon arriving home from work. The meal would be dished up unceremoniously, with conversation kept to a minimum. As one informant put it, people should not talk at meals, "out of respect for the food." Mealtime was not used as an occasion for strengthening family interaction.

Such a high degree of role segregation parallels the general picture of conjugal roles and social networks uncovered by Bott (1955) in her London studies. The social worlds of our subjects and their spouses were connected only by virtue of their marital or free-union relationship. The daily routines of male and female did not overlap. The man would leave in the morning to go to work and spend the day away from home. If he did return home for lunch, his meal was served quickly so that he could return to his activities of the afternoon. He would usually pass the evening with his friends. Generally these friends would not come to his home or interact with his family. His peer relationships thus constituted a separate and discrete world of social interaction, a world that excluded the spouse. Hers was a narrower range of social relationships, centering principally on the home, her own children, her relatives (especially her mother), and a few friends and acquaintances. She did not share in her mate's world, nor he in hers.

MARIHUANA AND HOME LIFE

An analysis of smoking histories among users showed that all had smoked at home at least once but that stable smokers tended to do so most of the time. Smoking at home usually involved only the individual user, although, in a few cases, it could also include intimate marihuana–using friends.

Even among stable smokers, the use of marihuana in the home often had to be done with care. One stable smoker, who did not wish his children to become interested in his habit, described the following daily smoking environment:

Q: Now, in the house, you smoke alone? That is, is the wife there?
R: I actually catch them off guard, my children and my wife, so that they don't realize. I send them off to watch television, to the living room. Then I go into the bathroom, and while I'm defecating I'm getting stoned.

Those users who wished for their children to rise in social standing were most likely to take such precautions. Although they did not consider marihuana use itself to be a handicap in social mobility, they recognized the strong social stigma attached to it by the rest of Costa Rican society. Others, less concerned about such matters, smoked regularly in the presence of their families. They maintained that their children either did not notice or care or that they could not distinguish between marihuana and tobacco. About five stable smokers had cousins or brothers living nearby who would occasionally visit their homes to smoke marihuana, but this practice was far more common in the study sample. Spouses usually did not share in the smoking sessions. Marihuana use, then, tended to reflect and further strengthen the aforementioned role segregation between subjects and their wives.

For most users, marihuana smoking was exclusively part of the male social world. Nevertheless, women who lived with them, whether wives or mothers, were usually conscious of their habit. One street mover described his mother's suspicions as follows:

. . . And I arrive home stoned, and she [subject's mother] keeps looking at my face, but she doesn't say anything.
Q: Do you think she knows when you're stoned?
R: It seems to me she must suspect it, especially when I come home stoned to eat and I get there, and she says, "You're going to eat?" and sure, I eat heartily, and she says, "Hmmmmm."

On occasion, such suspicions can explode into a confrontation and temporary ejection from the home. Because this is so, the young street movers tended to avoid flagrant or obvious domestic use. Stable smokers, such as the one described earlier, ran no such risks, however. Their peace at home had been achieved through their status as household heads and principal wage earners and through their selection of a mate with whom they could reach an understanding about their habits.

NETWORKS OF FRIENDS AND ASSOCIATES

Because we identified and became acquainted with our study population through their informal social networks, we often learned about friends and associates before we learned about family. Our analysis of these networks was patterned after Mitchell (1969), whose conceptual framework focuses on morphology and interaction. The former includes anchorage, reachability, density, and range and defines the shape and structure of the network. The latter includes content, directedness, durability, density, and range and encompasses the kinds and nature of the social relations that take place within the network.

Morphology:

1. Anchorage: In order to enter the adult social world of working-class males in San José, we used key individuals and their personal networks as points of reference, or anchorage.

2. Reachability: Key people, such as our initial "anchors," tend to maintain a position vis-à-vis the relational groupings that permits them to know "what is happening." They know how to relay messages and are aware of functional links in the communication web.

3. Density: Networks may be seen as "loose-knit" or "tight-knit" depending on the degree to which members of an anchor's network know each other and interact among themselves. Among our study population we encountered both.

4. Range: Naturally, some persons know many people, others know few. However, the utility of a network does not depend on numbers alone. A single well-placed contact is worth many drinking buddies in a moment of legal crisis.

Interaction:

1. Content: This feature of network relationships categorizes network interactions in terms of kinship obligations, economic assistance, religious participation, the camaraderie of friendship, or others. Within any given network, content may be single-stranded or multistranded.

2. Directedness: This feature characterizes the direction and subordinate-superordinate dynamics of network interaction. Equivalent reci-

procity is one possible variation of directedness; patron–client relationships represent another.

3.   Durability: The continuity of network interaction is described through this attribute. If relationships are continually active, they are considered manifest. If not, they are considered latent.

4.   Intensity: Intensity suggests the importance of the network links to the participating individuals, indicating to what degree they are willing to honor their obligations encompassed in their network relationships.

5.   Frequency: This attribute describes how often and with how many other network participants contacts occur in a day, a week, a month, or a year.

Because they were located through networks, the entire matched-pair subject population could be organized into eight relational systems, with a residual category including only ten subjects who were located by our office staff and seven who could not be clearly placed in any one of the eight groupings. Here we shall describe only four of the networks as examples, one for each of the three types of marihuana users, plus a single representative of nonusers. The first to be described is that of a pastoralist-escapist whom we shall call Mauro.

Mauro's Network

We were fortunate to have met Mauro early in the fieldwork. Tall and lean with an easy manner and unsuspicious nature, he was open to us and cooperative in sharing what he knew about his neighborhood, a residential area near the central city. Regular work was not his forte, and income was therefore uncertain. But since he still lived with his mother in spite of being in his late twenties, this was no real problem. Unmarried and unattached, he maintained his primary social contacts with friends.

Mauro's relational system provided eight subjects for the final sample. Most, like himself, were users of marihuana. One of the two nonusers selected from the network was Mauro's brother, the other a neighborhood friend from childhood.

The network consisted of young men who were as yet unmarried, whose financial responsibilities and obligations were as yet unformed, and for whom the most important activity of the day was sharing relaxing moments with friends. All held jobs, but none could be said to have had a career. Rather, they moved about in the city, quitting a job whenever they wished, finding another when they needed one, but maintaining a secure social base in their home neighborhood, regardless of where they happened to work or live at the time.

Mauro was a leader in this informal grouping, a status largely due to his position as "elder." He could be found in the morning sleeping at home and in the afternoon in his house, at the corner, or working. Persons looking for him would visit these places or leave a message with his mother or a friend on the corner. He was never too far away. His primary zone of interaction included a group of twelve men, younger than he, who all knew each other and interacted together whether Mauro were present or not. Density, therefore, was high. However, each of the members of the network participated in other networks as well, consisting mostly of family and work relationships. These were kept separate, and participation in Mauro's network was hidden to avoid ridicule for wasting time with suspect company.

The range of Mauro's network was limited and homogeneous; all members were younger than he. As all were relatively unconnected to official San José, they were of little utility to each other in times of need, except as confidants and providers of moral support. The network was limited in scope, being centered on an agreeable but undynamic elder who facilitated interaction by being easily accessible.

The principal content of the relationship was recreational; thus, the network was activated only when work schedules, weather, and circumstances permitted. Members coming together could be as few as two and as many as seven or eight. A typical pattern was to meet at Mauro's house and discuss what to do. Such discussions would stimulate preparations: a shave, a clean shirt, fresh socks, or perhaps a splash of after-shave if the goal were a dance or nearby regional fiesta. If it were to sit, talk, and smoke marihuana in a nearby coffee grove, the preparations would be less elegant. Often Mauro himself would decide what the group would do, a decision usually accepted by all. If that decision included smoking marihuana, Mauro would organize the collection of a *puesta,* or stake, with which to purchase the drug, and he would subsequently control distribution. The directedness of the transactions tended to be one-sided, with Mauro assuming a dominant position and keeping for himself more than an equal share of the booty.

Since recreation constituted the single-stranded content of the network, its durability depended on circumstances propitious for such activity. Because many conditions could impede this type of group effort (e.g., work, weather, other commitments, passing arguments), the network was activated only sporadically; in some weeks, members would assemble several times; in others, not at all.

In times of crisis, when one of the network participants might be arrested or hospitalized, Mauro would show up at our office to see whether we could help, considering us his most highly placed contact with the authorities. His network had no knowledge of people of real influence or strategic bureaucratic placement.

The two pastoralist-escapist marihuana smokers selected for the matched-pair study were introduced to us through Mauro. As they discussed their marihuana use, they emphasized outings with other members of the network and their lack of confidence to perform work tasks or function normally under the influence of the drug. This tendency to avoid working or non-smoker-dominated social contexts while stoned is unique among Costa Rican smokers and will be discussed in greater detail in Chapters 6 and 7.

The next network, describing a group of street movers, varies substantially from that described above. Unlike Mauro's pastoralist-escapist friends, these people did not activate their network for the primary purpose of smoking marihuana. Instead, they turned to the drug in the natural course of daily events.

Carlo's Network

Carlo, a young man in his early twenties, was the first subject contacted in the study. Our mutual encounter was fortuitous, since Carlo introduced us to dozens of individuals who provided valuable information and further contacts. Though his personal network provided only five subjects for the study, these five men were especially valuable in that they constituted prime examples of "street-mover" consumers of marihuana. Like Carlo, they were all shoeshine men who practiced their trade daily in downtown streets. In spite of their mercurial personal lifestyle and "street-mover" smoking behavior, their work in general was characterized by standardized patterns and regular hours.

Exceptionally bright, with easy humor and witty conversation, Carlo was able to convince many potential subjects in his network of shoeshine men that we were no risk to them. They, like him, were consumers who had learned to use the drug in the street at a very young age after leaving their parental home.

Carlo's first conversation with us was open, candid, and included many details of marihuana use and of his own personal involvement. Given the illegality of such use, his openness was quite remarkable and, over time, became striking when contrasted with the elaborate measures taken by subsequent informants to verify our identity before taking us into their confidence. His generosity, cooperation, and affability were the very traits that had won him loyalty and respect among his informal relational group. Carlo's close relationship with them facilitated our movements and contacts among his entire circle of friends and acquaintances.

Though Carlo's immediate group of co-workers might have appeared to the casual observer to be nothing more than a transitory, fleeting street-corner aggregation, it had a long history of occupational stability. Some members of the group had worked on the same park corner for twenty-five years and had developed regular clientele, standardized work patterns, and regular hours of operation. There was a wide range of ages; the youngest men were in their early twenties, the oldest in their late forties. One was married, two lived in free union, and two, including Carlo, were single. Generally they had no work other than cleaning shoes; however, Carlo himself had recently begun working sporadically in regional fiestas.

One of the occupational hazards of the group was police harassment, which was based in many cases on supposed enforcement of vagrancy laws. This often took the form of rounding up shoeshine men from all over the city, regardless of the stability of their work habits. These roundups meant imprisonment for the men until witnesses could certify that they were not vagrants but responsible self-employed entrepreneurs. To that end, we served as witnesses for Carlo's colleagues on numerous occasions, particularly after the minister of security publicly declared that shoeshine boys were a public menace and disgrace.

The range of Carlo's personal network was facilitated by the central location of his work. Masses of people passed through the park daily, creating the opportunity for literally hundreds of interactions in a single day. Because their work was located at the vortex of San José social movement, Carlo and his co-workers served as major conduits for urban communication. They were not only highly reachable in terms of their own personal networks but also very instrumental in making contact with other interlocking social networks. Carlo was always well-informed, and he kept us abreast of new developments, introduced us to many contacts developed through his park associations, and referred us constantly to people and places throughout the metropolitan area.

Carlo's total personal network, then, was large and diverse. Through a relative of his who worked for an attorney, he had access to many people in the justice department, contacts which proved very useful at times of police harassment. On occasion, his relative had taken legal steps to release Carlo and his friends from jail when they had been charged with vagrancy; at other times, friends of Carlo had been sentenced to prison for serious charges (e.g., selling marihuana and theft), and Carlo's contacts through his relative had provided dramatic assistance.

Although extensive in scope, these secondary zones of Carlo's network were characterized by low density, for the people passing through his "office" generally did not know each other. Density was much greater in his relations with his immediate circle of co-workers, his primary zone of interaction. Within that circle, all the men knew each other and were linked together by ties of work, friendship, recreation, and economic assistance. A rift between two brothers who worked in the park had slightly disrupted group cohesion, but most of the men viewed the discord as a family concern involving only the two brothers. For the most part, camaraderie and cooperation characterized the group.

The content of Carlo's primary zone of interaction (his circle of co-workers) was multistranded. Members of that circle shared moments of both recreation and work daily. They had known each other for years and thus shared many experiences from their youth, such as adventures in the reformatory and in the street.

Interactions at work tended to assume the form of highly structured dyads, generally of a reciprocal nature. For example, the men would often collaborate to coax an unsuspecting client to play *chapas,* a bottle-cap variant of the pea and shell game familiar to county fair midways. One of the men would shine the intended victim's shoes, while the other would engage his shoe-shining colleague in *chapas* and a betting tournament. The latter would pretend an attempt at locating the wad of paper his partner had skillfully moved about under one of the three bottle caps. Through such a demonstration, the two would try to entice their prey to enter the game. When successful, they would inevitably outwit him, and the winnings would be split equally.

There were many alternatives for recreational interaction. These included going to someone's room to play cards and talk, hiking through coffee groves at the edge of the city, and going to a downtown dance hall to drink, dance, and meet girls. In Carlo's secondary network (i.e., his contacts who pass through the park) interaction was much less intense. Carlo had the skills and contacts needed to make it effective, but he was more interested in enjoying his co-workers' company than in becoming a social entrepreneur. Thus, his extensive network remained largely dormant.

Carlo and his shoe-shining comrades were generally far less cautious about their selection of marihuana-smoking environments than were Mauro's pastoralist-escapist smoking companions. Sometimes they smoked on busy street corners, demonstrating their highly developed skills of concealment. At other times they smoked in downtown bars and rooming houses, places where they were also vulnerable to discovery and possible arrest. They also would on occasion make an excursion to a suburban coffee grove and there smoke their marihuana. Above all, they looked at marihuana as a vehicle for reciprocity and enjoyment.

With Carlo, as well as with other street movers we knew, both marihuana use and general lifestyle tended to be mercurial. Carlo's fellow shoeshine men would experience times of modest plenty when their *chapazos* were working well and their customers were tipping. But their business was also subject to inclement weather, and they themselves were subject to police harassment and frequent arrest. Paralleling the quixotic nature of their lifestyle was their uncertainty in terms of perceived effects of their marihuana use. By their own account, the drug could bring extreme pleasure in such primary activities as eating and sex and in such secondary activities as dancing or soccer. But it could also bring cold sweats, vomiting, and the sick feeling of being close to death. As we probed into the details of their smoking habits, it became eminently clear that such unpredictable effects were directly related to the precariousness of the settings in which street movers used the drug. This we shall discuss at length in Chapter 6.

Renardo's Network

As a non-marihuana-smoking day laborer, Renardo's network stood in sharp contrast to the preceding two. In his late thirties, Renardo was lean, muscular, and agile, the result of playing soccer for his entire life. He lived in a squatter settlement near a stable residential neighborhood. Renardo, his spouse, and his children shared a ramshackle wooden house with his father, his siblings, and his nephews—a dozen persons in all.

Like his father, Renardo worked in construction, an activity shared by most of the men in his network. Renardo and his father were prominent persons in their neighborhood. His own prominence stemmed from active participation in neighborhood affairs; for example, he had organized the citizen's committee that had brought utilities to the settlement, had created the impetus to build the small neighborhood chapel which doubled as a meeting hall, and continued to promote efforts to improve the area.

Renardo's network contributed six subjects to the final sample, all nonusers of marihuana. Except for Renardo himself, all these men were in their early to late twenties. All but three lived in free union with their spouses and had at least two children each. Two were formally married, and another was struggling to save enough money from his construction job to get married, an event which seemed to be postponed continually.

Although their housing was noticeably more humble than was common in the more stable residential areas from which we drew most of our subjects, individuals living in this settlement did not talk about their patently low standard of living. Rather, they saw their situation as a way of saving money on rent and remarked that the exercise of squatter's rights had permitted relatives to locate near each other and thus realize an important goal. The neighborhood had been established along a road that passed through a coffee grove. It was a line settlement with coffee trees behind and in front of the row of houses, providing a campestral atmosphere for the area and a touch of beauty appreciated by the residents. The road was unpaved, however, and became a sea of muck in the eight-month rainy season. All these physical features conditioned the interactions of the residents. The line configuration was especially important, however, for the kinds of interaction patterns which the members of Renardo's network had developed.

When we first met men from the settlement and sought information about the area and its residents, most of them referred us to Renardo and his father. This led us to consider them as natural leaders in the settlement's male informal relational system. We were relieved to discover that they were cooperative and open. We found Renardo to be a real network anchor because of his role as captain of the neighborhood's soccer team. Younger players and friends would constantly come to his house to talk, watch television, and discuss the team interaction that was facilitated by the fact that Renardo's house was situated near the middle of the line settlement.

Renardo's network was vibrant and solid. Interaction was daily, due to the fact that everyone leaving or entering was forced to pass by other network members' houses and thus could easily transmit messages or news. Yet the network was limited in range. In projects led by Renardo, such as campaigns to buy uniforms for the soccer team, the network had not been very successful; its members had simply lacked the resources and contacts for realizing their goals. Renardo's father had managed to obtain government support for utilities, but in other projects, such as informal fund-raising drives, he had not been successful. Although very persistent in dealing with formal institutions (e.g., government agencies), he had great difficulty organizing informal coalitions.

The ties between Renardo and the members of his network were multistranded, dealing with community organization, friendship, sports, and other recreational activities and reinforced with kinship links between Renardo and members of these informal relational groupings. Although the social style of the groupings was generally characterized by reciprocal and casual interaction, this pattern was often modified during formal rituals such as those of a soccer game. At such times, all would defer to Renardo, the field captain, or to his father, the team manager. The weekly schedule of these games, the frequent practices, and the daily social contacts about neighborhood concerns made the network a durable, manifest structure with a high degree of intensity. When Renardo was injured recently, network members provided considerable moral support as well as physical assistance. During his homebound convalescence, they were particularly supportive, many visiting him daily to keep him informed of current happenings.

The interactional patterns of the settlement, as reflected in the relational structure of Renardo's network, seem modeled more after the pattern of a small rural town than of a bustling urban enclave. This, however, was not surprising. Most of the settlement's residents had been reared in rural areas and had migrated to the city in recent years, bringing with them patterns of customary behavior associated with the rural relational systems from which they came.

The orientation of Renardo's social network toward work, community action, and sports seems wholesome and positive indeed, when compared with the hedonism of Mauro's pastoralist-escapists or Carlo's activities of petty gambling fraud. Still, there is a large category of users, representatives of which comprised more than half (twenty-three out of forty-one) of the matched-pair sample, that does not differ at all sharply with nonusers. The next network described is that of a "stable smoker." It will stand in contrast to the first two user networks—those of Mauro and Carlo—and will in fact resemble the networks of nonusers far more than those of pastoralist-escapist and street-mover users.

Nacho's Network

Nacho resided in a small town approximately thirty minutes from downtown San José. We met him through one of the anthropologists' neighbors, and he, in turn, introduced us to his circle of friends, five of whom were selected for the final sample. His house served as the center for an elaborate transport business that shipped vegetables to several markets throughout the country. This business provided an exceptionally high income for Nacho and his associates, the latter comprising his circle of intimate friends. All were very heavy users of marihuana and thus provided additional examples of economically stable consumers.

Nacho and his friends were established businessmen, good providers for their families, and very serious about their futures. Their use of marihuana was only one aspect of their daily interactions and was woven into social exchanges focusing on financial affairs. They were often observed smoking marihuana while discussing business opportunities, the feasibility of different ventures, and future plans.

Of the entire study population, these men were the most difficult to organize for the different medical and psychological examinations, largely because of the demanding schedule of their shipping business. Each week they made two round trips to a northern province, runs which took up most of the week. The remaining time was spent resting and planning the next week's trips. The amount of capital required for these ventures was impressive, suggesting high cash flow and a successful business. Of all the study's subjects, whether user or nonuser, the men in this network had the highest incomes. All were in their late thirties and were either married or in a stable union with children. Some had been married for ten years, another indication of the group's stability. They spent their free time with each other in their homes, usually smoking large amounts of marihuana. Their wives were often present, and though they did not join the men in smoking marihuana, they did share in the conversation.

Nacho and the men in this relational group were uniformly ambitious. They were quite concerned about their children's success in school and saw formal education as helping these children continue the families' social and economic ascent, which they themselves had initiated.

While Nacho's network was wide-ranging, due to his extensive business dealings, his primary social world centered on a small group of five business associates. This primary zone of interaction constituted a highly interactive, friendly group characterized by total density. All its members were closely linked to Nacho, but they also interacted with each other independently of him. At one point during the research, an altercation between two of the men (not including Nacho) did create some intragroup tension; the dispute was soon settled, however, and had little effect on the general cohesiveness of the group.

As the principal anchor for this relational group, Nacho was not as helpful as other anchors previously described. But this was largely because he was difficult to reach. He was often on business trips, had no phone, and lived far enough from the center of San José to make communication difficult.

The content of Nacho's interactions with his close associates was multistranded and included business, family, and recreation. A common recreational activity was to spend an evening in the home of one of the men; such an occasion would find the men relaxing and smoking marihuana cigarettes the size of cigars. Conversation would proceed amiably, with general good humor and casual interchange. In such informal situations, interactions would be reciprocal. In business, however, Nacho and one other associate assumed a superordinate stance in their interaction with others in the group. This dominant posture stemmed from the fact that these two men had a higher capital investment in the transport business than did the others.

Interactions among Nacho's primary network were highly manifest and intense, as reflected in the members' successful joint effort to develop the transport business. Such cooperative endeavor brought them together frequently and was reinforced by their close personal relationship.

MARIHUANA AND THE ADULT SOCIAL WORLD: AN OVERVIEW

To Nacho and his friends, marihuana smoking had a markedly calm and businesslike quality not seen among other kinds of users. These upwardly striving entrepreneurs smoked marihuana routinely as they discussed prospective business ventures and even while transacting business. Their recreational smoking usually took place in the home or in other private smoking environments where they were not worried about arrest or discovery. Stable smokers like Nacho tended to emphasize the routineness of their marihuana smoking and the evenness with which they could handle the effects of the drug. They pointed out emphatically that they felt marihuana helped them to do many things better, including work tasks, sporting activities, reading, writing, conversing, and listening. Rather than using marihuana as an escape from everyday dreariness, as did the street movers and the pastoralist-escapists, they approached marihuana as an aid in relating to the even, steady life they led.

The two realms of the working-class urban Costa Rican male's adult world discussed in this chapter have been family relations on the one hand and informal social-network relations on the other. Together, they give some idea of the variety of settings in which marihuana users are likely to smoke. By relating these settings to the many subjectively perceived effects of marihuana use (as will be done in considerable detail in Chapter 6), we begin to understand basic relationships between marihuana use and lifestyle. Nacho's family and friends contributed to the stability of his lifestyle, and his marihuana smoking was intimately related to both. It is not surprising that he regarded the effects of marihuana as predictable and controllable:

Q: Do you get more inspired when you smoke?
R: Yes.
Q: How?
R: Let's say you haven't smoked for a while and then you smoke. You feel different. . . . For me, marihuana, for whatever purpose you want it, if you set the tone and concentrate on what you're doing, it works for anything. . . . If I want not to sleep, with marihuana I don't sleep.

For Nacho, marihuana did what he wanted it to do, and he was reasonably confident about the outcome of each smoking session.

On the other hand, Carlo could not be so certain about the effects he would obtain when he smoked marihuana. He wanted the experience to be pleasureful, and it sometimes was quite so, but he realized that it might not be, just as he recognized the risk of arrest when he smoked on the street corner or the fact that he might not win in his *chapa* game. Although neither activity promised a totally reliable outcome, knowledge of this fact did not dampen Carlo's enthusiasm either for marihuana smoking or for trying to lure tourists into a *chapazo*. And therein lay the fundamental difference between Carlo's and Nacho's marihuana use. Both derived desired effects from smoking the drug, but Nacho had the social and economic wherewithal to ensure the security of both his life and his marihuana smoking, and Carlo could not be so certain about either. Perceived effects, as we shall see in Chapter 6, correlate directly and strongly with such differences in settings and expectations.

The four examples of networks discussed here represent important segments of the adult social worlds of three basically different types of users and of ordinary lower-class nonusers. Mauro's recreationally oriented and often latent network allows for a pattern of marihuana use that is often dormant and becomes active usually when a specific recreational occasion presents itself. Carlo's network, although more often manifest than Mauro's, still fosters an association between marihuana and recreation. Renardo's network illustrates how, in spite of poverty, stability and upward striving can be achieved. And Nacho's demonstrates that such stability and ambition is by no means limited to nonusers. In spite of their business acumen and success, Nacho and his friends turn to marihuana to facilitate both work and relaxation.

6/ Smoking Environment and Effects

The various smoking environments chosen by marihuana users are closely related to their relative control over social environments. By sifting through participant observation data, life-history materials, and marihuana-use interviews, we were able to identify thirteen kinds of marihuana-using environments.[1] Each segment of transcribed marihuana-use interviews was examined for descriptions of smoking environment and subjectively perceived effects, as these were reported by the individual subjects. In all, 578 different context accounts of smoking environments were counted by the scorer, with 527 described effects of marihuana smoking. The reasons the number of effects was not identical to the number of smoking contexts was that sometimes two effects were named for a single environmental setting and sometimes settings were named but no accompanying effects described. The scorer kept an individual user's tally for effects named and environments cited.

In the analysis, smoking environment was defined as the place where the user felt the effects described or where he actually smoked the marihuana. Most often the two were coterminous. However, users sometimes smoked *in preparation* for an activity in a place where it would be too risky to smoke; to eliminate confusion, we have scored this as equal to an effect felt in the actual place where the marihuana was smoked.

Preparatory smoking was a normal procedure for some of our users. One stable smoker, for example, mentioned his preparation for work:

> At times, I haven't got stoned, and I feel a bit donkey-headed, and maybe I have to assemble a control box like that one there, or maybe with twenty-four circuit breakers. Well, each breaker carries a line, and there's a diagram with instructions to assemble the box, and I feel donkey-headed and I can't do it. Then I leave it and don't assemble it. The next day, I come to work well-toasted . . . and shortly afterward the box is assembled.

This smoker maintained that preparatory smoking made him a more effective and willing worker. Another user explained preparatory smoking as follows:

116

When I'm going to talk to the mayor or some official, first I smoke and get stoned, and then I go talk. The same with a lawyer. I like to smoke before talking, because then, with my batteries in, I'm "pure life." I spend day and night smoking weed.

The above texts were scored for two smoking environments and one effect each. The first example was scored for "home alone" and "work alone" environments and the "work better" effect. The second was scored for "home alone" and "street alone" environments and the "improves performance" effect (see Table 60).

Stable smokers like the ones quoted above usually had a private place where they did their preparatory smoking undisturbed. Others not so fortunate secluded themselves and smoked all the material they had in order not to risk being caught with possession. This kind of smoking was not in preparation for any specific activity but rather for street wandering, bar hopping, or dancing. One young user explained his preparatory smoking thus:

Most of the time you could say [that I smoke] accompanied, because alone it's difficult. I buy [material]. I do . . . and find an empty field, and I smoke, since I don't like to carry that stuff around. So what I do is, I go to a place, and I smoke it right there, and I come out of there simply with what I've got in my head.

Carrying marihuana in one's head (*la llevo en la jupa*) is a use style that appears in most users' accounts. It is safe and, except for a very perceptive observer, undetectable. Preparatory smoking is a way for the marihuana smoker to enjoy the effects of the drug in any context he wishes.

In our analysis of smoking set, certain kinds of similar environments were combined into a single category, especially when they were reported infrequently. For example, smoking in school was combined with smoking alone at work, because smoking in school was reported seldom and the nature of the smoking environments in both cases was similar. In both, the user was forced to hide his smoking from supervisory authority and required to function in the same manner as nonsmokers.

Once basic smoking environments were identified, they were tabulated with citation instances in the life-history materials and marihuana interviews. When a new environment was found during the sifting of the transcribed interviews, it was either included in a separate category or combined with one of the existing categories. Bar and dance hall were kept separate because bars were less open smoking environments than dance halls. Prison, as a smoking environment, was so unique that it was included in spite of the few instances in which it was cited by our sample.

To give an adequate idea of the scope and nuance of these smoking contexts, each context included in the final tables deserves a brief description. They will be listed in order from "safest" and "lowest risk" to "most open" and "highest risk."

Home alone. The smokers in our sample cited this smoking environment more than any other. Of the 578 enumerated smoking environments, 128, or

22.1 percent, were in the "home alone" category. All references to smoking alone in one's own or one's family's home were scored for this category.

Work (school) alone. This was another relatively closed environment, cited in 11.9 percent of the cases. The "work alone" category was scored when the user described an instance of smoking by himself while on the job or in school.

Work in group. This category was scored when the user mentioned a smoking environment in which he and his working companions smoked together while on the job. Of the cited environments, 6.1 percent were coded in this fashion.

Home in group. This environment could be either in the subject's own home or in the homes of his friends, but it had to connote smoking with other users. This category accounted for 7.1 percent of all cited environments.

Vehicle. Since all these citations were for group smoking, this category was not separated into solitary and social subunits, as were the "work" and "home" environment categories. The "vehicle" context accounted for only 2.4 percent of all environments cited, but since the "ride" in a car or truck was seen by many users as one of the most pleasant smoking environments, we separated it from the countryside contexts described later.

Countryside alone. One does not have to go very far from the center of San José to find small groves of trees or coffee plantations where he can smoke in relative quiet. Users cited this smoking environment in 2.2 percent of cases.

Street alone. Solitary consumption of marihuana on the streets of San José was cited by users in 8.1 percent of all named user environments. Variations of this environment included ducking into a theater restroom to smoke a quick joint, smoking in the restrooms of a downtown café, and smoking while walking along a dark side street.

Countryside group. When users described experiences where several of them resorted to the coffee groves and nearby rivers for peaceful smoking sessions, these experiences were scored in the "countryside group" category. With 11.4 percent of the total responses enumerated, it was the fourth most frequently cited smoking environment mentioned by our user sample.

Street group. The second most cited smoking environment was the street-corner group that smoked marihuana together. Of all smoking environments cited, 18.3 percent were so categorized. There was always a certain conspiratorial quality in this kind of smoking context; smoking style would vary in accord with the business of a particular context. Concealment of the yellow marihuana cigarettes was practiced *de rigeur,* reaching its most sophisticated form on the busiest corners of downtown San José.

Bar. This smoking environment representing 4.3 percent of the reported total, could be either open (that is, of easy access to nonsmoker and police) or closed. If "open," the bar did not provide any security measures for its customers, so smoking style was much more like street smoking. If "closed," the bar provided at least enough vigilance for the clientele to be able to smoke more or less openly.

Pensión-brothel. This environment was difficult to differentiate from "home alone" because several subjects lived or had lived in boardinghouses similar to those used in the prostitution trade. The "*pensión*-brothel" category refers to *ad hoc* rental of single rooms for relations with prostitutes and for smoking. Usually the subject described a situation where he was alone with his girl or with one or two companions. Of the reported smoking environments, 4 percent were of this nature.

Dance hall. The dimly lit, pulsating lower-class dance hall is an extremely open and therefore risky environment for smoking marihuana. It was cited by our subjects relatively few times (1.5 percent of all citings). We felt it worthy of some attention as a separate category because of the extreme openness of the environment and the presence of women, neither of which are found in most bar smoking contexts.

Prison. By far the smallest category of smoking environments in number and percentage of responses (0.6 percent), the prison was included because of its uniqueness. The two kinds of prison cited were the central penitentiary and a detention center.

When ranked from most frequently to least frequently cited, the thirteen smoking environments fell into the following order:

Home alone	22.1%
Street group	18.3%
Work alone	11.9%
Countryside group	11.4%
Street alone	8.1%
Home in group	7.1%
Work in group	6.1%
Bar	4.3%
Pensión-brothel	4.0%
Vehicle	2.4%
Countryside alone	2.2%
Dance hall	1.5%
Prison	0.6%

Cross-tabulation of user type with these smoking-environments tests and gives considerable reinforcement to the user typology presented in Chapter 5. Table 58 illustrates in a straightforward manner the proportion of each smoking environment report attributable to each type of smoker.

Smoking-context reports were given in slightly different frequencies for each user type. Stable smokers mentioned an average of 12.4 specific smoking contexts, with a range of 6 to 25. Street movers spoke of anywhere from 7 to 34 different smoking contexts with a mean per subject of 16.5. Pastoralist-escapists reported a mean of 14.5 smoking contexts.

In order to adjust for the variation in frequency of smoking-environment citations among the three user types, we have standardized all the scores in Table 59, using a formula where the total for Row A is divided by ten times the number of subjects in Row B, or vice versa. Because of the small size of the pastoralist-escapist group (only two), we were forced to lump these with the street movers, who, as we mentioned earlier, are similar to the pastoralist-escapists in their use of "open-air" smoking environments. Thus, the standardization formula for the stable-smokers row would read: $293/(23 \times 10)$, which yields a factor of 1.274. The individual scores for each smoking environment were then multiplied by the standardization factor, yielding a standardized score for the stable-smoker row. When a similar operation was performed on the street mover/pastoralist-escapist row, the scores in each row could then be compared using a binomial procedure (Blalock 1972).

Table 59 illustrates the results of this operation. The "home alone" column holds high scores for the stable smokers, while the street movers and pastoralist-escapists show low scores for that same column. The two latter user types do at times have access to the home as a smoking environment, but to a much lesser degree and with much less security than the stable smokers. A test of significance shows this result to be significant at the .001 level.

Other closed environments listed show the same differences among the three user types, with the exception of the "vehicle" column. There, the fourteen citations are evenly distributed between stable smokers and street movers. This smoking environment is probably more accessible to the street movers than the other closed environments. A test of statistical significance yields a p value of .075, further supporting this conclusion.

Stable smokers obtain low scores in all open environments, and the difference is marked in all but one column. For the bar environment, they have a fairly high score, which could be the result of chance variation, coupled with the fact that the bar could in fact be a closed environment, depending on the vigilance measures taken by the manager. The low score that is most striking for the stable smokers is that for "street group" environments. Stable smokers are responsible for only 9 percent of all described "street group" environments, while street movers gave nearly 90 percent of these descriptions. This difference was found to be statistically significant at the .0001 level and indicated clearly that the stable smokers tend to avoid these very open and risky smoking environments.

Street movers have strikingly low scores in all the columns where the stable smokers have high scores. Only in the "work alone" column do they approach each other. Thus we have a clear bipolar trend. The street mover tends not to smoke marihuana in the closed secure environments that seem to be havens for stable smokers. The exception of the "work alone" environment may be explained by the fact that the street mover can have more access to this kind of smoking environment than to the other environments named so frequently by stable smokers. Such access does not require much social dominance or special experience. Why street movers and pastoralist-escapists have low scores at all for the "work alone" category may be explained by the fact that they work less, change jobs more often, and thus would be less likely to report smoking while on the job.

High scores appear for street movers and pastoralist-escapists in eight of the thirteen smoking-context columns that represent the more open environments for smoking marihuana. The "street group," "bar," "*pensión*-brothel," and "prison" smoking contexts show high scores that differentiate street movers and pastoralist-escapists from the stable smokers. Street movers were the only members of the sample who cited smoking experience in prison, probably reflecting the fact that they had a much more active history of trouble with the authorities than did the other two types of smokers. Smoking on the street in groups was the most often described smoking environment for street movers, and it was also the easiest way to be identified as a smoker by police and the rest of the community. The following quote from a stable smoker explains why he avoided open smoking environments:

> When I am stoned I don't like any kind of argument or trouble; nothing, because I'm a loner. Along with that, I'll tell you something else; I've almost never been in jail. Only once they took me from downtown San José, but that was just because I happened to be there. I had just gotten here. I was in a bar with a friend named Jughead and with two boys who have color [are known to the police] drinking beer when somebody said, "Dragnet." They did a dragnet, but I knew one of the officers in the station house, and I said, "Hey, don't you see who they're taking in? You know that I'm a worker; I'm no thief; I'm no bum." And he said, "Don't worry. We'll have you out of there fast." And so it was. They got me right out of there and that's the way it was. When they came to get me they said, "Don't ever run around with those boys again, because those two dudes are 'colored'; they're punks, thieves, and if you run with hoods like that you'll get the same 'color.' "

Such an attitude was common, especially among the stable smokers who held steady, blue-collar jobs.

Gilberto, a young street mover from our sample, had a preferred smoking environment in his street-corner gang. He was unable to smoke at home because his mother was militantly antimarihuana and, if she would catch him smoking, she was likely to throw him out of the house. Gilberto resorted to the only smoking environment in which he felt he had some control. There was always a tinge of defiance of the authorities in his descriptions of smoking in the street. He observed the conventions of concealment assiduously. When in his element on the street corner, he exuded a confidence and outspokenness that disappeared in the presence of his mother or older brothers.

Other street movers were even more audacious and skilled, choosing smoking environments of which Gilberto would be afraid. They smoked on the street because they had few other places where they could smoke. Filiberto, a young street mover with more experience in street ways, described how he could bring himself to smoke even with strangers:

> Q: Aren't you afraid to smoke with strangers?
> R: No, what's to scare you? Almost always you smoke with other "burners" and if you don't do it with them, well, you don't smoke. If somebody's not from your crowd, how can you be afraid to smoke with him if he is a "burner"?

Street movers did not seem to be concerned about their identification with other smokers. Indeed, they seemed to be resigned to the risks of such identification.

Referring to Table 58 again, the pastoralist-escapist group had only three cells that hinted at a difference from the street movers. "Countryside alone," "street alone," and oddly enough "dance hall" contexts were named in a relatively high frequency by the pastoralist-escapists. "Countryside group" and "street alone" had by far the highest number of citations.

Generally, pastoralist-escapists showed a tendency not to mention the closed smoking environments in which stable smokers used marihuana, while eschewing the risky open environments frequented by the street movers. The single exception was their frequent mention of, and therefore high positive score for, the "dance hall" category. The following excerpt from one pastoralist-escapist's interview illustrates the dance hall's attraction for this otherwise reclusive variety of Costa Rican marihuana user:

Q: Where do you dance?
R: The Broken Mug is where I generally hang out. [Names several working-class and low-life dance halls.] . . . And, shoot, I don't even go outside. I get the urge to keep dancing, and I'm blasted and fantastic! I'm a dancing fiend. . . . I really like the atmosphere.

Pastoralist-escapists did not smoke in most of the closed smoking environments. For some reason, the most risky of the open smoking environments did not attract them either, with the exception of dance halls, where they sought female companionship and escaped in music and dance. This left them solitary street smoking and the countryside as viable alternatives.

Paco, the older of the two pastoralist-escapists included in the sample, once visited our office after hours and asked if it would be all right to smoke there. When asked why he did not want to smoke in the street, he replied that he did not wish anyone to be able to identify him as a marihuana smoker, or, as he put it, "I don't want to be painted that way" ("No quiero andar con pinta"). We asked Paco if he would smoke in the house if his in-laws, with whom he lived, were not there. He replied that he knew smokers who smoked with their families present but that they were "a bunch of mud-faces who respect neither their ladies nor their pups" ("Son un montón de carebarros [sic] que no respetan ni a sus doñas ni a sus cachorros"). This kind of attitude contributes to the separation of pastoralist-escapists from other kinds of users.

Figure C shows the contrasts in the proportions of the various smoking-environment description counts for the three smoker types. During the interview on marihuana use, stable smokers spent most of their time talking about closed smoking environments, while the street movers concentrated much more on open environments. Pastoralist-escapists showed a marked preference for open but relatively low-risk environments, with countryside environments accounting for nearly 40 percent of all contexts cited.

This does not mean that these percentages represent the actual smoking time that the three types of users spend in each respective environment. It does, however, suggest trends that reinforce the validity of the basic typology. Pastoralist-escapists do not totally avoid smoking on the street or in other high-risk situations. Street movers occasionally get to smoke in their own homes or homes of others. Stable smokers may occasionally have smoked marihuana in street groups. But each user type has certain modal tendencies in selecting his smoking environment.

The answers to several specific inquiries in the marihuana-use interview reinforce this impression. In answer to the question "Under what social circumstances do you smoke?" the subjects responded in the following manner:

Do not smoke in social circumstances	5 (12.2%)
Smoke in low-risk circumstances	24 (58.5%)
Smoke in general social circumstances (parties, bars, in the street, etc.)	12 (29.3%)

The fact that, in responding to the above question, 70.7 percent of the users indicated some uneasiness in smoking by limiting it to the lowest-risk environments suggests that pure street movers are slightly less numerous than indicated by the previous analysis. However, a check of individual scoresheets, taking into consideration the borderline cases between stable smokers and pastoralist-escapists, revealed no such discrepancy. Table 58, correlating user type with smoking environment, further reinforces this point. Figures contained in the first eight environment columns, representing the lowest-risk smoking environments listed, constitute 71.4 percent of the total.

Almost all members of the sample said that they at times met with friends for the specific purpose of smoking marihuana; only five of the forty-one users said they did not. When asked with whom they smoked most of the time, the sample of users responded thus:

With relatives	4 (9.8%)
With friends	20 (48.8%)
With work companions	8 (19.5%)
Alone	9 (21.9%)

These data seem reasonable in light of Table 58, since all smokers at times chose solitary marihuana-smoking contexts. Smoking alone was the easiest way to reduce the risk of discovery. Most users indicated they cared enough about jeopardizing their smoking that they often sought low-risk environments; the 44.3 percent (see p. 119) overall total for solitary contexts is thus not surprising. Yet, the fact that 55.7 percent of all contexts mentioned were social where other smokers were included indicates that, in spite of risks, social contexts were the most preferred, when all is said and done.

Nearly 90 percent of all smokers said they had smoked either while on the job or immediately before, so that they were under the influence of marihuana during their work. This led to the expectation that the percentage of work-context smoking-environment descriptions in the marihuana-use interview material would be much higher than it in fact was. If everyone smoked at work, then why did they not talk about it as much as they did about home or other recreational contexts? It may be that the subjects attempted to give exciting stories about their marihuana experiences and thought the work contexts too ordinary and humdrum to be worthy of much attention.

The majority of marihuana use appears to have been reclusive and timid, not defiant in nature. At most, 39 percent of our sample could be identified as flaunters of Costa Rica's societal and legal conventions. For the most part, users were cautious about the people they smoked with and the places they smoked in. The majority took precautions to prevent discovery by authorities or hostile relatives.

The immediate effects of marihuana smoking would seem to depend as much on user set and expectation as on sheer physiological response. User and observer reports yielded sixty-eight distinguishable effects for which cannabis was assumed to be the cause. Although subjective in nature, they do clearly represent the perceived effects of marihuana use in the study population. In all, these total 527. All but eleven of these could be easily clustered, and they are cross-tabulated with smoking environment in Table 60. Below is a brief description of each effect category, including criteria for scoring.

1. *Bad for eyes.* This effect was cited relatively few times. It included blurred or distorted vision, irritation, some combination of the two, or eye redness.

2. *Good for asthma.* Subjects naming this effect either suffered from asthma themselves or had friends or relatives who used the drug to relieve asthma symptoms.

3. *Dry mouth, rough throat.* Although one of the "universal physiological effects," it was mentioned relatively few times in the interview materials. All users in our sample regularly suffered from dry mouths and red eyes, yet in our interviews they seemed not to give these effects much importance.

4. *Nerves (+ and −).* Subjects attributed both a calming and a disruptive effect to marihuana use. When they attributed greater tranquility to marihuana use, this was scored as +. Minus was scored when subjects said that they had "nerves"[2] as a result of smoking.

5. *Sweat, cough.* Although these effects could also be called "universal," they did not receive much attention from the users either. Because they appeared together in all the interview materials, they have been combined in the coding categories.

6. *Relieves aches and pains.* Users mentioned this effect only twice, and both times it was associated with working situations. The back and the legs were the areas relieved.

7. *Heat.* This effect involved a sensation of heat coursing through the body but was not necessarily connected with rapid heart rate. It was described simply as "heat in the entire body."

8. *Bad for lungs.* Only two users reported that heavy marihuana use damaged the lungs.

9. *Muerte blanca ("white death").* In the life-history interview materials, this was the fourth most frequently cited effect. Most cannabis literature refers to it as a "panic reaction." It represented 7.2 percent of all effect descriptions and will be described in greater detail later in this chapter.

10. *General "blahs."* A negative reaction to smoking large quantities of marihuana, this effect was rare. Users who experienced it claimed not to feel sick, just mildly subnormal.

11. *Marihuana hangover.* Also relatively rare, the marihuana hangover occurred on the morning after a night of very heavy indulgence. The symptoms were much the same as those of an alcohol hangover, with dry mouth, headache, and queasy stomach.

12. *Sleep (+ and −).* Most users said that marihuana helped them sleep more soundly. Some went as far as to claim that they could not get to sleep unless they smoked at least one cigarette before bedtime. Only two claimed that marihuana had a deleterious effect on their sleep.

13. *Sex (+ and −).* The third most frequently cited effect (7.8 percent of the total) was sexual performance and enjoyment. All but one user citing this effect claimed that it was positive rather than negative. Their specific comments in this regard will be presented later with considerable detail.

14. *Food appetite and enjoyment (+, −, and 0).* In addition to the many users citing positive and negative effects, two users claimed that marihuana smoking had no effect at all on appetite or food enjoyment (0). Since the impact on food appetite represents more than 10 percent of all described effects, it will also be described in greater detail later in this chapter.

15. *Work performance (+ and −).* The single most frequently mentioned effect was that on work performance. Thirty-eight users claimed that marihuana smoking affected work performance positively, while nineteen claimed the effect was negative. The positive effects had to do with endurance, work enjoyment, and care or concentration on job tasks, while negative ones were problems with short-term memory and concentration. Chapter 7 will explore in detail the relationship between work performance and marihuana smoking.

16. *General performance (+ and −).* This category of effects deals with performance situations outside of institutional settings. Such contexts include street transactions, card games, police evasion, and sports activities, especially soccer games. The positive descriptions were only slightly more numerous than the negative ones.

17. *Sing better.* Another rare effect, this was claimed only by nonprofessional singers in the sample, and the singing was always done in the home.

18. *Time on the job goes faster.* In contrast to the usual claims by North American users that time slows down while one is smoking marihuana, Costa Rican users who smoked on the job claimed that work time went faster if they were intoxicated with marihuana. Although this effect was reported only rarely, its contrast with the claims of other smoking traditions makes it of special interest.

19. *Uncontrollable mirth.* The participant observation materials contained references to this effect in far greater frequency than did the interview materials. This would indicate that laughter and gaiety were observed by the field team fairly often but that the users did not consider them very important. Goode (1970) shows this effect to be quite important among North American users.

20. *Passive audience.* We scored this effect when the user described a marihuana-intoxicated state in which he felt more like watching than doing. Television and movies were the usual objects of interest, but sometimes users mentioned watching other people in a bar or watching a sporting event or simply watching people pass by on the street.

21. *Antiboredom.* Fewer than 1 percent of the effects described in the interview materials were of this nature. Smokers reporting this effect usually described their "high" as livening up their approach to an otherwise unstimulating social environment.

22. *Everything rosier.* One of the more frequently cited effects (5.2 percent of all described effects), this refers to a general feeling of well-being in everyday situations. Surroundings that would otherwise be very unpleasant become at least bearable after smoking marihuana. Once the "high" is achieved, existence in general is less sad and burdensome, and prospects are more hopeful.

23. *Alcohol comparison (+ and −).* None of the marihuana smokers in our sample said alcohol was better than marihuana, but a few said it was about the same. Most agreed that marihuana intoxication was better than alcohol intoxication. They based this judgment on the degree of self-control maintained by the marihuana user as compared to the drunk, and on the absence of physical dependency on the part of the marihuana user, which they contrasted with the chronic alcoholic's constant desperation for a drink. Since users often had considerable experience with alcohol use on very heavy levels, they had a strong experiential basis for making such comparisons.

24. *Behavioral compensation.* This smoking effect was scored when users described social contexts in which they had to conceal the fact that they were under the influence of marihuana. According to these descriptions, an experienced smoker of marihuana could usually disguise his intoxication well enough to keep those around him (except perhaps other experienced smokers) from discovering that he had been smoking. In the strictest sense, this is not an effect but rather a masking of effect. Still, behavioral compensation helps to define the extent to which the user feels he has control over his actions, and thus may help delineate the perceived limits to self-control as they relate to marihuana use.

25. *Fright ("susto").* This refers to a state similar to a mild form of shock, brought on by a sudden frightening experience. It is rare, but usually it has a direct connection with the appearance of narcotics police where the user is smoking. In one case, it was related to the user's nearly having a traffic accident. This effect was scored only when it was apparent that the user felt his reaction to fright to be exaggerated because he was under the influence of marihuana at the time of the frightening experience.

26. *Active participation.* This category covers many recreational contexts; it is the opposite of the passive-audience category. Effects described in the interview materials where the smoker felt that marihuana was the cause for exuberant and unselfconscious physical activity were scored into this category. Plunging with abandon into a game of soccer, or swimming or dancing tirelessly, were the most frequently cited instances of this effect.

27. *Fight.* One of the rarer effects mentioned in the interviews was fighting. The two users who described this effect claimed that the drug made them "touchy" and easy to offend. Both users had bellicose life histories.

28. *Act idiotic.* This is the opposite of the behavioral compensation category, and it should be noted that this effect was mentioned only twice in 516 effect descriptions. The two individuals reporting this effect claimed to

do stupid (but not necessarily harmful) things while under the influence of the drug.

29. *You isolate yourself socially.* In four instances, users described a reaction to marihuana smoking in which they paid no attention to the people around them. Rather than conversing, the users experiencing this effect remained wrapped in their own thoughts, not bothering to acknowledge the presence of others around them.

30. *You become socially more aggressive.* Users described an equal number of instances in which they became more outgoing as a result of marihuana smoking. Using marihuana to give courage to start conversations with strangers was the form in which the users described this effect.

31. *Helps to face the day.* This effect was recorded only when users indicated that their normal day was not properly started unless they smoked marihuana at first rising. Such an effect is similar to the "everything rosier" category, but the user shows special need for the drug in order to cope with daily problems. It should be noted that the users who cited this effect were in extremely difficult situations when they experienced it.

32. *Floating sensation.* Very few users mentioned a floating sensation in their descriptions of marihuana's effects. This reflects the general impression of our field anthropologists that users in our sample did not have a particularly reverent or awestruck perception of marihuana and its effects. When the floating sensation was cited, those who mentioned it claimed that their heads felt strange and their steps light.

33. *Music sounds better.* This was not a universally perceived effect, but it was widespread among our sample group. Users claimed to enjoy music more after smoking marihuana; they felt it helped them listen more acutely and appreciate subtleties that they could not hear when not under the influence of cannabis.

34. *Nothing.* Seven instances were described where the user smoked marihuana but felt no effect of any kind. Five of these occurred in the street-group context.

35. *Perception altered.* Very few of the effects described were scored in this category. In order to be so scored, the user had to describe a perceptual distortion of vision or hearing. Changes in shapes and sizes, and unusual loudness of noises, were the usual forms of these effect descriptions.

36. *Conversation (+ and −).* Most users said that their conversation improved under the influence of marihuana. They considered their manner of speech to be more fluid and confident while stoned. They also claimed that, with marihuana, they were able to handle complex conversational topics with greater ease. Those who thought that marihuana hurt the quality of their conversation mentioned problems of remembering the exact topics of conversations and their tendency, when intoxicated, to speak for long periods on trivial matters.

37. *Thoughts more profound.* Many of the smokers in our sample considered marihuana to be an aid to concentration. Some users said they used

marihuana to help them concentrate on a single problem. Others said that they derived more enjoyment from reading when stoned.

38. *One becomes creative.* A few of our users, despite their working-class status, claimed that marihuana led them to be more creative, either in writing or in painting. They said that some of their leisure smoking had helped them design a house, write an autobiography, or paint a picture.

39. *Bad for memory.* Some marihuana users claimed that marihuana has a deleterious effect on memory, both short-term and long-term. This effect was cited specifically for work settings and usually involved losing count in some repetitive task. Users' perceptions of long-term memory problems were less defined.

These thirty-nine effect categories include almost all kinds of smoking experiences mentioned by more than one respondent. Nine effects mentioned only once have not been listed, in the interest of clarity.

In an effort to simplify and clarify the relationships between environment and effect, the thirty-nine listed above have been grouped into categories (see Table 61). Effects 1–8 were grouped into "physiological effects" and included all effects that users perceived as changing their bodies in some way. Effects 9–11 were placed in a "bad trip" category, since they refer to the three kinds of bad experiences connected with use of the drug. Effects 12–14 are related to appetites, and 15–18 to work and performance. Effects 19–31 include all those involving a change in behavior or state of mind, and effects 32–39 cover marihuana-induced changes in specific senses and in cognitive processes.

In Table 62 a standardization process similar to that used in Table 59 was employed to make the scores in each cell comparable from one effect to another. To derive the standardization factor for a given row, the multiple of all other rows was divided by 2×10^8. For example, to derive the standardization factor for the "physiological effects" row, $45 \times 111 \times 89 \times 8$ was divided by 2×10^8, which yielded a factor of 2.33. Each cell in the "physiological effects" row was then multiplied by this factor to produce a standardized score. When a similar operation was performed for each effects type, the scores in each column could be compared with each other.

The first column in Table 62 shows that the physiological and appetites effects occur with relatively high frequency in the "home alone" smoking environment. In contrast, the work and performance effects occur in a markedly high frequency in the "work alone" environment.

The general pattern, then, seems to be that users tended to match subjective effects with elements that were characteristic of the environments in which they smoked. In other words, the marihuana smoker would build his effect experience on what he found at hand. We find, for example, that "physiological" effects were mentioned for solitary or closed smoking environments more often than for open or social environments. The user, when alone, took what was within reach, in this case his own body functions, and associated it with the effect experienced from the smoking of the drug.

Table 63 contains standardized scores that make comparisons between rows and columns possible. The circled scores in the table are those that are notably high. The symbols placed below the circled scores indicate whether they are high in comparison to the other scores in that row or the other scores in that column or both. We can see that the effect types that occur in high frequency relative to their respective column in the "home alone" environment are also high relative to their respective rows. This means that physiological and appetites effects occur more often in the "home alone" environment than the other kinds of effects, and that they make up a high percentage of all physiological and appetite effects for all environments. The same may be said for the work and performance effects group and its correlation with the "work alone" environment.

The "bad trip" group of marihuana-smoking effects shows marked high frequency in the most open and risky smoking contexts (see circled scores in Table 63). Given the fact that more than 80 percent of "bad trip" descriptions are *muerte blanca,* or "white death," we may hypothesize that such a reaction may derive in large part from the insecurity and fear associated with open smoking environments. "White death" is the Costa Rican equivalent of what is known in the United States as "panic reaction." The Costa Rican term is colorful and very hyperbolic, since no user lived in terror of a real demise. Most users treated "white death" as a completely routine and ordinary phenomenon, curable with a cold soft drink or a glass of sugar water.

Marihuana smokers in our sample had had widely varying experiences with "white death" during their long user careers. Only fifteen individuals, or 36.6 percent of the matched-pair users, claimed never to have experienced this unpleasant effect. The rest had had "white death" four times or less. Only one claimed to have experienced "white death" more than eight times.

At the onset of "white death," the user begins to feel dizzy and cold, breaking into cold sweats and feeling the need to defecate and urinate. One subject described the symptoms as follows:

> You feel kind of faint. Maybe you're sitting and you feel dizzy, dizzy, dizzy, and you see some things backward and everything begins to spin, and you often begin to vomit, and other times, well, almost always you feel like vomiting. But many times you feel faint and you play strongman and you sit for a while and it passes.
> Q: How long does it last?
> R: Well now, it varies; it's quick. It could last at most an hour, maybe a half hour—at most an hour.
> Q: How does one feel? Is there pain?
> R: No, no pain, but you're out of control, like everything's spinning, like dizzy. Everything spins a lot, you know, spinning, spinning, spinning. It gets you like that.

There is no real dread reflected in these observations, simply distaste for the experience. The subject continued to describe an onset situation:

> Once I was lame in this foot, and I went to my brother-in-law's who smokes. . . . We bought a roll and we smoked it between the two of us, twelve each, but because I was hurting in this foot, right (I had the foot infected) I was lame and surely all that didn't agree with me. . . . There I went, walking or hobbling to the bus stop. I was all right up to there, but when my foot heated up,

and when I got to the bus stop, I had to grab a post; I saw everything spinning, and you begin to sweat icy streams, and you stay that way, soaked, and see everything spinning, dizzy. Then that passes, and you stay white, white, white.
Q: White death.
R: Laughs.

Finally he offered his own theory on the cause of that onset:

> . . . Well, the white death many times . . . happens to you because you're weak. There's no need to smoke fifty, or even two or three. If you're weak somehow, it can disagree with you . . . although you may not feel it, or even realize, but many times you have a weakness in the body and then it [marihuana] disagrees with you.

Although the above description is characteristic, there was great disagreement among the users in our sample about the cause of "white death." Some believed that smoking marihuana in excess would cause it. Others found that smoking after alcohol consumption, a phenomenon to be discussed later in greater detail, caused them to suffer "white death." Most users thought that some physical or mental weakness, when combined with marihuana smoking, could cause it. "You must get your mind right before smoking," said one informant of long experience. "If you're depressed or sick, the white death grabs you."

The observed appearance of a user who is going through "white death" is very similar to that of a victim of mild shock. The subject's face becomes pale, and he usually rests his head in his hands. If he is given a soft drink at this point, he will be back to normal in a few minutes. If not, he may vomit or rush off to relieve himself. His companions joke about his weakness and lack of resistance while they go about the mundane business of securing a soft drink or other curing preparation. If none of these is found, the "white death" victim is escorted home to where he can lie down and "sleep it off." This is very different from the North American pattern of elaborate supportive companionship, which is intended to help the panic-reaction victim to cope with his reaction psychologically. Although Costa Rican users think that the cause of "white death" may be either psychological or physiological, the cure they offer is physiological and direct.

The reported distribution of the effects we have called "appetites," encompassing food, sex, and sleep, seems to reinforce the idea that whatever is at hand commands the most attention among users. Tables 62 and 63 show that the "home alone" and the *pensión*-brothel" contexts have strong correlation with appetite-related effects. At home, users have direct access to resources that may be used to satisfy the need for food, sex, or sleep. Some go to *pensión*-brothels for food or sex. Others, if this interpretation is valid, would seem to search for appetite satisfaction in the context of "countryside groups" and "street groups."

Users generally claimed that both their sex appetites and their food appetites were increased as a result of smoking marihuana. Twenty-nine, or 70.7 percent of the sample, responded that marihuana increased food appetite, while only nine said that it had no effect and two that it had a negative effect. One pastoralist-escapist claimed that he preferred not to smoke before eating but only after, since he considered the high more important than his eating pleasure. He believed that eating after smoking reduced the effect of the marihuana. He expressed his belief this way:

Q: You like smoking after eating?
R: Right, first eating. If it's time for me to feed, first the feed and then the weed. If I get stoned and then feed, sure I feel sharp, like a guillotine, but I de-stone myself, understand? It takes away the weed. It's like getting stoned and down-ing a soft drink or a beer or something like that. Who knows what causes that. . . . On the other hand, if I feed and afterward I get stoned, you should see what a hit! I'm stoned just fine.

Only among the very heaviest users did we find that there was no per-ceived effect on food appetite. Often these individuals had begun their smoking careers with increased appetite effects, but later they had discovered that mari-huana smoking no longer affected their appetites. Negative effect on appetite was rarely found among the users. Lalo was one of two exceptions:

. . . I caught, how should I say it? Like a mania that dried up my hunger. No. How is it? Like indigestion . . . I . . . well, began not to eat except at night. . . . I drank coffee and smoked marihuana and I smoked white [tobacco] cigarettes in quantity. . . . I drank coffee and smoked marihuana, nothing else. . . . The only thing that bothered me was that I got indigestion at normal eating times during the day. . . . Like today, I haven't eaten anything, only I drank coffee six times.

Lalo's loss of appetite for food was very unusual and must have been influenced by his unhappy life situation. Since his mother had been a prostitute and mari-huana vendor during his childhood, Lalo had usually been left to his own devices when it came to eating. This resulted in irregular meals of poor quality with sporadic periods of no food at all. As Lalo's mother continued her pattern of neglect, Lalo's eating habits became set in such a way that his present-day eating style, with its poor nutritional quality and irregularity, strongly resembles that of his childhood. It should come as no surprise that at the time of the study Lalo had dietary and digestive problems; it is doubtful that they could be due simply to his marihuana smoking.

Thirty-four users claimed that sexual appetite and performance were posi-tively influenced by marihuana. Six claimed that marihuana had a neutral effect on sex, and only one said the effect was negative. Users claimed that marihuana increased their desire for sexual contact even if it did not necessarily lead to orgasm. In many of their accounts, they emphasized tactile stimuli. One user claimed that he preferred not to have sex when he was intoxicated with marihua-na because under the influence he tended simply to lie snuggled next to his sexual partner and not do anything.

The most frequently cited effect of marihuana smoking on sex was in-creased endurance. Users claimed that erections were maintained longer and were easier to obtain while under the influence of the drug. Paco provided a colorful description of this effect:

But the best thing is to be mounted on top [in the sex act] because you get a sensation that's so strange and so delicious that really, I think everything trembles, and it's delicious. That stuff's strange because with the weed your member thickens, who knows why? You get harder, stiffer when you're stoned, because the chicks that I've had when there's weed, well, they say, "What a brute!" On the other hand, when I'm not stoned and I'm doing it, they don't make as much noise, but when I'm stoned, they can't endure it.

The idea that women prefer men to be "high" during sexual contact was very common among users. A stable smoker described it similarly:

Q: What effect does it have on sex?
R: Well, marihuana gives you more resistance, that is, you last longer, ehhh! You dilate. Well, I dilate. On the other hand, without it, it's less; with it you last long. Normally, it's not the same. There are women who like to be with a man like that. There are women who get stoned and they like to be with a man who's stoned so they last longer.

Although the above accounts were typical of users' assessments of marihuana's effects on sex, a lone user said that excessive use could be deleterious to both sex appetite and sex performance. He found erection difficult with heavy doses of the drug:

Q: Would you have more or fewer sexual relations when you've smoked more than you usually do?
R: Well, about the same. . . . Actually, when I smoke very much I can't get anything up, because when you're well-toasted . . . you're hopeless [literally, "in the street"]. You can't get it up.

This subject smoked with his wife, however, often attaining very heavy dosage levels. He found that lighter dosages of marihuana could be stimulating sexually, just as did the other users cited above.

Six users claimed that marihuana had a neutral effect on sex. They tended to be heavy users and stable smokers. Tonio, one of these stable smokers, was a case in point:

Q: Do you think marihuana has effects on sex?
R: Well, many people say that it does, but I think it's normal.
Q: There aren't changes?
R: There aren't changes for me, personally.
Q: No more pleasure or anything?
R: No.

Whether stoned or sober, Tonio was not very active sexually, but the user who provided the following quote was extremely active:

Q: What in your opinion are the effects that marihuana has on sex?
R: Well, I never paid much attention to any of that. It's the same to me with or without marihuana.

This individual's use was so heavy and so constant that it was difficult to decide whether or not he had an adequate basis for comparison between sexual experience during marihuana intoxication and marihuana-free sexual contact. Nevertheless, his indifference to the drug in combination with sex provides sharp contrast to the testimony of the first two users cited.

Sleep has been included in the appetites category because it is an everyday experience which takes on a special pleasureful sense when combined with the psychotropic effects of marihuana. Being a need as undeniable as food, its universality cannot be questioned. In review materials, there were seventeen citations of effects on sleep. Generally, the users testified that marihuana smoking has a positive effect on sleep, and one even claimed that he had to smoke before going to bed. In the overall sample, a slightly but not significantly higher number of users said they slept well and soundly all the time. Thirty-one users claimed not to have any sleep disturbance at all, while nine had occasional sleep disturbance and one claimed to be an insomniac. Interview materials contained only two citations of negative effects of marihuana on sleep, both of these in connection with occasional sleep disturbance. Other sleep disruptions among marihuana users occurred often in connection with alcohol use.

Marihuana smokers were slightly less in agreement about the effects of smoking on work performance than they were about effects on sex or food hunger or sleep. In general, they considered the effect on work to be positive. To our question "Has marihuana ever impeded your working at full capacity?" only eleven of the forty-one users responded that at one time or another this had happened. To the reverse question, "Has marihuana ever helped you work better?" only nine replied negatively whereas thirty-two replied positively.

It may seem circular to argue that marihuana smokers mentioned work-related effects most frequently in connection with work-related environments, but it is important to do so in view of existing beliefs about the drug, particularly in Costa Rica. The common belief in Costa Rica is that marihuana smokers are moved by the effects of the drug to commit criminal acts, such as rape, robbery, and assault. However, we are seeing that the rule among Costa Rican users is simply to emphasize what they have at hand while under the influence of cannabis. If that happens to be work, the user either smokes on the job or smokes just before work, and in this way passes his day tranquilly. Following this argument, if some crimes are committed under the influence of marihuana they may simply represent the activity of a criminal who happens to smoke marihuana. Rather than being causal to the crime, marihuana smoking may be simply incidental to it.

The behavior and sensation category of effects is a large one. Among others, it includes active participation, uncontrollable mirth, behavioral compensation, fighting, and social isolation. These effects were most frequently mentioned in conjunction with open smoking environments.

To understand the breadth of this category, users' descriptions of some of the category's most frequently cited effects can be useful. Active participation was mentioned fifteen times in the user texts and is aptly illustrated by the following account:

> . . . In Puntarenas, I got there and got stoned on the beach, and I jumped into the water, and when I finally realized what was happening, I found I was under the pier, swimming like an idiot. . . . Luckily, there was a little boat, a fisherman

there, and they pulled me out, because if it had been up to me, I would have kept on going.

Other examples of enthusiasm for physical activity while under the influence of marihuana included dancing, playing soccer, and walking in the country.

The effect that we have called "everything rosier" was mentioned twenty-seven times in our interview texts. The majority of these citations were given in connection with the most frequently mentioned environments: "street alone," "home alone," and "street group." Paco's comments illustrate the euphoria that users often attributed to marihuana smoking:

Q: Why do you think you've kept smoking marihuana so long?
R: Well, because I dig it. In every sense, it sends the mind in so many directions, right? You feel more "pure life," as if you'd taken some super nourishment.
Q: Does it help you in some way?
R: Only in the sense that I'm inspired. I feel like another person, in another world. Sure, you feel like somebody else, man. Like right now, I'm bored, well, without weed, without anything, noodling it out [referring to the interview situation], but now if I should get hold of a reefer, I'd get stoned. Now I'm somebody else, understand? Everything is groovier, you get into another wavelength.

Uncontrollable mirth, so often described by other user populations, especially in the United States, was not mentioned very frequently by our Costa Rican users. All ten citations (out of a total of 516) were in conjunction with open group-smoking situations in the country or in the city streets. In such situations, the users would often tell jokes and clown, with the explicit purpose of provoking mirth.

Even though North American users often report the "passive audience effect" (Goode 1970: 153–155), references to it by our Costa Rican user sample accounted for only 2.8 percent of the total. The more recreational attitude toward marihuana use prevalent among the North American users probably accounts for the difference.

On seventeen occasions in the interview material, marihuana and alcohol were compared. Marihuana was judged superior to alcohol in thirteen of these occasions and more or less the same in the remaining four. In no interview did a subject assess marihuana as worse than alcohol. Generally, the tone of the comments was that users felt they were in greater control of their faculties and actions when intoxicated with marihuana than with alcohol. One of the younger smokers put it this way:

Well, you know that I have several friends in the *barrio* [names friends]. . . . With *guaro* [liquor] they get the urge to raise a fuss, to punch it out with somebody. Even I, when I down a few drinks, and I'm with them, I also get the urge. . . . Well, why should I let somebody hit them? On the other hand, when I'm stoned . . . at least I don't go around raising a fuss with anybody.

The theme of not enjoying the company of drunks was often heard in talking to users. Even though they themselves drank, they found the characteristic, numbed intractability of the drunk unpleasant.

Users also spoke of the aftereffects of alcohol and how they compared unfavorably with those of marihuana. One stable smoker was quite pejorative in his description of the physiological effects of alcohol:

> I tell many people: "Smoke marihuana, don't drink *guaro*. Don't you see that with *guaro* you don't wake up well? You even vomit blood." I've seen him, and he heaves and Wha! Wha! and he wakes up still Ay! Ay! On the other hand, marihuana doesn't do any of that.

Those who thought of alcohol and marihuana as equal did not partake in great quantities of either drug. They thought of each as a *vicio* (vice), and this to some extent controlled their actions. Even though they used both, they viewed both with mild disapproval. Such users were not given to excesses in anything and often claimed that they would have liked to have given up marihuana for economic and legal reasons.

The effects we have designated "cognitive and perceptive" form a medium-sized cluster and account for 14.6 percent of the total number of effects mentioned. Table 63 shows that cognitive and perceptive effects have strong positive correlations with "home in group," "countryside group," and "countryside alone" smoking environments, but only for the column percentages. This means that the cognitive and perceptive effects group tends to have greater-than-expected frequencies for certain groups of smoking environments, although not for any given single environment. The specific ones for which high correlations exist are for the most part social in nature and relatively free of risk.

Musical enjoyment is one of the cognitive and perceptive effects. In general, users found that listening to music was more enjoyable after smoking marihuana. "Rides" in the country and gatherings on the street corner were often accompanied by a small radio. Smokers also resorted to the company of the radio during solitary marihuana-smoking sessions, as in the case of Lalo:

> Q: What do you like to do best when you're stoned?
> R: When I'm stoned, you know what I like? To go to bed with the radio by the bed and listen to music, like classical,[3] because I like music like that, and also youth music [rock]. And I turn on the radio, hopefully I'm alone, just me, and I do that every night.

The two most often cited cognitive and perceptive effects were "conversation" and "thoughts more profound." Of the twenty-two total references to the conversation-altering effect, eighteen dealt with improved conversation, while four described a loss of conversational ability. Those who found improvement emphasized the facility with which they expressed their ideas. One noted that he preferred to be stoned when talking to officials or to his lawyer because he found technical conversations more manageable. In some of our first experiences in the field, users would demonstrate their linguistic dexterity and maintenance of control by performing difficult feats of recall and diction, using several forms of Costa Rican pig Latin.

Some users maintained that the effects of marihuana caused a deterioration in the quality of conversation. The usual complaint was that users could not remember what they are saying or that they did not bother to talk at all when they were stoned. One stable smoker discussed such conversational ills in the course of his marihuana-use interview:

> . . . They [marihuana smokers] seem a little like parakeets or parrots. They all want to talk at the same time . . . maybe you're saying something and they don't give you time to finish.

"Chattiness" as described above was often associated with reduced work effectiveness, but more frequently the smoker found improved facility in both conversation and work.

Twenty-nine citations of the "thoughts more profound" effect appeared in the life-history and marihuana-use interview materials. They tended to appear most frequently (seventeen out of twenty-nine citations) in connection with the "home alone" and "workshop alone" smoking environments. Users believed that marihuana affected concentration, memory, and free association so that they could think more clearly, with important insights. One stable smoker expressed his increased facility this way:

> It [marihuana] nourishes my thoughts for the things I do . . . be it a benefit . . . be it a way to get things done . . . I have a big thought. It provokes big thought . . . for example, it makes me wiser. . . . I think everything out better.

The phrase "I concentrate better" was heard also in connection with work and other kinds of performance. Some users claimed, much as the Jamaican *ganja* smokers quoted by Rubin and Comitas (1975), that they could sit down with a difficult problem, smoke marihuana to concentrate, and reach a solution. One user, a stable smoker, claimed that he was able to read more effectively with marihuana:

> . . . I have my room where I live. I start to read magazines. I like to read many magazines. I like to concentrate on a magazine that is attractive and good. There are police magazines on the F.B.I. and I particularly like them.

Although this subject's reading matter consisted of comic books and pulp novels, other subjects demonstrated good reading skills based on little educational opportunity, often surprising the field team with their conversation on world news events and political issues.

Table 64 contains a cross-tabulation of user types with the effects list presented earlier in this chapter. Stable smokers cited an average of 12.5 different types of effects, while street movers cited 13.3 and pastoralist-escapists cited 13.0. All six physical effects were cited in higher frequencies by the stable smokers. In Table 65, which shows only significant or near-significant differences, we can see that when standardized scores are compared for the physiological effects, relatively few differences between stable smokers and street-movers/pastoralist-escapists approach statistical significance. When the entire group of physiological effects is compared for the two user types, as in Table 66, we see that the difference in citations is significant at the .07 level of confidence. This may be interpreted as a tendency on the part of the stable smokers to cite physiological effects. We have noted earlier that stable smokers tend to smoke in closed and often solitary environments, and that these environments account for a high percentage of all physiological effects cited. It would seem, then, that stable smokers tend both to experience more physiological effects and to smoke in environments that are conducive to those kinds of effects. Although the smoking environment may not "cause" the onset of a specific effect, it would seem to heighten the likelihood of such an effect.

A characteristic scenario of marihuana use leading to physiological effects is as follows: Mario, a stable smoker who lives with his wife and two children, takes the bus home from his job as a construction worker at about 5:00 P.M. Since yesterday was payday, on his way home from work he is able to buy a roll of twenty-five marihuana cigarettes with what was left over from household expenses and rent. After a light evening meal of rice and beans with a small salad, Mario excuses himself to go to the bathroom. He often chooses this place for smoking, because he does not like to smoke in front of the children. As he relieves himself, he lights a marihuana cigarette made of the contents of two that he had bought. He notices shortly after inhaling the first *toques* (touches) of his marihuana cigarette that his heart is beating faster and that some of the physical aches caused by his strenuous work are beginning to disappear. His nerves, somewhat tense from the risky business of procuring his marihuana and transporting it to his house, now begin to calm. He finishes his cigarette and his hygienic functions and returns to the front of the house. There he may watch television or listen to the radio for an hour or so before retiring for the night.

Since Mario averages only two or three marihuana cigarettes per day, this may be his only use during the day. Typically, the effects he mentions are physiological and soothing.

In contrast to these are the "bad trips" frequently mentioned by street movers. Both marihuana hangover and "white death" were cited in significantly higher frequencies by the street-mover/pastoralist-escapist group, with p values in Table 65 of .001 and .005 respectively. But enhanced appetite effects were also frequently experienced by this group, particularly in conjunction with *pensión*-brothel contexts. Using the scenario descriptive approach again, let us examine a hypothetical case: Filiberto, a street mover, after a day of shining shoes in the downtown area, finds he has fifty colones in his pocket. He had arranged earlier in the day to smoke together with a friend that night, so he hurries out to a place where he knows he can buy two rolls of marihuana cigarettes for forty colones. Having made the purchase, he meets his friend at a soda fountain near the center of town and discovers that the friend has invited two women to smoke with them. The group's main problem is finding a place in which to smoke. One of the women offers her boardinghouse room, and they agree to smoke there, also agreeing on a fee for the women's sexual services, since both are prostitutes. The fee will be low because the men will also share their marihuana. Filiberto opens one of the rolls, hands out single cigarettes to the women, and apportions three each to himself and his friend. He combines the contents of his three cigarettes and smokes the resulting *puro* as he jokes with his companions and listens to the *cumbia* music blaring from the transistor radio that belongs to one of the prostitutes. Once Filiberto has finished his *puro*, he begins to feel the marihuana in his head, and the jokes become so funny that he can barely stop laughing. He rolls another *puro,* and as he smokes he notices that the prostitutes are becoming more affectionate. During sexual contact with his female companion, Filiberto finds that ejaculation is delightfully delayed and that when it comes it is excruciating. Filiberto now rolls another *puro,* this time with the contents of six street-size cigarettes, smoking without a word. One of the prostitutes says she is hungry, and so Filiberto dresses to go to a corner soda fountain. He eats several *gallos*[4] and as many sweets as his remaining funds will buy. All four eat hungrily but silently, sometimes commenting on the delicious-ness of their food. The *gallos* taste wonderful to Filiberto. He feels he can describe each separate flavor in great detail. The food has caused the effects of the marihuana to wear off, so Filiberto and his friend each light up a *puro* of six. The prostitutes are now both asleep, so Filiberto and his friend divide up the remaining eight cigarettes of the fifty they had brought to the room. Five or six hours have elapsed since they met in the soda fountain, and in that time the four have consumed forty-two marihuana cigarettes. Filiberto saves his remaining four for the morning after and walks to his own boardinghouse, not far from the center of San José.

The above account is based on a combination of various users' descriptions of the *"pensión*-brothel" smoking environment and the kinds of effects they feel during smoking sessions in such places. Several features in the account are common to many of the more hedonistic marihuana usage styles. First, a male smoking companion is present, and at times there may be as many as three or four companions. Second, the quantities of marihuana smoked are relatively high, as in this case where each of the men smoked eighteen cigarettes apiece. Third, the women involved are usually prostitutes. Fourth, the food is always in the form of snacks and treats rather than a stable meal. These features, in combination, give the overall impression of concentrated pleasure-seeking on the part of the users.

Positive or at the most neutral effects on "work and performance" appear in low frequencies in the interview materials of street movers and pastoralist-escapists and in correspondingly high frequency in the interviews of stable smokers. These differences may reflect the contrast between the pleasure-seeking and the daily-regimen approaches to using the drug. The stable smoker uses marihuana to help him get through a workday or to help him recover from everyday stress, while the street mover and the pastoralist-escapist assigns recreational and plea-sure-seeking values to his marihuana smoking.

"Behavior and sensation" effects do not show differences that are as clear-cut among user types. Perhaps this is because "behavior and sensation" emerged as a catchall residual category that contains some diametrically opposed effects (see the left-hand column in Table 64). Many of these effects were mentioned only a few times, so chance skewedness could also be the cause of the variation observed. Stable smokers may have been reflecting self-confidence about their marihuana-related social behavior in their positive scores for social aggressiveness and social isolation.

The final group of effects, "cognitive and perceptive," contains two that were mentioned fairly frequently. The first, "conversation," has both positive and negative components. Table 64 shows that both pastoralist-escapists and street movers mentioned the negative impact of marihuana on conversation more often than did stable smokers. Most of the latter indicated that their smoking increased their facility with words and spoken ideas. Yet when these scores were standardized, the differences turned out not to be statistically significant.

In Table 67 we have encapsulated the marihuana-use characteristic of each user type in terms of smoking environment and frequently experienced effects. Pastoralist-escapists appear to have been the most reclusive and self-conscious of the three types. They tended to avoid the open sorts of smoking environments frequented by the street movers and to have had little access to the secure, closed environments the stable smokers preferred. Effects reported by the pastoralist-escapists did not show strong tendencies for specific areas of emphasis. The table also reveals some basic differences between stable smokers and street movers. The latter saw marihuana as a drug of enjoyment and recreation. Their conversation about the drug was heavily loaded with sexual exploits, feasts, scrapes with the law, and other adventures, all recounted with a savor that contrasted sharply with the comparatively bland accounts of stable smokers. Compare the following stable smokers' account of sexual function under the influence of marihuana with Paco's vivid description cited earlier (p. 131):

Q: What effect does it have on sex?
R: Effect? Well, yes, that, yes.
Q: Is it good?
R: Yes.
Q: How?
R: Gee, well, normally . . . yes, it works as one wants, see? At times you feel, let's say. . . . How should I tell you? A lack of spirit, see? Because at times you get nerves, see? But that [marihuana] gets rid of them. . . . It comes out well; you work well.

The everyday flavor of this subject's description of marihuana's effect on sex typifies the stable smoker's approach to marihuana itself. To the stable smoker, marihuana is an ordinary part of everyday life having several functions that he considers pleasant and useful. These include work efficiency and enthusiasm, physical well-being, and skill in conversation and thought processes. Appetites and thrills receive some attention from the stable smoker, but they are not his most important topics in discussing marihuana.

Stable smokers use marihuana where they feel it is safe: in their own homes, at work, or in familiar closed environments. Street movers smoke the drug in much more risky and often dangerous environments, and they emphasize the sensual and adventuresome qualities of their smoking. As a result of constant vigilance, and in many cases real fear, they also suffer panic reactions more frequently. Pastoralist-escapists reject the street movers' choice of smoking environment, but they share a basically recreational approach to using marihuana.

To illustrate these points further, we shall now present three marihuana-use scenarios, one for each type of user, in which each type will be participating in preferred environments. These scenarios have been constructed from combinations of various field experiences and personal accounts and do not correspond to any single user in the sample.

Guille, a pastoralist-escapist, finds that it is now afternoon and he still has not had the opportunity to smoke marihuana all day. With only 5 colones in his pocket, he has little chance of buying enough marihuana for what he considers to be an effective dose; prices of individual cigarettes are between 1.25 and 1.50 colones. He searches the streets of his *barrio* and eventually manages to find three other boys who all have roughly the same amount of money. Together they are able to make what they call a *puesto* (bank) of 25 colones, which is sufficient to buy a "roll." Since Guille is the oldest and most experienced of the group, he is chosen to procure the marihuana. They all agree to meet in a deserted coffee grove nearby, where they can smoke in peace. Guille buys the marihuana and hurries through the streets of the *barrio* to the edge of the coffee grove where his smoking companions are waiting. They cross a stream and climb the wall of a ravine to a small clearing, and there they sit down to smoke. Guille passes three cigarettes each to his companions and keeps the rest of the "roll," making for himself a *puro* of his three. The others, being less experienced with the drug and therefore more cautious, smoke single cigarettes. As they smoke, all comment on the quality of the material, coughing intermittently and cracking jokes. By the end of the first round of smoking, all are laughing and coughing. Guille rolls himself another *puro* of three as his companions begin smoking their second cigarette. All inhale deeply and continue to keep the smoke in the lungs longer. About halfway through the second *puro,* Guille begins to feel that his head is floating, and he realizes he has reached his effective dose level. The group has settled down to story-telling, and Guille gives an account of a film called *Joe*, in which many of the actors use drugs. He describes in detail how the protagonist smokes his first marihuana through a hookah, noting that the actor inhaled just like one of the younger of the present smoking companions, who is duly embarrassed and kidded about the comparison. Suddenly they hear a figure moving through the grove, and all start and visibly tremble, but the figure moves on without stopping. Conversation now breaks off, and each user continues to smoke in silence. By now, Guille has finished eight cigarettes, more than his share. The others have had half that amount but show no desire for any more after finishing their fourth each. After offering the remaining cigarettes and being refused, Guille pockets them. At the beginning of the afternoon he had financial prospects for only three or four cigarettes, but he ends up through the "bank" arrangement consuming thirteen. The other boys, who all live at home, now are beginning to feel hungry and get up to leave. They separate at the edge of the coffee grove two hours after they met there, and walk silently to their individual homes.

Guille says that he prefers to smoke alone but that financial necessity forces him to smoke with a group. He seems to enjoy the company of these younger smokers and participates actively in their joking and conversation. Later, as he achieves heavier dosage, Guille's chatter and joking break off, and he becomes more pensive. Finally he goes home to eat, an action that often ends the effects of smoking. Given the resources at their disposal, the group hide themselves as well as possible when a stranger appears; the fear that passes through all of them is apparent. When they return to their homes, their families may or may not notice they have been smoking marihuana, or they may search for subtle clues such as red eyes and unusually hearty appetites.

Gilberto, a street mover, has been out of a job for about two weeks, but today he managed to find a half day's hauling work in the market. His earnings were twelve colones, of which he gave half to his mother as a contribution to the household food budget, keeping the other half for his own use. By 7:00 P.M. it is dark; Gilberto leaves the house after his evening meal, ostensibly on a minor errand. He climbs the hill to a corner toward one extreme of the *barrio* where his friends are gathered. One friend is currently selling marihuana on a small scale, and he tends to sell individual cigarettes at low prices because Gilberto helps serve the customers who come by. There are about ten people on the corner tonight, including one woman and males ranging in age from forty-three down to thirteen. As Gilberto approaches, he smells the aroma of burning marihuana in the air around the group. He exclaims in a manner of salutation that when he was four blocks away he said to himself, "Those mud-faces are smoking marihuana! I can smell the stuff from here!" He is greeted by the group not warmly but with profuse jocular acknowledgments of his presence. He approaches Yogui, the friend who is now selling marihuana, and asks if he can buy five marihuana cigarettes with his five colones. Yogui begins to object, saying they cost him more than that, but Gilberto reminds him of earlier *galeta* (runner) services rendered and eventually obtains Yogui's consent to the low price. Because they are among longtime smoking companions, Yogui makes the sale right there on the street corner without any complicated exchange procedures. Gilberto immediately wraps three into a ball covered with cellophane and puts them into his pocket. He unrolls the other two and combines their contents into a single paper, first removing seeds, which he believes cause headaches. The extra paper is burned as it is discarded, because the narcotics police believe the presence of yellow paper sufficient evidence to justify a twenty-four-hour jail term for "suspicion." Gilberto lights up his *puro* of two and inhales very deeply. He does not exhale for a long time, periodically sipping small gulps of air to help him maintain the marihuana smoke in his lungs. He holds the cigarette inside his cupped hand so that the glow from the ash cannot be seen from a distance. Not many vehicles pass this corner in the *barrio*, but any pair of headlights that approaches elicits a readying of defenses. These include preparation to swallow or discard each individual's marihuana, depending on the tightness of the situation. Most headlamps are false alarms, and business goes on as usual.

As Gilberto finishes his *puro,* he begins to notice he is feeling "toasted," warm and glowing. The dingy surroundings begin to look softer and more appealing. A group of three girls pass by the corner on the far side of the street, and the smoking group shouts minor flirtations across to them. Gilberto shouts, "Turn around and look at me, so I can die happy." After the girls are gone, one of the older users in the group begins to describe in lurid detail what he would do if he were alone right now with one of those girls. Gilberto listens. He thinks to himself that none of them except Alberto would have the courage even to walk up and talk to those girls, and Alberto does that only with girls he already knows. Still, Gilberto feels very good; he removes another cigarette from his cellophane ball and prepares it for smoking. He had used his last tobacco cigarette, making a *taco* to finish off his first marihuana cigarette; after rerolling his marihuana cigarette, he steps into a nearby corner store to buy five more tobacco cigarettes with his last colón. Gilberto rounds the corner to rejoin the smoking group just as he hears a flat voice say, "Narcotics police, don't move!" The faces of his companions blanch and assume a look of abject terror. One of the boys swallows the cigarette he is smoking. Then, the voice laughs and says, "It's only Lefty, fellows." The whole group laughs weakly at the joke, but when one of them says he swallowed a cigarette in reaction to Lefty's prank, everyone explodes in gales of laughter. Gilberto returns to his marihuana, noting that this cigarette is barely getting him back to the feeling he had achieved at the end of the first *puro*. He makes another *taco* to finish his marihuana butt; the transition from the harsh, acrid taste of the marihuana to the smoother qualities of the tobacco is always pleasureful. Since it is now 9:30 and he has an appointment in the morning to talk to a foreman about working in construction, he decides it is time to go home. He says good-bye to his companions and moves down the hill to his house. He has smoked three marihuana cigarettes during the past two and a half hours.

Alejandro is a stable smoker who specializes in interior carpentry for house builders. He awakens at 5:00 A.M., just before sunup, and smokes two marihuana cigarettes he had prepared the night before for this purpose. He feels that smoking helps him endure the cold of the shower he takes every morning and prepares him for the day's work. After a breakfast of bread and coffee, he leaves the house by 6:00 to be at the site by 6:30. He carries five marihuana cigarettes with him to work. At 11:30, while his companions at work are eating, he finds a secluded spot at the site where he can quickly fashion and smoke a *puro* of two cigarettes. He begins working before the others are finished eating because he says that marihuana fills him with energy. He continues vigorously until mid-afternoon, when he finds himself slowing down. Saying that he wants to investigate something under the house, as he crawls beneath the floorboards to look at the location of some concrete supports, he rerolls and smokes another marihuana cigarette. Since it is now 3:00 P.M., he estimates that this last dose will make the remaining ninety minutes of his workday pass more rapidly.

Alejandro leaves work at 4:30 and arrives home by 5:00. His wife has a large meal waiting for him. He eats what is in effect his only meal of the day and rests at home until his cousin comes by the house at 6:30. This cousin is Alejandro's most regular smoking companion. According to the cousin, the local marihuana dealer has just received a good batch of Limonese variety, so they decide to go and buy a small pouch. They must walk two miles to this dealer's house, where they are able to purchase a half ounce with their fifty colones. The cousin has some rolling paper, so they go to his house to smoke. Alejandro decides to make a super *puro* from a whole sheet-width (8½ inches) of paper. He rolls the *puro* into roughly the thickness of a soda straw, using for this purpose the amount of picadura normally used for eight street cigarettes. He smokes and smokes, always inhaling deeply and exhaling as little marihuana smoke as possible. His cousin rolls a *puro* of more modest size and smokes in the same way. The radio is tuned to a station that specializes in soft boleros, the music Alejandro calls "classical." They both listen and experience a soothing and restful sensation. The two smokers talk quietly of the day's activities, and Alejandro speaks of the additions he plans to make on his house and several plans for future employment when his present contract expires. His cousin listens and nods. At 9:00, the cousin is almost asleep, and so Alejandro leaves for his own home to watch television for an hour before joining his wife in bed. He is finishing a day in which he smoked perhaps more marihuana than usual because of the large purchase. The rest of his share of the purchase, which was divided evenly, will last him two or three days.

This last account emphasizes the kinds of effects and smoking environments found in the stable smokers' self-reports on marihuana use. The generally closed and secure atmosphere in which Alejandro smokes marihuana contrasts sharply with Gilberto's edgy and constantly vigilant street situation. While Gilberto risks arrest with every smoking session, the process of procuring and using marihuana is routine and calm for Alejandro. Alejandro has specific uses for his marihuana, both as a work enhancer and as a relaxer at the end of the day. Gilberto has the general purpose of getting stoned in a social recreational setting. Both know what they want their marihuana to do for them, and they seldom are disappointed. Their reliance on marihuana to enhance any type of experience is shared by the majority of users.

Costa Rican smokers seldom reported feeling the effects of marihuana without having smoked. Of the forty-one users for whom we have interview materials, only eight spoke of this phenomenon. Seven of these attributed such "flashbacks" to mental processes that led to a replication of the marihuana "high." For some, autosuggestion was the cause:

> You feel as if you were stoned, see? Well, thinking that, since you're accustomed, see, to being stoned the majority of the time, then perhaps in a moment when you think of something you get into the same state.

The single user who attributed flashback to a physical condition claimed that it was due to exposure to heat. When he had experienced it, he was working at his usual job as a baker and was required to spend a period of time near the ovens. After a few minutes, he had begun feeling as if he had smoked marihuana, even though he had not smoked. Yet he usually smoked marihuana in his bakery, so on-the-job stimuli and experiences were closely associated with his habit. Thus, even here, the "flashback" experience would seem related to autosuggestive processes. Users seem to associate specific experiences or mental states with the marihuana "high," and when they are reexposed to such experiences or mental states, they may experience the onset of marihuanalike high. Even to those who do experience it, however, flashback is rare. Most Costa Rican users have no idea that it could occur.

The mixture of marihuana with alcohol often generates effects that are very different from those of either alone. When users in our sample were asked what "crossing the cables" (mixing marihuana and alcohol) did to them, most said it did nothing. Only four thought that such a mixture brought good effects, and two said that the mixture drove them crazy and defined this craziness as fighting and getting into trouble with the police. Three said they suffered from "white death" when they mixed the two substances. Two subjects stated that "crossing the cables" brought on nausea, and two said the combination put them to sleep. One affirmed that when marihuana and alcohol were taken simultaneously, the effects of marihuana were doubled. In sum, twenty-six users reported that the combination of marihuana and alcohol led to unpleasant experiences, four found that it led to pleasant experiences, five failed to distinguish any special effects, and six claimed never to have mixed the two drugs.

NOTES

1.   Cross-tabulations were made in a manner similar to that used for user type and smoking environment, running user type and smoking environment against effects mentioned. Field notes again provided a baseline for defining the range of effects to be listed. Then, the life-history and marihuana-use interview transcriptions were sifted one by one to extract the number of times each effect was mentioned by the subject and to add any effect that had not yet been recorded. An internal check for accuracy in recording was provided by the fact that each effect was recorded twice, once in the effects-versus-user-type tabulation and once in the effects-versus-smoking-environment tabulation.

2.   "Nerves" (*nervios*) refers to a whole spectrum of psychological or physiological nervous disorders recognized by the Costa Rican lower class.

3.   On the basis of many interviews and conversations, we find that for most working-class Costa Ricans "classical" music really means the traditional Latin romantic ballads, or *boleros*.

4.   *Gallos* are tortillas topped with shredded cabbage and hard-boiled egg or a piece of meat or sausage or fried bologna. They cost about seventy-five céntimos apiece (U.S.$0.09).

7/ Marihuana and Work: Users at School and on the Job

Most chronic marihuana smokers in Costa Rica turned to the drug during either adolescence or late childhood. In the matched-pair sample, the mean age of initiation to regular use was 15.2 years, with a range of from 9 to 26 (see Table 68). "First taste" occurred, on the average, one year earlier—that is, at 14.2 years of age (Table 69).

The reasons given for the delay between first taste and initiation to regular use were varied, but they focused basically on bad or neutral reactions to the experience. Of the forty-one users in the matched-pair sample, fourteen reported disagreeable reactions in this regard, twelve reported no effect at all, two were indecisive, and thirteen reported agreeable experiences. Many users were very decisive in describing their negative reactions to their "first taste." One claimed he had suffered from "white death" nine consecutive times when he had originally tried marihuana:

R: Nine times I had the white death. Nine.
Q: And those were one after another?
R: All. One after another.
Q: Over how long a period between the first time and the ninth?
R: Gee . . . Let's say two months . . . but then, you see, my head, how hard-headed about something I am, see? . . . Any other person after three times says "No more" but I kept on until I dominated it. And I dominated it so that now . . . gee . . . we smoke a roll between two of us and I have great capacity.

This man's perseverance in spite of repeated unpleasant effects indicated that something stronger than the allure of the drug itself had led him to continue. Though extreme, his case was not totally unique. Over one third of our matched-pair sample had persisted and become regular users in spite of initial negative reactions.

Since marihuana is not presently considered to cause physical dependence, especially in dosages of "first taste" use, it would seem advisable to consider other possible influences that may have led potential users to continue trying the drug until they had learned to handle it. One of these, without a doubt, is peer-group pressure. Most working-class children who end up as chronic marihuana smokers seem to have passed through a period in their lives during which they were in intensive contact with the culture of San José's streets. There they were exposed to older and more experienced people who exerted influence on them both by example and by active counseling and inclusion in street-type activity. Under such tutelage, young potential users constantly heard that marihuana smoking could be an excruciatingly pleasureful experience and that it was not at all harmful to the body. They also were offered the drug repeatedly, thus receiving ample opportunity for "first taste" experiences and continued use. Among the users in our matched-pair sample, 72.5 percent were introduced to marihuana by people older than they. In two thirds of the cases, the first joint was offered by a person older by five years or less, and in one third by six years or more.

Another important factor stimulating prolonged use would appear to be the desire for new and/or defiant experiences. Many users told us of their original wish to achieve a psychotropic state. One claimed that he had begun marihuana use "for the luxury of calling myself a marihuana user." Another so liked his initial experiences that he forced a vendor to continue to supply him by threatening to report him:

> . . . I said to him, "What is that you're smoking?" "Ah," he said, "They're cigarettes but I'm not giving you any because that stuff can cause you harm." I said, "Give me some so I can try one." "Well, I'll give you one, but don't tell." I smoked some and I liked it. After that I often came by and said, "Don't you have one of those? Give it to me or sell it to me." And so I began. . . . Later I would say . . . "If you don't sell it to me, I'll tell the police you have some."

Adolescence, then, is a crucial period that gradually separates users from nonusers. Computer analysis of life-history materials shows that during that period, users in the matched-pair sample experienced significantly more ($p = .01$) social and economic decline of status than did nonusers. They also were significantly ($p = .002$) less likely to have had full-time jobs. There is no evidence that these conditions were caused by marihuana smoking. Rather, both the conditions and the smoking itself would appear to have their roots in important aspects of the users' adolescent situation and seem to tend to reinforce one another. As we have already seen, users tended, either by force or by their own choice, to leave their childhood home at an age earlier than nonusers (see Chapter 4). A young adolescent trying to make his own way without help and at times without even a proper idea of how to survive would have more reason to seek psychotropic escape. Recall of the adolescent situation given us by users lends credence to this interpretation.

An indicator of the almost irresistible pressures of the social environment and psychotropic need in establishing the marihuana habit may be found in the time lapses between "first taste" and the beginning of regular use (see Table 70). Although the mean lapse for users in the matched-pair sample was one year, more than 50 percent had begun regular smoking either immediately after or within one year of their "first taste" experience. All but three of the seventeen who had waited longer before initiating regular use had delayed no more than three years. The delays of these remaining three were four, five, and seven years. There would appear to be no relationship between the nature of first-taste experiences (i.e., good, bad, or indifferent) and these delays.

During their life-history interviews, all users in the matched-pair subsample were asked if marihuana use had made any difference in their lives. Thirteen indicated that the drug had somehow improved their quality of life, eighteen reported no long-term effect, either positive or negative, and one was totally ambivalent. None said that the net effect of marihuana use *per se* had been harmful. A small number of users, however, did think that use of the drug had led to more intense contact with criminal elements, which in turn had led to problems with the police, jail, and continued lowering of social status and self-esteem. The following passage typifies this view:

> . . . Suspicion, nothing more. The only thing about suspicion is that they grab you. Now and then when I'm coming home from the movies, straight home, and I'm with some other companions, what do they do? They search everyone and send us to jail. . . . Then what they do is give us a bad night.

Of the users who shared such opinions, very few actually had records of incarceration. Yet, by way of contrast, some individuals with the very worst records of arrest and incarceration perceived marihuana to be a positive influence on their lives.

During their first few years of use, practically all users had gone through an initial period of street-mover-style smoking. Although the general tendency had been to gravitate toward the stable-smoker style over time, some users never did so, and others assumed that style only briefly, returning quickly to their original street-mover patterns. An example of the movement from one smoking style to another is José. He began smoking as a pastoralist-escapist, meeting his first smoking companions at the swimming holes he frequented as a young adolescent.

> I would go to the rivers and with a gang of four or five, kids too, but more "with it" streetwise, you know. . . . I had been submissive in the house, but after I made these friends I became libertine, street-oriented, only in the street, the pastures, the coffee groves, that is, I spent more time in the coffee groves.

He later married and adopted a pattern of smoking in his workshop but seldom around the house. At the time of our interviews, José saw marihuana as helping him get through the day's work and very little else. He had maintained his stable-smoker patterns for more than fifteen years.

Martín was a stable smoker who had begun his smoking career very much in the street-mover style. In fact, he still associated with street movers, even though he seldom smoked with them. His first experiences with marihuana had occurred before he was married, when his lifestyle had been that of the young street mover without family. Martín at first had lived in boardinghouses (*pensiones*) and cheap hotel rooms, and he had smoked wherever he could, usually with street groups. As he had grown older and experienced a few "suspicion" arrests, he had decided that smoking alone in coffee groves (*cafetales*) was a safer policy:

> I do it alone because, as they say, "A solitary ox grazes better." I go alone, and if they [the police] should grab me in a coffee grove, well, I was defecating. But if there are two of us, they say we're smoking marihuana or performing acts of sodomy. That's why I go alone.

Finally, when Martín had married, he had taken to smoking in his own home, out of sight of his family. At the time of the interviews, he had smoked primarily in a "home alone" environment for more than twelve years.

Some users never move out of the pattern set during their first years of smoking. Roberto, who was forty-three at the time of the interviews, had begun late, at age twenty-four. Roberto's immersion in the street ambience of San José had begun during late childhood and early adolescence, but instead of embracing marihuana use at that stage in life, he had begun to use alcohol. He had had many opportunities to try marihuana before age twenty-four, but for reasons known only to him he had not pursued the drug. When he finally had tasted marihuana, he had continued despite repeated negative reactions until he had achieved an acceptable psychotropic effect. By then Roberto had established a street-oriented lifestyle which continued with only brief interruptions up to the time of the interviews. He smoked marihuana just about anywhere, in street groups, coffee groves, *pensión*-brothels, whenever marihuana was available. Roberto had remained a street mover during his entire smoking career, and at the time of the interviews a change in that pattern could not be foreseen. His drug-use pattern had been set during the crucial adolescent period; his initial drug of choice had been alcohol, and the adoption of marihuana had been only a continuation of that pattern.

AT SCHOOL

Many factors contribute to the development of drug habits. One of the most important is the school experience.

For years, the Costa Rican educational system has been a source of national pride. The extravagant claims of 90 percent literacy notwithstanding, the system has achieved a high level of success, compared with other Third World countries; if offers educational opportunities to all Costa Ricans who desire them. Children usually begin school at age seven, and attendance up to the sixth grade level is universally required. Although enforcement is lax, the vast majority of Costa Rican children do attend at least part of the required six years. In many cases, children have the same teacher throughout primary school. Because this is so, some teachers could remember our subjects and their behavior with considerable detail.

We were able to retrieve complete elementary-school records for only seven pairs of subjects in the matched-pair sample. The average age for beginning regular use among the smokers in this group was 12.4 years, exactly the same as for first taste. This is somewhat younger than the corresponding ages for the matched-pair sample as a whole.

Of the seven users, three had begun smoking marihuana regularly before terminating their schooling. Their school records show no difference in performance before and after beginning to use the drug. Copa, for example, had begun using marihuana at age eleven, the year *after* he had failed fourth grade, the only failure on his school record. His teacher for fourth and fifth grades reported that he was at times unruly and ill-spoken but that he was not a bad student and that he produced work slightly above average for the grades in which she taught him. She remembered clearly when he had begun marihuana use, and she saw no relationship between it and his school performance.

Javier had begun to use marihuana at age nine, due to his very early immersion in street life, selling *empanadas* to earn money for his family. He had managed to continue school through sixth grade, and his performance as evaluated by his teacher had remained almost rigidly consistent for his entire school career. Javier described the effect of smoking marihuana on his performance in the following passage:

> I went to school well stoned all the time. I would take along two or three joints. I'd smoke them in the bathrooms. All the time I was on top of the teacher, watching her and listening to what she was saying. I concentrated when I was stoned in class; I was interested. The proof is that I was one of the most efficient students, because I was always concentrating. My examinations almost always turned out well.

Arnoldo had begun smoking marihuana at age twelve, also after failing a grade. His performance evaluations show no before-and-after differences, either positive or negative, and he had continued school until he had finished sixth grade.

The opinion that marihuana actually helps in schoolwork was not unusual among the majority of users for whom complete school records were unavailable. The following is an example:

> Q: That thing about the mind, you said that marihuana gives you more activity.
> R: Yes, more activity of the mind. That was at first. I saw that I was studying with enthusiasm and I remember that I studied enthusiastically and it got to be more and I'd get up in the morning to study and I would go to the dealer's . . . and I bought one for the morning and I would learn everything and my mind opened up. It gave me capacity.

Although the three available school records for users who smoked marihuana while still in school do not substantiate such claims, neither do they indicate the contrary. None of the three indicates changes in performance levels after the initiation of marihuana use. All three of these early users for whom complete school records exist finished their first six years of school, and absence records were within normal limits, as may be seen in Table 71. In fact, overall, their mean number of absences was considerably lower than the mean number for nonusers.

Four of the users in this small group for which complete records exist had begun smoking marihuana after leaving school. The first of these, Tito, had failed third grade twice before finally passing. He had quit school after completing third grade and had begun smoking marihuana a year later. His poor performance and problems in social adjustment thus antedated his turning to the drug. A major factor contributing to these problems could have been overzealousness on the part of his parents. Tito claimed that when he did his homework his parents would stand over him and hit him every time he made a mistake.

Carlos had begun marihuana use two years after dropping out of primary school. By that time he had successfully completed five grades, with one failure in the third. His performance records show that he had maintained a barely passing average for those grades he did pass and that he had dropped slightly below that level during his failing year. The principal of his school, after giving an accurate description of Carlos and his early life history, said that Carlos had been a disciplinary problem while attending school and had been considered by his teachers to be innately bad. Carlos's problems in school had clearly preceded his marihuana use.

Of all the users for whom complete records were found, Heriberto had the fewest years of school. He had attended and passed the first and second years and dropped out in the third, never to return again. We were fortunate to be able to speak with Heriberto's teacher for those two years, and we found her familiarity with his home situation remarkable. Heriberto's schoolwork had not met average criteria for grade promotion, and he had been irregular in turning in assignments. The teacher said that she had allowed Heriberto to advance because she had known about his difficulties in the home, including frequent fighting between his parents and heavy drinking on the part of his father and his paternal uncle. She had noticed often that he was listless in class and dozed from lack of sleep during the night. On the playground, Heriberto's manner of play had been rough and physical compared to that of the other children. He had failed to show the affection toward his teacher that is normal for Costa Rican boys of that age. In sum, the teacher had seen in Heriberto the symptoms of a disturbed child from a troubled home. Not long after dropping out of school, Heriberto had left that home. He had not begun to smoke marihuana, however, until six years later, when he was fifteen years old and an established street-adolescent with a growing police record.

Betoel had also begun smoking marihuana during adolescence after leaving school. In a situation very similar to that of Heriberto, Betoel had failed second and third grades and finally dropped out after passing to fourth. The principal of the school remembered him and his brother, noting that both had been extremely unruly and difficult to control. She had been familiar enough with Betoel's home situation to be able to describe the severe alcohol problem that had existed when Betoel was a child. In her words, "Those boys slept as often in the streets or coffee groves as they did in their own homes." Betoel did not begin marihuana use until two years after he had left school. By then, his experience in the street was considerable and his independence was fully established.

Although it would be of no value to compare the seven users' school records with those of the nonusers' on a one-to-one basis, a general perusal of the control group's school careers will give some idea of the overall differences and similarities between the two. Generally, the nonuser group experienced slightly more success in their primary-school careers than did the user group. More of them progressed straight through their first six grades without failures. Nevertheless, Roberto, a nonuser, had the single most ignominious record of academic performance—three consecutive failures in the second grade. His first-grade instructor noted that Roberto had been sickly and introverted. The principal of the school said that the grading system at the time Roberto attended had been harsh and often unjust and that similar children do not receive that kind of treatment today. After failing third grade, Roberto had stopped attending.

Roger, another nonuser, had gone through all six grades of elementary school in an orphanage, where his attendance had been naturally perfect but his performance consistently mediocre. His teacher described him as docile and well-behaved, with no outstanding qualities, either bad or good. He and all the other nonusers except Roberto had managed to finish elementary school, however, in contrast to only three of their seven user counterparts.

We hinted earlier that familial problems were probably the strongest forces leading to incomplete primary schooling on the part of individual marihuana users. It should be noted, however, that similar problems existed in the families of some of the nonusers who eventually finished sixth grade. Roger, for example, had been very neglected during his first six years of life. His mother had finally decided to place him in an orphanage so he could receive more attention and socialization than she was able to give him. Being an illegitimate child, and left to his own resources most of the time, he had become unruly, roaming the streets and often not coming home at all. His entry into the orphanage gave more regularity to his life, prevented his permanently embracing the street way of life, and forced him to complete his basic schooling.

Trinidad and Enrique had lived in households where the father was an alcoholic. Even so, they had finished elementary school. Their rural residence removed them physically from the possible attractions of street life, so that they may have maintained their pattern of school attendance simply because they lacked other options.

Many who were later to become regular marihuana users had alternatives to school attendance at an early age. Of the seven users for whom we found complete school records, all had left their parental homes at least temporarily by age twelve. Of the seven nonusers for whom such records were available, only one had shared this experience, and he had gone to a carefully supervised orphanage. In some ways, then, these seven pairs would appear to be a microcosm of the larger matched-pair sample. To a significant degree ($p = .03$), users in this sample reported rowdiness and mischievousness in school more than did nonusers. Yet, in terms of academic performance the two groups were very similar. There were no significant differences in number of years completed or number of years attempted.

The preceding suggests that problems in the life cycle precede and directly contribute to the initiation of marihuana use. Disruptive school conduct and inadequate academic performance are often symptomatic of problems in a potential user's home, family life, and general living environment. Among such individuals, exposure to the urban street culture both presents opportunities and provides encouragement for beginning and continuation of use. Yet we find no evidence that marihuana smoking *per se* impedes academic performance. Some users, in fact, claim that such use actually helps it.

ON THE JOB

Both users and nonusers tended to begin working at an early age. Among our matched-pair sample, the mean age at which users began work was 12.0 and that at which nonusers began was 12.3. Slightly over half the subjects in the sample stated that these early job demands had forced them to drop out of school.

In Costa Rica, the fluctuating market for small-shop and artisan labor makes job turnover frequent and continuous. One difficulty we had in our research was keeping track of some of the subjects who were constantly shifting their place of employment. A man who was working as a shoemaker one week might be in construction the next. One who was a cab driver by night might be a transporter of vegetables during the day. We found that, to make a living wage, most of our subjects had to develop a repertoire of generalizable skills, an alert sense of where the job possibilities existed, and a coterie of helpful contacts.

Within this framework, nonusers attained more stability than did users. Over the years, they also received more promotions and raises ($p = .005$) and, as a group, were more upwardly mobile. The first temptation is, of course, to attribute these differences to marihuana use. Some of the differences were marked. During adolescence, nonusers tended to obtain full-time employment and users part-time or sporadic employment ($p = .002$), and this trend continued into adult life, where users tended to have less full-time employment ($p = .001$) and significantly more frequent job changes ($p = .01$).

Patterns of other economic activity seem also to point to greater disorder and marginality among users. In terms of income and expenditures, users spent either as much as or more than they earned to a significantly higher degree ($p = .005$) than did nonusers. Users also tended not to have material goods, whereas nonusers owned houses, appliances, and sometimes even motor vehicles. Nonusers, probably due to their involvement in installment purchases, were more likely to be in debt than their user counterparts ($p = .002$).

In all, nonusers appeared more strongly to connect with working-class economic activity than did the users with whom they were matched. They worked full-time and bought more durable consumer goods, for which they often went into debt. Users were more likely to work part-time or not at all, and some regularly engaged in illegal business transactions, a type of activity studiously avoided by the nonusing group.

Such a series of contrasts between users and nonusers would appear to corroborate the amotivational syndrome hypothesis of McGlothlin (1968), Smith (1970), and Kolansky and Moore (1972). Personal experience with the subjects over a two-year period, however, led the field researchers to suspect that other factors were involved. In order to test whether this were so, a dosage comparison was conducted, using mean daily dosage figures collected for all users in the matched-pair sample and comparing these with materials from the life-history interviews. The hypothesis underlying this operation was that if marihuana use were the cause of sporadic work histories and marginal economic activity, then the heaviest users would have the most sporadic work histories and the most questionable economic backgrounds.

The results did not at all support the hypothesis that higher dose levels are correlated with the poorest work records or the most marginal economic activity. The reverse, in fact, was found to be the case for several key variables. Users who had worked full-time during adolescence were smoking an average of 10.7 marihuana cigarettes per day at the time of the study; those who had worked part-time as adolescents were now smoking an average of 7.8; those who had worked only occasionally as adolescents were now smoking an average of 7.9.

Job changes, when correlated with various levels of marihuana use, yielded similar contrasts. Those who had steady jobs or who were self-employed were smoking more than twice as many marihuana cigarettes per day as those with more frequent job changes or those who were chronically unemployed (see Table 72).

A comparison between dosage level and character of work (full-time, part-time, seasonal) revealed no great dosage differences among various categories of the employed but marked dosage differences between the employed and the unemployed. Those who worked were smoking nearly twice as much marihuana per day as those who were unemployed. Among the employed, in spite of their high level of use, full-time workers were in the clear majority. See Table 73.

In terms of constancy of employment, heaviest users were the most stable. Those who reported no periods of unemployment were averaging 12.4 marihuana cigarettes per day (see Table 74). The length of unemployment showed a similar relationship to level of use. Those who had the shortest periods of unemployment were the heaviest users of marihuana.

Data on economic activity were on the whole less easy to interpret than the data on work history. Those who smoked the most tended to overextend their expenditures more than those who smoked less. Mean daily consumption for those who spent more than they earned was 11.0 cigarettes per day, as opposed to 9.7 per day for those who spent their earnings and nothing more. Users who spent less than they earned smoked an average of only 7.5 cigarettes per day. In part these figures can be explained by the cost of marihuana itself. By Costa Rican standards, the drug is expensive. At an average cost of one colón per cigarette, those who smoked eleven per day were spending nearly 80 colones a week. If they earned no more than 900 colones per month (a good working wage), one fourth of their income went for marihuana. Understandably, such individuals could easily become overextended.

A consideration of material possessions and property ownership sheds additional light on the matter. Those users who had accumulated some material goods and property were smoking an average of 14.3 marihuana cigarettes per day, whereas those who lacked such goods and property were smoking an average of only 7.7. This parallels income versus expenditures figures given above and would appear to be logical. Among the working class, those persons who try to accumulate material goods are the very ones who tend to incur installment debts.

Data up to this point seem to indicate that heavy marihuana use actually contributes to job stability and work performance. A consideration of illegal economic activity, however, beclouds the point. Users with the greatest access to and use of marihuana would appear to be those with the heaviest involvement in illegal economic exchange. Among smokers whose dominant economic activity was illegal or extralegal in nature, daily consumption averaged 14.5 cigarettes. Among those who turned to this kind of activity only to supplement their incomes, the average was 7.4. Among those who reported no illegal or extralegal economic activity, it was 8.2. Much of this illegal activity, of course, would revolve around the marihuana trade itself.

At best, then, a comparison of levels of marihuana use confuses the question as to whether the drug leads to poor work records and disordered finances. Users with the heaviest levels of consumption change jobs less frequently than moderate or light smokers and hold full-time rather than part-time jobs. They are more likely to own material goods, but they are also more likely to overextend their incomes and to be involved in illegal or extralegal economic activity. So conflicting are these findings that we can reach no firm overall conclusions, the single exception being that level of consumption would appear to be related more to relative access than to individual preference.

User typology yields much clearer relationships, perhaps because it reflects major trends in the entire life process. We find, for example, that all but one of the street-movers/pastoralist-escapists* in the matched-pair sample had spent their childhoods in the urban atmosphere of the city. Yet, of the twenty-three stable smokers in the sample, only thirteen were raised in San José, with ten growing up either in rural areas or in provincial towns. The difference is statistically significant ($p = .004$) and reinforces the concept that the former had opportunity for immersion in urban street culture at an earlier age than the latter. Significantly more ($p = .05$) street-movers/pastoralist-escapists were also likely to have been left to their own devices in the urban environment during childhood.

The smokers' own assessment of their childhood behavior provides additional insights into basic differences. To a highly significant degree ($p = .001$), street-movers/pastoralist-escapists claimed that they had been rowdy in school more than did stable smokers.

Childhood delinquency even further differentiates the two categories. Street-movers/pastoralist-escapists tended to have early history of vandalism and thievery to a significantly greater extent ($p = .01$) than did stable smokers. Even while still in school, many of the former were already beginning to attract the attention of police.

Work during adolescence also sets stable smokers apart from street-movers/pastoralist-escapists. Significantly ($p = .05$) more of the latter had held steady jobs during adolescence. This accords with what we know of life in the streets, where instead of working one spends his time *jugándosela* ("playing it out"). The true street mover avoids work and seeks instead an "angle" or a

---

*For the sake of economy of analysis, we have combined the two into a single category, based on their similar social positions and stages in life.

scheme to get something from nothing, through such activities as the shell game, gambling, "watching" parked cars, shining shoes, or dealing in small amounts of marihuana. Most street movers had embraced this way of life by the time they had reached adolescence.

An important indicator of the order with which an individual manages his adult life is the presence or absence of economic ascent. Here the differences between street movers/pastoralist–escapists and stable smokers is statistically significant at the .05 level of confidence. Stable smokers tended to experience increasing levels of income during their adult work histories, while street movers tended either to remain at the same level or to drop in earning power as adults. This would seem to be the logical consequence of the stable smokers' steadier work history both as adolescents and as adults.

Full-time versus part-time and other forms of work as an adult also differentiates strongly between street movers/pastoralist–escapists and stable smokers. Nineteen out of twenty-three stable smokers worked full-time, as opposed to only five out of eighteen street movers/pastoralist–escapists. The contrast is statistically significant at the .02 level of confidence.

Duration and frequency of unemployment both indicate that stable smokers are significantly different from the street movers in their approach to work responsibility. While only one of the eighteen street movers/pastoralist–escapists experienced no periods of unemployment during his adult work history, thirteen of the twenty-three stable smokers could make that claim. Street movers/pastoralist–escapists were unemployed more frequently than were stable smokers ($p = .01$) and their periods of unemployment were significantly ($p = .02$) longer.

Although the street mover and pastoralist–escapist types were first described in terms of their style of marihuana use, a style which contrasts sharply with that of stable smokers, they could just as easily have been described in terms of their approach to work. In general, stable smokers believed strongly that marihuana smoking had a positive effect on how they functioned at their jobs. The comments of one stable smoker evoke memories of Popeye and his spinach:

> Sometimes I'm doing a job in construction and all the time the boss comes by and says to me, "Look, what's wrong with you today that you're so clumsy and you can't mix cement?" I say, "Sonofabitch, here comes that billy goat around to bug me." And one time as he's coming around again, I say, "I'll be right back. I'm going to the bathroom." . . . And don't you see I was upset because I couldn't do the work. And I head for a little coffee grove nearby and I smoke three *aparati* and after a while I've done the work.
>
> And the boss comes by and says, "Man, now you did it. You spent a long time at lunch, but that's okay 'cause you got the work done."

Although street movers and pastoralist–escapists also claimed that marihuana could have a positive effect on work performance, they did not do so as consistently as stable smokers or with as great a frequency. They also more frequently perceived marihuana to be detrimental to work. One was emphatic in his opinion:

Q: Do you think that it [marihuana] screws up work, or does it come out the same, or what?
R: No, you draw into yourself. You get into this trip of drawing into yourself.

Sure, don't you see that you're into your own trip and if you have to, well, you seem like a zombie. Really it's ugly to work like that. I don't like to work stoned. I like to work straight. Afterwards I'm pooped, then yes. That stuff tastes better.

During the two years in which we maintained contact with him, this individual went through six different jobs and was unemployed for a total of at least six months. The fact that his level of marihuana use was somewhat lower than that of most permanently employed stable smokers would seem to indicate that something other than marihuana was responsible for his job insecurity.

To recapitulate, we have seen that the chronic user tends to begin his habit at a point of particular transition and stress, usually during adolescence. Pressures and encouragement from his peers, coupled with the desire to experience a psychotropic state, push him into a pattern of chronic use. In the process, the lure of pure pleasure would seem relatively unimportant; many reported their "first taste" experiences with marihuana as negative or neutral.

Rather than demonstrating that beginning to use marihuana has a negative effect on academic performance, school records (when available) suggest that chronic users had adjustment problems long before they had begun to use the drug. Work histories indicate that job stability and heavy marihuana use go hand in glove, thus strongly challenging the amotivational hypothesis. The most important factors contributing to satisfactory academic and work performance would appear to be social and cultural in nature. In comparing street movers/pastoralist–escapists with stable smokers, we find that differences between user and nonuser groups with regard to these crucial variables can best be explained by the presence of street movers in the user sample.

The common Costa Rican image of the chronic marihuana smoker is that of the street mover. He is uncouth and street-wise. He is given to the vices in general and will do many things that decent people will not, just to finance his vice. He seldom works.

Such an image fails to take users like Hector into account. Hector is a laborer in a bakery where he has worked for the last three and a half years. He has a wife and two children for whom he is the only means of support. Hector never smokes at home or in the street or in public places. He does smoke, however, in the bathroom at the bakery, where he works from five in the afternoon until three in the morning. He claims that marihuana makes his work go faster and the night pass more quickly. Hector represents the majority of marihuana smokers in our matched-pair sample, twenty-three to eighteen.

8/Chronic Use and Health

SUBJECT HEALTH STATUS

Medical History

One of our first tasks, once the base sample was identified, was to make an initial assessment of the subjects' health status. To that end, a standard medical history was obtained from each subject. Responses to several questions were significantly different for users and nonusers (see Table 75). The former more frequently reported episodes of involuntary weight loss, and the latter more frequently indicated concern with obesity. Users also more often reported adverse reactions to drugs than did nonusers.

In response to questions about changes in food appetite, users more often reported both increased and diminished appetite than did nonusers. Responses to questions about gastrointestinal symptoms indicated that users also experienced indigestion, nausea, and abdominal pain more frequently than nonusers. In the battery of questions that did not relate to eating or the digestive tract, there were relatively few responses that differentiated users from nonusers; the only differences were that users often reported having suffered serious head trauma, jaundice, and excessively frequent urination.

Users indicated more frequent use of barbiturates and tranquilizers. They also reported the number of tobacco cigarettes and the years of smoking as higher, and the use of hallucinogens and inhalants such as gasoline as more frequent. Although the reported differences were statistically significant, except for tobacco the overall use of alternate psychotropic substances was very limited. Only two users and seven nonusers reported employing barbiturates or tranquilizers as frequently as once a week, fourteen users and eleven controls reported employing one of these as often as once a month, and twenty-three users and three controls reported having employed them in the past but not at the time of the study. Hallucinogens such as LSD or mescaline had been employed by fifteen users. Nine reported casual use of these substances in the past, six reported past use as often as once a month, but all denied current use. One member of the control group reported daily use of hallucinogens in the past but no current use. Inhalation of gasoline or paint thinner to obtain a "high" was reported by nineteen users and two controls. Three users claimed they had employed such vaporizing intoxicants as often as daily, eight as often as once a month, and eight as an occasional casual experience. Two members of the control group claimed past daily use of such intoxicants. All denied current use. The mean years of tobacco use was 17.8 for the users and 13.3 years for the controls (p .001). The mean number of tobacco cigarettes per day at the time of the study was estimated as 21.3 by the users and 17.9 by the controls ($p \leqslant .03$).

The Physical Examination

Since our intent was to measure the chronic rather than the acute effects of marihuana, *all* examinations in the physical and psychological battery, except the sleep EEGs, were conducted in the early morning. Subjects were instructed not to use marihuana after 10:00 the previous evening, were picked up by taxi between 5:30 and 6:30 A.M., and were being actively examined by 7:00 A.M. The number of subjects scheduled for any given day was always small (one, two, or three) so that delays could be avoided.

On the physical and eye examinations, a number of abnormalities were found that were not of sufficient seriousness to exclude the subject's continued participation in the research. Among users, one had an anal fistula and seven had unilateral testicular atrophy. Six of the seven cases of atrophy could be attributed to mumps or to trauma to the scrotum. One individual who suffered from the condition was unaware of it until the time of examination. In the control group, only two individuals were found to have testicular atrophy, and in both instances it was unilateral. Other conditions discovered in the control group were: chronic otitis media in two instances, a history of peptic ulcer in another two, and bilateral muscle atrophy in the lower extremities attributed to old poliomyelitis in one subject and renal stone in another. Hyperemia or dilatation of the conjunctival blood vessels was found in forty (47.6 percent) of the marihuana users and in fifty-six (35.9 percent) of the nonusers. Pterygium was present in eight (9.52 percent) of the users and in only three (1.92 percent) of the nonusers.

As a group, the marihuana users had significantly lower weights and lower mean systolic blood pressure. Mean diastolic blood pressure for the users was not significantly lower, however. Table 76 summarizes these findings.

Laboratory Tests

The users had a lower mean hematocrit than the controls and a higher mean of prothrombin times. They also had a lower conjugated bilirubin level and lower serum albumin levels, but neither difference was significant at the .05 level of confidence. Serum globulin levels, however, were significantly lower in the users ($p \leqslant .02$). With the remaining laboratory tests, there were no statistically significant differences (see Tables 77 and 78).

Examination of stools for evidence of intestinal parasites revealed no significant differences in the overall rate of infestation, based on one stool examination per subject. Thirty-eight of the users and eighty-one of the controls had positive stool examinations for parasites. Eleven users and thirty-five controls had more than one parasite in the stool.

Further analysis was conducted to see how well the presence of eosinophilia in the stained blood smear correlated with the finding of intestinal parasites in the stool. Only twelve of the thirty-eight users with positive stool examinations for parasites had eosinophilia, defined as a percentage of eosinophilia of 4 percent or higher in the blood smear. Twenty-three of the control group of eighty with intestinal parasites had eosinophilia. Eosinophilia was also present in thirteen users and eighteen controls who did not have stool positive for parasites (see Tables 79 and 80).

Electrocardiography

Ten of the users and twenty-two of the nonusers had abnormalities of their electrocardiograms, but in no instance was the finding diagnostic of a serious cardiovascular defect. Only two individuals were excluded from the study because of cardiovascular disease. When standard measurements of the rate, P-R interval, QRS-T complex, the Q-T interval, and the electrical axis in the frontal plane were made, no significant differences were found between users and controls (see Table 81).

Relevance of Initial Findings

The cluster of positive responses from the medical history relating to upper alimentary tract symptoms activated by food intake is noteworthy in light of the fact that those who were subsequently selected for the matched-pair sample indicated more frequent past concern about the availability of food and had more often experienced outright hunger. Whether intermittent episodes of hunger had led to more awareness of related gastrointestinal symptoms such as nausea, indigestion, and abdominal pain cannot, however, be determined from these data.

The more frequent history of jaundice in the user group was not reflected in an increase in physical or laboratory findings of liver disease in the user group. If anything, data indicated the contrary. The mean bilirubin levels in the user group of both the base and matched-pair samples was lower than among their controls.

The higher percentage of users who experienced increased frequency of urination might be related to their higher incidence of positive serological tests for syphilis (see p. 162 below). Gonococcal infections are common in Costa Rica, and one would expect that they would be more prevalent in individuals with active or treated syphilis than in those with no evidence of syphilis. Although no subjects had active symptoms of gonorrhea at the time of examination, it is likely that the incidence of acute gonococcal urethritis, as well as nonspecific urethritis, was higher in the user group than in the controls. If so, the reported difference in incidence of difficulty of urination could be explained on that basis.

We have no explanation for the difference in reports of blows to the head. Our anthropologists found no evidence of greater physical violence among the users, neither did the medical history reveal any possible causes for the reported trauma. One could conjecture that there might be a correlation between this finding and the higher number of arrests for drug possession in the user group, but our data can neither confirm nor deny the possibility. It seems worth noting that when we selected our matched pairs and controlled for occupation the differences disappeared. This led us to suspect that head trauma could be related to occupational hazards.

One important finding to come out of the medical histories was that the use of drugs other than marihuana was higher in the user group. Although the use of hallucinogens is not common in Costa Rica, barbiturates and other hypnotic agents are readily available without prescription. One would expect that Costa Rican marihuana users would more frequently use other drugs, for this would conform to what we know of drug users in other cultures (Blum and associates 1970: 245–275; Coggins and Lipman 1972: 29–33). The association between marihuana smoking and the previous or concurrent use of tobacco cigarettes has also long been noted (Shafer 1972: 42).

Significant differences in mean body weight between smokers and controls have not been emphasized in previous studies, in spite of the fact that mean weights for users in the Jamaica study were seven pounds less than for their controls (Rubin and Comitas 1975: 232). With our Costa Rican base sample, the mean difference of 3.14 kilograms (6.9 lbs.) might have been related to the lower income and more frequent bachelor status of users. They might simply have had less food available to them on a regular basis. In this regard, it is important to note that the weight difference did not appear in the matched-pair population, where occupation and marital status were controlled.

Systolic blood pressure, but not diastolic or mean blood pressure, was lower in the user group (115 mm Hg vs. 118 mm Hg; $p = .04$). Although a number of studies have reported mild decreases in blood pressure as an acute pharmacological effect of marihuana, the difference in the present case can be better explained by the lower weight of the users than by the direct effect of the drug on the cardiovascular system. Mean blood pressures were not reported in the Jamaica study but were described as being "within normal ranges" for both users and controls.

Hematocrit levels averaged less in the user group than in the controls, even though hemoglobin levels were not statistically different. Since these two tests should corroborate each other, we have no explanation for this discrepancy. Only one subject was severely anemic, and the mean levels for both groups were well within normal limits. These findings contrast with those of the Jamaica study, where higher hemoglobin and hematocrits were found in the users.

Although prothrombin times were slightly longer in the user group than in the controls, the differences were minimal even though statistically significant. In the absence of other differentiating factors related to blood coagulation and liver function, we have no explanation for this difference.

The tendency toward lower bilirubin levels in the users is brought out more strongly when these levels are compared in the matched-pair sample, where users had lower total and conjugated bilirubin levels, the latter difference being significant at a confidence level of .05. Reese Jones and his co-workers in San Francisco found that bilirubin levels declined in healthy young males who were given daily oral doses of up to 240 milligrams of Delta 9 THC in acute toxicity studies. These levels returned to normal promptly upon cessation of the drug (Personal communication).

Evaluation of intestinal parasites in relation to eosinophilia was carried out as an indirect measure of immunologic responsiveness. There is increasing evidence that eosinophilia is dependent on cell-mediated immune responses (Zucker-Franklin 1974: 10–12). If cell-mediated immunity were suppressed by marihuana use, as suggested by Nahas et al. (1974: 419–420), one might expect this impairment to be reflected in suppression of the eosinophilic response in these very long-term, heavy users. But there were no significant differences in the presence of eosinophilia in the user and control group, whether intestinal parasites were present or not—though we might have found that some subjects with eosinophilia in the absence of intestinal parasites actually had parasites had we examined more than one specimen per subject.

Evaluation of the electrocardiograms showed no detectable pattern. Only ten of the twenty-two abnormalities found in the tracings are regularly associated with heart disease, and these ten were found more frequently in the nonuser group than in the user group. The numbers are too small to draw statistical inferences.

In a recent review of the cardiovascular effects of marihuana, Clark (1975) found T-wave changes reported in studies of acute effects where ECGs were done, and in one study he found transient P-wave changes. The Mendelson study (Mendelson, Rossi, and Meyer 1974) reported "minimal" electrocardiographic effects, and the Jamaica study (Rubin and Comitas 1975) found "minor" ECG abnormalities in 30 percent of both marihuana smokers and controls, although it suggested that this high incidence of abnormality was related to cardiomyopathy rather than to marihuana use. The question of the effect of marihuana on persons with coronary artery disease continues to be an open one. One study demonstrated decreased exercise tolerance in patients with angina pectoris after smoking one marihuana cigarette. The present research, by excluding subjects above age fifty, eliminated those who would most likely have arteriosclerotic heart disease with symptoms of myocardial ischemia. Thus it sheds no further light on the possible effect of marihuana on persons with such disease. Further studies of the effect of marihuana smoking in experienced smokers with evidence of coronary disease are indicated.

Screening for Potential Matched Pairs

One of the major conditions for matching users and nonusers was that both groups be free of general pathologies which might affect the results in projected specialized tests. The excluded conditions were not related to the possible effects of marihuana use itself, but they might have distorted our interpretations had they not been eliminated. The potential effect of tuberculosis on pulmonary function, for example, could have caused abnormalities in the pulmonary test battery which could not reasonably have been attributed to the effects of marihuana smoking. Because we were interested in subtle central nervous system functions and changes that could be attributed to marihuana use, we were also concerned that syphilis not be present in the matched-pair group. The well-recognized effects of central nervous system syphilis could have distorted the findings in the neuropsychological test battery, the electroencephalogram, and the visual-function tests. Good color vision was essential for participation in the visual-function studies; hence, all subjects with impaired color vision were also excluded from the matched-pair study. Because binocular vision was necessary for the visual-function studies, with a degree of visual acuity that would be comparable in the matched pairs, we also selected out individuals with defects in visual acuity that could not be corrected to 20/40 or better.

In addition to the above, subjects with a diagnosed disease not suspected to be related to marihuana use were excluded from further participation in the study. For example, subjects with a history of alcoholism who were found through the physical examination and laboratory studies to have abnormalities indicating liver disease were diagnosed as having cirrhosis of the liver and hence not continued in the study. But subjects with minor abnormalities of one or more laboratory tests which did not lead to diagnosis of a specific disease process, or those with minor abnormalities of their chest X-ray or electrocardiogram, were maintained in the study as potential subjects for the matched-pair tests.

Conditions Diagnosed for Which Subjects Were Excluded from the Study

Using the criteria listed above for exclusion of subjects from the matched-pair study, the following defects were identified and diagnoses made:

The commonest sign of abnormality was a positive serological test for syphilis. This was found in twenty of the marihuana users and seventeen of the controls. The difference was statistically significant ($p = .01$).

The next most common abnormality was pulmonary lesions compatible with tuberculosis. These we found in eight users and seventeen controls. The difference was not statistically significant.

Three users and thirteen controls were found to have defective color vision, for which they were dropped from the study. Defects in visual acuity that were not correctable to 20/40 or better were found in four marihuana users and four controls. The difference was not statistically significant.

A diagnosis of serious disease was made in twelve of the total sample. Three of these were users, and nine were controls. One of the users and four of the controls had two or more causes for exclusion from the study. Diseases diagnosed in the user group were as follows. One had a severe anemia, with hemoglobin of 9.4 grams per 100 milliliters and a hematocrit of 32 volumes percent; the cause of the anemia was not determined. The second subject had diffuse enlargement of his thyroid gland, with elevations of his white-blood-cell count and erythrocyte sedimentation rate. The third was diagnosed as having subnormal mentality by the neurologist on the basis of his mental-status examination, but he would have been excluded in any case because of a positive serological test for syphilis.

Among nonusers, two subjects were found to have chronic alcoholism with cirrhosis of the liver; both had low serum albumin with reversal of the albumin-globulin ration. One had further evidence of liver impairment with elevation of his blood sugar, serum glutamic pyruvic transaminase, and serum bilirubin. This individual also was found to have an impaired performance on the mental-status examination. Three nonusers were diagnosed as having impaired performance on the mental-status examination, two of whom were also excluded on the basis of abnormal chest X-ray suggestive of pulmonary tuberculosis. Three were found to have serious cardiovascular diseases. One had severe hypertension and electrocardiograph evidence of enlargement of the heart. A second had coarctation of the aorta that had been diagnosed previously. Both these subjects had impaired color vision, which also would have led to their exclusion from further participation in the study. A third subject had mitral insufficiency with X-ray evidence of secondary pulmonary complications of that disorder. Finally, one subject was found to have severe renal disease with proteinuria, urinary casts, elevation of his blood urea nitrogen level and hypoalbuminemia with reversal of the albumin-globulin ration. All subjects with identified diseases were referred to appropriate clinics for further diagnostic study and treatment, and all subjects with impaired visual acuity that was correctable with eyeglasses were furnished with suitable corrective lenses, thus enabling them, if otherwise qualified, to continue to participate in the matched-pair study.

In all, 37 of the 84 users and 56 of the 156 controls were excluded from consideration for matched-pair selection because of these abnormalities (see Table 82).

Subjects Excluded for Behavioral Reasons

During the initial medical screening, eleven subjects failed to complete the test battery or were found to have inaccurate histories of marihuana use. Since for all of them we had obtained the medical history, physical examination, and laboratory tests, however, these results were included in the data for the main sample of 240 subjects. The subjects were then excluded from consideration for the matched-pair study (see Table 83).

Comparative Health Status in the Matched-Pair Subsample

Review of the items from the medical history, physical examination, and laboratory study of the matched pairs reveals that they differed from the base sample in only three areas other than the ones for which exclusions had been consciously made:

1. Responses to the question about adverse or allergic reactions to food were different in that nonusers showed more positive responses ($p = .02$). A second item in the history which differentiated the groups was the response to the question regarding low back pain. The nonusers again gave more positive responses to this question ($p = .05$).

2. On the mental-status section of the neurological examination, a larger percentage of nonusers performed poorly in abstracting or generalizing thoughts. This test was based on asking a subject the meaning of a common proverb familiar to most Costa Ricans. Nonusers were more concrete in their interpretations ($p = .05$).

3. In the laboratory studies, there was confirmation of the pattern established by the base sample. Prothrombin times were longer in the users than in the controls ($p = .001$), and total bilirubin, total serum globulin ($p = .02$), and alpha 1 globulin ($p = .01$) were lower. The differences in beta and gamma globulin noted in the main sample were less apparent in the matched pairs, although there was a tendency for all fractions to be lower.

Analysis of blood-sugar levels two hours after a 100-gram glucose load also revealed differences between the users and their controls. Among users, mean postglucose blood-sugar level was 67.9 milligrams per deciliter (standard deviation 21.0) and among controls it was 59.0 milligrams per deciliter (standard deviation 13.4; $p = .05$).

Because of contradictory reports on the acute effect of marihuana on blood-glucose levels, five subjects whose two-hour postglucose blood sugars were equal to or lower than their fasting levels were given a five-hour oral glucose-tolerance test along with their matched controls. The results showed no significant differences in the glucose-tolerance curves of the two groups (see Figure D).

Health-Screening Summary

Health screening of the base population of 240, using a standardized medical history, a physical examination, a battery of laboratory tests, a chest X-ray, and an electrocardiogram allowed us to develop a sample of long-term marihuana users matched with a nonusing sample, none of whom had clinical manifestations of common Costa Rican maladies such as tuberculosis, syphilis, intestinal parasites, and alcohol abuse. Only minor differences were found between users and nonusers. The former reported more gastrointestinal symptoms in the past, more concern about maintaining adequate body weight, and more use of substances of abuse than did nonusers. Their concern about body weight was reflected in the results of the physical examinations, where the mean body weight of the users in the base sample was significantly lower than that of nonusers. In the subsequent matched-pair sample, however, where occupation and marital status were controlled, this difference did not appear.

Other findings that differentiated between users and nonusers were that the former had slightly lower systolic blood pressure, more frequent presence of pterygia, and more frequent atrophy of one testis. Our data are insufficient to establish a cause-and-effect relationship between chronic use and the first two of these conditions, even though proven acute effects of marihuana smoking include transient lowering of blood pressure and hyperemia of the conjunctivae. Nor can we attribute the greater incidence of unilateral testicular atrophy in users to the effects of chronic use. In all but one case this could be traced directly to mumps or trauma.

Laboratory studies revealed only minimal differences. Among users, the mean hematocrit and bilirubin levels were lower and prothrombin times were slightly longer. Yet all these were within normal limits. The most striking contrast between the two groups was that among users laboratory evidence of past exposure to syphilis was much more common, in spite of the fact that the physical examination revealed no evidence of organ damage due to syphilis in either group.

A number of abnormal chest X-rays, suggestive of pulmonary tuberculosis, were found in both users and nonusers, but with no significant differences between the two groups. Statistically significant differences did not emerge from analysis of the electrocardiograms either. In the end, we were forced to conclude that neither the general physical examination nor the laboratory studies revealed a clear pattern of health impairment which could be attributed to the chronic effects of marihuana use.

SPECIAL STUDIES

Visual-Function Tests*

Although the visual-function tests showed several statistically significant differences between users and nonusers, these were too small to be clinically significant. All findings from both groups were within established limits of normalcy. Relative to the nonuser group, however, users showed increased basal lacrimation, increased intraocular pressure, increased photosensitivity, decreased dark adaptation, decreased color-match limits, and decreased Snellen acuity. These differences were associated with statistical probabilities of from $p = 0.7$ to $p = 0.01$ and are presented in Table 84. There were no significant differences between users and nonusers in incidence of pathological fundus signs, conjuntival hyperemia, pterygia, or color-match midpoints.

There are threads common to most of these findings and reports of previous research on the acute effects of marihuana use on eye function. Among these are symptoms typical of many irritative states of the anterior segment of the eye (Eakins et al. 1972; Bhattarcherjee 1975). Excellent general descriptions of these symptoms have been presented by Duke-Elder (1964, 1966). Table 85 compares these common symptoms of eye disease with the conditions we found in the user group as well as with reports from the literature on acute use.

*Portions of the visual-function test results were published earlier in *Investigative Ophthalmology and Visual Science* 16 (8), pp. 689–699.

In eye disease, conjunctival hyperemia is typical of many irritative states and has been documented repeatedly as a result of acute marihuana use (Hepler et al. 1972; Valk 1973; Thomas and Chester 1973). Among chronic users in our matched-pair sample, however, the profound hyperemia characteristic of the acute user was not found; in fact, clinically determined conjunctival hyperemia was only slightly more frequent in the users than in the nonusers. Perhaps what we were seeing was an adaptation to chronic use, dissipation of the condition, masking of the condition, or an unusually high incidence of hyperemia in our nonusing control subjects. The data are insufficient to indicate which of these might be the case.

Light sensitivity or "photophobia" is common in irritations of the anterior segment of the eye (Duke-Elder 1964). Its pathophysiology, however, is poorly understood (Walsh and Hoyt 1969). Although there was no quantitative measure of light sensitivity in our tests, the high frequency of reflex withdrawal of user eyes from the light used to excite pupillary constriction tends to suggest heightened sensitivity on the part of the user group. In addition, there was a statistically significant difference in brightness limits and color-match limits for the anomaloscope tests. An increase in subjective brightness sensitivity in the user group could account for their unusual performance on the anomaloscope-based color measures.

As compared with nonusing controls, an apparently optically uncorrectable acuity deficit was found in the users. Acuity is often slightly to greatly decreased in anterior-segment disease. This may be due to many causes, not the least of which are slight changes in the refraction or transmission characteristics of the various optical layers of the anterior segment, usually from edema. In acute users, reduced Snellen and Vernier acuity has been reported by several researchers (Levander et al. 1974; Shapiro 1974; Valk 1973), though not by all (see Hepler et al. 1972).

Intraocular pressure elevation and elevation of protein content of the aqueous humor is also a corollary of diseases of the anterior segment of the eye (Eakins et al. 1972). Green and Pederson (1973) have reported protein damping into the anterior chamber in the isolated rabbit anterior segment which was treated with Delta 1 THC.

Our observation of increased intraocular pressure in users conflicts with several reports of decreased intraocular pressure as an acute effect in nonchronic users. In the absence of more data, there is no clear explanation for the discrepancy. It may be related to varying degrees of "experience" in the subject samples that have been tested. Flom et al. (1975) replicated previous findings of reduced intraocular pressure in acute smokers with little use experience but found little or no intraocular pressure change in subjects with extensive use history. This would suggest that the "experience" variable is an important one that should be taken into consideration in future studies.

Disease or trauma of the anterior segment of the eye appears to be closely related to prostaglandin production. If prostaglandins and their release are specifically inhibited, the irritative response in the eye (see Table 85) does not occur (Neufeld, Jampol, and Sears 1972; Neufeld and Sears 1973). Green and Bowman (1974) have reported, however, that Delta 9 THC inhibits the formation of prostaglandins. If this is correct for all products of THC, it is unlikely that prostaglandin production can be directly responsible for the signs of irritation which may be seen in the acute phase of marihuana consumption. Yet, in the absence of other information we must also consider the possibility that in the long-term chronic user there is a prostaglandin rebound or hyperproduction during periods of abstention. The moderation of prostaglandin effects of physiology which could occur during adaptation to ten years of use are difficult to guess. As in cigarette smoking, the important question is "What trends are set, the results of which will not be clearly seen for another fifteen to twenty years?"

The visual and ocular signs that we discovered in these chronic users may also originate directly or indirectly from neurophysiological effects. Changes in pupil dimensions, vasomotor activity, accommodation, and lacrimation are discussed classically in association with the balance between sympathetic and parasympathetic divisions of the autonomic nervous system (Walsh and Hoyt 1969). Recent findings also imply that there may be neural control of intraocular pressure (Cox et al. 1975; Macrie and Cevarino 1975). Even heightened brightness sensitivity may have specific neural origins, especially under the influence of THC (Bieger and Hockman 1973).

All these considerations are, however, based on rather minimal differences between users and nonusers. When we assess our findings as a whole, we must conclude that we found no evidence that chronic marihuana use has any serious detrimental effect on eye function. At most, the findings indicate the presence in users of a very mild, nonspecific irritation of the anterior segment of the eye.

Sleep EEG-EOG Studies

ADJUSTMENT NIGHTS

The first night for each subject participating in the sleep EEG–EOG studies was considered a period of adjustment, and the resulting data were analyzed independently. For these nights we obtained usable data from a total of twenty-seven matched pairs (see Table 86). Two parameters were found to differentiate significantly between users and nonusers:

1.   REM Period Length
On the average, users had longer REM periods than nonusers ($p = .05$).
2.   Percent Stage 1 REM
Subjects in the marihuana-user group had a greater percentage of Stage 1 REM sleep, on the average, than their matched controls ($p = .05$). This seems to reflect simply the fact that users had longer REM periods in general.

POSTADJUSTMENT NIGHTS

Adequate data were obtained on postadjustment nights for thirty-two matched pairs (see Table 87). Here three parameters yielded statistically significant differentiation.

1. Sleep Latency 1

This parameter measured the time between "lights out" and the first appearance of Stage 1, sometimes employed as *the* measure of sleep latency. Users had a significantly longer sleep latency 1 than did their controls ($p = .01$). The other two measures of sleep latency gave similar but not statistically significant evidence of differences between the two groups.

Variability among subjects for all three sleep-latency measures was considerably greater for marihuana users than for controls, during both postadjustment and adjustment nights. Although one could hypothesize that this variability was related to differences in use levels of marihuana, testing of this hypothesis failed to establish such a relationship.

2. REM Period Length

Users had longer REM periods, on the average, than did their controls ($p = .05$). The difference was in the same direction as that obtained on the adjustment night, although smaller in magnitude.

3. Percent Stage 1 REM

Again we find that users had a greater percentage of Stage 1 REM than did their controls ($p = .05$) and that this was directly related to the fact that users had longer REM periods in general.

One of our basic questions was whether lifestyle rather than marihuana smoking *per se* might account for these differences, few though they were. To answer it, we turned to the paradigm of users and levels of use developed earlier in the study, and we incorporated these into a multivariate linear hypothesis model. The results are summarized in Table 88. Levels of use and the designations "stable smoker" and "street mover/pastoralist-escapist" apply, of course, only to the marihuana-using group. As a heuristic device for completing the analysis, however, controls were arbitrarily assigned the categories of their matches.

The comparison of use levels and lifestyles within the user group yielded no instances of statistically significant differences, indicating that neither factor was responsible for the minor differences in sleep patterns we found through the studies. Statistically significant differences, however, did emerge between those control subjects who were paired with stable smokers and those who were paired with street movers/pastoralist-escapists. The former had longer time in bed, more sleep-period time, more total sleep, more sleep stages, more REM periods, and lower percent stage 3 than the latter. The tendency among smokers was in the opposite direction. Our tentative conclusion is that by their very nature these statistically significant differences must be attributable entirely to chance factors in subject selection.

NIGHT-TO-NIGHT VARIABILITY COMPARISONS

Standard deviations of night-to-night variability were calculated on the basis of four consecutive nights of observation for each of the twenty-two pairs for whom we were able to obtain that many nights of usable laboratory data.

Median and mean estimates of these standard deviations for both groups of subjects are shown in Table 89. When comparisons were made between the two groups using the Wilcoxon signed rank test, only one parameter indicated differences in variability. Users had twice as much night-to-night variability in Sleep Latency 1 as did their controls. The average for the former was 21.9 minutes and for the latter only 11.1.

CORRELATIONS BETWEEN SMOKING AND SLEEP

The most impressive result of the sleep EEG-EOG study is the lack of evidence of major disturbances of sleep patterns in individuals who have smoked marihuana for ten to twenty-seven years and who continued their daytime smoking during the study (see Table 90). This does not necessarily imply that the sleep brain function of long-term marihauna users is the same as that of nonusers, but it does raise certain questions about the nature of the drug's long-term effects.

The seeming normality of our subjects' sleep patterns could be the result of insensitivity of the sleep EEG-EOG to marihuana effects, changes due to the two-hour prebedtime abstinence period imposed on the chronic marihuana smokers, the development of tolerance to the drug by sleep brain mechanisms, or a true lack of change in individuals using marihuana chronically and continuously at the levels characteristic of our subjects. Although it is certainly possible that the sleep EEG-EOG is not sensitive to long-term marihuana effects, sleep EEG-EOG patterns *do* show clear changes as a function of age (Williams et al. 1974), *are* typically altered by drugs (Kay 1973), and *are* abnormal in many mental and physical diseases (Williams et al. 1974). In addition, previous studies of bedtime administration of marihuana and THC have suggested the occurrence of drug-related changes in the sleep EEG-EOG.

It is possible that, although marihuana may have certain effects on sleep brain mechanisms, the abstinence period before bedtime was sufficient to allow either normal functioning to be reattained or recovery processes producing apparent normality to become operative. Yet, though the absence of acute effects might be explained in this fashion, it seems unlikely that residual effects of long-term chronic use would be so immediately reversible.

A third possibility is that the brain, when exposed chronically to a centrally acting substance such as marihuana, has sufficient plasticity to readjust its function so as to give the appearance of normality (i.e., develop tolerance). A fourth possibility is that there are in fact no residual effects on sleep brain function of long-term marihuana smoking or continued daytime smoking at levels characteristic of our subjects. Only through further research will we be able to know which of these explanations is closest to the truth.

The only significant EEG-EOG variables differentiating our user group from the nonuser group were the users' ability to fall asleep and their REM sleep. On the average, the users' sleep latency 1 on postadjustment nights was twice as long as that of their controls. Yet the user group contained fewer subjects reporting any sleep difficulty before the study than did the control group. It may be, then, that the extended sleep latency in users was the result of our enforced two-hour prebedtime abstinence period. If users were accustomed to smoking at or before bedtime, the abstinence requirement could have disturbed their routine enough to make it difficult for them to fall asleep. Another possibility is that anxiety associated with sleeping in the laboratory delayed sleep onset. Use of marihuana is illegal in Costa Rica, and the sleep study was conducted in a government hospital. Several users verbally expressed great concern that their anonymity be preserved, and all users may have felt this concern to a greater or lesser extent. We know that one of the first-night effects of sleeping in the laboratory is a reduction in the amount of REM sleep (Rechtschaffen and Verdone 1964; Agnew et al. 1966), a phenomenon usually attributed to anxiety concerning the strangeness of the sleeping environment and the recording procedures. Yet, if anxiety were present prior to sleep onset in our user subjects, it was not sufficiently strong after sleep onset to reduce REM percent below control levels.

Although statistically significant, our users' increases in REM percent and REM period length were very small on the average and would not usually be considered clinically significant. Even a normal subject may show larger changes from just one night to the next; yet the fact that the significant changes in these REM characteristics were observed on both the adjustment and the postadjustment nights indicates that they were not spurious. On the average, on all study nights users spent more time in bed and more time asleep than did controls. Since REM sleep occurs predominantly during the latter part of the night, and since successive REM periods tend to be longer, this extra sleep in users probably contained relatively high amounts of REM sleep. Further contributing to their elevated REM percent might have been the two-hour prebedtime abstinence period.

The apparent discrepancy between the results of this study and the results of previously reported acute studies is not at all surprising. Our study was a naturalistic one of very long-term users. Daily marihuana use continued as usual during the study, except that smoking was stopped at least two hours before bedtime. Thus, any *true* drug effects would have had to have been a mixture of residual effects from a median of fifteen years of drug use and smoking during the day. What we may be seeing is evidence that the acute, short-term effects of the drug are different from those of long-term use.

Special Pulmonary Studies

From administration of the Chronic Bronchitis Questionnaire of the British Medical Research Council, modified for the Costa Rican setting, the only statistically significant difference to emerge between users and nonusers was that users perceived that their work was lighter than did nonusers. A difference in height was found, although not statistically significant; users were, on the average, 1.5 centimeters shorter than nonusers. Since marihuana use was not usually begun before growth was achieved, this was interpreted as suggesting earlier epiphysial closure associated with malnutrition, possibly related to the fact that users had left home earlier than had nonusers. Lung growth, as judged from vital capacity values, was apparently not affected.

Since height is the strongest determinant of predicted normal pulmonary values (Morris et al. 1975), differences in this regard directly affected these values. Although the absolute values for volumes and flows did not differ significantly between groups, users had a tendency toward larger values calculated as percent predicted.

A strong tendency appeared suggesting that the users had larger indices of small-airway patency (FEF_{75-85}), especially after use of a bronchodilator. Considering their level of exposure to tobacco, both users and nonusers had relatively well preserved volumes, flows, and parenchymal function (D_{CO}). That mild-to-moderate bronchitis was present in both groups is suggested by the changes after the bronchodilator aerosol administration, but these too were not statistically significant.

Users had not experienced the loss of ventilatory function that might be predicted from an extrapolation of the horizontal study of Tashkin et al. (1976). The results suggest that there may be a tendency for concomitant marihuana smoking to counteract the known effects of tobacco cigarettes on small airways. Although the superior functioning of these airways in users does not reach the statistical level of significance, at least it cannot be said of the users that they have suffered an additive of synergistic decrement in pulmonary function over that attributable to tobacco alone (see Table 91).

Plasma Testosterone Studies

Of our forty-one matched pairs, thirty-eight yielded satisfactory plasma samples for testosterone level analysis. Results (see Figure E) were first analyzed by using the paired t-test for each user and his matched control, and based on the mean value of two testosterone determinations for each subject. The result was a t of 0.39, with 37 degrees of freedom, $p = .10$. The analysis was then repeated using the lowest testosterone value for each subject. Here the result was a t of 0.75, with 37 degrees of freedom, $p = .10$, with group means for the thirty-eight users of 564.06 nanograms per deciliter (SD 159.42) and for the controls of 549.37 (SD 166.07). The difference between the two means was not significant.

In an attempt to see whether a dose-related effect was present, those users whose daily average was ten or more marihuana cigarettes were then compared with their matched controls. The mean testosterone level in these thirteen users was 522.8 nanograms per deciliter (SD 175.71) and in the controls 550.31 nanograms per deciliter (SD 117.82). Again the differences were not statistically significant.

Four of the seven users who, in our initial medical screening, had been discovered to have unilateral testicular atrophy were included in the matched-pair sample and hence formed part of the plasma testosterone study. The testosterone levels of these four subjects yielded a mean of 592.8 nanograms per deciliter (range 485–715), while their matched controls had a mean of 593.0 nanograms per deciliter (range 415–698). Again the differences were not statistically significant.

Except for 1 to 3 percent which circulates in the free state, testosterone is attached to a carrier protein, a beta globulin, in the plasma. Since the marihuana users had more of a tendency toward lower beta-globulin levels than did the nonusers, the plasma testosterone levels in those users with beta-globulin levels below the mean level of the group were compared with the plasma testosterone levels of those with beta-globulin measurements higher than the mean for the group. There was no difference between the two.

These findings are hard to reconcile with those of Kolodny's Saint Louis research (1974). Our user subjects had smoked marihuana for longer periods of time and in larger quantities than those recruited for the Saint Louis study. The fact that their testosterone levels were not significantly lower than those of their matched nonusing controls mitigates against a cause-and-effect relationship between long-term use and lowered testosterone levels. It may be that, over time, there develops a tolerance to marihuana that overcomes whatever inhibitory action it may have on the hypothalamic-pituitary axis or on the end organ, the testis, or it may simply be that the effects Kolodny measured were transitory in nature. A concurrent study by Reese Jones, in which Delta 9 THC was administered orally every four hours, has indicated that decrements in testosterone levels following ingestion of THC are only transient (personal communication). When THC administration is discontinued, the individual's testosterone levels return to his original baseline. This might explain why our results are more in agreement with other recent findings by Mendelson, Kuehnle, Ellingboe, and Babor (1974).

Transient decrements in plasma testosterone levels which remain within the normal range, as found by Kolodny et al. and Jones et al. (personal communication), would not be expected to affect sexual function, protein anabolism, or secondary sexual characteristics in the adult male. Such decrements would be of more concern in the adolescent male. Yet the mean age at which our subjects began marihuana use was 15.2 years, and the earliest was 9.

Our health-screening examination failed to find diminished masculine features in any subject. Although measures of sexual function require more detailed and focused studies than were done in the survey, procreative function was tested by asking each subject how many children he had fathered. The responses indicated a mean of 2.6 children for users and 2.6 children for controls. These findings cast serious doubt on cause-and-effect relationship between marihuana smoking and plasma testosterone levels in long-term users.

Nutritional Studies

A nutritional survey of the matched-pair sample revealed that 60 percent had a diet deficient in calories (see Table 92). Mean caloric intake was only 63.6 percent of the INCAP standard of 2,900 calories per day. Ten percent of the sample reported diets deficient in protein. All cited rice and beans as their primary protein source; in combination, the two provide all the essential amino acids. Seventy-one percent of the sample were deficient in vitamin A intake, whereas only 8 percent were deficient in intake of iron. Deficiency of fat intake was present in all but 7 percent of the subjects. Although underreporting such intake could explain this finding in part, even reasonable upward adjustments to account for the amount used in cooking failed to raise these levels to minimum daily requirements for most subjects. Reported intakes for vitamins B_1 and B_2 indicated that 13 percent of the sample were deficient in B_1 and 21 percent in B_2. Forty percent of the subjects reported diets deficient in niacin. Vitamin C intake was highly variable on a daily basis, with 29 percent of the sample having dietary deficiencies.

Comparison of marihuana users and nonusers indicated no measurable differences in diet quality, nor did the meal environment differ basically between the two groups. In both respects, variation within the groups was greater than that between the two.

GENERAL RESULTS OF BIOMEDICAL STUDIES

A basic rationale for studying marihuana in places like Costa Rica is that the use of all drugs, marihuana included, is subject to cultural biases. Our study has shown that customs, environment, family, and individual personality characteristics not only govern use but color effects as well. The results suggest that even long-term physiological response may be influenced by the social and cultural setting.

Given the striking differences in family background which separated the marihuana users from their controls, the general health status of the two groups turned out to be remarkably alike. The few minimal differences that did emerge in no way impaired users' ability to function on a day-to-day basis. Although the method used to identify subjects for the study tended to minimize inclusion of individuals with gross functional impairments, general health status and neurological, pulmonary, and visual function tended to be good in users and nonusers alike. The absence of differentiating features in the results of the special tests is all the more impressive when one considers that the chronic users were also regular users of alcohol and tobacco, with rare individual exceptions. To the extent that marihuana use is harmful to physical health, one might expect synergistic effects in individuals using all three substances regularly for prolonged periods of time. The apparent absence of such synergism casts doubt on the purported harmful effects of marihuana smoking on pulmonary, brain, visual, and testicular functions.

9/ Neuropsychological and Personality Correlates

The possibility of permanent changes in brain function and personality after prolonged cannabis use is an issue that has generated considerable controversy in scientific, legal, and political communities (Hollister 1971). In North America, this controversy has been unnecessarily intense because of overpublicized studies that have serious methodological shortcomings (see Brecher 1974; Zinberg 1976). Two recent studies (Campbell et al. 1971; Kolansky and Moore 1971) often cited as evidence for permanent brain damage and personality changes (amotivational syndrome) employed poly-drug users and failed to include nonusing control groups. Several subjects in the Campbell et al. study had a history of neurological trauma, while the sample in the Kolansky and Moore study was selected from a psychiatric ward. Other methodological factors, including the relatively low frequency and duration of cannabis use in North American users, limits generalizations from studies that report null results (e.g., Grant et al. 1973).

Several cross-cultural studies have been conducted in countries where cannabis use is more prevalent and less associated with poly-drug use. These projects—in Egypt, Greece, and Jamaica—more appropriately address the issue of long-term changes in brain function, intelligence, and personality after prolonged and heavy cannabis use. Here we will briefly review and critique each of these studies and compare their results with those we obtained in Costa Rica. By doing so, we hope to clarify and resolve some of the intense controversy that continues to prevail on this issue.

EGYPT

In Egypt, cannabis use (hashish) has long been prominent among some lower-class segments of the population. Consumption by some Egyptians has been estimated as high as 200 milligrams of THC daily. The mean THC content of Egyptian hashish, about 3 percent by weight (Souief 1976), is much higher than the mean THC content in North American preparations, which are only about 1 percent by weight. Egypt has considerable potential for cannabis research, and a large project directed in that country by Souief (1971, 1976) has provided evidence pertaining to possible long-term changes in brain function and personality.

The sample used for the Egyptian project consisted of 850 hashish users, who had consumed the drug from five to thirty years, and of 839 nonusers. All subjects were selected from Egyptian prisons, with the user group comprising all males convicted for hashish use and imprisoned during the period from June 1967 to March 1968. Controls were defined "as those subjects who never took hashish or any other narcotic substance" (Souief 1971: 17). The average age of the user group was thirty-nine years; the average age of the nonuser group was thirty-three years. While the distribution of urban–rural subjects and percentage of skilled laborers was approximately equal between the groups, 60 percent of the user group and only 54 percent of the nonuser group were illiterate. Only six users had a high school degree, whereas forty-four controls possessed high school certificates and an additional nine had some type of university degree.

Brain Function

Those aspects of the Egyptian study pertaining to brain function and intelligence consisted of twelve "objective tests" measuring perceptual speed and accuracy, distance and time estimation, digit span, reaction time (to Rorschach cards I–IV), and visual-motor abilities (Bender gestalt). The test battery was similar to those employed in some acute studies which have reported transient changes in cognitive function. Analysis of the sixteen test scores generated by the battery revealed significant differences on ten variables, with users performing more poorly on eight of the ten. These differences occurred on three of the four perceptual speed tasks, on the Trail Making Test (Part A, not Part B), on the digit span backward test (not forward or total), and on the Bender gestalt test. Souief (1976: 338) concluded from the differences that prolonged cannabis use produces subtle deficits in the cortical level of arousal.

Personality

Studies concerned with personality and mental health were limited and stemmed basically from the administration of separate interviewing schedules to users and nonusers. Although the interviews were largely devoted to patterns of consumption and the subjective effects of hashish, some findings pertaining to personality and to lifestyle are of interest. There was a strong tendency for users to seek out other drugs (opium, alcohol, tobacco, and caffeine) that act on the central nervous system. Users were more likely to come from single-parent families and families with consuming parents. Users exhibited a higher frequency of divorce in the past (6 percent vs. 2 percent). More nonusers were arrested for non–cannabis-related activities (14 percent vs. 6 percent). Not surprisingly for a prison sample, 79 percent of the users stated that they wished they could stop taking hashish.

Discussion

The Egyptian project, while large-scale and chronic in its focus, contained a number of methodological problems that raise serious questions concerning Souief's conclusions (Fletcher and Satz 1977). User and nonuser groups clearly differed on age and literacy, with the differences favoring the nonuser group. The potential influence of the literacy differences is illustrated by the absence of significant differences in the "Upper Egyptian" analysis, where users had a higher literacy level (Souief 1971). Consumption of other narcotics was uncontrolled in the user group (30 percent used opiates), and a higher percentage of users regularly consumed alcohol (22 percent vs. 9 percent). Separate interviewing schedules were devised, indicating that subject identity as user or nonuser was not concealed from examiners. The extent to which findings from a prison sample generalize to the entire population of Egyptian users is questionable, especially when interviews concerned the crime for which users were arrested. Finally, statistical problems associated with the bias toward rejection of the null hypothesis in large samples (Bakan 1971) could make very small group differences "significant." This possibility was certainly apparent in the interview data but could not be determined for the objective test data. Nonetheless, in such a large sample statistical significance does not necessarily imply psychological significance, just as group differences do not necessarily imply deficits or dysfunction. More appropriate statistical analyses, making better use of the large sample, would help clarify the rather unclear status of the Egyptian project as it pertains to brain function and personality. Further clarification could be provided by appropriate matching on literacy, age, poly-drug use, and other independent variables that separate user and nonuser groups.

GREECE

The results of the Greek study (Stefanis et al. 1977) provide some evidence concerning the long-term effects of cannabis use on brain function and personality. The Greek sample consisted of forty-seven chronic hashish users and forty controls matched for age ($\bar{X} = 42$), family origin, education, residence at birth, and upbringing. Users had smoked an average of twenty-three years, beginning at an average age of seventeen years. The THC content of Greek hashish was about 4 to 5 percent by weight, and users were exposed to as much as 200 milligrams daily (Boulougouris et al. 1976).

Brain Function

This project employed only a brief psychometric battery for an acute study based on a subsample of twenty chronic users ($\bar{X}$ age = 44) who had smoked hashish for an average period of over twenty-five years (Dornbush and Kokkevi 1976). Simple tests of perceptual motor ability were administered thirty and seventy minutes after consumption of different cannabis preparations (0–180 mg THC). The major finding of this study was that, after twenty-five years of hashish use, Greek users revealed an acute pattern of response similar to American short-term users who consumed up to 25 milligrams of THC. The authors concluded: "The heavy long-term use of Cannabis does not qualitatively change the general patterns of response in acute use that are exhibited by, as yet, occasional short-term users" (ibid. 1976: 321). These results were buttressed by a separate acute study with this subsample, in which EEG changes were qualitatively similar to those exhibited by acutely intoxicated American volunteers (Fink 1976) and in which no differences were found between the Greek users and nonusers for resting EEG patterns.

Personality

Assessments of the mental health of the Greek user groups were obtained via semistructured social histories, mental-status examinations, and information gathered from home visits, civil authorities, and previous psychiatric records (Stefanis et al. 1976). The results revealed that more users than nonusers (38 percent vs. 17 percent) had "mental disorders." The differences were most prominent for personality disorders (26 percent vs. 8 percent), especially of the antisocial type (11 percent vs. 0 percent). In interpreting these findings, Stefanis et al. (1976) pointed to harsh governmental restrictions on hashish use and suggested that cannabis use in Greece "may be considered as another form of antisocial behavior more likely to occur in people with a personality disorder" (ibid.: 62). In other words, the authors viewed cannabis use as an expression of deviance and not as a causal factor in the behavioral problems of their users. These impressions were strengthened by the absence of a relationship between amount of hashish consumption and incidence of behavioral disorders.

Discussion

It is difficult to assess the neuropsychological portions of the Greek study. The important issue, namely, the long-term effects of cannabis on users in a drug-free state, was not addressed in any detail. The major finding was that the acute effects of the drug in heavy chronic users with over twenty-five years of experience appeared qualitatively similar to those of occasional users with far fewer years of experience.

The personality and mental-health studies shared many of the problems associated with interview-based methodology in North American drug research. Separating antecedents and consequences of cannabis use as it relates to personality development and group differences (Halikas 1974) presents considerable interpretative difficulties under an interview format. Although more emphasis was placed on the social and cultural context in which hashish use took place, it could not be determined whether behavior disorders and other sociocultural differences between groups were attributable to hashish use *per se* or to societal attitudes and restrictions concerning such use. Objective psychological tests would have provided additional information on the personality traits of the user and nonuser groups. This assessment would seem particularly important considering the high incidence of psychopathology reported for both the user group and the nonuser group.

JAMAICA

The Jamaican project represented a comprehensive effort to determine the long-term effects of cannabis use on higher brain function and personality. It lasted three years, was multidisciplinary in nature, and was carried out in a country where marihuana (*ganja*) use for recreational, medicinal, and other purposes is endemic in the lower working classes (Rubin and Comitas 1975). The only results of the project that will be discussed here are those deriving from portions of the neuropsychological, personality, neurological, psychiatric, and anthropological evaluations.

The sample evaluated in Jamaica consisted of sixty adult males from the lower working classes (largely rural). Thirty of these subjects had been heavy smokers (at least three times weekly) during the last seven years. The average duration of use was 17.5 years at a frequency of seven spliffs daily. The THC content in marihuana samples provided by the users averaged 2.96 percent by weight, and users ingested about 60 milligrams daily. Users were matched with nonusers for age ($\bar{X}$ = 34 years), socioeconomic class, and residence. Although no controls had been heavy smokers in recent years, all but twelve subjects had had some experience with cannabis, with initial experience occurring as early as eight and as late as thirty-six years of age. Use of other drugs, including alcohol, was infrequent in the sample and the Jamaican lower class as a whole.

Brain Function

An extensive neuropsychological and intellectual evaluation was conducted on these groups (Knights, in Rubin and Comitas 1975). These measures, administered during a seven-day drug-free period of hospitalization, were largely derived from the Halstead-Reitan neuropsychology battery and included a Wechsler Adult Intelligence Scale (WAIS). Analysis of these data failed to reveal consistent significant differences between users and nonusers. Resting EEGs conducted during the hospitalization period also failed to reveal differences between the groups (Beaubrun and Knight 1973).

A separate neuropsychological and psychophysiological study (Bowman and Pihl 1973) unrelated to the Jamaican project was performed on two other Jamaican samples of users (N = 30) and nonusers (N = 24). This study matched user groups more carefully on age, sex, social class, alcohol use, intelligence, education, and modernity. Again, despite this careful matching and the use of multivariate statistical procedures, no significant differences emerged between the user groups.

Personality

Personality evaluations were based on objective personality tests and interviews by resident psychiatrists (Rubin and Comitas 1975). Results based on the Eysenck Personality Inventory and a projective test, the Lowenfeld Mosaic Test, revealed no differences between user groups. Similar null results were obtained for psychiatric interviews and mental-status examinations (Beaubrun and Knight 1973).

Discussion

The Jamaican project constituted a major breakthrough for cross-cultural drug research. The combination of field-based social-science evaluation and hospital-based clinical evaluation made possible a powerful and thorough examination of the effects of cannabis on the individual and his society. Neuropsychological and personality studies were much more extensive than those conducted in Egypt and Greece. Nevertheless, the project produced no evidence for changes in brain function or personality.

The fact that the neuropsychological and personality phases of the Jamaican project were more extensive than those conducted in Egypt and Greece does not mean that design, test selection, and data analysis could not have been improved. Serious reservations, which have not been adequately addressed by any previous chronic study, can be directed to the neuropsychological phases of this project.

First, no attempt was made to standardize the neuropsychological test battery for use in Jamaica *prior* to the experimental study. The authors reported that some of the subtests of the WAIS had to be omitted because of obvious cultural bias (Knights, in Rubin and Comitas 1975). Yet other tests, presumably with equal bias, were not excluded. Knights explained his reasoning as follows:

> These tests are not culture free, but since the primary concern was to determine differences between the smokers and non-smokers, this was not considered a limiting factor, on the assumption that any cultural bias in the test items would be similar and consistent for both groups. [Rubin and Comitas 1975: 111.]

This reasoning would not follow, however, if a floor or ceiling effect occurred on several of the tests. If the tests were too difficult or too easy for both groups, possible differences between groups could be masked by these artifacts.

Second, virtually no attempt was made to include measures of short-term memory, under distraction, for verbal and perceptual functions. This omission is particularly significant in view of reports of memory and time disturbances in some cases of chronic marihuana usage (Kolansky and Moore 1971). Also, disturbances in short-term memory are known to occur as primary symptoms after lesions to different structures and systems of the brain (Luria 1973).

Third, the methods of analyses employed in the Jamaican project were all univariate statistical tests, which present problems when multiple measures are used (Hummel and Sligo 1971). Multivariate statistical procedures would have been more appropriate for two reasons. The first reason is that multivariate procedures take into account the dependent structure prevailing among a number of correlated measures. Groups that are not significantly different on a series of univariate tests may differ on a multivariate test. The second reason for using multivariate procedures concerns greater control of the probability of group differences because of chance (type 1 error rates) by reducing the number of univariate tests applied to the data (ibid. 1971).

A fourth problem is that no attempt was made to evaluate the long-term neuropsychological effects within the user group as a function of frequency and duration of use. This evaluation would have helped to rule out possible within-group differences in the chronic users.

Costa Rica

In Costa Rica, serious attention was given to the preceding methodological considerations. Prior to any evaluation of the matched-pair sample, a preexperimental phase was conducted to ensure that the neuropsychological and intellectual measures employed were appropriate for the culture. In particular, an attempt was made to eliminate the possibility of psychometric artifacts (floor and ceiling effects) that could obscure possible differences between users and non-users. The preexperimental phase permitted the evaluation of those tests most likely to be influenced by cultural factors (e.g., verbal learning and memory tasks). On the basis of that evaluation, a neuropsychological and personality battery was selected for the experimental phase (matched-pair study) in order to evaluate a wide range of abilities. Many of the tests chosen for the battery are used in standard neuropsychological and personality evaluations in North America, and some have been used in acute studies where they have revealed transient changes. Statistical evaluation of group performance in the experimental phase was quite intensive, including computer-based multivariate analyses of variance and covariance. Variables concerning frequency and duration of use were given special consideration, so that possible group differences would not be overlooked because of heterogeneity within the user group.

Preexperimental Phase

To deal with the issue of culture-fairness, a sample of eighty-six native Costa Rican males was administered the initial neuropsychological battery. In general, subjects in this pretest group were members of the working class soliciting services from the Ministry of Health in San José. None was considered for either the base sample or the matched-pair sample.

Analysis of the pretest results revealed that Costa Rican performance on the neuropsychological battery was generally comparable to performance by subjects in the United States (see Fletcher et al. 1975). Some tests showed evidence of ceiling effects and were discarded from the final battery. The intelligence test used initially (IPAT Culture-Fair Scale) proved difficult for many Costa Ricans and may have produced a floor effect under the timed conditions employed. In a subsequent study (see ibid. 1975), two additional intelligence tests, Raven's Coloured Progressive Matrices and the Puerto Rican standardization of the WAIS were administered to thirty subjects from the preexperimental sample. The results indicated that the WAIS was most appropriate for use in Costa Rica, probably because of the fact that it had been standardized for a Spanish-speaking population.

Experimental Phase

The experimental phase consisted of the administration of the final test battery to the matched-pair sample. The purpose of the operation was to determine whether chronic use of marihuana is associated with any disturbance in neuropsychological, intellectual, and personality spheres. In addition to the neuropsychological and intellectual measures selected from the pretest, two personality measures were employed: Form E of the 16 Personality Factors Questionnaire (Cattell et al. 1970) and an Incomplete Sentence Test. The final battery was as follows:

A. Verbal Memory and Learning

1. Logical Memory (Wechsler Memory Scale)

Logical Memory consisted of two short paragraphs of narrative nature devised by the consulting psychologist in San José (Dina Krauskopf), using material that was culturally homogeneous for the population to be examined. The paragraphs were read to the subject (one at a time) in Spanish, and the subject was asked to relate to the examiner the content of the passage immediately upon hearing it for the first time. Scores were based on the number of phrases correctly remembered or approximated for each of the two paragraphs. After a ninety-minute interpolated delay, the subjects were again asked to repeat to the examiner the content of the two paragraphs that they had heard earlier. Thus, two scores were obtained; one for immediate short-term verbal memory and one for delayed short-term memory.

2.   Word Learning (Williams Memory Battery)

This was a verbal learning task consisting of five trials with a set of Spanish words of extremely low frequency of use. These words were read along with a definition to the subject. On each trial, the subject was required to recall the appropriate definition for the stimulus word. A score was obtained consisting of the total number of errors committed across five trials.

3.   Delayed Recall (Williams Memory Battery)

This was a measure of retention. The subject was shown a card with nine line drawings of common objects. After a ten-minute delay, he was asked to name the objects. For each picture not recalled spontaneously, a prompt, or clue, was given. If the subject failed to name the correct picture, he was shown a sheet with the original nine drawings and six others. Failure to select the appropriate drawing was labeled an error of recognition. Scoring consisted simply of the total number of errors in the three recall conditions.

B.   Nonverbal Memory and Learning

1.   Rey-Davis (Williams Memory Battery)

The Rey-Davis was a test of nonverbal learning and was an excellent measure of visuo-spatial ability. In this test, the subject was required to locate and remember the location of just one of nine pegs on four boards. Five trials were conducted with the pegs in this position. The score consisted of the total number of errors across all trials.

2.   Facial Recognition Memory Test

The Facial Recognition Memory Test (Milner 1968) was a test of memory for nonverbal stimuli (faces). The subject was presented with a card containing twelve photographs of unfamiliar men and women, which he was asked to study for forty-five seconds. At the end of this time period, the photograph was removed and an interpolative task of approximately one and a half minutes was presented. The subject was then presented with a photograph of twenty-five pictures of unfamiliar men and women and asked to identify the twelve who had appeared in the first photograph. Scores were reported in terms of number of photos correctly identified.

3.   Benton Visual Retention (Benton 1963)

This was a measure of reproduction memory. The subject was shown a drawing of a common geometric figure, which he viewed for ten seconds. The figure was then removed, and after a five-second delay the subject was asked to reproduce the figure graphically. Reproductions were either correct or incorrect, with a correct reproduction receiving a score of 1. Total score was the number of correctly reproduced figures. The test has proven to be useful in detecting mild disturbances in writing ability (agraphia) and voluntary movements (apraxia) following brain injury.

C.   Somatosensory-Perceptual and Motor Functions

1.   Tactual Performance Test (Halstead-Reitan Neuropsychology Battery)

This task (Reitan 1964), as modified and administered in the Satz Neuropsychology Laboratory, was designed to test unilateral tactile learning and central nervous system integrity. It provided an indirect measure of transfer capabilities from the dominant to the nondominant cerebral hemispheres. By eliminating all visual and auditory cues, the subject was required to pick up ten wooden geometric shapes and place them in a formboard in a fifteen-minute interval, using first the preferred hand and then the nonpreferred hand. Evidence of the transfer of learning from the dominant cerebral hemisphere to the nondominant cerebral hemisphere was demonstrated by a significant reduction in the time required to perform the task with the nonpreferred hand.

2.   Finger Localization Test (Benton 1959)

This task was composed of three parts which, when combined, measured the subject's ability to integrate and report sensory stimulation. Part I measured unilateral and bilateral differentiation between digits, something that should be easy in the absence of cortical dysfunction. The fingers of each hand were numbered one through five, beginning with the thumb; stimulation by touching the finger in question with the tip of a pen or pencil, out of the subject's range of vision, was reported by number. Part II required the subject to identify the finger stimulated by pointing to the same finger represented on a diagram of each hand. Part III required the subject to identify a letter of the alphabet which was traced on his fingertip. Scores were reported in terms of the task and were combined for total errors in terms of right and left sides.

3.   Finger Oscillation Test (Halstead-Reitan Neuropsychology Battery)

As a measure of fine manual ability, the Finger Oscillation Test (Reitan 1969) was given. A version of this test was also given in Jamaica. In our version, the subject was required to depress a key rapidly for ten seconds, using his index finger. A Veeder-Root counter recorded the frequency with which the key was depressed during the time interval. Four ten-second trials per hand were administered; scores were summed and averaged over trials for each hand. Difference scores between hands were used to determine the degree of manual laterality (Satz et al. 1967).

D.   Wechsler Adult Intelligence Scale

Three intelligence tests were employed in the preexperimental phase: the Culture-Fair Intelligence Test of Cattell, Raven's Progressive Matrices (Raven 1965), and a Spanish version of the Wechsler Adult Intelligence Scale (Wechsler 1968). The latter was found most appropriate for a Costa Rican working-class population. Because of restrictions on the amount of testing time, it was administered according to the Satz-Mogel Short Form Procedure (Satz and Mogel 1962). This procedure uses all eleven WAIS subtests and scales. It has been used in a variety of settings, including Costa Rica (ibid. 1962; Mogel and Satz 1963; Goebal and Satz 1975).

E.   Personality

1.   16 Personality Factors Test (16 PF; Cattell et al. 1970)

This was a test constructed on the basis of factor analyses of literally thousands of questionnaire items, self-ratings, and behavior ratings. The sixteen basic personality factors making up the test constitute a portion of the twenty-four to thirty primary factors discovered from the factor analytic studies and which presumably form the basic dimensions of the normal adult personality. Table 93 lists the factors making up the test, along with a brief description of each factor.

2.   Sentence Completion Test

In this test, the subject was faced with the task of filling out incomplete utterances with the *first content that came to mind*. The answer yielded information as a product not of an introspective effort but of an association of ideas. In constructing the test, we selected verbal forms most familiar to working-class males in San José and attitudinal areas of proven interest to our research. The major areas explored through the test were social relations, for which we elicited attitudes having to do with the interpersonal sphere in general, heterosexuality, friends, and work; psychotropics, for which we elicited attitudes having to do with the use of alcohol and marihuana; and personal identity, for which we elicited attitudes having to do with personality dynamics, such as fears, guilt, frustration, attitudes toward the past, the future, goals, and self-image.

Brain Function

Table 94 presents the means, standard deviations, ranges, and results of the univariate t-test for each of the sixteen major variables making up the neuropsychological analysis. They indicate that, in general, there were no significant differences between users and nonusers. The finding is reinforced by the fact that multivariate analysis of the same material also failed to uncover significant differences (Hotelling's T^2 = .67; 16 and 65 df; p = .82).

Closer inspection of the data merely highlights the similarity in performance between users and nonusers. Table 95 presents the descriptive statistics and univariate t-tests for the Williams Scale for the Measurement of Memory. It reveals a tendency for the user group to perform more poorly than the nonuser group on Word Learning, Delayed Recall, and Rey-Davis subtests. Figure F plots the mean number of errors in Word Learning for each group across the five trials making up the test. While there was a trend for the user group to perform more poorly, it is obvious that both groups showed similar learning curves on this memory task. A similar finding is evident on the other test of verbal memory, Logical Memory. While there was a nonsignificant trend for the user group to perform more poorly, Figure G shows that the two groups actually responded similarly to the immediate and delayed conditions of the test (see also Figures H and I). Similar findings were apparent on the Rey–Davis subtest.

In Table 95, one can see a nonsignificant trend for the user group to perform more poorly. However, Figure J, which plots mean errors for each group across the five trials of the task, shows that learning curves were quite similar for the two groups. Because the Rey–Davis presumably measured a nonverbal aspect of memory (spatial), it is interesting to compare performance on this task with the Facial Recognition Memory Task (see Table 94). Again there was a slight though nonsignificant trend for users to perform more poorly (see Figure K). In general, the results of the memory tests, across different stimulus materials, show no significant differences in memory and learning between users and nonusers.

In looking more closely at the results for the somatosensory-perceptual tasks, the absence of significant univariate differences is even more apparent. Table 96 reports the descriptive statistics and univariate t-tests for the different components of the Halstead Tactual Performance Task. On the six different scores obtained for this task, no significant group differences emerged. Instead, as Figure L (time) and Figure M (errors) show, transfer of learning from right hand to left hand was clearly present and similar for both groups. Table 97 presents descriptive statistics and univariate t-tests for the different portions of the Finger Localization Test. Differences between groups, none of which are significant, occur inconsistently, with no general trends appearing (see Figure N).

Considering trends in the data on the sixteen major variables in the neuro-psychological battery, it appears that on eleven of these variables the user group performed more poorly (see Figure O). This finding, however, merely highlights the importance of the multivariate test on all sixteen variables. The fact that this test was not significant should lend caution to interpreting trends which may appear in the data.

Intelligence

Our insights into the possible effect of chronic marihuana use on intelligence come basically from a comparison of performance on the subtests and scales making up the WAIS. Table 98 presents the means, standard deviations, ranges, and univariate t-tests for each of the WAIS subtests ($N = 11$) and Scales ($N = 3$). These fourteen variables were also combined for a multivariate test, which was not significant (Hotelling's $T^2 = .88$; 14 and 67 df; $p \leq .58$). Similarly, the univariate t-tests were not significant. The user group had a higher though nonsignificant mean subtest performance on six of the eleven subtests and a slightly higher Verbal and Full Scale IQ. Once again, performance of the two groups was quite similar. This is clearly illustrated in Figure P, which plots mean subtest scatter for both groups. The difference in scatter, particularly in the Performance subtests, is not remarkable; further, as Figure Q shows, Verbal, Performance, and Full Scale IQs are quite similar for both groups.

Personality

Table 99 presents the means, standard deviations, ranges, and univariate *t*-tests for each of the sixteen personality factors. Only one *t*-test was significant, that for factor $Q_1(t = 2.35; p \leq .02)$, a factor associated with a conservatism-liberalism dimension of personality. However, the fact that the multivariate test for all sixteen variables was not significant (Hotelling's $T^2 = .57$; 16 and 65 df; $p \leq .89$) minimizes this finding. Figure R, which reveals the personality profiles of the two groups on the standard clinical scoring form, shows that the two groups endorsed very similar behavior in responding to the test items.

Similar results were obtained when the primary factors were converted into second-order factors (see Tables 93, 100, and 101). As Table 101 and Figure R show, there were no significant univariate differences between user and nonuser groups. In view of this finding and the general direction of the experimental results, it is not surprising that the multivariate test was also nonsignificant (Hotelling's $T^2 = .36$; 8 and 73 df; $p \leq .95$). The personality profile of the two groups turned out to be similar both for the sixteen primary factors and for the eight second-order factors.

Sentence-completion analysis was consistent with these findings. In supplying stubs for the incomplete sentence stems, users more frequently spoke of traumatic incidents in their past and were more optimistic about the future. They gave greater value to friendship and more emphasis to the sexual aspect of man-woman relationships. But otherwise, users and nonusers fully shared a common outlook on life.

An independent analysis of the sentence-completion materials by individuals not involved in the collection of data and using an entirely different analytical framework confirmed that users and nonusers shared basic personality traits. When researchers in the Social Psychology Laboratory of the University of Chicago applied the Loevinger technique (Loevinger 1970) for assessing levels of ego development, they found no differences between users and nonusers.

Level of Use and Lifestyle as Distinguishing Factors

To further refine our analysis and avoid missing possible relationships between specific types of marihuana use and brain function, intelligence, and personality, we broke the user group into categories reflecting frequency and duration of use and user lifestyle.

Two use-level groups were formed by dividing the total matched-pair user population according to the median number of cigarettes consumed daily. The median, obtained from EEG log reports and the nutritional survey, turned out to be 7.7 cigarettes per day. The subject at the median was discarded, leaving twenty users who smoked on the average less than seven cigarettes daily as low users and those twenty who smoked more than seven cigarettes per day as high users. Three comparisons were made: between high users and their matched controls, between low users and their matched controls, and between low users and high users. The results are presented in Table 102. The table reveals some univariate differences between high and low users versus their controls. However, the absence of significant differences on multivariate tests makes interpretation of apparent univariate differences meaningless. Overall, the findings indicated that level of marihuana use has little influence on performance in the neuropsychological, intelligence, and personality battery.

In assessing the relevance of user type, the original paradigm was again collapsed into two categories: street movers/pastoralist-escapists and stable smokers. Eighteen subjects fell into the first category, twenty-three fell into the second. Univariate and multivariate significance tests were computed between the first category and their matched controls, between the second category and their matched controls, and between the two categories themselves. Table 103 presents the results.

In the comparison between street movers/pastoralist-escapists and their matched controls, we found no significant differences, either univariate or multivariate. A comparison of stable smokers and their matched controls also failed to reveal differences on neuropsychological or intellectual variables. However, we did find a significant multivariate difference with regard to personality on both the 16 PF *primary* factors (Hotelling's $T^2 = 2.45$; 16 and 29 df; $p \leq .02$) and the *second-order* factors (Hotelling's $T^2 = 2.21$; 16 and 29 df; $p \leq .05$). Furthermore, significant univariate differences were found for primary factors H ($t = 2.61$; 22 df; $p \leq .02$), L ($t = 2.40$; 22 df; $p \leq .03$), and Q_I ($t = 2.42$; 22 df; $p \leq .02$), and the second-order factor Q_{VIII} ($t = 2.40$; 22 df; $p \leq .02$). Stable users, by comparison with their controls, were more Venturesome (H+), Suspicious (L+), Radical (S+), and Conscientious ($Q_{VIII}+$).

When street movers/pastoralist-escapists were compared with stable smokers, several differences also emerged. On the Neuropsychological Test Battery, stable smokers were slower than street movers on the Tactual Performance Task ($t = 4.04$; 39 df; $p \leq .05$) and made more errors on the Finger Localization ($t = 3.66$; 39 df; $p \leq .06$). The multivariate test, comprising the sixteen neuropsychological variables, however, turned out to be not significant (Hotelling's $T^2 = .82$; 13 and 27 df; $p \leq .63$).

The WAIS also revealed some interesting univariate differences. The stable smokers scored significantly lower than the street movers/pastoralist-escapists on the Picture Completion subtest ($t = 11.64$; 1 and 39 df; $p \leq .002$) and they had a lower Performance IQ ($t = 5.54$; 1 and 39 df; $p \leq .002$). Once again, however, the multivariate test on all fourteen variables was not significant (Hotelling's $T^2 = 1.50$; 14 and 26 df; $p \leq .18$).

In the personality sphere, only one significant difference emerged. Street movers/pastoralist-escapists obtained a higher mean score on Factor H, a factor associated with Venturesomeness ($t = 6.45$; 1 and 39 df; $p \leq .01$). This finding is interesting in light of the fact that stable smokers scored higher on Factor H than did their matched controls. On this basis, one might also expect a difference on Factor H between users and nonusers. That such a finding was not obtained underscores the precariousness of interpretations based solely on univariate analysis. No significant multivariate difference was found between street movers/pastoralist-escapists and stable smokers on the 16 PF primary factors (Hotelling's $T^2 = 1.45$; 8 and 32 df; $p \leq .22$). Nevertheless, the fact that differences emerged when we analyzed the results of the psychological test battery by user lifestyle, especially between stable smokers and controls, suggests that there is some substance to the user lifestyle paradigm.

Discussion

The psychological phase of our research represents the most recent attempt to examine the effects of chronic marihuana use on higher brain function and personality. Considerable effort was devoted to avoiding the methodological problems hampering previous chronic studies. Subject selection was rigorous, and variables confounded in other studies—such as socioeconomic class, use of other drugs, educational level, and medical status—were controlled by careful screening and matching. The size of the matched-pair sample was sufficiently large to permit the use of more powerful multivariate statistical procedures.

In developing our testing procedures, the problem of culture-fairness was addressed as a primary issue. Initial attempts at standardization were made with a Costa Rican sample, to ensure an absence of ceiling and floor effects. This permitted the use of tests that purport to measure storage, retrieval, and organizational processes in short-term memory and that are commonly considered to be culturally biased. These we felt were vital to the neuropsychological assessment. Finally, variables relating to level and pattern of intake were investigated, so that subtle effects attributable to marihuana use would not be masked by the heterogeneity of these variables within the user group. Despite taking such precautions with regard to data analysis, sample, and test selection, we failed to uncover significant differences between user and nonuser groups—even in those subjects who had consumed cannabis for over eighteen years.

In the neuropsychological and intellectual evaluations, this absence of group differences was consistent with findings reported in chronic cannabis studies in Greece (Stefanis et al. 1977) and Jamaica (Bowman and Pihl 1973; Rubin and Comitas 1975). The fact that these studies involved different sampling and geographical groups and additional neuropsychological and intellectual tests lends support to our null results. Such null results are in clear contrast to the results of neuropsychological research on chronic alcoholics, where deficits have been found clearly apparent in many users (Tarter 1975).

In the personality area, our findings are in basic accord with those obtained in Jamaica and in controlled studies in the United States. The latter have looked into a variety of variables pertaining to personality-trait differences (Krug and Henry 1974), behavioral disturbance (Halikas 1974), and academic achievement (Hochman and Brill 1973; Mellinger et al. 1976), and include longitudinal assessments of personality change (Jessor 1976). Although the U.S. studies revealed no significant behavior disturbances that could be attributed to chronic marihuana use, personality differences between marihuana users and nonusers were apparent. Like the differences emerging from our own study and from that of Jamaica, however, those found in controlled U.S. studies did not seem to implicate cannabis use as a causative factor. Differences in family structure, socialization, and peer contact, all of which had placed potential users in contact with segments of society in which marihuana use was prevalent, were apparent in almost every case and preceded use of the drug (Halikas 1974). All this suggests that habitual cannabis use may be viewed more appropriately as an *expression* of deviance than as a *cause*. One major task awaiting future drug research is clearly that of separating personality factors which *antedate* drug use and lead a person to engage in drug use from personality factors which are *consequences* of such use.

Our results should not be taken to indicate that, in Costa Rica, marihuana use is an insignificant social or personal event with no influence on individual behavior. We have only to examine the carefully collected anthropological data for contraindicative evidence. We have seen, for example, that there are at least three different marihuana lifestyles in the country. Comparing users representative of these varying lifestyles revealed some interesting differences in personality, presumably as a function of attitudes and concerns about marihuana use itself. Thus, those users who were characterized by stable family and work histories (stable smokers) were also apparently more venturesome, liberal, suspicious, and had more superego strength than did their nonusing controls. Such findings can be directly related to the nature of marihuana use in Costa Rica. In order to employ the drug in a country where such behavior is illegal and often associated with irresponsibility, personality traits such as liberalness and venturesomeness would assist in adapting marihuana use to one's behavioral repertoire. Furthermore, to engage in this behavior successfully, that is, while maintaining good family and job relations and without police harassment, one would have to be conscientious at work and sufficiently aware of the social and legal complications so as to avoid behavior that would jeopardize a "stable" pattern of use. Thus, at least in the stable-smoker group, marihuana use was found to be related to a series of fairly coherent response styles, reflected as personality traits in the 16 PF.

We make no pretense that our findings either will be or should be taken as the final chapter on the long-term effects of cannabis use on human adaptive functions. Neuropsychological tests provide only indirect measures of higher brain functions. Further research awaits continued development in the neurosciences of more subtle techniques for directly measuring these processes. Also, neuropsychological research on higher cortical function in chronic users has been largely atheoretical. Specific tests of models of the acute influence of cannabis on the brain (e.g., Tinklenberg and Darley 1975) might reveal interesting findings in chronic users.

The possibility that subtle deficits in higher adaptive functions may be associated with chronic cannabis use cannot be excluded on the basis of current cross-cultural evidence. Such a deficit could be extremely rare or difficult to detect. No cross-cultural study has addressed satisfactorily a problem common to cancer research. Lung-function tests, in the absence of prospective studies, often reveal no differences between cigarette users and nonusers, probably because most subjects afflicted with cancer due to chronic tobacco use have previously died. When evaluating these possibilities, however, the rigorous selection procedures used in the present study must be considered.

Our field studies represent one-shot probes in which users were examined on one occasion. Follow-up studies of the same group of subjects would be extremely helpful in documenting the *process* of chronicity. Indeed, it is hoped that, increasingly, prospective longitudinal studies will command adequate funding and the dedication of qualified researchers. There is no substitute for repeat observations on the same subjects over time, preferably *before* and *after* exposure to marihuana. This type of design would settle, once and for all, the delicate issue concerning precursor variables in personality and subtle changes in brain function following chronic cannabis use.

10 / Cannabis: Cause or Correlate?

Because of the complexity of marihuana use, the contradictions that presently surround our understanding of it, and the fact that strong opinions are held both for and against the drug, studies which include both sociocultural and medical research yield insights that could not be obtained through the pursuit of either alone. Although the literature on the drug is enormous, most falls into one of only five categories: its pharmacognosy, studies of acute pharmacological effects in animals and man; surveys of "institutional" populations such as prisoners or university students; journalistic and impressionistic accounts of users; and attempts to summarize and synthesize the literature. Few studies have attempted to examine the long-term effects of marihuana in a natural setting, combining both social science and biomedical approaches, and rarely has sufficient attention been paid to the impact of the cultural context and the need for adequate control groups. Most studies limit consideration of such matters to one or two variables: age, sex, occupation, or race. Compounding these problems is the tendency for opinion- and policy-makers, when they attempt to draw conclusions from the results of research, to ignore or only casually mention the implications of sampling procedures. Thus we find small-scale studies treated as seriously as large-scale studies, and studies that pay no attention to the sampling problem treated as seriously as those in which sampling and control procedures were scrupulously developed (NIDA 1974: 114; Maugh 1974: 683).

The importance of the cultural dimension in drug use, and the difficulty of locating, in the United States, a population of chronic marihuana smokers who were not at the same time poly-drug users, led us to choose Costa Rica as our research site. We worked there in a metropolitan, urban setting among a lower-class population that exceeded in size the population of any similar study in either the United States or abroad.

In addressing ourselves to the numerous hypotheses advanced by others, we paid close attention to the sociocultural setting and to sampling problems, and we used a broadly gauged methodology emanating from a variety of disciplines. Thus, we explicitly attempted to overcome the weaknesses of previous studies and to address ourselves to the traditional criticism of cross-cultural research. The anthropological team that developed the study sample and carried out the sociocultural studies was widely experienced in both Latin American and urban research. The medical and psychological personnel were binational, and the clinical work was undertaken by the Costa Rican team. The choice of Costa Rica as our research setting proved to be a happy one. Officials were remarkably cooperative, professionals were highly skilled, and the population of users was nearly ideal in that their use was heavy, long, and unmixed with other drugs save only alcohol and tobacco.

Though chronic users abound among the Costa Rican working class, the history of cannabis in the country is a shallow one. What sparse documentation does exist indicates that the drug was introduced less than one hundred years ago, very likely through groups of railroad construction laborers who were brought from Panama in the 1880s after de Lesseps had abandoned the French plans for an Isthmean canal. Chinese and Jamaican members of this labor group were reputed to have planted and smoked cannabis soon after arriving in Costa Rica. During the same period, there were some scattered attempts to establish a fiber industry based on hemp, but these projects never flourished. Historically, there has been some use of cannabis as a medicinal plant, mainly for treatment of asthma. Presently the drug is used, mainly in cigarette form, by a broad cross section of the working-class population in urban areas and to some extent in coastal banana plantations.

Although an undetermined amount is imported from Panama, Colombia, and Mexico, most marihuana used in Costa Rica is grown in the country itself. Production occurs in scattered plots in the tropical lowlands of the country, generally in remote areas. The crop is brought to market in a variety of ways, usually in small and large quantities of picadura, the chopped leaves and flowers of the plants. The picadura is later rolled into cigarettes by urban wholesalers and retailers. Yellow wheat paper is most commonly used for this purpose. Despite attempts of the Costa Rican government dating back to the 1920s to control the substance, marihuana is readily available to users. Attempts at control since 1970 have included the establishment of a special narcotics police unit. Confiscations and arrests have not produced any notable deterrent to production or use of the drug but have caused the price to consumers to fluctuate.

The potency of Costa Rican marihuana was tested by sending thirteen street samples collected over a two-year period to United States' laboratories for analysis under special permit from the Costa Rican and United States governments. THC content of the samples varied from 1.27 to 3.72 percent by weight. Since in Costa Rica marihuana cigarettes are generally sold in "rolls" of twenty-five that average close to five grams each, a single standard joint would contain about 200 milligrams of material. Users in our sample smoked a mean of 9.6 cigarettes a day (median of 7 and range of 2.5 to 40). On occasion, however, we observed a single individual going through as many as eighty in a twenty-four-hour period.

The average Costa Rican user in the sample had smoked regularly for 16.9 years. Since he smoked about ten cigarettes a day, he was exposed to less Delta 9 THC (about 40 mg) than his Moroccan, Indian, or Egyptian counterparts. The heaviest user in our sample, however, smoking an average of forty cigarettes a day, had a level of Delta 9 THC exposure on a par with heavy hashish smokers in Morocco and India and as reported among United States military personnel in Europe at 160 milligrams per day.

Costa Rican interest in and knowledge about marihuana has risen sharply since 1968, coinciding with a general rise in interest in Europe and North America. Prior to 1968, the country's most pressing drug problem was considered to be alcoholism and the illegal production of alcohol. Today, most accept that it is marihuana.

This change in public attitude reflects a perceived increase in marihuana use by young people of the middle and upper classes on an occasional recreational basis. Fears about possible deleterious effects of marihuana smoking have been and are regularly fueled by sensationalist newspaper reports and by the fact that what was traditionally assumed to be just a lower-class trait and associated with undesirable behavior is now being more widely accepted.

There is little evidence that heroin, cocaine, and similar substances are used much in Costa Rica. Police and Ministry of Health records show that 98 percent of all arrests and drug seizures, aside from those for illegal alcohol, concern marihuana. Estimates and studies show, however, that clandestine production and consumption of unlicensed cane alcohol equals that officially sanctioned and that alcoholism is a major social and economic problem, especially among the working-class population. Tobacco use in Costa Rica is also widespread; the vast majority of Costa Rican men are tobacco smokers.

Longtime marihuana users accept its use as harmless and acceptable behavior and regard the recently developed public attitudes about marihuana use as unjust. In contrast, nonusers accept, without question, the pejorative assertions made in the news media about the drug.

THE STUDY SAMPLE

Our subjects were all permanent residents of metropolitan San José, capital of Costa Rica and a city of some 437,000 inhabitants. They were all male, lived in forty-five of the city's working-class residential *barrios,* and constituted a stratified and purposive sample, since random procedures were impossible due to the illegality of the drug.

During the first year of the study, 84 users and 156 nonusers were chosen and studied, sociocultural and biomedical interviews and examinations being conducted with each. During the second year, a subsample of 41 users and 41 matched nonusers was chosen for in-depth studies in several areas of inquiry. Matches were made on the basis of six characteristics: occupation, educational level, marital status, age, and levels of tobacco and alcohol consumption. In this fashion, many environmental and social factors were controlled (see Table 1).

In terms of income, the base sample of 84 users and 156 nonusers represented all but the lowest and highest deciles of San José's population and, in average socioeconomic status, ranked in the middle of the working class. Its range of occupations was typical of urban economic life: 24 subjects were in commerce, 32 in transportation, 129 were in artisanal or building trades, and the rest were in service occupations. As a group, the subjects tended to earn a little less than the average incomes projected for their *barrios,* but their incomes fell entirely within normal ranges.

In terms of social characteristics, the sample was remarkably homogeneous. Users were differentiated* from nonusers in only ten of fifty-four variables examined in the initial phase of the study. There were no significant differences with respect to religion, political activity, educational levels achieved, involvement in work as children, present family structure, unemployment, family size, or numbers of children produced. Initial differences were found with respect to earning capacity (users earned slightly less), arrests (users had been arrested more frequently), imprisonment (users had been in jail and the reformatory more often), and in family of socialization (more users had been reared by surrogate parents).

The matched pairs derived from this original sample largely reflected the patterns of the larger group. As we came to know them better as individuals, however, we discovered that similarity in structure often disguised dissimilarity in content. Detailed knowledge of this content came only after intensive work with the eighty-two individuals comprising the matched-pair population.

CHILDHOOD AND FAMILY

Early family structure of future users and nonusers was basically similar. Its rural origins were evident in behavior patterns such as early work for children and close extended-kin relationships. These relationships carried over into the city, where social life concentrated on extended family ties much more than on neighbors and other *barrio* residents, with relatives often living in the same or adjacent *barrios* and even next door to one another.

The average size for the families of orientation of both groups was about five, a number that generally included both parents. Although many kinsmen were present from time to time, in terms of long-term patterns each family tended to remain economically independent, receiving assistance from relatives only in crisis situations, and then only to a limited extent. Although most fathers regularly worked and supported their families, mothers tended to be the dominant social figures during childhood, and many worked full-time, especially those whose sons later became marihuana users. In general, most subjects of both groups felt that their childhood and homelife had been satisfactory and that they had been fairly treated, even spoiled. Most had begun some type of work by the age of twelve.

The typical family of both groups was not involved in community affairs, showed little interest in religion, and was seldom concerned with politics. In spite of their command of primary loyalties, families socialized and celebrated their kinship and common life only to limited degrees. Few meals were eaten together, seldom were friends brought home, and family parties occurred only at Christmas or an occasional birthday. Males developed their lives outside the home, the result being that their social networks were largely independent of

---

*Statistically significant differences $p \leq .05$.

family ties. Females, especially mothers, held the home together. In keeping with this key role, mothers were idolized and revered.

These, then, were the similarities. But there were differences that very early in the life cycle began clearly to separate future users from future nonusers. In other words, specific clusters of circumstances and experiences seem to have predisposed certain individuals toward marihuana use during the first years of their existence. These tended to be circumstances and experiences that led to marginality and psychic or physical stress. Thus, more users than nonusers grew up in the city. More left their parental home, and at an earlier age. More suffered from inadequate diet and housing. More had mothers who worked full- or part-time outside the home and who either controlled or helped control the family finances. More had abstemious mothers. More had fathers who were inactive in community life and who failed to assume any role of leadership. More had siblings who were given preferential treatment. And more came from families that were downwardly mobile. More also related poorly to basic institutions of socialization, such as school and church. More engaged in mischievous behavior at school, had a high rate of absences, and were expelled. More users than nonusers engaged, as children—and before the onset of marihuana use—in delinquency such as petty theft, and fewer worked full-time.

One of the most significant findings was that 36.6 percent of the users had been sentenced to the reformatory, as opposed to 0.0 percent of the nonusers. This suggests strongly that the reformatory itself must have contributed to the development of the marihuana habit. It seems striking that, although 17.1 percent of the nonusers spoke of committing delinquent acts during adolescence, not a single one was sentenced to the reformatory. Of the users who committed such acts, 83.3 percent were sentenced. It may be that, *because* of their use, users were early pursued by the authorities, for being designated as *"marihuanos"* would have made them vulnerable police subjects. And their problems would have been compounded by their leaving home—a step taken by the majority by at least mid-adolescence. One whose primary reference group is other street youth is vulnerable in the extreme.

We see, then, that even before reaching adolescence, users were developing along different lines than nonusers. By and large, they were individuals who came from weakly constituted families, who had absent and moralistic mothers, who suffered from disciplinary inconsistencies and sibling rivalry, who lived in poverty, and who had begun to have serious problems with the major institutions of society such as schools and other formal organizations. Yet there is no clear pattern indicating that marihuana led to these problems. The opposite, in fact, would seem to be the case. Of those nine users who left home at age twelve or earlier, eight began smoking after taking that crucial step, and one began simultaneously. Of those who left home between thirteen and sixteen years of age, six were already smoking, six began at the time they left home, and three began smoking later. None said that their reason for leaving home was marihuana use; most cited economic problems.

What these figures clearly indicate is that, rather than being a cause of marginality and stress, marihuana use is the result. Other differences between the early lives of users and nonusers serve only to reinforce this conclusion. Whereas only 29 percent of users stayed with their parents until marriage or never left their parental home, some 66 percent of nonusers did so. In contrast to nonusers, then, most users were on their own by the time they were in their late teens, independent of family ties and responsible only to themselves. That they valued such independence seems confirmed by the fact that, quite different from nonusers, they seldom married in their teens.

Because many identical experiences and circumstances appear when we consider alcohol consumption instead of marihuana use, it seems evident that these conditions led to drug use, and not vice versa. Childhood experiences of men who, at the time of our research, were moderate and heavy drinkers closely resembled those of the marihuana-user population. Heavy and moderate drinkers were significantly more inclined, as children, to have been unruly in school, to have had frequent fights, to have been excessively absent from classes, to have been indulged at home, and to have been generally unhappy. They tended to have had an early hostility to authority and institutional controls and to have abandoned their parental home significantly earlier than those who became light drinkers or abstainers. Why some individuals with troubled early lives turned to alcohol while others turned to marihuana is not clear, however. In the urban ambience of San José both of these options were readily accessible. The difference between them was that inebriation was not illegal and thus offered no risks, whereas marihuana use was the opposite.

During the adolescence of all subjects, whether users or nonusers, peer groups constituted important social alternatives to home life and school life. Most boys had "run" with street gangs and cliques at one time or another, but users had clearly been more committed to such activity. Generally, such peer groups had assumed primary importance among those who left home; they literally had become the school of hard knocks, where individuals acquired social habits and experiences not taught in other institutional arrangements. Thus the street was the classroom for models of drinking behavior, sexual relations, marihuana smoking, street-survival techniques, and occupations, where experimentation was encouraged in employment, sex, and personal "style."

ADULTHOOD

Despite the tendency of nonusers to gain regular employment earlier, the work profile of the subjects in both groups during adulthood was, in some ways, similar. For both groups, the average at the onset of regular work, either full- or part-time, had been twelve years. The need to work in the support of their families was the principal reason given by both groups for leaving school. All subjects had been involved in a variety of trades and jobs through time.

Significant differences in job histories were numerous, however. Users changed jobs more frequently and had been forced into more part-time or temporary employment, or even unemployment. Users also had longer periods of unemployment, enjoyed fewer salary raises and promotions, and were significantly more likely to have engaged in extralegal activities to supplement their low income. They had fewer debts, saved less money, and were less likely to own substantial material goods than nonusers.

Although users were slightly different with respect to their greater involvement in consensual unions, their families of procreation were, in general, similar in structure to those of nonusers. Both* had the same average number of children (2.6), although users tended to have somewhat longer lasting relationships with their wives or consensual mates than did nonusers. Users also tended to help their spouses in the home more than did nonusers. In general, both nourished hopes that their offspring would enjoy an equal or better socioeconomic status than their own.

More users than nonusers lived in apartments. They also tended to move their residences more often than did nonusers and to spend more free time with their friends and less with their families. As a general rule, they were less involved in formal institutions than were nonusers and thus less likely to be leaders in any kind of organization, less likely to participate in political clubs, and less likely to attend church.

During their adult life, users were detained, jailed, and involved in legal entanglements more than nonusers. Since their use of the illegal drug clearly made them more vulnerable, understandably more users than nonusers viewed the legal system as unjust and expressed a general distrust of other people.

The overall picture that emerges with respect to users, then, is one of an accumulation of negative experiences: childhood problems with authority, unhappy home lives, early entry into street life, reform school, arrests, increased vulnerability to police activity, lack of regular employment and advancement, and a haunting sense of inferiority *vis-à-vis* their siblings. The pattern these men were developing in their adult life was replicating, in large part, that from which they had suffered as children. They were offering weak role models for their own offspring, taking little part in civic and community life and tending to delegate the management of household finances to their wives. They were also spending more of their free time outside the home than were nonusers.

But users did not present a uniform pattern in all these respects. Street movers were those who most differed from nonusers. Stable smokers, however, who constituted the majority of the user sample, were characterized by family situations, patterns of employment, income, debt, and accumulation of material possessions very similar to those of the nonusers. This provides a further convincing indication that circumstances and personal experiences, rather than drug use *per se,* were the primary cause of the marginal behavior of the street movers.

MARIHUANA USE

In examining the effects and circumstances of marihuana use among the user population, we found that the typology used of stable smokers, street movers, and pastoralist-escapists was an important one. Stable smokers had a mean age of 33.9; street movers of 28.1; and pastoralist-escapists of only 22.5 Each of these three types favored a specific smoking environment. Stable

*In the matched-pair sample.

smokers liked to smoke at home or on the job, street movers on street corners in a group, and pastoralist-escapists in secluded rural settings.

Of the user group as a whole, 9.8 percent preferred to smoke with relatives, 48.8 percent with friends, 19.6 percent with work companions, and only 9 percent alone. Most appeared to be reclusive and timid rather than defiant in their attitudes toward use. At most, 29 percent of the sample could be identified as open flaunters of Costa Rican societal and legal conventions. For the most part, users were cautious about people and places around which they smoked.

Thirty-nine different effects were described by one or another of the users. Each tended to be associated with a specific type of environment. For example, "physical effects" tended to be associated with "home alone" environments, "increased appetite" with home or boardinghouse environments, and "muerte blanca," or panic reaction, with the insecurity and fear of open street smoking. Generally, users said that marihuana smoking helped them get to sleep. Most also said that it increased their appetite for food and enjoyment of sex. Approximately three fourths reported that it helped them work better, one of the major reasons given for marihuana use. Uncontrollable mirth, so often described by other user populations, was cited infrequently as a reaction—only 10 times out of a total of 516 citations. Euphoria was spoken of 27 times, generally in connection with the most popular smoking environments: street alone, home alone, and street with group. When asked what they liked to do best while smoking marihuana, twenty-seven of the forty-one in the user group talked of engaging in active sports, recreation, or work, and seven spoke of doing things with friends. Only seven mentioned preferring passive behavior, a contrast to a common effect of marihuana smoking reported by U.S. users.

In comparing marihuana with alcohol, users overwhelmingly claimed that the former was superior because in their view it was not physically harmful and, rather than making them more aggressive, it calmed their nerves. In contrast to the depression and confusion caused by alcohol, they felt that marihuana improved conversation and led to clearer thought and deeper insights.

Just as we found there was a clear relationship between context and effect, so we found an equally clear relationship between effect and user type. Physical effects were cited in significantly higher frequencies by stable smokers, and appetite and bad-trip effects were cited more frequently by street movers. The latter seemed to look to marihuana for escape from their ordinary routine. Stable smokers, on the other hand, had established a way of life which included marihuana use as part of their everyday routine: instead of using it to escape from their preoccupations, they perceived it as an amenity to make their routine more bearable or satisfactory.

All three types of users agreed that the mixture of marihuana with alcohol could generate effects very different from those of either alone. Such mixture, known as "crossing the cables," was believed to lead usually to unpleasant experiences.

Most users had begun regular smoking of marihuana during late childhood or adolescence ($\bar{X}$ = 15.2 years). Seventy-five percent had been initiated to the drug by persons older than themselves, in most cases members of their street-side peer groups. The fact that many suffered bad trips with their first marihuana experiences had not discouraged them from trying again or from developing into chronic users. Not a single user claimed that marihuana had been harmful in his life. Nor did any user see any relationship between his own well-being, social mobility, and use of the drug.

Complete school records could be found for only seven of the forty-one matched pairs in the subsample. These records showed no differences in school performance which could be related to use of the drug. Users who had began smoking marihuana while still students claimed unanimously that it had helped them in school. In no case did marihuana use appear to have been a cause for school dropout or failures. Although users more consistently remembered that they had been unruly in school, this was not reflected in the documented performance of the seven matched pairs for whom records could be found. Nor was there a significant difference in these seven pairs with regard to the number of years of school attempted or completed.

If marihuana use leads to poorer social adjustment, irresponsible behavior, and lack of motivation, one would expect that the heavier the use the greater such problems would be. The opposite, however, turned out to be the case. The heavier the use, the more stable the employment record was, the fewer the periods of unemployment were, and the more likelihood there was that the user was enjoying the benefits of a long-term, full-time job. Heavy users were more likely to engage in deficit spending than light users, but they also owned significantly more material goods, in this respect paralleling the practices of the nonusing group and following a pattern common to other ambitious, working-class Costa Ricans. Part of the affluence of heavier users would appear to be attributable to the fact that they were more involved in illegal or extralegal economic activity than were lighter users, much of this illegal activity involving the distribution of marihuana and thus offering greater accessibility to the drug as well as to higher earnings.

When the three basic lifestyles of users were cross-tabulated with specific sociocultural variables, some highly significant correlations emerged. Street movers and pastoralist-escapists were on their own in childhood earlier and more frequently than were stable smokers. Street movers and pastoralist-escapists claimed to have been more rowdy in school, to have engaged more frequently in illegal and rebellious behavior such as vandalism and theft, and, during adolescence, to have held significantly fewer steady jobs. By comparison with stable smokers, street movers and pastoralist-escapists were experiencing significantly less upward mobility as adults, less full-time employment, more frequent unemployment, and longer periods of unemployment. The employment records of stable smokers resembled those of nonusers. Understandably, stable smokers claimed—more frequently than did street movers—that marihuana has positive effects on work.

In sum, among our user sample, marihuana smoking had begun in adolescence, and its initiation had usually been related to periods of transition and stress. The vast majority of users had serious adjustment problems long before they began to use marihuana. These problems had been more serious with future street movers than with future pastoralist-escapists or stable smokers. In fact, so overwhelmingly had the most serious problems been experienced by the street-mover group that we can say that most significant differences between users and nonusers in the work history were due to the inclusion of street movers in the matched-pair subsample. Street movers, however, constituted less than 50 percent of the user sample. Most marihuana smokers in our matched-pair sample were stable smokers, "invisible," solid, productive citizens.

We see, in this carefully controlled sample population, that the numerous significant differences found in adult behavior between users and nonusers are highly correlated with different kinds of socialization experiences. The vast majority of these antedated marihuana use and more adequately explain the differences found in the two groups today than does marihuana use itself. This supports similar findings from studies of user populations in the United States (NIDA 1974: 13; Halikas et al. 1971: 692–694), where longitudinal studies of high school and college youth indicate that probability of use can be predicted by variables such as attitudes approving deviance, lack of religious participation and involvement, social support for drug use, friends' approval of use, deviant behavior, and more intensive petting behavior (Jessor et al. 1973: 5–15). All these variables, except possibly "petting" (the higher incidence of syphilis among users does suggest greater promiscuity), coincide strikingly with the preconditions we observed in the childhood and adolescence of future chronic users in San José.

Another common finding in U.S. studies is that students reporting delinquent behavior are more likely to use marihuana than those not reporting such behavior (Johnston 1973). The Costa Rican data are superficially similar. As we have already seen, however, delinquency and other antisocial behavior on the part of users may be explained solely by early life experiences, without the need to introduce marihuana as an explanatory factor.

The fact that marihuana use among working-class males in San José is invariably learned in the street also coincides with the findings of several studies previously reported. In these studies, peers rather than parents are the important influence on an individual's attitude toward the drug (NIDA 1974: 23; Kandel 1978). Yet it cannot be said that, as in the United States, "the greater the involvement with marihuana, the greater the likelihood that those with whom one associates are also marihuana users, and, therefore, the more justified one is in expecting tolerance towards one's own marihuana use" (NIDA 1974: 23; Fisher 1972: 9–10; 1973: 5–12). Style of use among Costa Ricans varies greatly. Some of the heaviest users are stable family men who live much to themselves and who smoke in solitude. All users are in constant contact with nonusers through their personal social networks. We did not find any compulsion among users to reduce such contacts.

Many studies have spoken to the issue of drug-use proneness among marihuana smokers. Smith (1974) found that children who were regular cigarette smokers were more likely than nonsmokers to use marihuana later. Also, an earlier, nationwide study of high school students found that those who use marihuana were more likely to use alcohol and other psychoactive drugs than were their non-drug-using peers (Johnston 1973). The 1974 NIDA report on marihuana and health repeatedly states that the more heavily a user smokes marihuana, the greater the probability he has used or will use other drugs.

Among Costa Rican working-class men we found similar relationships. Heavy marihuana users tended to be heavy tobacco users as well, and many also used alcohol heavily. The fact that, in our final sample, users and nonusers were matched for tobacco and alcohol consumption meant that, during analysis of the life-history materials, no significant differences emerged in this respect. But, in building that sample, the field anthropologists had great difficulty finding non-marihuana-using controls because of the heavy tobacco and alcohol consumption of many members of the user group.

One thing not confirmed by the Costa Rican data is the movement from marihuana to other drugs such as amphetamines, barbiturates, heroin, LSD, and cocaine. Although these substances were available, users showed little interest in them. Nor does there appear to have been much use of more potent cannabis substances. The reason given by users was that they could simply smoke more marihuana if they wanted stronger effects.

Another finding from U.S. studies that is questioned by the Costa Rican data is that the greater involvement with marihuana, the greater the need to perceive others as involved and hence the greater the likelihood to expect tolerant reactions from others (NIDA 1974). The attitude of a sizable minority of Costa Rican users (39 percent) was definitely ambivalent. Although they continued to use the drug, they did not uncritically justify its use. Many clearly stated that marihuana was preferable to alcohol but that it would be better to use neither, and their hope was that their children would abstain from both.

Another finding from the United States *not* confirmed by the Costa Rican materials is that of parental influence on use. It was observed in the United States that the highest rates of marihuana usage were found among adolescents whose parents—particularly mothers—had been drug users (Kandel 1978). We were unsuccessful in obtaining hard data on use of prescription drugs among the parents of our subject group, but we did obtain data on use of tobacco, alcohol, and illicit drugs. No differences emerged with regard to fathers, but in the case of mothers, there were two. There was a statistically significant trend ($p = .02$) for the mothers of future marihuana users to abstain totally from alcohol, and there was a nearly significant trend ($p = .07$) for them to abstain from tobacco as well. Only one mother was reported to have used marihuana. Other statistically significant and possibly related trends were that mothers of future users were more likely to work full-time outside the home and to be capricious in rewards and sanctions to their children.

Reasons Costa Rican users gave for using marihuana were to some degree like those given by U.S. users. As with their U.S. counterparts, Costa Rican users tended to have low self-esteem and a high level of experience and adventure-seeking (Baskett and Nysewander 1973). And as in the United States, Costa Rican users sought, through the drug, attainment of a state of well-being, instant achievement, relaxation, easier social interaction, avoidance of boredom, psychological support for dealing with pain and discomfort, rebellion or rejection of parental values, a search for purpose, a way for organizing experience, an aphrodisiac, and an adaptation to life (NIDA 1974: 23–24). One thing they did *not* seek was mystical or religious experience.

In all, Costa Rican users attributed thirty-nine effects to the drug. Each was differentially related to setting and user's lifestyle, and together they were perceived in a very different order of popularity or hierarchy from that found among U.S. users. Many of these effects were variations of heightened perception. Marihuana was said to enhance one's enjoyment of food, sex, work, music, conversation, and even involvement in physically active sports. This may reflect a real physiological response. The sensation of heightened, selective perception has been frequently reported by U.S. users and is receiving increasing validation from the findings of electroencephalographic research (NIDA 1974: 10).

Although some users reported that marihuana was impairing their short-term memory processes, this was *not* confirmed by the neuropsychological battery. Lack of agreement between the test results and user perception may be attributable to the fact that users were reporting their *acute* reactions whereas the test battery was designed and administered to measure *chronic* effects. No hard data were obtained regarding the effect of marihuana use on driving ability. However, some of the user subjects did earn their living by driving trucks, buses, or taxis, and some preferred to drive while under the influence of the drug. Although many subjects attributed greatly increased appetites to marihuana use, the nutritional studies uncovered *no* significant differences in food intake between users and nonusers.

Many other studies have dealt with the effect of marihuana on human aggression. The general conclusion is that, unlike alcohol, marihuana suppresses aggressiveness, dominance, and competition among all nonstressed animals, man included (NIDA 1974: 8, 80, 61). A large body of anecdotal material consistent with this conclusion was provided by our user subjects. Some had turned from alcohol to marihuana specifically to become less aggressive. But there would appear to have been sociocultural precedents. As a group, marihuana smokers had had significantly fewer fights during adolescence than moderate and heavy alcohol users.

Because no time-motion studies were made, it is impossible to say whether there was an increasing depression of work output at successively higher levels of marihuana use. However, a clear inverse relationship was found to exist between stability of work and level of use. The heaviest users had the highest incomes, the least unemployment, and the most stable job histories of the entire user group. They also more frequently reported that their preferred activity while intoxicated was to work.

As with Jamaicans who used the drug primarily as a work adjunct, Costa Rican users did not usually report the "high" sought by American recreational users. Not a single user reported hallucinations, although many did report a panic reaction known locally as "white death," related not to level or potency of dosage but to the physical and psychological state of the victim. Treatment was purely physical—a high-sugar-content drink—and recovery was quick and assured. The quick recovery is reminiscent of that reported by Chopra and Smith for victims of "Cannabis psychosis" in Calcutta, India (Chopra and Smith 1974).

There was a great deal of anecdotal evidence for the buildup of tolerance. Well-experienced users never fell victim to "white death." Instead, they described in considerable detail how they had learned to handle the drug. The heaviest user, averaging forty marihuana cigarettes per day, managed a very successful business with eight employees.

No reports or observations of withdrawal symptoms were collected. Users, even those who had stopped marihuana use for varying periods of time because of lack of funds, travel, or imprisonment, categorically denied that they ever occurred. They contrasted the lack of such symptoms in the case of marihuana with their presence in the case of alcohol and tobacco.

Overall, very few subjectively perceived adverse effects were reported or observed over the two-year period. The most common of such effects described in the extant literature are pathological intoxication, acute cannabis psychoses, subacute and chronic cannabis psychoses, and residual conditions including flashbacks (Negrete 1973). Only two such conditions were observed or self-reported for the user population: pathological intoxication ("white death"), and flashback (reported very rarely). There was absolutely *no* indication of severe intoxication, acute cannabis psychoses, or subacute and chronic cannabis psychoses, in spite of heavy, prolonged usage of fairly potent material. Nor was there a single report of "freaking out," that is, being overcome by an outside force or will that was evil or hostile in intent (Tart and Crawford 1970: 701–704).

In areas of personal and social life, marihuana use was not shown to result in behavior that impaired the individual's ability to function as a regular member of his society. The significant differences found between users and nonusers tended to have their roots in events antedating marihuana use. Where deviant behavior was encountered, marihuana appeared to be more a correlate than a cause.

As found among working-class men in San José, marihuana use would seem to function, then, largely as a device to cope with daily routines and problems. In sociocultural terms, the basic problem deriving from use would be police harassment and possible imprisonment. Secondary problems would be the financial drain caused by the cost of an illegal substance, and the type of peer group with which one associates when he engages in illegal behavior. We found no other clear evidence of marihuana-caused interference in the normal functioning of adult, working-class males.

PHYSICAL AND PSYCHIC HEALTH

Among the original sample of 84 users and 156 nonusers, gastrointestinal complaints were more common in the former than in the latter, as were symptoms of frequency of urination. Marihuana smokers more often used other drugs of abuse such as barbiturates and vaporizing substances, but their overall level of use was quite low. Although the differences were minimal and both groups were within normal limits, users yielded lower means for weight and systolic blood pressure. Pterygium was present in more users than nonusers, as was atrophy of one testis, though the latter was attributable to mumps or trauma in all but one of the users so affected and in all the nonusers. Users had more surgical scars than did nonusers, but specific causes for the scars were not determined.

Differences in clinical laboratory findings were minimal between users and nonusers in the base sample. Users tended toward lower levels of hemoglobin and hematocrit, a finding that merits further study. The other minor differences in laboratory findings—prolonged prothrombin times and lower serum globulin in the users—though not previously found in either acute or chronic studies, would also merit further research.

Chest X-ray and standard electrocardiograms revealed no significant pathological patterns among the marihuana users which would distinguish them from the control group. Patterns of infestation with intestinal parasites were similar in both groups. A basic measure of cell-mediated immunity, the eosinophilic response to parasitic infestation, was no less vigorous in the users than in the controls.

These initial health-screening data from 240 subjects were reanalyzed for those subjects comprising the matched-pair sample of forty-one users and forty-one controls. The only major physiological differences to emerge were that two-hour postprandial glucose levels were significantly higher in the forty-one users than in the controls. The values of both groups, however, were within the normal range. Subsequent five-hour glucose-tolerance tests on five of the matched pairs failed to reveal significant differences. Our overall conclusions were that in this matched-pair sample there was no demonstrable impairment of glucose metabolism.

Although detailed visual-function studies failed to demonstrate clinically significant differences between users and nonusers, there was an array of findings in users which suggested increased irritation of the anterior segment of the eye. These included photosensitivity, decreased dark adaptation, decreased visual acuity using the Snellen test, and decreased acuity at different levels of illumination. Because the findings were not statistically significant as a group, further studies on chronic cannabis users will be required before firm conclusions can be drawn. It may be that any increased irritation of the anterior segment of the eye is due simply to exposure to a greater amount of smoke *per se*.

Sleep electroencephalographic studies revealed very few differences. Rapid eye movement periods, percentage of total sleep time in Stage 1 REM, and sleep-latency time were significantly longer in users than in nonusers, and night-to-night variability in sleep patterns was greater. None of the deviations in users was outside the range of normal, however. Deviations were distinctly *less* abnormal than those demonstrated among heavy alcohol users.

Studies of ventilatory function in the entire matched-pair sample and of pulmonary parenchymal function in a subsample of twenty pairs yielded no significant differences between users and nonusers. Although there was a tendency for users to have milder airways changes than their controls, there was physiological evidence of bronchitis in both groups.

No difference in plasma testosterone levels was found between the user and nonuser groups. Nor could we discover any correlation between heavier marihuana use and lower testosterone levels. Not even unilateral testicular atrophy appeared to affect the levels. Men having one healthy testis enjoyed levels as high as those having two.

There was no difference between the users and the nonusers in total nutrition or in the various nutritional elements. However, wide variations occurred within each group from subject to subject.

No significant univariate or multivariate differences were found on the sixteen variables derived from the neuropsychological test battery. The results of memory, somatosensory-perceptual intelligence, and personality tests were strikingly similar for the two groups. Users had slightly lower performance on the neuropsychological tests and slightly higher performance on the intelligence subtests, but in neither battery were these differences statistically significant.

Further analysis of the neuropsychological test data in search of differences possibly related to level and type of use also failed to reveal significant differences. However, reanalysis of the 16 PF did document some personality differences between street movers and stable smokers that tended to support the validity of our characterization of their two rather distinct lifestyles.

Marihuana and Life Processes: Some Unanswered Questions

No single study can provide all the answers, but it can offer insights for the evaluation of previous research and point the way for hypotheses to be tested in the future.

Because of the importance of family behavior and environment in determining marihuana use, the role of women should receive far more attention than it has in the past. The experience of Costa Rican users suggests that women are of critical relevance during the early stages of the life cycle and that these stages directly affect all subsequent ones.

Psychological and biomedical studies of women users continue to be rare. Had we looked at females instead of males, would our results have been substantially different? Only by doing so at some future date will we know the answer.

One of our principal objectives was to identify gross or subtle changes in major body and central nervous system functions which could be attributable to marihuana. We failed to do so.

Some of our results, however, do suggest directions for additional research. The lower body weights of subjects in the base sample correspond with a like trend in the Jamaican study. Research by Mendelson, Rossi, and Meyer (1974), showing regular gains in weight over a three-week period of regular use, suggests that fluid retention was the cause. Does longer use bring about such tolerance that fluid retention no longer occurs? The relationship between body weight, carbohydrate metabolism, and insulin activity in chronic users is still far from clear.

Why does chronic inhalation of marihuana smoke not exert synergistic effects on the damage to small airways caused by tobacco smoke? Users in our matched-pair sample smoked marihuana *in addition to* as many tobacco cigarettes as did their matched nonusing pairs. Yet their small airways were, if anything, a bit healthier than their matches. We must tentatively conclude either that marihuana has no harmful effect on such passages or that it actually offers some slight protection against harmful effects of tobacco smoke. Only further research will clarify which, if either, is the case.

The absence of effects on plasma testosterone levels, procreative ability, and sexual potence suggests that impairment of sexual function caused by long-term marihuana use must be subtle if it exists at all. But the final answer will come only after more careful and more detailed studies of the matter have been made.

If marihuana use persists in individuals of older ages, another series of questions arise. What is the effect of such use on individuals with those common chronic diseases for which there is as yet no cure? Arteriosclerotic heart disease, peripheral vascular disease, chronic lung disease, the common cancers of lung, breast, and colon, and diabetes will in the future be as great a cause for concern in the developing countries as they are now in the industrial nations of Europe, North America, and the Far East.

The Costa Rican data cast in doubt any relation between chronic use and higher cortical functions. But could there be subtle deficits that would become apparent after even longer years of continued use? Only longitudinal research could give the answer.

Given the climate of debate in the United States today, one of our most difficult tasks is to look at the whole matter of psychotropic drugs objectively. From our Puritan past we have inherited a tradition of duality. Things and actions are good or bad. People are either saints or sinners, and problems can be brought under control through simple prohibition. The reality we face, however, is far more complex. Whether we like it or not, we are dealing with many shadings of gray, and into this amorphous category falls the question of marihuana.

How we handle this substance in our society is of concern to us all. Of those psychotropic drugs considered illegal by our courts and codes, marihuana is the one most widely used. Its popularity is such that, among some elements of our society, the law is openly flaunted by the majority.

In the politicized and emotionally charged atmosphere surrounding marihuana use, far too much research has been marred by the predetermined stances of the researchers. Much that claims to be research is barely above polemics. Fully aware of this problem, we tried to look as objectively as possible at the consequences of long-term, heavy use. We employed natural as well as clinical settings, and used an unprecedented number of carefully matched subjects. Our measures were as thoughtfully chosen as we could make them. None of us who directed the project had any preconceived notions as to what we might find. We were entering a new field of research and were willing and anxious to accept any data or insights that might emerge.

Many of us were frankly surprised that we were unable to uncover any real consequences of prolonged use of the drug. Indeed, some of the physicians and psychologists on our team were sincerely disappointed at the lack of significant differences between our controlled population of users and nonusers. Their first reaction was that they would have nothing to say, and this they found frustrating after the enormous amount of effort and time they had invested.

But *no* findings in science are in themselves findings—indeed, findings of the most important type. For years, those of us who made up the research team had assimilated the pseudoscientific reports of the popular press to the effect that marihuana use, over time, could lead to a frightening array of deleterious effects. We had, frankly, expected to find at least *some* of these in our research. Yet the fact that we did not is entirely in keeping with results of the only other serious studies of chronic effects in which intervening sociocultural variables have been properly controlled—namely, those studies carried out in Greece and Jamaica. Had we looked at almost any other substance, alcohol for instance, we would have found more effects than we found with marihuana.

We cannot scientifically take our nil results as final, for techniques change and future researchers will undoubtedly ask different questions. We have ever present the realization that years of research were carried on before scientists concluded overwhelmingly that tobacco was a harmful substance. Yet, on the basis of our research we are convinced that if chronic marihuana use leads, in the long run, to deleterious effects, these must be subtle indeed.

One thing our research does clearly show is the difficulty of separating sociocultural determinants from physiological determinants. We ask ourselves how much of the supposed effects of drugs in our society today are really the result of peculiar sociocultural or idiosyncratic conditions. Far too much research in the field of drugs has been based on subjects picked randomly from the streets or from a student or other "captive" population with either no thought or very little thought as to how nondrug factors in their lives may have caused some observed anomaly or behavioral deviance. Other research has made simple extrapolations from laboratory studies of animals or cells to the human scene. In the case of marihuana, a single active ingredient—THC—has been administered, and this often far in excess of any normal human dosage. Our hope is that we are collectively rising beyond such crudity in research design.

A commentary on the state of drug research is the fact that our final study population of forty-one users and forty-one nonusers is the largest to date for which more than three sociocultural variables have been controlled. So poor is the understanding among the scientific community of the need and difficulty of establishing such controls that our findings have already been attacked by some as being nonrepresentative because of the "smallness" of the sample. From these same attackers we have been told that recruiting a controlled sample is a "simple matter."

Controlling for basic sociocultural variables is far from simple. For example, to obtain 24 matched pairs for a current study by Carter of the effects of traditional coca use in Bolivia, more than 1,500 individuals had to be interviewed and screened. And only after settling on the 24 pairs could more serious research begin in terms of prior conditions that had led to use or nonuse of the drug. The implication of such facts, of course, is that social science cannot be an afterthought if we are ever to obtain comprehensive and satisfactory answers to the drug question. It must be an integral part of each piece of research that deals with human beings.

As these lines are being written, the marihuana debate is taking on renewed vigor in the United States. The state of Florida has greatly increased its programs of control, to the end that it cease to be identified as the major port of entry for marihuana emanating from various parts of Latin America and the Caribbean. In viewing these developments, we cannot but ask ourselves whether the cure may not be worse than the disease. We are convinced that had we worked with inmates in the state prison who had been sentenced because of their involvement in marihuana we would have found some visible effects emanating from their incarceration. With our tightly controlled Costa Rican sample, we could find none that we could unequivocally attribute to prolonged use.

Marihuana is a psychotropic, and it does have certain *acute* effects. These we have not addressed, for they have been and are being thoroughly researched through other largely clinical studies. The general consensus, among both scientists and users, is that these effects are mild indeed when compared to our most popular and thoroughly legal drug—alcohol.

We no longer have the prerogative of deciding whether marihuana will be used in American society. It is being used, in spite of the controls and laws.

What the American public must eventually decide is whether it wishes to permit another legal drug. And in doing so, it must weigh the effects—many of which are deleterious from the individual standpoint—of the present legal structure against the effects of marihuana itself. But it must exercise caution to distinguish between supposed effects—often sensationalized in the mass media—and those effects proven through solid, scientific research.

Correlation is not synonymous with cause and effect, and those officials responsible for our laws must take great care never to confuse the two. They must question the *a priori,* the sampling techniques, the laboratory procedures, and the extrapolative validity of all reports that pass as science. They must realize that any serious attempt at unraveling the drug dilemma will require extreme care in sampling procedures, detailed observations in natural settings, strict controls, and totally appropriate physiological, biochemical, and psychological measures. They must abandon the comfortable position of taking seriously only those scientific results that agree with their particular point of view, and they must consider divergent, even conflicting, findings. Then they must exercise their best judgment in determining whether and how we need to alter our laws.

While this may be a utopian dream, the fact is that ours is a society with faith in and support for scientific research. Our plea is simply that this research be used—indeed, that there be a far more serious partnership between scientists and policymakers than there has been in the past. In terms of drug research and policy, this would mandate more multidisciplinary, closely coordinated studies of drug use in living situations, the careful control of basic social and cultural variables, willing response on the part of scientists to questions raised by policymakers, the formulating by scientists of questions policymakers should address, and constant dialogue among all parties concerned. Even if all this can be accomplished, it will come to naught unless the American public can learn to accept facts more dispassionately than it does at this time. Only then can we hope to move from the present morass of opinion and alarm to the firmer ground of reason.

Lexical Appendix

Lower-class, urban Costa Ricans have a slang of their own which they employ as a symbol of group cohesion and as a means for excluding outsiders. The lexicon for this slang is constantly undergoing revision. One of its richest variants is that used by marihuana smokers. This appendix, containing some of the more common terms of that variant, indicates how easily the smoker can communicate discretely with a fellow initiate. It also conveys something of the way smokers perceive the world. The actual terms used and their literal meanings are given here in italics; the "street" or *pachuco* meanings follow in roman.

Abanico (Fan)   Main door leading directly to different wings in a prison.

Abrió (Opened).   To declare everything to the police, to confess.

Algo (Something).   Marihuana.

Allá adentro (Inside there).   In the penitentiary.

Allá viene la gente (There come the people).   There come the police. Warning sign to tell smokers the narcotics police are approaching.

Amigos solo los de abajo (Friends only the lower ones).   Phrase used to indicate that there are no friends, that you can only count on your testicles.

Amontonado (Piled up).   Free union marriage.

Anda con color (Has color).   Means someone who is marked by police and is persecuted and taken to jail frequently on suspicion of possession or use of marihuana.

Aparato (Apparatus).   Marihuana cigarettes.

Asistentes (Assistants).   Inside the penitentiary those prisoners who are well behaved will be trusted by the guards and they serve to run errands and "assist" them. It is through these men that the prisoners send word outside to have things brought in.

A todo perro flaco siempre se le pican las pulgas (Skinny dogs attract fleas).   The poor and humble are humiliated and taken advantage of by people better off than they.

Avispado (Full of bees).   Very active, alert.

Barra (Bar).   A group of friends, usually of the underworld.

Barrio militar (Military neighborhood).   A neighborhood where people cover up for each other. Even if they see someone doing something against the law, they don't tell on him.

Bautizada (Baptized).   Marihuana which has been adulterated with another substance.

Bicho (Insect).   Marihuana cigarette.

Blancos (Whites).   Tobacco cigarettes.

Boletas (Tickets).   Paper used to roll marihuana cigarettes.

Bomba (Bomb).   Marihuana.

Bombazo (Bomb explosion).   First alcoholic drink.

Borraja (Borage).   Material used by marihuana traffickers to alter purity of the drug.

Bote (Boat).   Penitentiary.

Brete (Fetter, work).   Work.

Bretear como un caballo (Work like a horse).   To work hard.

Buena soldada (Good pay). Ejaculation.

Burucha. Marihuana.

Cachiflin (Squib). Marihuana.

Caí (I fell). I fell into the hands of the police.

Caja de leña (Firewood box). Matchbox.

Caldo (Broth). Drink made out of extract of marihuana by boiling the drug.

Caldo de pollo (Chicken broth). Preparation made with paregoric—extracting the opium to make a crude form of morphine.

Cama (Bed). Trap.

Camarón (Shrimp). Temporary work.

Camaronear (To shrimp). To work at temporary jobs.

Cannabis (Cannabis). Most common name for marihuana in Costa Rica.

Cañazo (To hit with a cane stick). Blow. Also used to mean a gulp of liquor.

Carebarro (Mudface). A shameless person; a patient person who does not get upset often.

Cargar (To carry). To be carried to the penitentiary.

Carnita 'e pavo (Turkey meat). In good shape, in good health.

Cartonazo (A blow with a piece of cardboard). Name given to marihuana cigarettes sold in the penitentiary which are sometimes made with brown paper bags instead of regular paper; they are hard like a piece of cardboard. Also, a swindle.

Castillo blanco (White castle). Penitentiary.

Cerrado (Closed). Under the effects of marihuana.

Chamaca (Mexican term for girl). Girl.

Chamba (A lucky break). Work.

Chanti (Shanty). A hut.

Chapazo (Sheet of metal). Variation on the pea and shell game (see Chapter 5). A piece of paper is placed under one of two bottle tops, and the other person has to guess under which it is. Since it is easy to cheat, the victim usually ends up losing.

Chasco (Disappointment). Disappointment. A serious problem.

Chingas (Small amount). A small amount of money paid to participate in a gambling game. This money usually is kept by the person organizing the game. It is used also to name the last little piece of a marihuana cigarette, the butt.

Chirriado (Witty, merry). Under the effects of marihuana.

Chiviarse (For chivarse: to be annoyed). To be annoyed, or mad.

Chivo (Goat). A man who is supported by a woman, usually by a prostitute.

Chochando (Being senile). To be under effects of marihuana.

Chocho (Senile). Under effects of marihuana.

Chulo (Pimp). Pimp.

Chupado (Emaciated, gaunt). A way of smoking marihuana.

Cojones (Testicles). Testicles. *Se le fueron arriba los cojones (Testicles went up).* The person was very mad.

Colilla (Butt). Marihuana cigarette, usually the last piece.

Con las pilas puestas (With the batteries on). Same as *Cerrado* under the effects of marihuana.

Cuete (Firecracker). The stick used by policemen. Also, firearm.

Cruzado con tiburón (Crossed with shark). To mix marihuana with alcohol.

Descuidos (Carelessness). To steal.

Desmoto (Dismantle, to clear away). When effects of marihuana are over.

Diablo rojo (Red devil). Amphetamines.

Doctor chiringa. A quack doctor.

El doctor (The doctor). Marihuana vendor.

El hueco (The hole). Pronounced "gueco." Torture chamber in a jail.

El material (The material). Marihuana.

El que anda con lobos, lobo se hace (He who runs with the wolves turns into one). If you run around with people that have bad habits, you too will acquire them.

El que con lobos anda, a aullar se enseña (He who runs with the wolves, will learn to howl). If you run around with people that steal, you too will learn to steal.

El que es tonto ni dios lo quiere (He who is foolish not even God likes). One should not be too foolish because all doors will be closed to you.

El que receta (He who prescribes). A marihuana vendor.

El que tiene puede (The person who has things can do things). The person who has money can do what he wants.

El que me la hace me la paga (He who hurts me will pay). I take revenge on those who hurt me.

El sukia. Marihuana vendor.

Enchantar—derived from chanti. Smoke marihuana in a shanty.

Engaletado. Stashed away—referring to marihuana.

Enyugado (Joined by a yoke). To be tied down to a job or in marriage.

Es completa (Is complete). The ideal woman; one who has all the good qualities that a woman can have.

Esta carajada (This damned thing). Marihuana. Also, to point to something.

Estar en la onda (To be in the wave). To be part of a marihuana smoker's group. To feel the effects of marihuana. Those who are *en onda* are in the same "frequency," in radio language.

Estar muy cerrado (To be very closed). To be under effects of marihuana.

Estar (o sentirse) pijiado. To be under effects of marihuana.

Extraí (for straight). To have your liquor straight, without mixes.

Filo (Edge). Hunger.

Fogonata (Bonfire). When one smokes a lot of marihuana at a time.

Fumar trocha (To smoke a portion). To smoke marihuana.

Galetas Supply of marihuana. Also the runner who serves the marihuana dealer.

Gancho (Hook). The cheater who helps the trafficker to sell illegitimate marihuana (adulterated). Also, a person used by police to catch another.

Ganja (Ganja). Marihuana.

Gansear (To make an idiot out of a person). Trick played by the police on smokers, by putting some of their own marihuana in the smoker's pocket and then taking him to jail for possession.

Golpeado por la vida (Hit by life). Means that person has had a sad and struggling life.

Goma (Gum, rubber). State a person is in after drinking too much the day before, generally manifested in headaches and stomach disorders and thirst.

Gotera (Drip, trickle). Effects felt after effects of marihuana are over. Used also for feelings after too many alcoholic drinks, like *goma.*

Grifa (Marihuana). Marihuana.

Grifo (Tap, faucet). Marihuano. (*Marihuano* is the person who smokes marihuana). To be under the effects of marihuana.

Hacerme una maleta (To make me a suitcase). To fight or be in very close touch with a person.

Hacer un puesto (To make a stand). To get together a group of friends to buy marihuana and smoke it.

Hierba (Grass). One of the most common names for marihuana in Costa Rica.

Hierbas corrientes y fragmentos de ramitas (Ordinary grass and pieces of twigs). Materials used by traffickers to adulterate marihuana.

Jumo (Drunk). Drunk.

La amarilla (The yellow one). Marihuana.

La bandera (The flag). Excess piece of paper left at the end of a marihuana cigarette in order to smoke as much as possible. See Chapter 2.

La bonita (The pretty one). Marihuana.

La cachimba de Don Juan (Don Juan's pipe). Pipe used to smoke marihuana.

La cochinada (Filth). Marihuana.

La consiguieron (They got it). They stole it.

La cosa (The thing). Marihuana.

La crespa (The curly one). Marihuana.

La rubia (The blonde one). Marihuana.

La chinga (or la desnuda) (The naked one). The end of a cigarette, either regular tobacco or marihuana. One never finds a *chinga* from a marihuana cigarette because smokers do not throw them away, they stick them to the end of a tobacco cigarette and smoke all of them.

La fatídica (The ominous one). Marihuana.

La gente (The people). People from the narcotics police.

La isla (The island). The island of San Lucas, where the penitentiary is. (They arrested me and I ended up on the Island.)

La jodieron (They screwed her up). They stole from her. Also used to say a girl has been raped.

La muleta (The crutch). Pieces of wood used to hold the butt of a marihuana cigarette so that it can be smoked to the very end.

La negrita (The little black one). The patron saint of Costa Rica, the Virgin of the Angels.

La niña (The girl). A cocaine snort.

La que traba (The one who bonds, ties). Marihuana.

La que es fuerte, la que pica (The strong one, the one who pricks or itches). Marihuana. This is the most recent expression in Costa Rica.

Las tres (The three). A puff of any kind of cigarette.

La tenebrosa (The gloomy one, the dismal one). Marihuana.

La verde (The green one). Marihuana. A recent, frequent name used in Costa Rica.

La vida fácil (The easy life). Loose living, delinquent living, antisocial. To live without worries or effort or study or work.

Le pego el descuido (I stick you with the carelessness). I rob you.

Le recetaron (They prescribed something for him). They gave him marihuana.

Lipidia (Poverty). "White death." Sickness which produces sweats, diarrhea, and discomposure. A Panamanian expression.

Los de la onda (Those of the wave). Those who smoke marihuana.

Manteca (Fat, lard). Marihuana. A delinquent person would use the expression *mi manteca* to designate a loved one, especially his mother.

Mantequita (Diminutive for manteca: lard, fat). Marihuana. Another current common use in Costa Rica.

Marilú (A proper name). Marihuana.

Mariquita (A proper name). Marihuana.

Mata (Plant, bush). Marihuana.

Matando la tocola. Smoking the last piece of a marihuana cigarette.

Matar la culebra (To kill the snake). Kill time.

Médico (Medic, doctor). The person who "prescribes" or sells marihuana.

Monte (Woods). Marihuana, because it grows anywhere even in the woods and thus does not need special attention. Presently a very common name for marihuana in Costa Rica.

Morfo (Related to morphine, drugs). To smoke drugs.

Moscorrofia. Marihuana.

Mota (Speck, mote). Marihuana. Also very common nowadays.

Moteado (Speckled, mottled). A person under the influence of marihuana.

Motearse (To get oneself mottled). To smoke marihuana.

Motica (Diminutive for mota: mote or speck). Marihuana.

Música de onda (Music of the wave). Modern, pop music.

Nos metió a la chorpa. He put us in jail.

Nos caimos (We fell). We were caught, arrested. Once the police know about you; you "have fallen."

Pacientes (Patients). Marihuana buyers, in relation to "doctor" who sells it.

Pacos (Proper name). Policemen.

Pacho (Proper name). An unpleasant or ugly thing, incident or circumstance. Also, a bad joke.

Palo (Stick). A person who warns smokers in his neighborhood that the police are coming.

Pambelé. Type of cannabis preparation that comes in the form of a paste in the size and shape of a matchbox. To use it, you scrape what you want and smoke it. It is of good quality and comes from Panama.

Pegando descuidos (Negligence, carelessness, to stick someone with a negligent act). Steal.

Pelagatos (Poor devil, wretch). Poor.

Pelota (Ball).   Gang, group of friends.

Percanta.   Prostitute.

Pichones (Young pigeons).   Marihuana cigarettes.

Piecito (Small foot).   Friend.

Pijiarme.   Smoke marihuana. *Pijiada, pijeo,* and *pijearno* are also used.

Pitillos (Cigarette).   Marihuana cigarettes.

Pizote solo.   Alone. The *pizote* is an animal that runs in packs and is usually undernour-ished and hungry. But the *pizote* who runs around alone can get more food and is better nourished. So people who are like a *pizote solo* live better and have more and have fewer problems.

Puro colchón (Pure padding).   Indicates marihuana of bad quality or marihuana that has been "padded" with adulterants. It is used also to imply that something is no good or a conversation that has no depth or meaning.

Quedarse cerrado (To stay closed).   To be under the effects of marihuana.

Quemadero (Burning place).   Place where marihuana is smoked.

Quemadores (Burners).   Marihuana smokers.

Quemarla (To burn it).   To light a marihuana cigarette. To smoke it.

Quemón (Large burn).   Marihuana smoker.

Químico (Chemist, chemical).   Alcohol, alcoholic.

Recetar (To prescribe).   To sell marihuana. A client would approach a seller in the drug-store or "soda" and ask him: Do you prescribe?

Resguardo (Safeguard, protection).   Old marihuana inspection authorities.

Rollo (Roll).   A set amount of marihuana to be sold. Each rollo has twenty-five ciga-rettes and its price varies between 25 and 35 colones.

Sapo (Frog).   Person who accuses another one for no reason at all. A person who is a busybody repeating everything he hears or sees. Also used to indicate a member of the Civil Guard who dresses in green.

Sentirse bonito (To feel pretty).   To feel effects of marihuana.

Subidas (Ups).   A puff of a marihuana cigarette.

Sueño de opio (Opium dreams).   Illusion, ideal state.

Tabo.   Penitentiary.

Taco (Wooden peg, wad).   Empty end of a white tobacco cigarette which has been filled with marihuana.

Tapíz (Tapestry).   Drunkard. Also *tapiñar* or *tapiñea.*

Teja (Tile).   One hundred colones.

Tener color (To have color).   To be known by the police for a special reason, for smoking marihuana, for stealing, for vagrancy.

Tequioso (Burdensome, harmful).   Lively, spirited, badly behaved.

Tieso (Taut, rigid, erect, stiff).   Under effects of marihuana.

Tocola.   End of a marihuana cigarette.

Tostado (Toasted).   Toasted, a person who has smoked a lot of marihuana.

Tropa (Troup).   Group of friends, gang.

Tuanis.   Pretty, groovy.

Un bicho (An insect).   A marihuana cigarette.

Un ganso (A goose).   A member of the law who plants a marihuana cigarette on a person and then arrests him. Also *gansea* from the verb *gansear.*

Un lloro (A wailing, like in a funeral).   A roll of twenty-five marihuana cigarettes. *Lloro* is *rollo* in "backwards" talk, where syllables are reversed.

Un moto (Short for motorcycle).   A marihuana cigar.

Vamos a prenderla (Let's set fire to it).   Let's smoke marihuana.

Vengo empastillado (I am under the effects of pills).   To be drugged with pills.

Vicio-contrabando (Contraband vice).   To smoke marihuana, because it is against the law, like contraband.

Vicio-público (Public vice).   To drink alcohol and smoke tobacco cigarettes. They are "public" because they are legalized and even patented.

Ya se llegó (It has arrived).   To feel the effects of marihuana.

Yerba (hierba = grass).   Marihuana.

Yodo (Iodine).   Coffee.

Zoncha.   Marihuana.

Zopilota (Female buzzard).   Marihuana.

Figure Appendix

IMPLEMENTS EMPLOYED IN MARIHUANA USE

Pipa de paz (peace pipe)

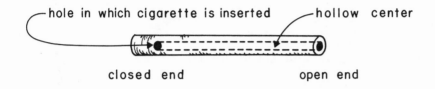

hole in which cigarette is inserted — hollow center

closed end   open end

Cachimba (pipe)

picadura or cigarette
placed here

stem

Coco Seco (dried coconut)

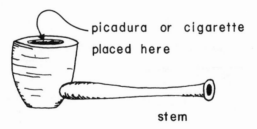

mouth placed around
small hole

marihuana

smoke

marihuana and live coals
placed in large hole

live coals

Figure A

Pipa de agua (water pipe)

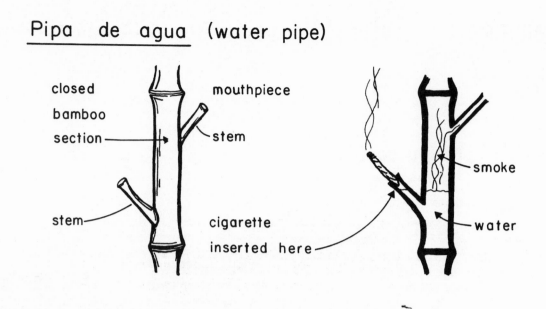

closed bamboo section

mouthpiece

stem

stem

cigarette inserted here

smoke

water

Caja de fósforos (matchbox)

hole into which cigarette is inserted

jacket

end to be removed

tray

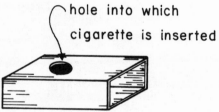

tray inserted into box

mouth placed here, and cigarette inhaled through box

Figure A (cont.)

Taco

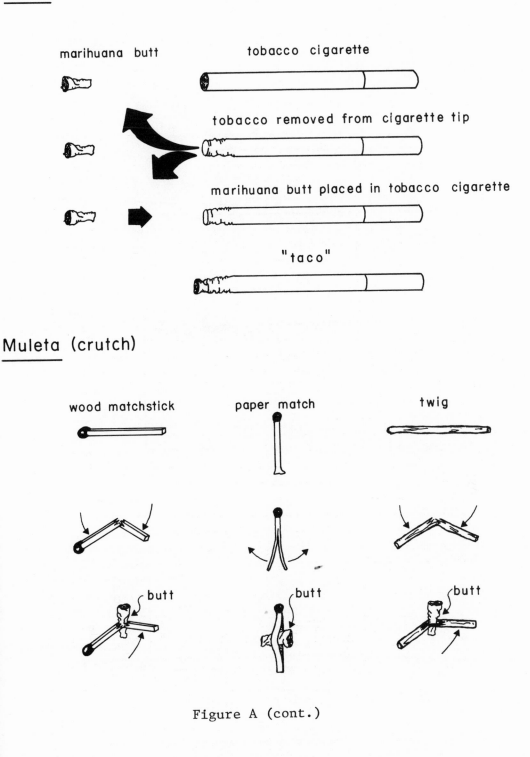

marihuana butt   tobacco cigarette

tobacco removed from cigarette tip

marihuana butt placed in tobacco cigarette

"taco"

Muleta (crutch)

wood matchstick   paper match   twig

butt   butt   butt

Figure A (cont.)

La Bandera (flag)

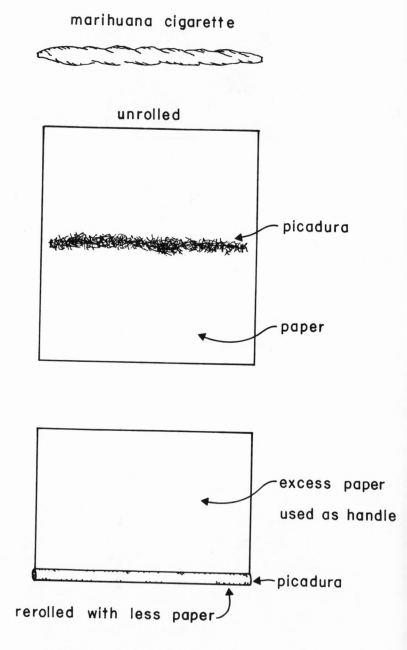

marihuana cigarette

unrolled

picadura

paper

excess paper
used as handle

picadura

rerolled with less paper

Figure A (cont.)

URBAN DISTRIBUTION NETWORK FOR MARIHUANA

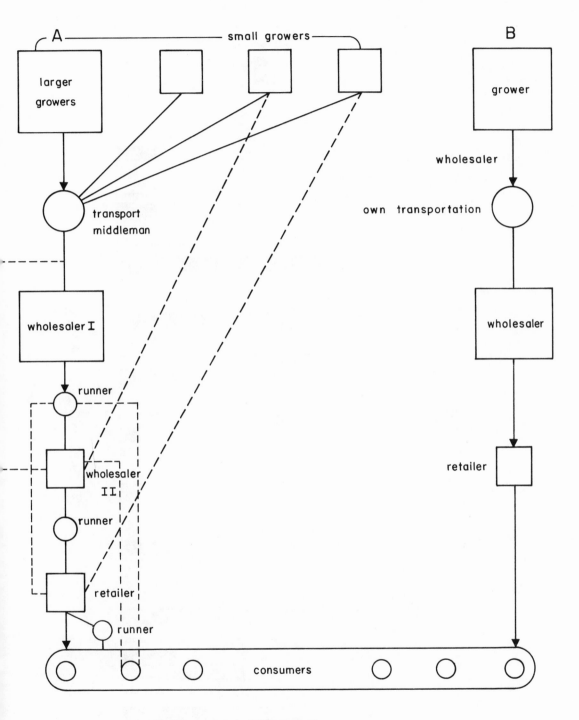

Figure B

USER TYPE AND SMOKING ENVIRONMENT

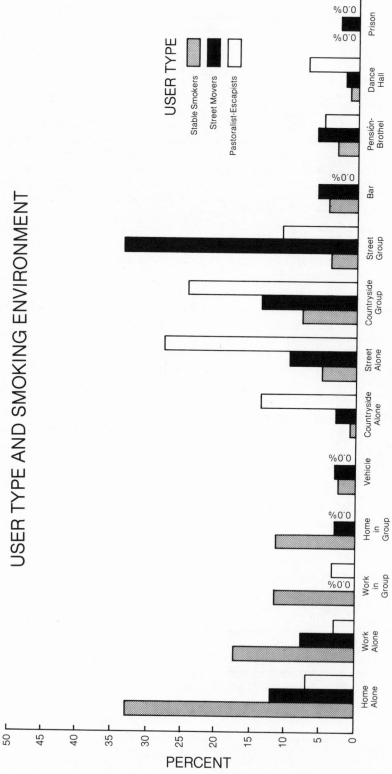

Figure C

GLUCOSE TOLERANCE TESTS

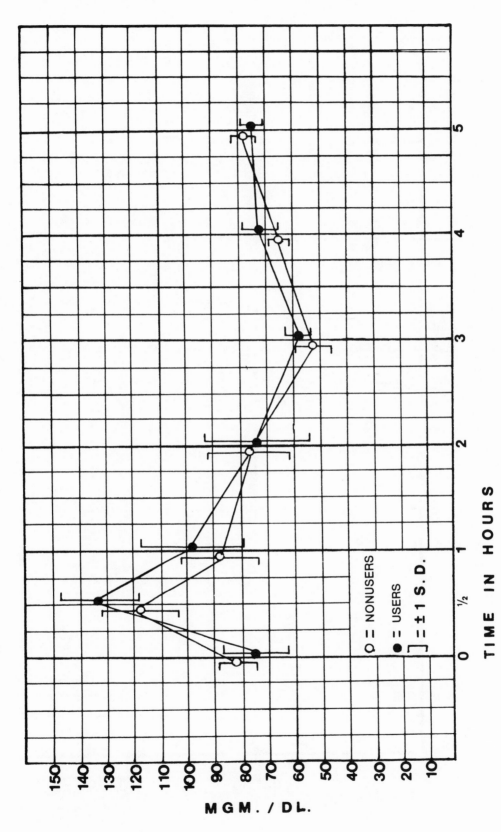

Figure D

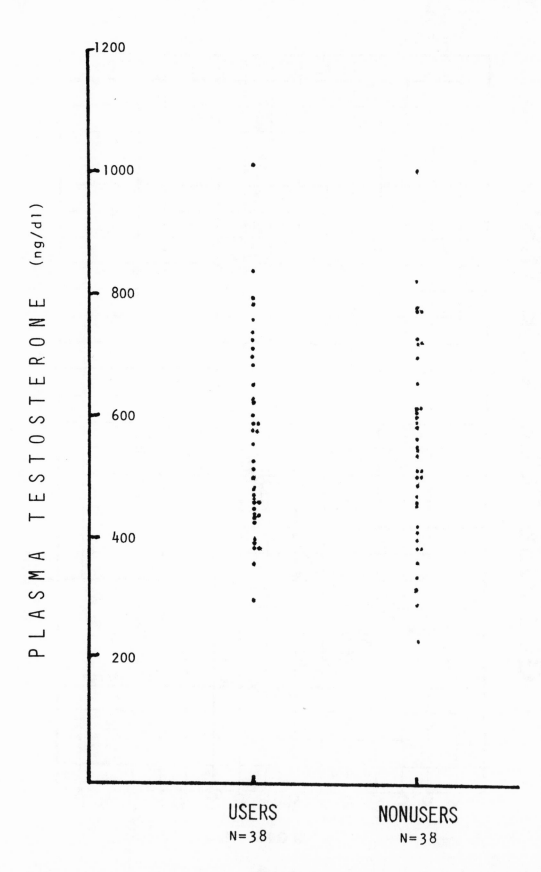

Figure E

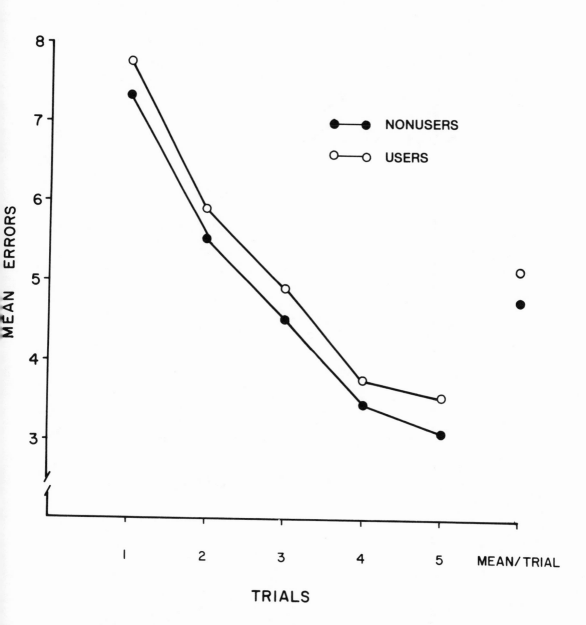

Figure F   Mean Error Recall X Trials and Groups on Word Learning Test
            Maximum Errors: 10 per trial

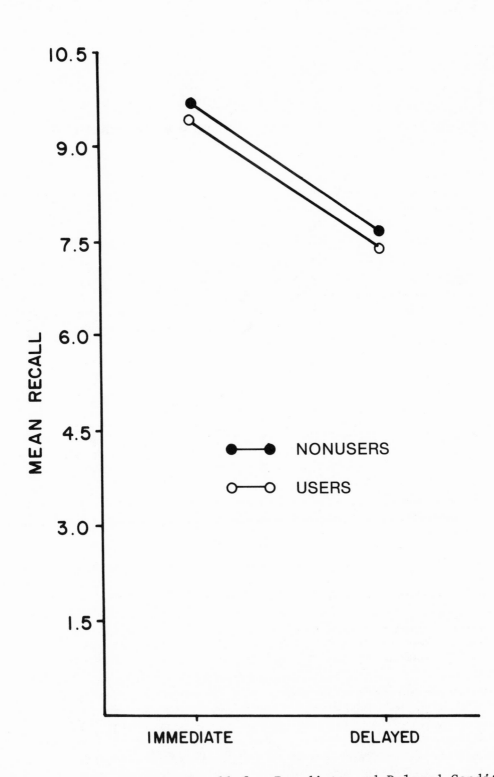

Figure G   Mean Correct Recall for Immediate and Delayed Conditions
                        X Groups on Logical Memory Test
                        Maximum Score: 22

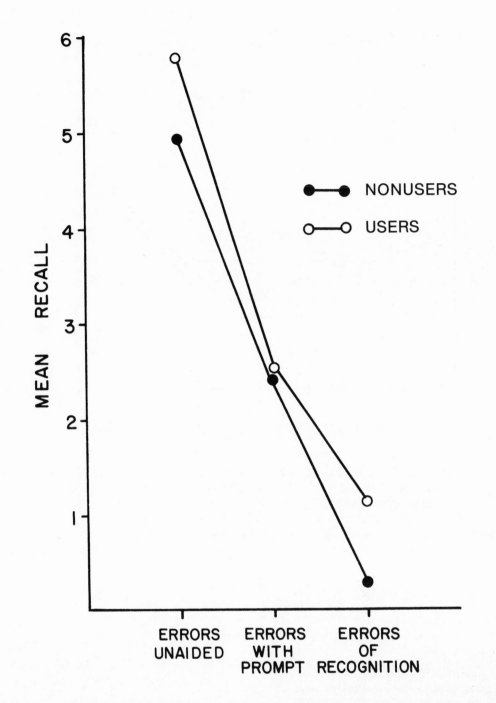

Figure H   Mean Error Recall X Type of Error and Groups on Delayed
            Recall Test
            Maximum Score: 9

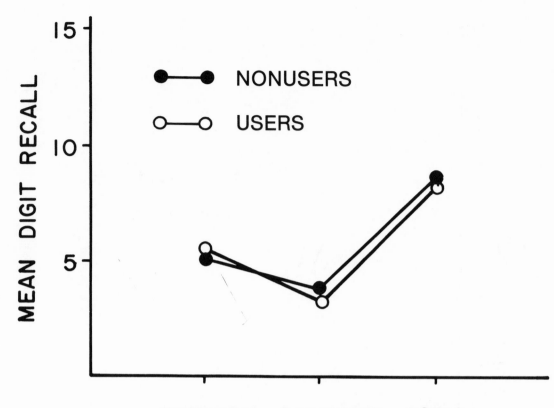

Figure I   Mean Digit Span (Raw Scores) from Williams Memory Battery
X Groups
Maximum Score: 16

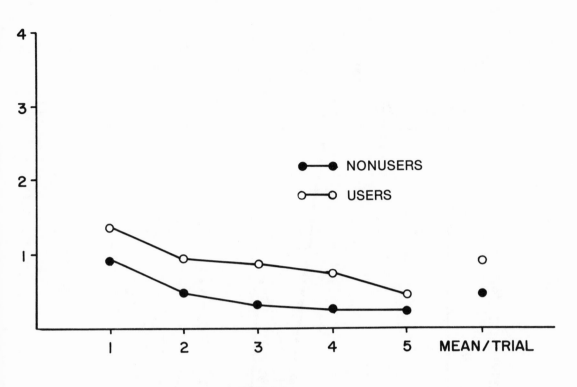

Figure J   Mean Recognition Error (Location) X Trials and Groups on
Rey-Davis (Nonverbal Learning) Test
Maximum Score: 4 per trial

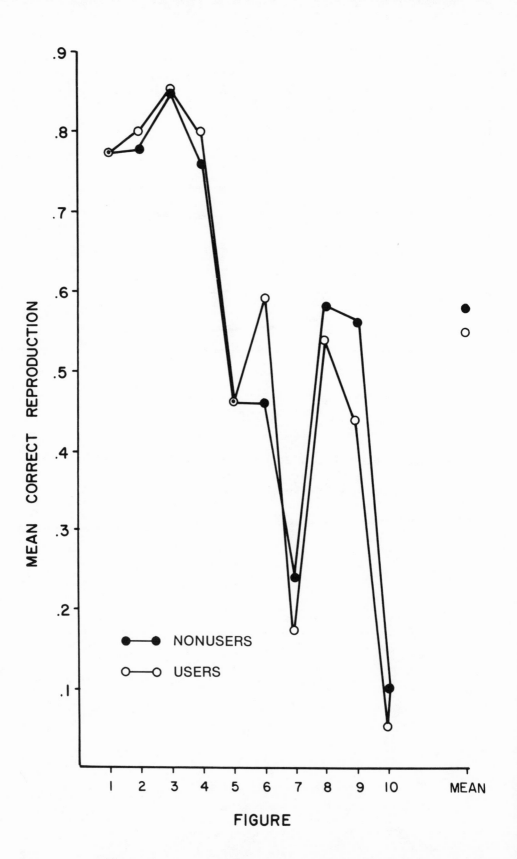

Figure K   Mean Correct Reproduction on Benton Visual Retention
            Test X Figures and Groups
            Maximum Score: 1.00 per Figure

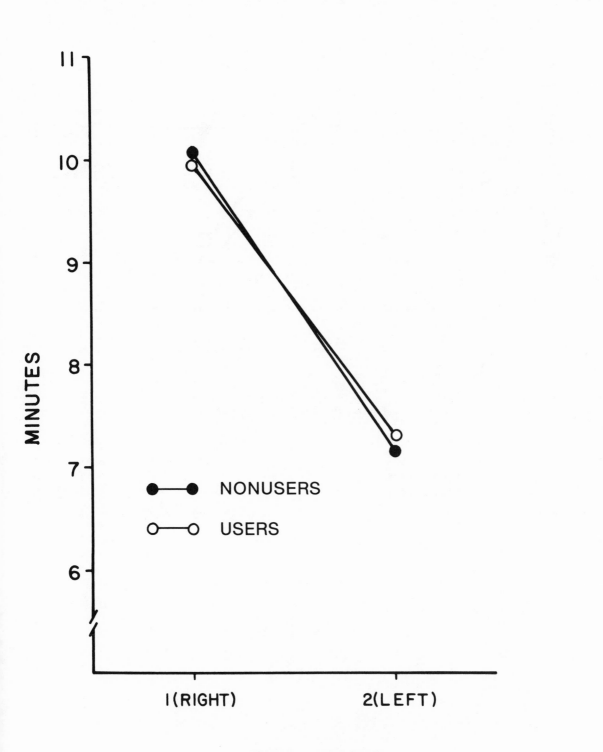

Figure L   Mean Transfer of Learning (Minutes) Between Hands on Tactual
            Performance Test X Groups
            Maximum Time per Hand: 15 min.

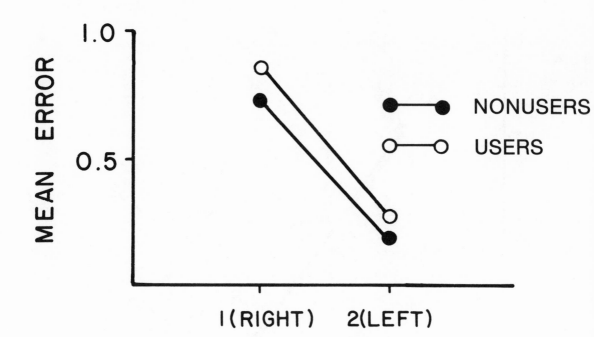

Figure M   Mean Transfer of Learning (Errors) Between Hands on Tactua.
           Performance Test X Groups
           Maximum Error per hand: 10

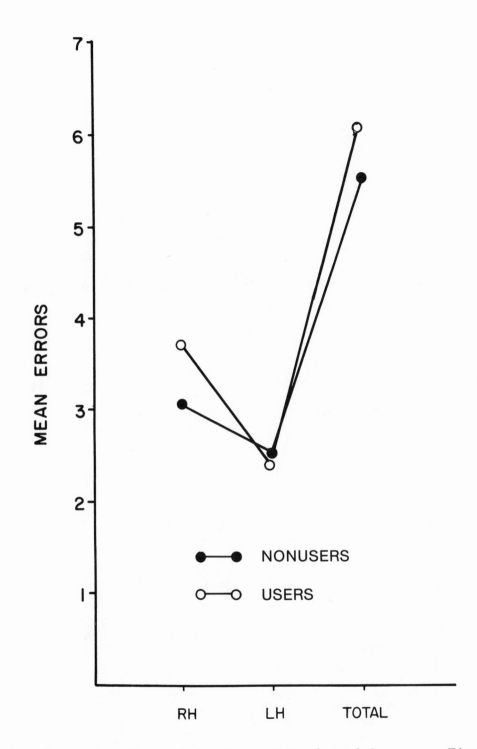

Figure N   Mean Recognition Error X Hands and Groups on Finger
            Localization Test
            Maximum Error per Hand: 20

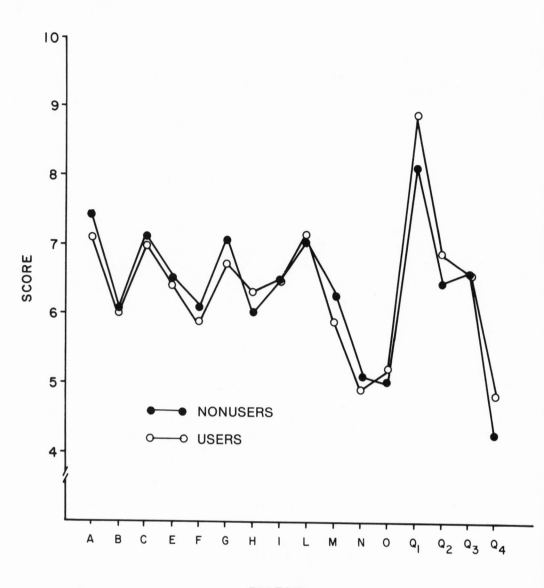

Figure 0   Mean Factor Score X Groups on IPAT 16 PF Test
                Maximum Score per Factor: 10

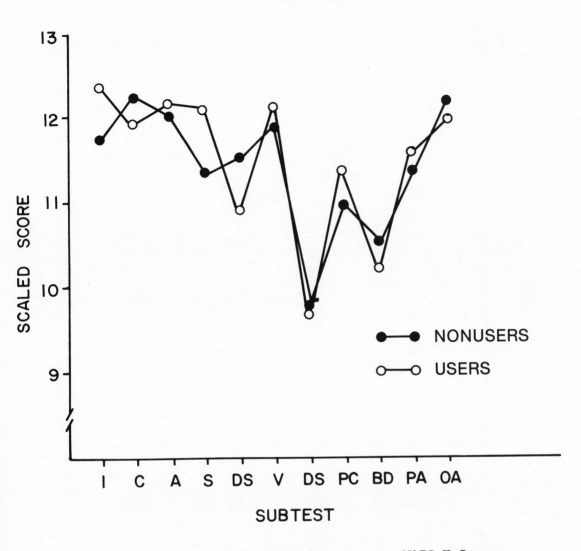

Figure P   Mean Subtest Performance on WAIS X Groups
                        Maximum Scaled Score per Subtest: 19

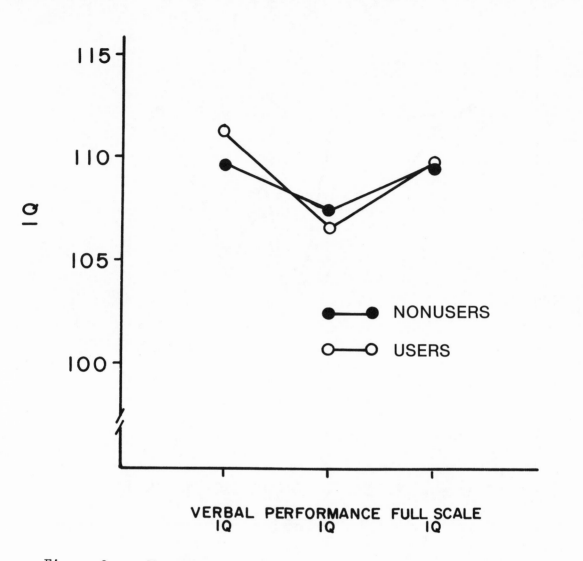

Figure Q   Mean Verbal, Performance, and Full Scale IQ on WAIS X Gro

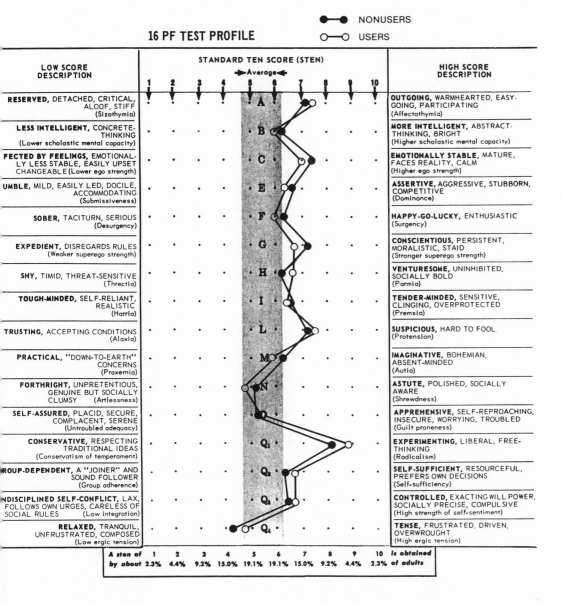

Figure R   Mean 16 PF Test Profile X Groups

Table Appendix

Table 1

Age, Marital Status, Education, Occupation, and Alcohol
and Tobacco Consumption for Base and Final Samples

Variables and Categories	Base Sample		Final Sample	
	Users N=84	Nonusers N=156	Users N=41	Nonusers N=41
Mean age	31.07	30.68	29.95	28.98
Marital status				
Formal and consensual marriage	53.6%	68.0%	64.0%	76.0%
Single	46.4%	32.0%	36.0%	24.0%
Education				
None	1.2%	5.2%	2.5%	0.0%
Incomplete primary	53.5%	35.9%	46.3%	39.0%
Complete primary	27.4%	33.3%	31.7%	39.0%
Incomplete secondary	16.7%	21.8%	19.5%	22.0%
Complete secondary	1.2%	3.8%	0.0%	0.0%
Occupation				
Unskilled	41.7%	41.0%	34.1%	26.5%
Skilled	58.3%	59.0%	65.9%	73.5%
Mean alcohol consumption*	9.68	8.92	8.512	8.829
Tobacco consumption				
Mean number of pack years	19.30	13.79	16.21	15.27

*On a 17-point scale.

Table 2

Decree Dealing with Marihuana Production
Decree No. 5, October 24, 1928

Article 1. Among the infractions against public health, as defined in
Chapter IV, Title VII, of the Penal Code, will be the
production, sale, purchase or transport for sale of
marihuana in any of its forms.

Article 2. Police and health authorities are authorized to confiscate
marihuana and to destroy seedbeds and fields of the plant.
The person or persons found disobeying this decree will be
subjected to the Penal Code and the Law for Protection of
Public Health.

Article 3. Whoever is proven to be the owner of a marihuana field,
regardless of its size, will be judged by the common
court in accord with Article 422 of the Penal Code;
whoever will be found working as a laborer in such a
field, or whoever will be found possessing the drug in
any form, including cigarettes, either for sale or for
his own use, will be forced to pay a fine of from five
to 120 colones by police or health authorities, in accord
with Article 150 of the Law for Protection of Public Health.

Table 3

Common Marihuana Types

Marihuana Type	Color and Smell	Consistency	Origin	Taste	Effects-- Remarks
La Negra	Black; "earthy smell"	Straight; fine seeds	Limón	Harsh; rasps the throat	Strong and immediate effect
La Rubia	Yellowish (blonde); "like a cut lawn"	Curly; many seeds	Limón	Smooth	Moderate, but "good high" and delayed actio
La Café	Brown; "little odor"	Straight; few seeds	San Isidro del General	Neither harsh nor smooth	Compara- tively weak
San Miguelito	Yellow to brown; "fusty, and stronger than tobacco"	Curly to straight; many seeds	Panama (via Limón)	Harsh	Strongest available

Table 4

Profits from Marihuana

Grower

Secures seed nearly free from last harvest of local vendor.

Invests four or five man-hours in cultivation of five or six cannabis plants (enough to produce a pound of dried material). Harvesting and drying occupy only a few minutes.

Taken to a transport middleman, he receives ¢300 to ¢600 for his pound (US $35-70).

or

Taken directly to San José, he receives ¢700 to ¢1,000 from a wholesaler II or retailer (US $82-117).

Transporter

Delivers marihuana to wholesaler I or II and receives ¢400 (US $47) to ¢700 (US $82) per pound (makes ¢100 gross profit per pound).

Wholesaler

Sells in one- or two-pound bags to the retailer for ¢600 (US $70) to ¢1,000 (US $117) per pound (makes ¢200 [US $23] per pound gross profit).

Retailer

Sells to consumers after twelve man-hours labor in rolling and adulteration realizing at least ¢1,600 per pound gross profit (before subtracting runner fees and paper [US $187]).

Note: The prices quoted above represent a range of prices encountered by the field team during two years of research. Prices, extremely sensitive to police pressure, may move from one extreme to the other in a period of only four months.

Table 5

Analysis of Marihuana
Mean Percent by Weight

Sample Number	Cannabi-chromene*	Delta 9 THC	Cannabinol
1	.25	2.49	.03
2	.19	2.34	.02
3	.19	1.27	.17
4	.21	1.33	.28
5	.18	3.41	.28
6	.08	1.62	.07
7	.15	2.86	.23
8	.10	2.53	.08
9	.24	3.72	.44
10	.09	1.60	.26
11	.13	1.78	.23
12	.16	1.87	.18
13	.17	1.67	.19

*These samples contain only trace amounts of Cannabidiol (50 nanograms).

Table 6

Extrapolations of Degree of Exposure to Delta 9 THC
Based on Cross-Tabulation of Sample Analysis Results
and Average Daily Consumption Levels*

Marihuana Smoked per day in Mg	Delta 9 THC Content in Mg/100 Mg (% by Weight)		
	Low 1.27	Mean 2.11	High 3.72
Low (2.5 cig./day) 500 mg	6.35 mg	10.55 mg	18.60 mg
Mean (9.6 cig./day) 1,900 mg	24.13 mg	40.09 mg	70.68 mg
High (40 cig./day) 8,000 mg	101.60 mg	168.80 mg	297.60 mg

*Since we cannot assume that the user absorbs all the Delta 9 THC when
he smokes, we must emphasize that these amounts indicate levels of exposure.
An approximate dosage level may be obtained by multiplying the cell amounts
by 0.50.

Table 7

Marihuana and Other Drug Confiscations

Item	Jan.-June 1972*	July 1972- June 1973*	July 1973- June 1975*	July 1973- June 1975†
Marihuana cigarettes	6,335	16,309	35,877	31,911
Picadura (kg)	4.1	97.3	242.8	342.9
Marihuana plants destroyed	4,150	667	2,053	6,598
Marihuana fields located	2	5	10	0
LSD doses	47	23	157	0
Cocaine (gm)	112	3,635	3,322	0
Cocaine (pills)	90	65	15	0
Barbiturates (pills)	0	0	584	0
Methodone (pills)	0	0	11	0

*Marihuana and other drug confiscations reported by the Department of
Narcotics, Ministry of Public Security, January 1972-June 1975.

†Marihuana officially registered and destroyed from all sources by the
Ministry of Health, July 1973-June 1975.

Note: The reason for the discrepancy in the data is that not all the drugs
reported as being confiscated by the narcotics police were in fact
registered and destroyed by the authorities in the Ministry of Health who
are officially charged with that responsibility. Because of this legal
obligation, and because much confiscated material comes from agencies
other than the police, we have used the official Ministry of Health reports
as the basis for most of our estimates.

Table 8

Marihuana Reported Confiscated by Police from 1950 to 1956

Year	No. Cigarettes	Kg Picadura
1950	273	368.8
1951	1,079	23.9
1952	3,678	351.3
1953	1,504	13.5
1954	1,845	6.3
1955	606	840.3
1956	1,603	261.1
Totals	10,588	1,865.2

Source: La Nación, February 17, 1957: 61.

Table 9

Arrests and Reported Drug Infractions
as an Index of Police Activity

Infraction	Jan.-June 1972*	July 1972- June 1973*	July 1973- June 1975*
Persons arrested for marihuana possession	161	367	3,107
Foreigner arrests for drug violation	0	0	216
Marihuana traffickers reported	0	0	1,137
Vagrants reported	0	0	366
Persons arrested using paint thinner	0	0	63
Cocaine possession arrests	3	6	0
Hashish possession arrests	0	5	5

*Drug and other infractions reported by the Department of Narcotics, Ministry of Public Security, January 1972-June 1975.

Table 10

Number of Newspaper Articles on Drug Abuse
La Nación, Prensa Libre, La República, Excelsior

	1970	1971	1972	1973	1974	1975
General Campaign against marihuana	0	200	39	23	8	12
Conferences dealing with marihuana	2	23	1	5	0	2
Arrest and trial of marihuana vendors	30	43	25	57	44	17
Arrests and trial of marihuana users	17	26	9	21	17	8
Destruction of marihuana crops	19	18	5	16	11	5
Foreigners involved in marihuana traffic	4	13	11	7	7	0
Marihuana use in other countries	5	23	7	16	2	4
Popular accounts of effects of marihuana use	2	29	5	7	0	1
Scientific reports on effects of marihuana use	0	10	2	2	5	0
Law dealing with marihuana	4	22	16	6	1	1
Narcotics officials dealing with marihuana	0	22	30	72	3	0
General campaign against all drugs	13	41	68	38	15	0
Arrests of traffickers in hard drugs and confiscation of hard drugs	5	8	68	19	12	12
Arrests of users of hard drugs and confiscation of hard drugs	0	4	0	1	1	0
Conferences dealing with hard drugs	0	4	6	1	1	0
Use of hard drugs in other countries	11	15	67	63	9	4
Law and narcotics officials dealing with hard drugs	0	5	48	12	0	0
General campaign against alcohol	1	40	15	16	10	16

Table 11

Population Growth in Metropolitan Area of San José, 1927–1973

Year	Costa Rica	Metropolitan Area	Percent of Costa Rica
1927	471,524	89,006	18.9
1950	800,736	179,736	22.5
1963	1,336,274	320,431	24.0
1973	1,820,000	436,862	24.0

Source: Ministerio de Obras Públicas y Transporte: 5.

Table 12

Housing

	Users*	Nonusers*
House	63.2%	78.0%
Apartment	23.7	4.9
Room	10.5	9.8
Squatter hut	2.6	7.3
Own	23.7	31.7
Rent	60.5	51.2
Borrow	13.2	7.3
Squat	2.6	9.8
Wood floors	71.1	73.2
Cement floors	21.1	4.9
Tile floors	5.3	19.5
Tamped earth	2.6	2.4
Zinc roofs	81.6	87.8
Ricalit roofs	10.5	9.8
Concrete roofs	2.6	0.0
Wood roofs	2.6	2.6
No answer	2.6	0.0
Glass windows and grates	13.2	14.6
Glass windows	57.9	65.9
Wooden shutters	23.7	14.6
None	5.3	4.9
Electric stove	55.6	72.5
Gas stove	11.1	5.0
Charcoal stove	13.9	15.0
Camp stove	11.1	5.0
None	8.3	2.5
Block walls	5.3	5.0
Block and wood walls	10.5	10.0
Wood walls	84.2	85.0
Bathroom		
present	94.7	95.1
absent	5.3	4.9
Running water		
present	92.1	95.9
absent	7.9	4.9
Electricity		
present	89.5	92.7
absent	10.5	7.3

*Although most figures are based on the total matched-pair sample of 41
and 41, some are based on different totals because of a small amount of
nonreporting.

Table 13

Distribution of Subjects According to Neighborhood Type

| | | Matched-Pair Subsample | | | | | | Base Sample | | | | | |
| | | Users | | Nonusers | | Total | | Users | | Nonusers | | Total | |
		No.	%	No.	%	Total	%	No.	%	No.	%	Total	%
I.	Central	9	22.0	3	7.3	12	14.6	15	17.9	16	10.3	31	12.6
II.	Stable residential; contiguous to central city	17	41.5	18	43.9	35	42.7	33	39.3	57	36.5	90	37.5
III.	Stable Residential; government housing projects	2	4.9	1	2.4	3	3.7	6	7.1	4	2.6	10	4.1
IV.	Satellite towns	2	4.9	4	9.8	6	7.3	11	13.1	27	17.3	38	15.8
V.	Peripheral Transitional	9	22.0	3	7.3	12	14.6	13	15.5	14	9.0	27	11.3
VI.	Squatter settlements	2	4.9	6	14.6	8	9.8	4	4.8	12	7.7	16	6.7
VII.	Rural communities	0	0.0	1	2.4	1	1.2	0	0.0	9	5.8	9	3.8
VIII.	Provincial cities and towns outside SJMA*	0	0.0	5	12.2	5	6.1	0	0.0	13	8.3	13	5.4
IX.	Unknown	0	0.0	0	0.0	0	0.0	2	2.4	4	2.6	6	2.5
	Totals	41	100.2	41	99.9	82	100.0	43	100.0	115	100.0	240	100.0

*SJMA: San José metropolitan area.

Paired t-test (for % in Totals columns) is 0.0; not significant.

Table 14

Mean Incomes for Barrios and Subjects
According to Typology
(1973 Census)

Neighborhood		Average Income* of Type	Average Income* for Subjects	Total No. of Subjects
I.	Central	1,589	924	31
II.	Stable residential, contiguous	883	728	90
III.	Stable residential, housing project	1,182	1,037	10
IV.	Satellite towns	1,206	999	38
V.	Peripheral transitional	948	762	27
VI.	Squatter settlements	--†	795	16
VII.	Rural communities	--†	857	9
VIII.	Provincial towns and towns outside San José metropolitan area	--††	348	19
Total				240

*Calculated in colones ($1.00 = ₡8.54).

†Barrio census element numbers not available.

††Not calculated.

p = .06.

Paired t-test (of first five results) is 2.74; significant at the .06 level.

Table 15

Economic Rank According to Income-Housing Index

Economic Rank of _Barrios_ Represented in the Sample (Based on Income-Housing Index); Decile Units*	Number of Subjects			
	Users	Nonusers	Total	Percent
1. (High) First Decile	--	--	--	--
2. Second Decile	5 (1)†	9 (0)	14 (1)	5.8 (1.2)
3. Third Decile	4 (2)	12 (3)	16 (5)	6.7 (6.1)
4. Fourth Decile	12 (6)	18 (2)	30 (8)	12.5 (9.8)
5. Fifth Decile	-- (0)	4 (2)	4 (2)	1.7 (2.4)
6. Sixth Decile	15 ( )	11 (2)	26 (10)	10.8 (12.2)
7. Seventh Decile	26 (12)	49 (16)	75 (28)	31.3 (34.2)
8. Eighth Decile	6 (3)	5 (0)	11 (3)	4.6 (3.7)
9. Ninth Decile	3 (1)	19 (9)	22 (10)	9.2 (12.2)
10. Tenth Decile	--	--	--	--
Other††	13 (8)	29 (7)	42 (15)	17.5 (18.3)
Totals	84 (41)	156 (41)	240 (82)	100.1 (100.1)

*Rank determined according to CESPO classification (Fonseca-Tortós et al. 1970).

†Number in parentheses indicates the number of subjects from the decile in the final matched sample.

††Persons whose residences were not part of _barrios_ ranked or were unstable at time of research.

Paired t-test (on two sample %s) is 0.01; not significant.

Table 16

Subjects Raised in Reformatory*

| | Users N=84 | | Nonusers N=156 | |
	No.	%	No.	%
Yes	6	7.1	1	0.7
No	74	88.0	141	90.0
No answer	4	4.7	14	8.9

*Entire childhood and educational experience; does not include those who were in reformatory for short periods.

X^2 is 5.672; significant at the .02 level.

Table 17

Subjects Raised by Surrogate Parents

| | Users N=84 | | Nonusers N=156 | |
	No.	%	No.	%
Yes	11	13.0	7	4.4
No	69	82.1	136	87.1
No answer	4	4.0	13	8.3

X^2 is 4.293; significant at the .05 level.

Table 18
Predominant Adults

| | Users N=41 | | Nonusers N=41 | |
	No.	%	No.	%
Father alone	4	9.8	1	2.4
Mother alone	8	19.5	9	22.0
Both parents	26	63.4	25	61.0
Other	3	7.3	6	14.6

X^2 is 3.41; not significant.

Table 19

End of Parental Relationship
During Period of Socialization

| | Users N=41 | | Nonusers N=41 | |
	No.	%	No.	%
Separation/divorce	10	24.4	7	17.1
Death	5	12.2	8	19.5
Never together	4	9.8	4	9.8
Did not end	22	53.7	22	53.7

X^2 is 2.69; not significant.

Table 20

Contact with Godparents

| | Users N=41 | | Nonusers N=41 | |
	No.	%	No.	%
Annual contact	10	24.4	13	31.7
Less than annual	11	26.8	17	41.5
No contact	18	43.9	11	26.8
No answer	2	4.9	0	0.0

X^2 is 3.32; not significant.

Table 21

Satisfaction with Childhood

| | Users N=41 | | Nonusers N=41 | |
	No.	%	No.	%
Positive	19	46.3	23	56.1
Negative	16	39.0	10	24.4
Neutral	6	14.6	8	19.5

X^2 is 2.05; not significant.

Table 22

Relationship Between Parents

	Users N=41		Nonusers N=41	
	No.	%	No.	%
Amiable	17	41.5	18	43.9
Hostile	6	14.6	2	4.9
Variable	6	14.6	13	31.7
No answer	12	29.3	8	19.5

X^2 is 4.36763; not significant.

Table 23

General Ambience in Home

	Users N=41		Nonusers N=41	
	No.	%	No.	%
Pleasant	16	39.0	19	46.3
Disagreeable	14	34.1	14	34.1
Neutral	11	26.8	7	17.1
Other	0	0.0	1	2.4

X^2 is 1.13; not significant.

Table 24

Father's Work

	Users N=41		Nonusers N=41	
	No.	%	No.	%
Full time*	29	70.7	28	68.3
Stable jobs*	23	56.1	25	61.0

X^2 for full time is 0.10; not significant.

X^2 for stable jobs is 0.24; not significant.

*Categories not mutually exclusive.

Table 25

Parental Punishment

| | Mothers | | | | Fathers | | | |
| | Users N=41 | | Nonusers | | Users N=41 | | Nonusers | |
	No.	%	No.	%	No.	%	No.	%
More than fair	10	24.4	6	14.6	13	31.7	11	26.8
Fair	20	48.8	26	63.4	18	43.9	16	39.0
Less than fair	8	19.5	9	22.0	4	9.8	7	17.1
No answer	3	7.3	0	0.0	6	14.6	7	17.1

X^2 for mothers is 1.73; not significant.

X^2 for fathers is 1.09; not significant.

Table 26

Parental Political Activity

| | Users N=41 | | Nonusers N=41 | |
	No.	%	No.	%
Work/vote	11	26.8	6	14.6
Vote only	16	39.0	18	43.9
No activity	11	26.8	11	26.8
No answer	3	7.3	6	14.6

X^2 is 1.47; not significant.

Table 27

Migration Patterns

(N=41 Users and 41 Nonusers)

	T1 %	T2 %	T3 %	Net T1–T2 %	Net T2–T3 %	Net T1–T3 %
Rural users	30	20	0	−10	−20	−30
Provincial town users	30	7	12	−23	+ 5	−18
San José users	29	73	88	+44	+15	+59
Unknown/No answer Users	11	0	0	0	0	0
Totals	100	100	100			
Rural Nonusers	38	34	2	− 4	−32	−36
Provincial town nonusers	23	14	12	− 7	− 5	−12
San José nonusers	30	49	86	+19	+37	+56
Unknown/No answer Nonusers	8	0	0	0	0	0
Totals	100	100	100			

Table 28

Adequacy of Food in Childhood

	Users N=41		Nonusers N=41	
	No.	%	No.	%
Less-than-adequate	18	43.9	8	19.5
Adequate	23	56.1	33	80.5

X^2 is 5.63; significant at the .02 level.

Table 29

Adequacy of Housing in Childhood

	Users N=41		Nonusers N=41	
	No.	%	No.	%
Less-than-adequate	16	39.0	8	19.5
Adequate	25	61.0	33	80.5

X^2 is 3.77; significant at the .06 level.

Table 30

Mother's Work During Childhood

	Users N=41		Nonusers N=41	
	No.	%	No.	%
Mother worked	26	63.4	18	43.9
Mother did not work	10	24.4	21	51.2
Unknown/No answer	5	12.2	2	4.8

X^2 is 6.06; significant at the .02 level.

Table 31

Finances Within Family of Childhood

	Users N=41		Nonusers N=41	
	No.	%	No.	%
Father controlled	16	39.0	22	53.6
Mother controlled or shared with father	23	56.1	14	34.1
Others controlled	2	4.9	5	12.2

X^2 is 4.42; significant at the .05 level.

Table 32

Leadership Roles of Father During Childhood
(e.g., Clubs, Church, Politics)

	Users N=41		Nonusers N=41	
	No.	%	No.	%
Was a leader	5	12.2	11	26.8
Was not a leader	32	78.0	22	53.6
Unknown/No answer	4	9.8	8	19.5

X^2 is 2.85; significant at the .09 level.

Table 33

Parental Preferential Treatment During
Childhood

	Users N=41		Nonusers N=41	
	No.	%	No.	%
Absent	16	39.0	25	61.0
Present for siblings	14	34.1	5	12.2
Present for ego	7	17.1	6	14.6
Unknown/No answer	4	9.7	5	12.2

X^2 is 6.30; significant at the .02 level.

Table 34

Socioeconomic Mobility During Childhood

	Users N=41		Nonusers N=41	
	No.	%	No.	%
Upward or static	27	65.9	34	82.9
Downward	14	34.1	7	17.1

X^2 is 8.4; significant at the .01 level.

Table 35

Mother's Use of Alcohol

	Users N=41		Nonusers N=41	
	No.	%	No.	%
Mother drank	6	14.6	17	41.5
Mother did not drink	30	73.2	23	56.1
Unknown/No answer	5	12.2	1	2.4

X^2 is 5.99; significant at the .02 level.

Table 36

Mother's Use of Tobacco

	Users N=41		Nonusers N=41	
	No.	%	No.	%
Mother smoked	10	24.4	19	46.3
Mother did not smoke	28	68.3	20	48.8
Unknown/No answer	3	7.3	2	4.9

X^2 is 3.22; significant at the .07 level.

Table 37

Education

Level of Education Completed	User N=84		Nonuser N=156	
	No.	%	No.	%
None	1	1.2	8	5.1
Some primary	44	52.4	56	35.9
Primary complete	23	27.4	52	33.3
Some secondary	14	16.7	34	21.8
Secondary complete	1	1.2	6	3.8
Unknown	1	1.2	0	0.0

X^2 is 10.196; not significant.

Table 38

School Behavior

	Users N=41		Nonusers N=41	
	No.	%	No.	%
Mischievous	23	56.1	15	36.6
Well-behaved	13	31.7	25	61.0
Unknown/No answer	5	12.2	1	2.4

X^2 is 4.28; significant at the .04 level.

Table 39

Expulsion from School

	Users N=41		Nonusers N=41	
	No.	%	No.	%
Expelled	14	34.1	5	12.2
Not expelled	22	53.7	35	85.4
No answer	5	12.2	1	2.4

X^2 is 7.04; significant at the .01 level.

Table 40

School Attendance

	Users N=41		Nonusers N=41	
	No.	%	No.	%
Frequently absent	19	46.3	10	24.4
Occasionally absent	8	19.5	11	26.8
Never absent (except normal illness)	9	22.0	18	43.9
Unknown/No answer	5	12.2	2	4.9

X^2 is 6.1; significant at the .05 level.

Table 41

Self-Perception of Childhood Conduct

	Users N=41		Nonusers N=41	
	No.	%	No.	%
Good	9	22.0	18	43.9
Fair-to-bad	32	78.0	23	56.1

X^2 is 4.47; significant at the .05 level.

Table 42

Home Abandonment/Age/Subsequent Marihuana Use

	Users N=41		Nonusers N=41	
	No.	%	No.	%
Left home 1-12 years	10	24.4	2	4.9
Left home 13-18 years	19	46.3	11	26.8
Stayed until marriage or never left	12	29.3	27	65.9
No answer	0	0.0	1	2.4

X^2 is 13.23; significant at the .01 level.

Table 43

Adequacy of Food/Abandonment of Home

	Less than Adequate No.	Less than Adequate %	Adequate or Better No.	Adequate or Better %	No Answer No.	No Answer %
Left home 1-12 years	7	8.5	5	6.1	1	1.2
Left home 13-14 years	12	14.6	18	22.0	0	0.0
Stayed until marriage or never left	7	8.5	32	39.0	0	0.0

X^2 is 8.24; significant at the .02 level.

Table 44

Delinquency

	Users N=41 No.	Users N=41 %	Nonusers N=41 No.	Nonusers N=41 %
Did commit delinquent acts	18	43.9	7	17.1
Did not commit delinquent acts	21	51.2	33	80.5
No answer	2	4.9	1	2.4

X^2 is 7.50; significant at the .01 level.

Table 45

Experience in Reformatory

	Users N=41		Nonusers N=41	
	No.	%	No.	%
At least one term served	15	36.6	0	0.0
Never in reformatory	26	63.4	41	100.0

X^2 is 15.99; significant at the .0001 level.

Table 46

Work During Adolescence

	Users N=41		Nonusers N=41	
	No.	%	No.	%
Full-time	26	63.4	38	92.7
Part-time or none	15	36.6	3	7.3

X^2 is 10.25; significant at the .002 level.

Table 47

Socialization Experience Profile:
Childhood, Ages 1-12

| Item | Presence or Absence of the Quality or Experience | | | | | | | | | | | |
| | Users | | | | | | Nonusers | | | | | |
	Manuel	Miguel	Marcos	Mario	Martín	Sum	Jaime	Julián	Jorge	Juan	José	Sum
Positive Factors:												
Reared by parents	x	0	0	x	x	3	x	x	0	0	0	2
Reared by mother	0	0	x	0	0	1	0	0	x	x	x	3
Reared by father	0	x	0	0	0	1	0	0	0	0	0	0
Favored and indulged	x	x	0	0	0	2	0	0	x	0	0	1
Primary school finished	x	0	0	0	0	1	x	0	0	0	0	1
Neutral Factors:												
Mother most important	x	0	0	x	0	2	0	0	0	x	x	2
Mother worked	x	0	x	0	0	2	0	x	x	x	x	4
Father most important	0	x	0	0	x	2	0	x	0	0	0	1
Reared in San José	x	0	x	x	0	3	x	x	0	0	x	3
Childhood employment	x	x	x	0	x	4	x	x	0	x	x	4
Negative Factors:												
Reared by surrogates	0	x	x	0	0	2	0	0	x	x	x	3
Father or stepfather alcoholic	x	0	0	x	0	2	x	x	0	0	x	3
Capricious & excessive punishment	0	0	0	x	x	2	x	x	0	0	0	2
Heavy discipline	0	x	0	0	0	1	x	x	0	x	0	3
Deprivation & negligence	x	0	x	0	0	1	x	0	0	x	x	3
Abandoned home (age)	9	0	6	0	0	2	0	0	0	0	0	0
Street life	x	0	x	x	0	3	0	0	0	0	0	0
Expelled from school	0	0	0	x	0	1	0	0	0	0	0	0
Downward family mobility	x	0	x	0	0	2	0	x	0	x	x	3
Reformatory	x	0	0	0	0	1	0	0	0	0	0	0
Marihuana use (age)	10	0	10	0	0	2	0	0	0	0	0	0
Sum of positive & negative factors in childhood:												
Positive	3	2	1	1	1	8	2	1	2	1	1	7
Negative	6	2	5	4	1	18	4	4	1	4	4	17

Table 47A

Socialization Experience Profile:
Adolescence, Ages 13-19

| Item | Presence or Absence of the Quality or Experience | | | | | | | | | | | |
| | Users | | | | | | Nonusers | | | | | |
	Manuel	Miguel	Marcos	Mario	Martín	Sum	Jaime	Julián	Jorge	Juan	José	Sum
Positive Factors:												
Continued childhood family	0	x	0	0	0	1	x	0	x	0	x	3
Good relations with mother	x	0	0	x	0	2	x	0	x	x	x	3
Good relations with father	x	x	0	0	0	2	x	x	0	0	0	2
Dependent on family	0	x	0	0	0	1	x	x	x	x	0	4
Regular employment	0	x	x	0	0	2	x	x	x	x	x	5
Attended school	0	x	0	0	0	1	x	x	x	0	0	3
Married	0	0	0	0	0	0	x	x	0	0	x	3
Civic activity	0	0	0	0	0	0	x	0	0	0	0	1
Upward mobility	0	0	x	0	0	1	x	0	0	x	x	3
Negative Factors:												
Family dissolved	0	0	x	x	0	2	0	0	0	0	0	0
Independent of family life	x	0	x	x	x	4	0	0	0	0	x	1
Heavy punishment	0	x	0	0	x	2	0	0	0	0	0	0
Abandoned home (age)	9	0	6	16	15	2	0	0	0	17	0	1
Street life	x	0	x	x	x	4	0	0	0	x	x	2
Expelled from school	0	0	0	x	0	0	0	x	0	0	0	1
Reformatory or prison	x	0	0	0	x	2	0	0	0	0	0	0
Criminal activity	x	0	0	0	x	2	0	x	0	0	x	2
Alcohol problem	0	0	x	0	x	2	0	0	0	0	0	0
Downward mobility	0	x	0	0	0	1	0	x	0	0	0	1
Marihuana use (age)	10	14	10	15	17	3	0	0	0	0	0	0
Sum of positive and negative factors in adolescence:												
Positive	2	5	2	1	0	10	9	5	5	4	5	28
Negative	4	2	4	4	7	21	0	3	0	2	3	8
Sum of positive and negative factors for full period of socialization, ages 1-19												
Positive	5	7	3	2	1	18	11	6	7	5	6	35
Negative	10	4	9	8	8	39	4	7	1	6	7	25

Table 48

Church Attendance

Frequency	Users N=84		Nonusers N=156	
	No.	%	No.	%
Once a week	6	7.3	34	21.9
2-3 times a month	2	2.4	8	4.9
Less than once a month	4	4.8	27	17.1
In fiestas	4	4.8	30	19.5
Does not presently attend	12	14.6	19	12.5
Never attended	37	43.9	27	17.0
No answer	19	21.9	11	7.3

X^2 is 47.567; significant at the .001 level.

Table 49

Occupation

	Users N=84		Nonusers N=156	
	No.	%	No.	%
Office worker	1	1.2	1	0.6
Seller	10	11.9	14	9.0
Farmer	1	1.2	2	1.3
Transportation worker	11	13.1	21	15.5
Artisan	39	46.4	90	57.7
Laborer	2	2.4	4	2.6
Service worker	14	16.7	15	9.6
Other	6	7.1	9	3.8

X^2 is 1.947; not significant.

Table 50

Subjects Reported Monthly Wages

Monthly Amount in Colones*	Users N=84		Nonusers N=156	
	No.	%	No.	%
0 - 399	15	17.9	12	7.7
400 - 599	18	21.4	17	10.9
600 - 799	18	21.4	37	23.7
800 - 999	11	13.1	35	22.4
1000 - 1199	12	14.3	19	12.2
1200 - 1599	5	6.0	24	15.4
1600 plus	1	1.2	9	5.8
No answer	4	4.8	3	1.9

X^2 is 5.673; significant at the .02 level.

Table 51

Subject Arrests Reported

	Users N=84		Nonusers N=156	
	No.	%	No.	%
Yes	68	81.0	51	32.7
No	15	17.9	103	66.0
No answer	1	1.2	2	1.3

X^2 is 99.65; significant at the .001 level.

*1 colon = US $ 0.117.

Table 52

Subjects Reporting Jail Experience

	Users N=84		Nonusers N=156	
	No.	%	No.	%
Yes	57	67.9	10	6.4
No	26	31.0	139	89.1
No answer	1	1.2	7	4.5

X^2 is 99.65; significant at the .001 level.

Table 53

Offenses Committed Leading to Imprisonment*

Type of Offense	Total Offenses -- 109 Users		Nonusers		Significance Level
	No.	%	No.	%	
Felony:					
Property	25	22.9	1	0.9	.001
Narcotic	49	45.0	1	0.9	.001
Other	16	14.7	8	7.3	.4
Misdemeanor:					
Manner	3	2.8	3	2.8	--
Narcotic	0	0.0	0	0.0	--
Other	2	1.8	1	0.9	ns

*Percentages are based on total number of offenses; some persons recorded
multiple offenses; p values are based on binomial distribution.

Table 54
Marital Status

	Users N=84		Nonusers N=156	
	No.	%	No.	%
Single	36	42.8	45	28.8
Married	14	16.6	82	52.6
Divorced	2	2.4	1	0.6
Consensual union	31	36.9	24	15.4
Unknown	1	1.2	4	2.5

X^2 is 32.454; significant at the .01 level.

Table 55

Number of Second Marriages

| | Users N=84 | | Nonusers N=156 | |
	No.	%	No.	%
Yes	26	30.9	92	58.9
No	54	65.2	62	39.7
Unknown	4	4.7	2	1.2

X^2 is 14.557; significant at the .001 level.

Table 56

Number of Consensual Unions Reported

| | Users N=84 | | Nonusers N=156 | |
	No.	%	No.	%
None	11	13.0	77	49.3
One	17	20.2	45	28.8
Two	14	16.6	10	6.4
Three or more	40	47.6	18	11.5
Unknown	2	2.3	6	3.8

X^2 is 64.257; significant at the .001 level.

Table 57

Courtship

| | User N=41 | | Nonuser N=41 | |
	No.	%	No.	%
Long-term (three months or less)	21	51.2	29	70.7
Short-term (more than three months)	9	22.0	2	4.9
No answer	11	26.8	10	24.4

X^2 for N of 31 (short-term vs. long-term) is 5.72; significant at the .02 level.

Table 58

User Type and Smoking Environment

User Type	Home Alone	Work Alone	Work in Group	Home in Group	Vehicle	Country-side Alone	Street Alone	Country-side Group	Street Group	Bar	Pensión-Brothel	Dance-hall	Prison	Row Total
Stable Smokers (N=23)	94	47	34	34	7	2	14	23	10	11	7	2	0	285
Street Movers (N=16)	32	21	0	7	7	7	25	36	93	14	15	4	3	264
Pastoralist-Escapists (N=2)	2	1	1	0	0	4	8	7	3	0	1	2	0	29
Column Totals	128	69	35	41	14	13	47	66	106	25	23	8	3	578 Grand Total

Table 59

User Type and Smoking Environment Standardized for Statistical Comparison*

User Type	Standardization Factors	Home Alone	Work Alone	Work in Group	Home in Group	Vehicle	Countryside Alone	Street Alone	Countryside Group	Street Group	Bar	Pensión-Brothel	Dance-hall	Prison	Standardized Totals
Stable Smokers (N=23)	1.274	119.7	59.9	43.3	43.3	8.9	2.5	17.8	29.3	12.7	14.0	8.9	2.5	0.0	362.8
Street Movers plus Pastoralist-Escapists (N=18)	1.583	57.0	34.8	1.6	11.1	11.1	17.4	52.3	68.1	152.0	22.2	25.3	9.5	4.8	467.2
p Scores		$p<.001$	$p<.001$	$p<.001$	$p<.001$	$p<.076$	$p<.001$	$p<.001$	$p<.001$	$p<.0001$	$p<.053$	$p<.001$	$p<.015$	$p<.036$	

*Standardization factor derived by dividing the other row total by 10 N_1.

Table 60

Cross-tabulation of Effects and Smoking Environments

Effects	Home Alone	Work Alone	Work in Group	Home in Group	Vehicle	Countryside Alone	Street Alone	Countryside Group	Street Group	Bar	Pensión-Brothel	Dance-Hall	Prison	Row Totals
Bad for eyes	3						3		1					8
Good for asthma	4													4
Dry mouth, rough throat	7	1	1						1	1				11
Nerves (+ calm)	6	3					1	1	2					13
– aggravate)	3								3					6
Sweat, cough	6	2	1		1			1	1		1			13
Relieve aches, pains		1	1											2
Heat			1		1		2		1					5
Bad for lungs	2													2
"Muerte blanca"	4	1	1	3	3	1	2	2	14	4	2			37
General "blahs"	2													2
Marihuana hangover									6					6
Sleep (+ helps)	12					1	1		1					15
– hinders)	2													2
Sex (+ better)	11						1	2	6		11			31
– worse)	1													1
Food appetite (+ inc.)	11	3	1				8	1	16		2			42
– decrease	5	2					1		2					10
0 neutral)	1								1					2
Work (+ helps)	2	39	2		1				1					45
– hinders)		6	4											10
General performance	1	4	2				2		3		1	2		15
(+better, –worse)		4	2		1		2	1	3					13
Sing better	2													2
Time on job goes faster		4												4
Mirth	4						1	3	2					10
Passive audience	2		1	1			1	3	3	2	1			14
Antiboredom			1			1			1	1	1			5
Everything rosier	9		1			1	6	3	7					27
Alcohol (+ better	8	2					2		1					13
= equal)			3					1						4

(Continued)

Table 60 (Cont.)

Cross-tabulation of Effects and Smoking Environments

Effects	Home Alone	Work Alone	Work in Group	Home in Group	Vehicle	Country-side Alone	Street Alone	Country-side Group	Street Group	Bar	Pensión-Brothel	Dance-hall	Prison	Row Totals
Behavioral compensation	1	2			1		3			1				8
Fright ("susto")							1	2						3
Active participation	2						2	4	4			3		15
Fight									1	2				3
Act idiotic	1		1											2
Isolate yourself socially	1	1	1	1										4
Socially more aggressive							2	2						4
Helps face the day	3												1	4
Floating sensation								1	1	1				3
Music better	4			1		1	1	1	3	1		1		13
Nothing			1	1					5					7
Perception altered		1						1	2					4
Conversation (+ better	2	3	3	5				3	2					18
— worse)						1	1		2					4
Thoughts more profound	10	7	3	1			3	2	2		1			29
One becomes creative	4							2						6
Hurts memory	1	4					1		1					7
Column Totals	147	90	31	13	8	4		30	107	13	18	7	1	516 Grand Total

Table 61

Simplified Tabulation of Effects and Smoking Environments

Effect Types	Home Alone	Work Alone	Work in Group	Home in Group	Vehicle	Country-side Alone	Street Alone	Country-side Group	Street Group	Bar	Pensión-Brothel	Dance-Hall	Prison	Row Totals
Physiological	31	8	4	0	2	0	6	2	9	1	1	0	0	64
Bad trip	6	1	1	3	3	1	2	2	20	4	2	0	0	45
Appetites	53	5	1	0	0	0	11	1	27	0	13	0	0	111
Work & Performance	5	57	10	0	2	0	4	1	7	0	1	2	0	89
Behavior & Sensation	31	7	7	2	1	1	17	15	26	7	0	4	1	119
Cognitive & Perception	21	12	8	8	0	2	7	9	18	1	1	1	0	88
Column Totals	147	90	31	13	8	4	47	30	107	13	18	7	1	516

Table 62

Cross-Tabulation of Environments and Effect Types

Standardized for Comparison Within Columns

Effect Types	Home Alone	Work Alone	Work in Group	Home in Group	Vehicle	Country-side Alone	Street Alone	Country-side Group	Street Group	Bar	Pensión-Brothel	Dance-hall	Prison	Standardization Factor[†]
Physiological	72.2*	18.6	9.3	0	4.7	0	14.0	4.7	20.9	2.3	2.3	0	0	2.33
Bad Trip	19.9	3.3	3.3	9.9	9.9	3.3	6.6	6.6	66.2	13.2	6.6	0	0	3.31
Appetites	71.1	6.7	1.3	0	0	0	14.8	1.3	36.2	0	17.4	0	0	1.34
Work & Performance	8.4	95.4	16.7	0	3.3	0	6.7	1.7	11.7	0	1.7	3.3	0	1.67
Behavior & Sensation	38.8	8.8	8.8	2.5	1.3	1.3	21.3	18.8	32.5	8.8	0	5.0	1.3	1.25
Cognitive & Perception	35.6	20.3	13.5	13.5	0	3.4	11.9	15.2	30.5	1.7	1.7	1.7	0	1.69

*Circled scores are markedly higher for a given environment than scores of other effects.

†Obtained by dividing the multiple of all other row totals by 2×10^8.

Table 63

Cross-Tabulation of Environments and Effect Types

Standardized for Both Columnar and Row Comparisons

Effect Types	Home Alone	Work Alone	Work in Group	Home in Group	Vehicle	Country-side Alone	Street Alone	Country-side Group	Street Group	Bar	Pensión-Brothel	Dance-hall	Prison
Physiological	103.5	43.6	63.2	0	123.9	0	62.8	33.0	41.2	37.3	26.9	0	0
Bad Trip	28.5	7.7	22.4	160.5	260.9	173.9	29.6	46.4	130.4	214.0	77.3	0	0
Appetites	102.0	15.7	8.8	0	0	0	66.4	9.1	71.3	0	203.8	0	0
Work & Performance	12.0	223.5	113.6	0	87.0	0	30.1	11.9	23.1	0	19.9	99.4	0
Behavior & Sensation	55.6	20.6	59.8	40.5	34.3	68.5	95.5	132.1	64.0	142.7	0	150.6	274.1
Cognitive & Perception	51.1	47.6	91.8	218.9	0	179.2	53.4	106.8	60.1	27.6	19.9	51.2	0

Legend: ○ means that the score is notably high.
– means that the score is notably high relative to other scores in the same row.
l means that the score is notably high relative to other scores in the same column.
+ means that the score is notably high relative to other row and column scores.

Table 64
Smoking Effects and User Types

Effects	Pastoralist-Escapists	Street Movers	Stable Smokers	Total
Bad for eyes	0	2	6	8
Good for asthma	0	0	4	4
Dry mouth, rough throat	0	5	6	11
Nerves (+ calms	0	4	9	13
- worsens)	0	3	3	6
Sweat, cough	2	3	8	13
Relieves aches, pains	0	0	2	2
Heat	0	2	3	5
Bad for lungs	0	0	2	2
"Muerte blanca"	1	20	16	37
General "blahs"	0	0	2	2
Marihuana hangover	0	6	0	6
Sleep (+ helps	0	7	8	15
- hinders)	0	0	2	2
Sex (+ better	2	18	19	39
- worse)	0	0	1	1
Food appetite (+ inc.	1	24	18	41
- decrease	0	4	6	10
0 neutral)	0	1	1	2
Work (+ helps	0	13	32	45
- hinders)	2	3	5	10
General performance				
(+ helps	0	6	9	15
- hinders)	0	6	7	13
Sing better	0	2	0	2
Time on job goes faster	0	0	4	4
Mirth	1	8	1	10
Passive audience	1	5	8	14
Antiboredom	0	2	3	5
Everything rosier	2	11	14	27
Alcohol (+ better	1	3	9	13
- equal)	0	0	4	4
Behavioral compensation	0	4	4	8
Fright ("Susto")	2	0	1	3
Active participation	1	5	9	15
Fight	0	3	0	3
Act idiotic	1	1	0	2
Isolate yourself socially	0	0	4	4
Socially more aggressive	0	1	3	4
Helps face the day	0	1	3	4
Floating sensation	1	1	1	3
Music better	2	7	4	13
Nothing	1	2	4	7
Perception altered	0	3	1	4
Conversation (+ better	0	6	12	18
- worse)	2	2	0	4
Thoughts more profound	2	7	20	29
One becomes creative	0	2	4	6
Hurts memory	1	4	2	7
Totals	26	206	284	516

Table 65

Significant Differences in Standardized Scores*
for User Type and Smoking Effects

Effects	Street movers/ Pastoralist- Escapists	Stable Smokers	Total	p score
Good for asthma	0.0	4.0	4.0	$p = .0600$
"Muerte blanca"	33.1	16.1	49.2	$p = .0050$
Marihuana hangover	9.5	0.0	9.5	$p = .0010$
Sex (+ better)	31.6	19.2	50.8	$p = .0200$
Work (+ helps)	20.5	32.3	52.8	$p = .0190$
Time on job goes faster	0.0	4.0	4.0	$p = .0600$
Mirth	14.2	1.0	15.2	$p = .0004$
Alcohol (= equal)	0.0	4.0	4.0	$p = .0600$
Fight	4.7	0.0	4.7	$p = .0400$
Isolate yourself socially	0.0	4.0	4.0	$p = .0600$
Music better	14.2	4.0	18.2	$p = .0100$
Conversation (- worse)	6.3	0.0	6.3	$p = .0100$
Hurts memory	7.9	2.0	9.9	$p = .0500$

*Standardization factor derived by dividing the other column total by $10n_i$.

Table 66

Effects Types and User Types: A Comparison
of Standardized Scores*

Effects Types	Pastoralist- Escapists and Street Movers	Stable Smokers	p score
Physiological	17.4	21.7	$p = .073$
Bad trip	21.3	9.1	$p = .011$
Appetites	43.4	27.7	$p = .009$
Work & Performance	25.2	28.7	$p = .080$
Behavior & Sensation	43.4	32.3	$p = .030$
Cognition & Perception	32.3	23.7	$p = .030$

*Standardization factor derived by dividing the other column total by
$20 n_i$.

Table 67

User Type, Effect, and Smoking Environment

User Types	Smoking Environments	Smoking Effects
Pastoralist-Escapists	Limited repertoire, choosing low-risk open environments. Favored environments are "countryside alone" "street alone" "countryside group" "dance hall."	Few clear emphases, but appetites and behavioral effects seem to be favored. Share lack of confidence in performance while under marihuana effects.
Street Movers	All open environments and some closed environments when available. Often seem to be flaunting the law. Favored environments include "street in group" "pensión-brothel" "bar."	Appetite effects clearly emphasized, with minor emphasis on behavioral effects. Striking preponderance of "bad trip" effects in general and "white death" in particular. Lack confidence in work performance while stoned.
Stable Smokers	Closed environments, heavily favoring the user's home and shunning the risky and open environments. Favored environments are "home alone" "work alone" "work in group" "home in group."	Emphasis placed on practical and every̅ₖ day nature of use, containing more accounts of purely physical effects and positive effects on work performance. Thought and conversation are also claimed to improve under the influence of marihuana.

Table 68

Age of First Regular Marihuana Use

Age at first regular use	Number of individuals
9	2
11	2
12	6
13	3
14	6
15	4
16	4
17	6
18	3
20	2
21	1
25	1
26	1

Table 69

Age of First Taste of Marihuana

Age of "first taste"	Number of individuals
8	1
9	3
10	1
11	3
12	4
13	5
14	5
15	7
16	5
17	2
18	1
19	1
20	1
21	1
25	1

Table 70

Time Lapse Between "First Taste" and Regular Use

"First taste" Impression	Lapse	No Lapse
Good	5	9
Bad, Indifferent	12	15

X^2 is .290; not significant.

Table 71

Mean Absences per Year

Pair of Subjects	Users		Nonusers	
	Excused	Nonexcused	Excused	Nonexcused
1	4.0	1.0	9.0	3.6
2	1.5	0.0	15.8	0.0
3	2.7	2.0	4.3	0.5
4	4.3	1.5	8.2	0.0
5	7.7	0.5	9.6	0.6
6	1.5	1.0	0.0	0.0
7	10.6	2.0	7.2	7.7

$\overline{X}$ is 4.6, 1.1 $\overline{X}$ is 7.7, 1.7

Table 72

Job Changes and Use Level

Job Changes	Use Level (in cigs. per day)
Does not work	6.2
Frequent (several times a year)	7.6
Occasional (yearly or less)	5.7
None	15.4

Table 73

Character of Work and Use Level

Character of Work	Use Level (in cigs. per day)	No. of Subjects
Full-time	10.0	24
Part-time	11.0	9
Seasonal	10.1	3
Does not work	5.4	5

Table 74

Constancy of Employment and Use Level

Periods of Unemployment	Use Level (in cigs. per day)	No. of Subjects
Frequent (several times a year)	8.2	16
Occasional (yearly or less)	8.6	12
None	12.4	13

Table 75

Responses to the Medical History (N=240)

	Users N=84		Nonusers N=156	
	No.	%	No.	%
Weight loss	25	29.8	22	14.1
Obesity	4	4.8	30	19.2
Reaction to drugs	21	25.0	26	16.7
Changes in appetite	22	26.2	10	16.7
Indigestion	11	13.1	5	6.4
Nausea	12	14.3	4	2.6
Abdominal pain	9	10.7	4	2.6
Jaundice	7	8.3	2	1.3
Frequent urination	12	14.3	1	0.6
Trauma to head	50	59.5	61	39.1

$\underline{p} \leq .05$ for all items.

Table 76

Comparative Findings on the Physical Examination

	Users N=84		Nonusers N=156	
	No.	%	No.	%
Body weight (kg)	60.29		63.43	
Systolic blood pressure (mm Hg)	115		118	
Pterygium	8	9.5	3	1.9
Abdominal scars	14	16.7	11	7.1
Testicular atrophy, unilateral	7	8.3	2	1.3

$\underline{p} \leq .05$ for each item.

Table 77

Results of Laboratory Tests
(N=240)

	User (N=84)		Control (N=156)	
	Mean	S D	Mean	S D
Hemoglobin (gms/dl)	14.60	1.08	14.82	1.05
Hematocrit (ml/dl)	45.39	2.81	46.35	3.00*
Leukocytes (1,000s/mm^3)	9.42	2.65	8.99	2.33
Segmented neutrophiles (%)	56.0	8.8	57.0	11.3
Lymphocytes (%)	36.0	8.4	34.0	8.9
Eosinophiles (%)	4.7	3.5	5.4	5.1
Monocytes (%)	2.4	2.3	2.0	2.0
Juvenile neutrophiles (%)	0.5	0.9	0.7	1.2
Metamyelocytes (%)	0.0	0.0	0.0	0.0
Myelocytes (%)	0.0	0.0	0.0	0.0
Basophiles (%)	0.1	0.4	0.1	0.3
Prothrombin time (secs.)	13.4	0.9	12.9	1.2*
RBC sedimentation rate (mm/hr)	10.4	8.2	9.0	7.0
Blood sugar, fasting (mg/dl)	73.6	11.0	75.5	11.0
Two-hour postglucose (mg/dl)	66.3	18.0	65.4	23.7
Urea nitrogen (mg/dl)	15.3	3.5	14.6	2.9
Alkaline phosphatase	3.5	1.7	3.6	1.5
Pyruvic transaminase (units/ml)	16.3	18.3	20.8	33.5
Bilirubin, direct (mg/dl)	0.16	0.14	0.19	0.14
Bilirubin, total (mg/dl)	0.48	0.25	0.53	0.29
Total protein (gm/dl)	7.72	0.79	7.77	0.50
Albumin	4.12	0.39	4.22	0.41
Globulin	3.42	0.39	3.54	0.39*
Alpha 1	0.43	0.09	0.52	0.09
Alpha 2	0.85	0.18	0.87	0.16
Beta	0.87	0.18	0.94	0.20
Gamma	1.29	0.34	1.27	0.26

*p values discussed in the main text.

Table 78

Urine Analysis N=240

	Users N=84		Nonusers N=156	
	Absent	Present	Absent	Present
Glucose	84	0	156	0
Protein				
Negative	68	0	143	0
Trace to 1	0	16	0	10
2 to 4	0	0	0	3
WBC, per HPF				
9 or less	0	75	0	144
10 or more	0	9	0	12
RBC, per HPF				
4 or less	0	83	0	152
5 or more	0	1	0	4
Casts	83	1	14	2

Table 79

Intestinal Parasites
(N=238*)

	Users N=83*		Controls N=155*		Totals	
	No.	%	No.	%	No.	%
Ancylostoma or Necator	7	8.2	14	9.0	21	8.8
Ascaris lumbricoides	5	5.9	9	5.8	14	5.8
Trichuris trichiura	9	10.6	26	16.8	35	14.6
Strongyloides stercoralis	3	3.5	4	2.6	7	2.9
Enterobius vermicularis	0	0.0	1	0.6	1	0.4
Hymenolepis nana	0	0.0	5	3.2	5	2.1
Entamoeba histolytica	2	2.4	8	5.2	10	4.2
Entamoeba coli	7	8.2	24	15.5	31	12.9
Endolimax nana	11	12.9	20	12.9	31	12.9
Iodamoeba buetschlii	1	1.2	4	2.6	5	2.1
Giardia lamblia	3	3.5	8	5.2	11	4.6
Trichomonas hominis	1	1.2	5	3.2	6	2.5

*One user and one control failed to submit stool specimens.

p values discussed in the main text.

Table 80

Intestinal Parasites and Eosinophilia

	Users N=83*			Controls N=155*		
Parasites Present	Eosino- philia	% Positive	Parasites Present	Eosino- philia	% Positive	
38	12	31.6	80	23	28.8	
Parasites Absent	Eosino- philia	% Positive	Parasites Absent	Eosino- philia	% Positive	
45	13	38.9	75	18	24.0	
Total:						
83	25	30.1	155	41	26.5	

*One user and one control failed to submit stool specimens.

Table 81

Electrocardiographic Abnormalities

	Users N=84	Controls N=156	Total N=240
Occasional A-V nodal extrasystoles	0	1	1
Isolated A-V nodal and ventricular extrasystoles	0	1	1
A-V nodal rhythm	1	0	1
Short P-R interval	0	1	1
Atrioventricular block, first degree	1	1	2
Wolff-Parkinson-White syndrome	0	1	1
Right bundle branch block, complete	0	2	2
Right bundle branch block, incomplete	6	8	14
Left ventricular hypertrophy	0	2	2
T-wave changes suggestive of ischemia	1	5	6
Prolonged Q-T interval	1	0	1
Total Abnormalities	10	22	32

Table 82

Subjects Excluded from Matched-Pair Study

	Users N=84	Nonusers N=156	Totals N=240
Defects in visual acuity	4	4	8
Defective color vision	3	13	16
Positive serological test for syphilis	20	17	37
Pulmonary lesion	8	17	25
Other serious disease	3*	9*	12
Total excludable defects	38	60	98
Total excluded subjects	37*	56*	93

*See text, pp. 162-163.

Table 83

Subjects Excluded for Causes Other Than Medical Abnormalities

Cause	Users N=84	Nonusers N=156	Totals N=240
History of abstention from marihuana found to be inaccurate	NA	2	2
History of marihuana use found to be inaccurate	1	NA	1
Alcohol abuse interfered with participation in testing	1	2	3
Failure to keep appointments	2	1	3
Failure to cooperate with medical test procedures	2	0	2
Totals	6	5	11

NA = not applicable.

Table 84

Summary of Findings of Comparison Between User (U) and Nonuser (N) Groups
(NS Indicates Large Deviation from Customarily Accepted Significance Level)

Test (Condition)	Finding	Level of Significance
Pupil response	U less than N	n.s.
Contributors to pupil data	U less than N	--*
Intraocular pressure	U greater than N	$p = 0.06$
Dark adaptation	U less than N	$p = 0.07$
Acuity vs. luminance	U less than N	$p = 0.07$
Color-match midpoint	U requires more red	n.s.
Color-match range	U less than N	$p = 0.01$
Brightness midpoint	U more than N	n.s.
Brightness range	U less than N	$p = 0.01$
Schirmer (lacrimal fluid production)	U more than N	$p = 0.02$
Fundus abnormality	U more than N	n.s.
Conjunctival hyperemia	U more than N	n.s.
Pterygia	U more than N	n.s.

*Resulting probability depends on analysis.

n.s. = not significant.

Table 85

Symptoms of Nonspecific Irritation of the Anterior Segment of the Eye and
Observations in Users and as Reported in the Literature

	In Eye Disease*	Trends in Chronic Users†	Acute Users
Conjunctival hyperemia	increased	slightly increased	increased
Light sensitivity	increased	increased	not measured
Acuity	decreased	decreased	conflicting reports
Intraocular pressure	increased	increased	decreased
Pupil diameter	decreased	slightly decreased	decreased
Lacrimation	increased	increased	decreased

*As described by Duke-Elder, 1964, 1966.
†No consumption for 4-10 hours.

Table 86

Comparison Between 27 Chronic Marihuana Users and 27 Age-Matched
Control Subjects on Each of 25 Sleep Stage Parameters
(Adjustment Night)

Parameter	Mean ± Standard Deviation		t Value & Significance
	Marihuana Users	Control Subjects	
Time in bed	420 ± 49	390 ± 68	+1.76
Sleep period time	390 ± 53	372 ± 65	+1.05
Total sleep time	381 ± 51	362 ± 64	+1.14
Sleep efficiency index	.908 ± .084	.930 ± .060	−1.25
Sleep latency	25.5 ± 27.8	15.2 ± 9.1	+1.73
Sleep latency 1	25.9 ± 27.7	15.2 ± 9.1	+1.80
Sleep latency 2	32.7 ± 31.6	21.2 ± 10.3	+1.71
Number of stages	38.3 ± 15.5	32.6 ± 12.6	+1.50
Frequency of stage 1 (x2)	21.2 ± 11.9	18.6 ± 9.2	+0.90
Number of awakenings	3.81 ± 3.51	3.15 ± 2.92	+0.74
REM period length	28.6 ± 7.3	23.0 ± 7.3	+2.68 ($p < .05$)
REM interval length	76.0 ± 29.8	72.2 ± 20.6	+0.62
Number of REM periods	3.44 ± 1.01	3.41 ± 0.84	+0.16
Percent stage 0	2.4 ± 3.2	2.6 ± 5.7	−0.20
Percent stage 1	7.4 ± 4.2	7.1 ± 3.8	+0.28
Percent stage 1 REM	23.5 ± 5.2	20.4 ± 6.1	+2.17 ($p < .05$)
Percent stage 2	55.9 ± 7.0	56.7 ± 10.8	−0.35
Percent stage 3	5.3 ± 4.0	7.4 ± 7.9	−1.21
Percent stage 4	5.4 ± 6.6	5.8 ± 7.8	−0.21
Latency stage 0	189 ± 172	216 ± 137	−0.63
Latency stage 1	0.4 ± 1.7	0.0 ± 0.0	+1.11
Latency stage 1 REM	104.2 ± 56.3	102.3 ± 50.0	+0.13
Latency stage 2	7.2 ± 6.7	6.0 ± 4.3	+0.77
Latency stage 3	114.8 ± 153.6	114.7 ± 159.7	+0.00
Latency stage 4	178.3 ± 176.6	193.9 ± 176.1	−0.41

Table 87

Comparison Between 32 Chronic Marihuana Users and 32 Age-Matched
Control Subjects on Each of 25 Sleep Stage Parameters
(Average of Postadjustment Nights)

Parameter	Mean ± Standard Deviation		t Value & Significance
	Marihuana Users	Control Subjects	
Time in bed	428 ± 54	406 ± 71	+1.43
Sleep period time	409 ± 50	394 ± 67	+1.07
Total sleep time	404 ± 47	390 ± 65	+1.03
Sleep efficiency index	.947 ± .048	.963 ± .025	−1.84
Sleep latency	16.1 ± 16.7	10.2 ± 7.6	+1.69
Sleep latency 1	21.9 ± 19.1	11.1 ± 8.0	+2.86 (p < .01)
Sleep latency 2	23.5 ± 19.2	15.9 ± 10.2	+1.83
Number of stages	32.4 ± 9.2	32.6 ± 6.8	−0.10
Frequency of stage 1 (x2)	16.8 ± 7.7	17.0 ± 5.5	−0.00
Number of awakenings	2.70 ± 1.99	2.29 ± 1.60	+0.90
REM period length	29.5 ± 4.6	26.8 ± 5.3	+2.04 (p < .05)
REM interval length	68.8 ± 12.6	66.6 ± 8.2	+0.71
Number of REM periods	3.99 ± 0.58	3.92 ± 0.78	+0.37
Percent stage 0	1.2 ± 2.2	0.9 ± 1.2	+0.81
Percent stage 1	6.4 ± 3.3	6.1 ± 2.2	+0.43
Percent stage 1 REM	27.5 ± 3.6	25.1 ± 4.1	+2.44 (p < .05)
Percent stage 2	54.3 ± 6.8	54.9 ± 7.9	−0.46
Percent stage 3	5.5 ± 3.0	6.3 ± 3.7	−1.02
Percent stage 4	5.1 ± 4.7	6.7 ± 5.9	−1.43
Latency stage 0	274 ± 106	268 ± 108	+0.23
Latency stage 1	5.8 ± 14.3	0.9 ± 3.8	+1.83
Latency stage 1 REM	82.0 ± 22.1	82.4 ± 28.4	−0.05
Latency stage 2	7.4 ± 4.4	5.7 ± 3.8	+1.40
Latency stage 3	94.4 ± 118.3	86.2 ± 118.1	+0.34
Latency stage 4	176.2 ± 151.8	153.0 ± 143.6	+0.78

Table 88

Effects of Subject Type and Use Level on Each of 25 Sleep Stage Parameters
(Average of Post-Adjustment Nights for 32 Pairs of Age-Matched Subjects)

Parameter	Marihuana Users						Control Subjects					
	Mean	Type		Use Level			Mean	Type		Use Level		
		Street	Stable	Lo	Med.	Hi		Street	Stable	Lo	Med.	Hi
Time in bed	430	444	416 ††	447	428	416	403	380 ††	427	410	371	428
Sleep-period time	411	425	398 ††	419	415	400	391	367 ††	416	398	363	413
Total sleep time	406	417	394 ††	415	411	391	387	363 ††	412	395	360	407
Sleep efficiency index	.946	.941	.951	.930	.962	.946	.962	.961	.963	.963	.971	.952
Sleep latency	16.4	16.3	16.5	25.0	11.1	13.1	10.3	11.1	9.4	9.2	7.8	13.9
Sleep latency 1	21.9 **	19.7	24.2	26.3	22.7	16.8	11.2 **	12.5	9.9	10.2	7.8	15.7
Sleep latency 2	24.0	25.1	22.8 †	34.5	18.6	18.8	15.9	16.5	15.3 †	14.1	12.2	21.4
No. of stages	32.5	33.9	31.1	29.2	33.1	35.2	32.2	29.8	34.7	30.8	31.5	34.5
Freq. of stage 1 (x2)	16.9	17.2	16.5	14.4	16.5	19.7	16.7	14.8	18.5	15.5	16.6	17.8
No. of awakenings	3.7	4.2	3.3	3.4	3.8	4.1	3.2	2.8	3.6	2.8	2.9	4.0
REM per length	29.6	29.8	29.4	29.6	31.1	28.0	26.9	26.5	27.2	28.5	25.2	26.8
REM int. length	69.2	71.0	67.5 †	71.2	69.4	67.1	67.1	68.4	65.8 †	65.3	68.6	67.4
No. of REM periods	3.99	4.03	3.95	4.01	3.92	4.04	3.88	3.51	4.25	4.03	3.56	4.05

(Continued)

†Significant Interaction Between Street/Stable and Users/Controls (p<.05).
††Significant Interaction Between Street/Stable and Users/Controls (p<.01).
**Significant Difference Between Users and Controls (p<.01).

Table 88 (Cont.)

Parameter	Marihuana Users						Control Subjects					
	Mean	Type		Use Level			Mean	Type		Use Level		
		Street	Stable	Lo	Med.	Hi		Street	Stable	Lo	Med.	Hi
Percent stage 0	1.3	1.7	0.9	0.9	0.9	2.1	0.9	0.7	1.1	0.6	0.7	1.4
Percent stage 1	6.3*	5.8	6.8	5.5	6.5	6.9	6.1*	5.7	6.5	6.0	6.3	5.9
Percent stage 1 REM	27.4	27.1	27.8	27.8	28.1	26.3	25.0	24.2	25.9	26.9	23.4	24.8
Percent stage 2	54.2	53.3	55.1 †	55.1	53.3	54.2	54.8	54.1	55.5 †	54.7	54.9	54.8
Percent stage 3	5.5	5.3	5.7	6.0	5.8	4.7	6.4	7.7	5.1	6.0	7.6	5.7
Percent stage 4	5.3	6.9	3.7	4.6	5.4	5.8	6.8	7.6	5.9	5.7	7.1	7.4
Latency stage 0	276	285	266	277	280	270	270	272	268	307	286	216
Latency stage 1	5.3	3.0	7.7	0.8	11.6	3.6	0.9	1.4	0.5	1.0	0.0	1.8
Latency stage 1 REM	82.1	82.5	81.6	82.2	85.4	78.6	82.6	86.0	79.3	77.8	82.0	88.1
Latency stage 2	7.6	8.8	6.3	9.5	7.5	5.7	5.7	5.4	6.0	4.9	4.5	7.5
Latency stage 3	90.9	67.0	114.8	74.8	77.8	120.0	81.8	47.4	116.2	77.1	76.8	91.5
Latency stage 4	174.5	151.8	197.2	211.9	143.5	168.3	149.4	121.9	176.9	143.4	160.3	154.2

*Significant Difference Between Users and Controls (p<.05).
†Significant Interaction Between Street/Stable and Users/Controls (p<.05).

Table 89

Night-to-Night Variability (Standard Deviations) Comparisons Between
22 Chronic Marihuana Users and 22 Age-Matched Control Subjects

Parameter	Median Estimate		Mean Estimate	
	Marihuana Users	Control Subjects	Marihuana Users	Control Subjects
Time in bed	2.9	5.3	15.6	15.2
Sleep-period time	11.7	9.7	27.2	15.9
Total sleep time	12.8	11.3	27.5	18.1
Sleep efficiency index	.026	.020	.046	.029
Sleep latency	8.0	4.8	23.0	7.3
Sleep latency 1	9.8*	5.0	31.7	9.8
Sleep latency 2	8.6	6.8	22.6	9.1
Number of stages	7.2	7.2	8.8	8.0
Frequency of stage 1 (x2)	3.3	2.8	3.9	3.1
Number of awakenings	1.1	1.0	1.4	1.2
REM period length	6.2	5.8	6.9	6.6
REM interval length	9.7	11.4	15.9	15.4
Number of REM periods	0.68	0.68	0.73	0.73
Percent stage 0	0.8	0.7	1.6	1.8
Percent stage 1	2.3	2.5	3.2	2.7
Percent stage 1 REM	4.4	3.8	4.8	4.6
Percent stage 2	5.5	5.1	5.9	6.1
Percent stage 3	2.6	2.9	3.2	3.8
Percent stage 4	3.1	2.7	3.9	4.1
Latency stage 0	106	85	126	125
Latency stage 1	0.0	0.0	22.7	6.5
Latency stage 1 REM	27.9	26.8	35.3	37.3
Latency stage 2	3.1	3.1	3.4	6.2
Latency stage 3	40.6	42.6	73.5	79.3
Latency stage 4	92.6	80.2	144	104

*Significant difference between groups ($p \leq .05$).

Table 90

Daily Smoking Behavior

Subject I.D.	Sleep Night							
	1	2	3	4	5	6	7	8
1	2	0	2	8	2	0	0	6
2	25	20	8	12	20	12	20	12
3	9	20		10	11	12		12
4	8	6	4	7	10	12	10	4
5	25	19	6	0	16	0	19	
6	15	15	24	26	25	26	24	12
7	6	2		1	0	10	3	4
8	25	20	18	24	22	27	26	24
9	15	18	25	20	26	25	24	22
10								
11	10	10	9		12	10	14	10
12	6	8	20	10	9	12	12	9
13	5	6	9	5	12	12	7	6
14	8	6	10	8	12	10	8	10
15	12	8	8	10	10	16	12	6
16	1	1	1	2	2	1	2	1
17	7	7	7	7	7	0	8	16
18	2	3	0	0	2	4	1	3
19	25		21	25	35	30		
20								
21	0	0	3	2	8	0	0	4
22	2	0	0	3	4	3	6	3
23								
24	8	6	12	1	3	4	12	14
25	25	9	8	15	14	8	10	12
26	2	1	3	11	9	6	8	10
27	5	7	10	8				
28	14	10	10	6	6	7	12	16
29	0	0	0	3	4	2	5	8
30								
31					6	10	4	12
32	0	0	2	6	4	0	0	8
33	6	8	0	0	12	10	3	11
34	0	6	8	12	0	0	10	14
35	0	3	0	2	4	6	6	4
36	6	5	18	3	25	0	4	8
37	6	4	5	8	12	15	15	13
38	0	8	6	10	2	0	12	0
39	0	0	8	10	0	3	8	10
40	7	6	7	6	10	16	10	8
41	0	0	3	10	14	6	10	11

Note: nights in boxes used in night-to-night variability calculations.

Table 91

Summary of Pulmonary Test Results

Means	Means, paired-t, and $\underline{p}$ values are tabulated below			
	Users	Nonusers	Paired-t Values	$\underline{p}$ Values
Age (years)	31*	31*	0.61	n.s.s.
Tobacco, lifetime packs	5,544	4,147	1.29	$\underline{p}$=.19
Height, cm	167.3	168.7	0.73	n.s.s.
Left home before age 16	58%	12%		$\underline{p}$=.05
Perception of work	Lighter	Heavier		$\underline{p}$=.05
FVC (1.)	4.38†; 4.43††	4.34†; 4.37††	0.26†; 0.43††	n.s.s.†; n.s.s.††
percent predicted	91.2; 93.3	89.7; 90.8	0.52; 0.86	n.s.s.; n.s.s.
FEV $_{1.0}$ (1.)	3.53; 3.57	3.45; 3.48	0.61; 0.73	n.s.s.; n.s.s.
percent predicted	94.8; 96.5	92.6; 93.3	0.61; 1.06	n.s.s.; n.s.s.
FEF$_{25-75}$ (1./sec.)	3.67; 3.91	3.425; 3.43	1.60; 1.49	$\underline{p}$=.11; .13
percent predicted	84.6; 89.9	74.7; 81.5	1.23; 1.47	$\underline{p}$=.23; .13
FEF$_{75-85}$ (1./sec.)	1.26; 1.36	1.11; 1.13	1.33; 1.82	$\underline{p}$=.19; .08
percent predicted	91.9; 98.1	79.6; 81.6	1.40; 1.78	$\underline{p}$=.16; .08
D$_{CO}$ (ml/min/mm Hg)	12.6	13.0	0.52	n.s.s.
percent predicted	83.7	86.4	0.51	n.s.s.

n.s.s. = Not statistically significant.

*The difference between the mean age recorded here and elsewhere in the report is a function of the fact that the pulmonary tests were the last tests run in the battery.

†Before bronchodilator.

††After bronchodilator.

Table 92

Intergroup Comparison Nutrient Intake; Above and Below 2/3 of Recommended Allowances

Nutrient		Stable	Smokers Street	Total	Controls	Totals
Calories:	above	9	5	14	18	32
	below	14	13	27	23	50
						(82)
Protein:	above	22	15	37	36	73
	below	1	3	4	5	9
						(82)
Retinol:	above	10	3	13	10	23
	below	13	15	28	31	59
						(82)
Iron:	above	21	16	37	39	76
	below	1	2	3	2	5
						(81)
Fat:	above	3	1	4	2	6
	below	20	17	37	38	75
						(81)
Calcium:	above	19	17	36	32	68
	below	4	1	5	9	14
						(82)
B_1:	above	21	13	34	37	71
	below	2	5	7	4	11
						(82)
B_2:	above	22	13	35	29	64
	below	1	5	6	12	18
						(82)
Niacin:	above	15	10	25	24	49
	below	8	8	16	17	33
						(82)
Vitamin C:	above	18	12	30	27	57
	below	4	6	10	14	24
						(81)

Table 93

Sixteen Personality Factors Test:
Primary Factors

Factors	Low Sten Score Description (1-3)	High Sten Score Description (8-10)
A	Reserved, detached, critical, aloof, stiff (Sizothymia)	Outgoing, warmhearted, easygoing, participating (Affectothymia)
B	Dull Low intelligence (Crystallized, power measure)	Bright High Intelligence (Crystallized, power measure)
C	Affected by feelings, emotionally less stable, easily upset, changeable (Lower ego strength)	Emotionally stable, mature, faces reality, calm (Higher ego strength)
E	Humble, mild, easily led, docile, accommodating (Submissiveness)	Assertive, aggressive, competitive, stubborn (Dominance)
F	Sober, taciturn, serious (Desurgency)	Happy-go-lucky, gay, enthusiastic (Surgency)
G	Expedient, disregards rules (Weaker superego strength)	Conscientious, persistent, moralistic, staid (Stronger superego strength)
H	Shy, timid, threat-sensitive (Threctia)	Venturesome, uninhibited, socially overprotected (Parmia)
I	Tough-minded, self-reliant, realistic (Harria)	Tender-minded, sensitive, clinging, overprotected (Premsia)
L	Trusting, accepting conditions (Alaxia)	Suspicious, hard to fool (Protension)
M	Practical, "down-to-earth" concerns (Praxernia)	Imaginative, bohemian, absentminded (Autia)
N	Forthright, unpretentious, genuine but socially clumsy (Artlessness)	Astute, polished, socially aware (Shrewdness)
O	Self-assured, placid, secure, complacent, serene (Untroubled adequacy)	Apprehensive, self-reproaching, insecure, worrying, troubled (Guilt-proneness)
Q_1	Conservative, respecting traditional ideas (Conservativism of temperament)	Experimenting, liberal, freethinking (Radicalism)
Q_2	Group-dependent, a "joiner" and sound follower (Group Adherence)	Self-sufficient, resourceful, prefers own decisions (Self-sufficiency)
Q_3	Undisciplined self-conflict, lax, follows own urges, careless of social rules (Low self-sentiment integration)	Controlled, exacting willpower, socially precise, compulsive, following self-image (High strength-of-self sentiment)
Q_4	Relaxed, tranquil, unfrustrated, composed (Low ergic tension)	Tense, frustrated, driven, overwrought (High ergic tension)

Table 94

Means, Standard Deviations, and Tests of Significance for
Neuropsychological Battery for User (U)
and Non-user (N) Groups

		Mean	SD	Range	t-value	prob.< t
Age	U	30.24	7.30	19-47		
	N	30.61	7.26	18-50		
Logical Memory Immediate	U	9.29	3.90	3-18	.53	.60
	N	9.66	3.61	4-17		
Logical Memory Delayed	U	7.38	3.65	1-15	.32	.75
	N	7.56	3.47	0-14		
Finger Oscillation Right Hand	U	45.54	8.14	26-60	.32	.75
	N	46.02	5.72	29-58		
Finger Oscillation Left Hand	U	43.54	6.50	29-54	.80	.43
	N	42.39	5.83	32-58		
Tactual Performance (minutes)	U	17'03"	5'01"	7'13"-30'	.66	.51
	N	17'45"	6'13"	8'36"-30'		
Tactual Performance (total errors)	U	1.24	2.79	0-11	.61	.55
	N	0.93	2.45	0-10		
Digit Span	U	8.46	1.35	6-11	.39	.70
	N	8.59	1.41	5-12		
Word Learning (errors)	U	25.80	11.79	3-48	.77	.45
	N	24.00	10.16	3-42		
Delayed Recall (errors)	U	9.56	6.79	0-29	1.48	.15
	N	7.63	5.03	0-25		
Facial Recognition Test	U	7.90	1.56	4-11	.34	.74
	N	8.00	1.16	5-10		
Finger Localization (total errors)	U	6.10	3.35	0-16	.68	.50
	N	5.59	3.53	1-16		
Benton Visual Retention	U	5.70	2.26	1-10	.12	.91
	N	5.66	1.93	0-9		
Rey-Davis	U	7.17	3.69	0-17	1.75	.09
	N	5.76	3.10	0-16		
WAIS Verbal IQ	U	111.07	10.04	85-139	.58	.57
	N	109.98	9.54	88-136		
WAIS Performance IQ	U	106.59	7.68	90-117	.28	.78
	N	107.17	11.57	84-132		
WAIS Full Scale IQ	U	109.22	8.09	88-124	.05	.98
	N	109.12	9.89	92-133		

Table 95

Means, Standard Deviations and Tests of Significance
for Williams Memory Battery for User (U)
and Nonuser (N) Groups

	Means	SD	Range	t value	prob.< t
Word Learning	U 25.80	11.79	3-48	0.77	0.14
	N 24.00	10.16	3-42		
Delayed Recall	U 9.56	6.97	0-29	1.48	0.15
	N 7.63	5.03	0-25		
Rey-Davis	U 7.17	3.69	0-17	1.75	0.09
	N 5.76	3.10	0-16		
Digit Span	U 8.46	1.35	6-11	0.39	0.70
	N 8.59	1.41	5-12		

Table 96

Means, Standard Deviations, and Tests of Significance
for Tactual Performance Subtests for User (U)
and Nonuser (N) Groups

	Mean	SD	Range	t value	prob.< t
RH time (min.)	U 9'48"	3'20"	3'11"-15'	.15	.88
	N 10'04"	3'12"	5'16"-15'		
RH errors	U 0.83	1.91	0.7	.24	.81
	N 0.73	1.88	0.8		
LH time (min.)	U 7'06"	2'37"	3'07"-15'	.35	.73
	N 7'14"	3'13"	3'20"-15'		
LH errors	U 0.26	1.11	0-6	.36	.72
	N 0.20	0.72	0-3		
Total time (min.)	U 17'03"	5'01"	7'13"-30'	.66	.51
	N 17'45"	6'13"	8'36"-30'		
Total errors	U 1.24	2.79	0-11	.61	.55
	N 0.93	2.46	0-10		

t-values represent test between E and C groups only.

E group (N=41); and C group (N=41); S group (N=86).

Table 97

Means, Standard Deviations, and Tests of Significance
for Finger Localization Subtests for User (U) and
Nonuser (N) Groups

	Mean	SD	Range	t value	prob. t
Part I					
LH errors	U 0.02	0.16	0-1	1.14	0.26
	N 0.10	0.37	0-2		
RH errors	U 0.29	0.75	0-4	1.65	0.11
	N 0.07	0.35	0-2		
Bilateral LH errors	U 0.93	1.06	0-2	0.10	0.92
	N 0.90	1.22	0-4		
Bilateral RH errors	U 1.00	0.95	0-3	0.22	0.83
	N 0.95	1.07	0-4		
Total Part I errors	U 2.24	2.06	0-9	0.49	0.63
	N 2.02	2.02	0-7		
Part II					
LH errors	U 0.12	0.40	0-2	0.24	0.81
	N 0.15	0.57	0-3		
RH errors	U 0.34	0.53	0-2	0.78	0.44
	N 0.46	0.78	0-3		
Total Part II errors	U 0.46	0.74	0-3	0.71	0.48
	N 0.61	1.09	0-5		
Part III					
LH errors	U 1.37	1.22	0-5	0.11	0.92
	N 1.39	1.14	0-4		
RH errors	U 1.85	1.48	0-5	0.79	0.44
	N 1.61	1.11	0-4		
Total Part III errors	U 3.22	2.32	0-10	0.46	0.65
	N 3.00	1.87	0-7		
Grand Totals; Parts I, II, and III					
Total RH errors	U 3.68	2.23	0-11	1.29	0.20
	N 3.05	2.02	0-8		
Total LH errors	U 2.41	1.51	0-6	0.34	0.74
	N 2.54	2.06	0-8		
Total RH and LH errors	U 6.10	3.35	0-16	0.68	0.50
	N 5.58	3.53	1-16		

Table 98

Means, Standard Deviations, and Tests of Significance for
WAIS Subtests and Scales for User (U) and
Nonuser (N) Groups

	Mean	SD	Range	t value	prob. > t
Information	U 12.34 N 11.76	2.58 2.56	8–17 8–17	1.22	0.23
Comprehension	U 11.88 N 12.22	2.70 2.10	2–16 8–17	0.74	0.46
Arithmetic	U 12.20 N 12.00	1.91 2.42	9–15 6–18	0.39	0.70
Similarities	U 12.05 N 11.32	2.22 2.62	4–16	1.44	0.16
Digit Span	U 10.89 N 11.46	2.12 2.68	7–16 6–18	1.08	0.29
Vocabulary	U 12.34 N 11.83	2.60 2.65	7–19 7–17	0.95	0.35
Digit Symbol	U 9.66 N 9.78	2.08 1.99	7–17 6–15	0.32	0.75
Picture Completion	U 11.32 N 10.93	2.83 4.03	6–18	0.51	0.61
Block Design	U 10.21 N 10.46	2.36 2.46	4–15 6–14	0.49	0.63
Picture Arrangement	U 11.49 N 11.37	2.89 3.60	5–17 1–19	0.21	0.83
Object Assembly	U 11.90 N 12.15	1.32 1.74	10–16 7–16	0.73	0.47
Verbal IQ	U 111.07 N 109.98	10.64 9.54	85–139 88–136	0.58	0.57
Performance IQ	U 106.59 N 107.17	7.68 11.57	90–117 84–132	0.28	0.78
Full Scale IQ	U 109.22 N 109.12	8.09 9.89	88–124 92–133	0.05	0.96

Table 99

Means, Standard Deviations, and Tests of Significance
for 16 PF Personality Test for User (U) and
Nonuser (N) Groups

Factor	Mean	SD	Range	t value	prob. < t
A	U 7.10	1.73	4–10	0.83	0.41
	N 7.41	1.75	4–10		
B	U 6.00	1.40	3–10	0.13	0.90
	N 6.05	1.69			
C	U 7.00	1.98	2–10	0.28	0.78
	N 7.10	1.61	2–10		
D	U 6.41	1.58	4–10	0.41	0.68
	N 6.53	1.40	4–10		
F	U 5.90	1.18	4–10	0.73	0.47
	N 6.10	1.70			
G	U 6.76	1.98	1–9	0.81	0.42
	N 7.07	1.71	4–10		
H	U 6.39	1.86	2–9	0.83	0.41
	N 6.02	1.89	3–10		
I	U 6.51	2.01	2–10	0.00	1.00
	N 6.51	1.73	2–10		
L	U 7.20	1.71	4–10	0.08	0.94
	N 7.17	1.73			
M	U 5.88	2.29	1–10	0.53	0.60
	N 6.15	2.13	3–10		
N	U 4.98	2.22	1–9	0.33	0.75
	N 5.12	2.02	1–9		
O	U 5.22	2.01	1–10	0.44	0.67
	N 5.02	1.82	1–8		
Q_1	U 8.88	1.62	4–10	2.35	0.02
	N 8.20	1.91	2–10		
Q_2	U 6.90	2.22	2–10	0.81	0.42
	N 6.54	2.13	2–10		
Q_3	U 6.63	1.88	1–9	0.12	0.91
	N 6.68	1.60	3–9		
Q_4	U 4.85	1.61	2–9	0.07	0.92
	N 4.83	1.84	2–9		

Table 100

16 PF Second-Order Factors

Symbol	Technical Title	Popular Level
Q_I	Exvia vs. Invia	Extraversion vs. Introversion
Q_{II}	Adjustment vs. Anxiety	Low Anxiety vs. High Anxiety
Q_{III}	Pathemia vs. Cortertia	Sensitivity/Emotionalism vs. Tough Poise
Q_{IV}	Subduedness vs. Independence (Promethean Will)	Dependence vs. Independence
Q_V	Discreetness	---
Q_{VI}	Prodigal Subjectivity	---
Q_{VII}	Intelligence (same as Factor B)	---
Q_{VIII}	Superego Strength (similar to Factor 6)	---

Table 101

Means, Standard Deviations, and Tests of Significance
for 16 PF Second-Order Factors for User
(U) and Nonuser (N) Groups

Factor	Mean	SD	Range	t value	prob. $< t$
Q_I	U 6.07	1.29	3.3–9.4	0.31	0.76
	N 6.17	1.48	3.6–10.0		
Q_{II}	U 4.73	1.39	1.9–8.7	0.17	0.87
	N 4.69	1.42	1.8–7.2		
Q_{III}	U 3.92	1.78	1.0–7.9	0.52	0.60
	N 3.74	1.67	1.0–7.7		
Q_{IV}	U 7.53	1.18	3.8–9.7	0.71	0.48
	N 7.35	1.10	5.4–9.9		
Q_V	U 4.35	1.41	1.0–7.4	0.61	0.55
	N 4.19	1.19	1.0–6.5		
Q_{VI}	U 6.62	1.41	3.2–8.9	0.36	0.72
	N 6.72	1.19	4.8–9.6		
Q_{VII}	U 6.00	1.40	3.0–10.0	0.13	0.90
	N 6.05	1.69	1.0–9.0		
Q_{VIII}	U 6.77	1.34	4.2–10.0	1.32	0.20
	N 6.38	1.32	3.4–9.5		

Table 102

Univariate Psychological Analyses X User Group

Groups	Neuropsychological			Intelligence (WAIS)			16 PF (Personality)		
	Variable	Prob.> t	Direction	Variable	Prob.> t	Direction	Variable	Prob.> t	Direction
High User (H) vs. Control (C) $N_H=N_C=20$	Left-Hand Tapping	.04	H faster	(none)			(none)		
Low User (L) vs. Control (C) $N_H=N_C=20$	(none)			Information	.05	L higher	Q_I (Radi-calism)	.03	L More Radical
				Object Assembly	.04	C higher			
High User (H) vs. Low User (L) $N_H=N_L=20$	(none)			(none)			(none)		

Table 103

Univariate Psychological Analyses X Typology Groups

Groups	Neuropsychological			Intelligence (WAIS)			16 PF (Personality)		
	Variable	Prob.> t	Direction	Variable	Prob.> t	Direction	Variable	Prob.> t	Direction
Street Mover (SM) vs. Control (C) $N_{SM} = N_C = 18$	(none)			(none)			(none)		
Stable (S) vs. Control (C) $N_S = N_C = 23$	(none)			(none)			H (Venturesomeness)	.02	S More Venturesome
							L (Suspiciousness)	.03	S More Suspicious
							Q (Radicalism)	.02	S More Radical
							Q_{VIII} Conscientiousness	.02	S More Conscientious
Street Mover vs. Stable (S) $N_{SM} = 18$ $N_S = 23$	Form Board (Total Time)	.05	S Slower	Picture Completion	.002	S lower	H (Venturesomeness)	.01	SM More Venturesome
	Finger Localization (Total errors)	.06	S more errors	Performance IQ	.002	S lower			

References

Academia de Geografía e Historia de Costa Rica
1952   Procedimientos. Año IV, 11:3–12.

Agnew, H. W. Jr.; Webb, W. B.; and Williams, R. L.
1966   The First Night Effect: An EEG Study of Sleep. *Psychophysiology* 2: 263–266.

Aranugo, Alcen Maynard
1959   *Medicina rústica, Brasiliana*. Volume 300. São Paulo: Companhia Editora Nacional.

Ardila Rodríguez, Francisco
1965   Aspectos médico-legales y médico-sociales de la marihuana. Tesis doctoral. Universidad de Madrid, Facultad de Medicina.

Ayala, Manuel Josef de
1930   *Mobiliario hispano-americano del siglo XVI. Colección de documentos inéditos para la historia de Ibero-América.* Tomo II. Madrid: Cia Ibero-Americana de Publicaciones, S.A.

Bakan, D.
1971   The test of significance in psychological research. In B. Lieberman, ed., *Contemporary problems in statistics*. New York: Oxford University Press. Pp. 147–162.

Baskett, G. D., and Nysewander, R. W.
1973   Drug use correlates. *Psychology: A Journal of Human Behavior* 10 (no. 1): 54–66.

Beaubrun, M. H., and Knight, F.
1973   Psychiatric assessment of 30 chronic users of cannabis and 30 matched controls. *American Journal of Psychiatry* 130: 309–311.

Benton, A. L.
1963   *The revised visual retention test*. 3d ed. New York: Psychological Corporation.
1959   *Right-left discrimination and finger localization: Development and pathology.* New York: Hoeber.
1955   Development of finger localization capacity in school children. *Child Development* 26: 225–230.

Bhattarcherjee, P., and Eakins, K.
1975   Inhibition of the ocular effects of sodium arachidonate. *Prostaglandins* 9: 175.

Bieger, D., and Hockman, C.
1973   Differential effects produced by Delta 1 Tetrahydrocannabinol on lateral geniculate neurons. *Neuropharmacology* 12: 269–273.

Blalock, Hubert M., Jr.
  1972   *Social statistics*. New York: McGraw-Hill.
Blum, R. H., and associates
  1970   *Society and drugs*. San Francisco: Jossey-Bass Inc. Publishers.
Bott, Elizabeth
  1955   Urban families: Conjugal roles and social networks. *Human Relations* 8 (no. 4): 345–384.
Boulougouris, J. C.; Liakos, A.; and Stefanis, C.
  1976   Social traits of heavy hashish users and matched controls. In R. L. Dornbush, A. M. Freedman, and M. Fink, eds., *Chronic cannabis use. Annals of the New York Academy of Sciences* 282: 17–23.
Bowman, Marilyn, and Pihl, Robert O.
  1973   Cannabis: Psychological effects of chronic heavy use. *Psychopharmacologia* 29: 159–170.
Brecher, E.
  1974   Marihuana: The health questions. *Consumer Reports*, pp. 143–149.
Campbell, A.; Evans, M.; and Thompson, J.
  1971   Cerebral atrophy in young cannabis smokers. *Lancet* 1: 1219–1224.
Cappa, Ricardo
  1890   Estudios críticos acerca de la dominación española en América. Parte Tercera. *Industria agrícola-pecuaria llevada a América por los españoles*. Gregorio del Amo, ed. Madrid: Librería Católica de Gregorio del Amo.
Cattell, R.; Eber, H.; and Tatsuoka, M.
  1970   *Handbook for the 16 P.F.* Champaign, Illinois: Institute for Personality and Ability Testing.
Chopra, G. D., and Smith, J. W.
  1974   Psychotic reactions following cannabis use in East Indians. *Archives of General Psychiatry* 30: 24–247
Chopra, I. C., and Chopra, R. N.
  1957   The use of the cannabis drugs in India. *Bulletin on Narcotics,* January–March, pp. 4–29.
Clark, S. C.
  1975   Marihuana and the cardiovascular system. *Pharmacology, Biochemistry and Behavior* 3: 299–306.
Cobo, Bernabé
  1891   *Historia del Nuevo Mundo*. Publicada por primera vez con notas y otras ilustraciones de D. Marcos Jiménez de la Espada. Sevilla: Sociedad de Bibliófilos Andaluces.
Coggins, W. J., and Lipman, J.
  1972   Use of illegal drugs in college. *Journal of Florida Medical Association*, pp. 29–33.
Cox, C. E.; Fitzgerald, C.; and King, R.
  1975   A preliminary report on the supraoptic nucleus and control of intraocular pressure. *Invest. Ophthal.* 14: 26–28.
Dornbush, R. L., and Kokkevi, A.
  1976   Acute effects of cannabis on cognitive, perceptual, and motor performance in chronic hashish users. In R. L. Dornbush, A. M. Freedman, and M. Fink, eds., *Chronic cannabis use. Annals of the New York Academy of Sciences,* 282: 313–322.
Duke-Elder, S.
  1964   *Parsons's disease of the eye*. Boston: Little-Brown. Pp. 230–233.
  1966   *System of ophthalmology*. Volume 19. St. Louis, Mo.: Mosby. Pp. 133–166.

Eakins, K.
1970   Increased intraocular pressure produced by prostaglandins E_1 and E_2 in the cat eye. *Exp. Eye Res.* 10: 87.
Eakins, K.; Whitelocke, R.; and Bennett, A.
1972   Prostaglandin-like activity in ocular inflammation. *British Medical Journal*, pp. 3–452.
El Diario de Costa Rica. Daily newspaper. San José, Costa Rica.
El Excelsior. Daily newspaper. San José, Costa Rica.
Fink, M.
1976   Effects of acute and chronic inhalation of hashish, marihuana, and Δ-9-Tetrahydrocannabinol on brain electrical activity in man: Evidence for tissue tolerances. In R. L. Dornbush, A. M. Freedman, and M. Fink, eds., *Chronic cannabis use. Annals of the New York Academy of Sciences* 282: 387–398.
Fisher, G.
1972/
1973   Personality characteristics ascribed to marihuana users by users and non-users. *Behavioral Neuropsychiatry* 4 (nos. 9–10): 5–12.
Fletcher, J. M., and Satz, P.
1977   A methodological commentary on the Egyptian study of chronic hashish use. *Bulletin on Narcotics* 29.
Fletcher, J.; Todd, J.; and Satz, P.
1975   Culture-fairness of three intelligence tests and a short-form procedure. *Psychological Reports* 37: 1255–1262.
Flom, M.; Adams, A.; and Jones, R.
1975   Marijuana smoking and reduced pressure in human eyes: Drug actions or epiphenomena. *Invest. Ophthal.* 14: 52–55.
Flores, M.; Mencu, T.; and Lara, M. Y.
1972   *Valor nutritivo de los alimentos para Centro América y Panamá.* Guatemala: INCAP.
Fonseca-Tortós, Eugenio; Adis-Castro, Gonzalo; Amador-Sanchez, Francisco; Hernández-Ureña, Rafael; and Thomas-Claudet, Pierre.
1970   *Algunos aspectos scoiográficos del área metropolitana de San José Costa Rica.* San José: Centro de Estudios Sociales y de Población, Universidad de Costa Rica.
Goebel, R., and Satz, P.
1975   Profile analysis and the abbreviated Wechsler adult intelligence scale: A multivariate approach. *Journal of Consulting and Clinical Psychology* 43: 780–785.
Goode, E.
1970   *The marijuana smokers.* New York: Basic Books, Inc.
Grant, I.; Rockford, J.; Fleming, T.; and Stunkard, A.
1973   A neuropsychological assessment of the effects of moderate marihuana use. *Journal of Nervous and Mental Disorders* 156: 278–280.
Green, K., and Bowman, D.
1974   Effect of marijuana derivatives on intraocular pressure in rabbits. Paper Presented at the International Conference on Pharmacology of Cannabis. Savannah, Georgia.
Green, K., and Pederson, J.
1973   Effect of Delta-1-Tetrahydrocannabinol on aqueous dynamics and ciliary body permeability in the rabbit. *Exp. Eye Research* 15: 499–507.
Halikas, J. A.
1974   Marihuana use and psychiatric illness. In L. Miller, ed., *Marihuana: Effects on human behavior.* New York: Academic Press. Pp. 265–302.

Halikas, J. A.; Goodwin, D. W.; and Guze, S. B.
  1971   Marihuana effects—A survey of regular users. *Journal of the American Medical Association* 217: 692–694.
Haring, Clarence Henry
  1939   *El comercio y la navegación entre España y las Indias en época de los Hapsburgos.* Paris: Brujas, Desclée de Brouwer.
Hepler, R.; Frank, I.; and Ungerleider, J.
  1972   Pupillary constriction after marijuana smoking. *American Journal of Ophthalmology* 74: 1185–1190.
Hochman, J. S., and Brill, N. Q.
  1973   Chronic marihuana use and psycho-social adaptation. *American Journal of Psychiatry* 130: 132–140.
Hollister, L.
  1971   Marihuana in man: Three years later. *Science* 172: 21–29.
Hummel, T., and Sligo, J.
  1971   Empirical comparisons of univariate and multivariate analysis of variance. *Psychological Bulletin* 76: 49–57.
Instituto de Nutrición de Centroamérica y Panamá
  1969   *Evaluación nutricional de la población de Centroamérica y Panamá: Costa Rica.* Guatemala: INCAP.
Jessor, R.
  1976   Predicting time of onset of marihuana use: A developmental study of high school youth. *Journal of Consulting and Clinical Psychology* 44: 125–134.
Jessor, R.; Jessor, S.L.; and Finney, J.
  1973   A social psychology of marihuana use: Longitudinal studies of high school and college youth. *Journal of Personality and Social Psychology* 26 (no. 1): 1–15.
Jiménez, Otón
  1971   Tonduzia. *Separata de Revista de Agricultura.* Mayo-Agosto, nos. 5, 6, 7, 8.
Johnston, L.
  1973   *Drugs and American youth.* Ann Arbor: University of Michigan, Institute for Social Research.
Kandel, Denise B.; Kessler, Ronald C.; Margulies, Rebecca Z.
  1978   Antecedents of adolescent initiation into stages of drug use: A developmental analysis. In D. B. Kandel, ed., *Longitudinal Research on Drug Use.* New York: John Wiley and Sons. Pp. 73–99.
Karniol, I. G., et al.
  1974   Cannabidiol interferes with the effects of Delta-9-Tetrahydrocannabinol in man. *European Journal of Pharmacology* 28: 172–177.
Kay, D. C.
  1973   Sleep and some psychoactive drugs. *Psychosomatics* 9: 108–118.
Knights, R.
  1975   Psychological test results. In V. Rubin and L. Comitas, eds., *Ganja in Jamaica.* The Hague: Mouton. Pp. 111–120.
Kolansky, A., and Moore, W.
  1972   Toxic effects of chronic marihuana use. *Journal of the American Medical Association* 222: 35–37.
  1971   Effects of marihuana use on adolescent young adults. *Journal of the American Medical Association* 216: 486–492.
Kolodny, R. C.; Masters, W. H.; Kilodner, R. M.; and Toro, G.
  1974   Depression of plasma testosterone levels after chronic intensive marihuana use. *The New England Journal of Medicine* 290: 872–874.

Krug, S., and Henry, T.
1974   Personality, motivation, and adolescent drug use patterns. *Journal of Counseling Psychology* 21: 440–445.
La Nación. Daily newspaper. San José, Costa Rica.
La Prensa Libre. Daily newspaper. San José, Costa Rica.
La República. Daily newspaper. San José, Costa Rica.
Leuchtenberger, C.; Leuchtenberger, R.; and Ritter, U.
1973   Effects of marihuana and tobacco smoke on DNA and chromosomal complement in human lung explants. *Nature* 242: 403–404.
Levander, S.; Binder, J.; Agurell, S.; Rader-Bartfai, A.; Gustafonen, B.; Leander, K.; Kindgren, J. E.; Ohloson, A.; and Tobisson, B.
1974   Pharmacokinetics of Delta-8-THC in man after smoking: Relations to physiological and psychological effects. Abstract in *International conference on the pharmacology of cannabis*. Savannah, Georgia.
Loevinger, Jane
1970   *Measuring ego development*. San Francisco: Jossey-Bass.
Luria, A.
1973   *The working brain*. New York: Academic Press.
McGlothlin, William H.
1968   The marihuana problem: An overview. *American Journal of Psychiatry* 125 (no. 3): 126–134.
Macrie, F., and Cevarino, S.
1975   Ciliary ganglion stimulation. I. Effects on aqueous humor inflow and outflow. *Invet. Ophthal.* 14: 28–33.
Mangin, William, ed.
1970   *Peasants in cities: Readings in the anthropology of urbanization*. Boston: Houghton-Mifflin.
Manno, J.; Kiplinger, G.; Scholz, N.; and Forney, R.
1971   The influence of alcohol and marihuana on motor and mental performance. *Clinical Pharmacology and Therapeutics* 12: 202–211.
Manno, J. E.; Kiplinger, G. F.; Haine, S. E.; Bennett, I. F.; and Forney, R. B.
1970   Comparative effects of smoking marijuana or placebo on human motor and mental performance. *Pharmacology and Therapeutics* 11: 808–815.
Matarazzo, J.
1973   *Weschler's measurement and appraisal of adult intelligence*. 5th ed. Baltimore: Williams and Wilkins.
Maugh, T. H.
1974   Marihuana: The grass may no longer be greener. *Science* 185: 683–685.
Mellinger, G. D.; Somers, R. H.; Davison, S. T.; and Manheimer, D. J.
1976   The amotivational syndrome and the college student. In R. L. Dornbush, A. M. Freedman, and M. Fink, eds., *Chronic cannabis use. Annals of the New York Academy of Sciences* 282: 37–55.
Mendelson, J. H.; Kuehnle, J.; Ellingboe, J.; and Babor, T. F.
1974   Plasma testosterone levels before, during and after chronic marihuana smoking. *New England Journal of Medicine* 291: 1051–1055.
Mendelson, J. H.; Rossi, A. M.; and Meyer, R. E.
1974   *The use of marihuana: A psychological and physiological inquiry*. New York: Plenum Press.
Milner, B.
1968   Visual recognition and recall after right temporal lobe excision in man. *Neuropsychologia* 6: 191–209.

Ministerio de Obras Públicas y Transportes
1973   *Características socio-económicas del área de estudio en 1973.* Informe técnico de trabajo No. 11. San José, Costa Rica.
Ministerio de Salubridad y Protección Social
1974   *Ley general de salud.* San José, Costa Rica: Imprenta Nacional.
1950   *Código sanitario.* San José, Costa Rica: Imprenta Nacional.
Mitchell, J. Clyde, ed.
1969   *Social networks in urban situations.* Manchester: Manchester University Press.
Mogel, S., and Satz, P.
1963   Abbreviation of the WAIS for clinical use: An attempt at validation. *Journal of Clinical Psychology* 19: 289–300.
Morales de Flores, Irma, and Chassoul Monge, Charles
1972   *Diagnóstico de alcoholismo: Conclusiones* (Encuesta Nacional de hábitos de ingestión de alcohol). San José, Costa Rica: Comisión sobre alcoholismo.
Morris, J. F.; Koski, A.; and Breese, J. D.
1975   Normal values and evaluation of forced end-expiratory flow. *Am. Rev. Resp. Dis.* 111: 755–762.
Nahas, G., et al.
1974   Inhibition of cellular mediated immunity in marihuana smokers. *Science* 183: 419.
National Institute on Drug Abuse (NIDA)
1974   *Marihuana and health: Fourth annual report to the United States Congress from the Secretary of Health, Education and Welfare.* Washington, D.C.: United States Government Printing Office.
Negrete, J. C.
1973   Psychological adverse effects of cannabis smoking: A tentative classification. *Canadian Medical Association Journal* 108: 195–196.
Neufeld, A.; Jampol, L.; and Sears, M.
1972   Aspirin prevents the disruption of the blood aqueous barrier in the rabbit eye. *Nature* 238: 158.
Neufeld, A., and Sears, M.
1973   Prostaglandin and eye. *Prostaglandin* 4: 157.
Partridge, William L.
1974   Exchange relationships in a community on the north coast of Colombia with special reference to cannabis. Ph.D. dissertation. Gainesville, Florida: University of Florida.
Patiño, Victor Manuel
1969   *Plantas cultivadas y animales domésticos en América Equinoccial: Plantas introducidas.* Tomo IV. Cali, Colombia: Imprenta Departamental.
Pérez Cabrera, Ricardo
1938   *Sinopsis de medicina vegetal.* San José, Costa Rica: Imprenta Borrase Hnos.
Raven, J.
1965   *Guide to the Standard Progressive Matrices, Sets A, B, C, D, and E.* London: H. K. Lewis.
Rechtschaffen, A., and Verdone, P.
1964   Amount of dreaming: Effect of incentive adaptation to laboratory, and individual differences. *Percept. Mot. Skills* 19: 947–958.
Reitan, R. M.
1969   *Manual for administration of neuropsychological test batteries for adults and children.* Privately published by the author. Indiana Press.
1964   *Manual for administration of neuropsychological test batteries for adults and children.* Neuropsychological laboratory. Indianapolis: Indiana University Medical Center.

Rodríguez, Cecilia, and Terán, Elena
1967   Aspectos históricos y urbanos del area metropolitana de San José de Costa Rica. Tesis presentada en la Facultad de Ciencias y Letras de la Universidad de Costa Rica para obtener el grado de licenciatura en Geografía, San José, Costa Rica.
Rubin, V., and Comitas, L., eds.
1975   *Ganja in Jamaica*. The Hague: Mouton
Ruiz, Hipólito
1952   *Relación histórica del viage, que hizo a los Reynos del Perú y Chile el botánico don . . . en el año 1777 hasta el de 1778, en cuya época regresó a Madrid*. Segunda edición, enmendada y completada en todo lo que le faltaba, según la copia definitiva inédita, del Manuscrito de D. Hipólito, hallada y copiada en el Departamento Botánico (Historia Natural) del Museo Británico, por el Dr. Jaime Jaramillo Arango. Publicado por la Real Academia de Ciencias Exactas, Físicas y Naturales de Madrid. Madrid: Talleres Gráficos de Cándido Bermejo.
Sáenz Maroto, Alberto
1970   *Historia agrícola de Costa Rica*. Publicaciones de la Universidad de Costa Rica. Serie Agronomía No. 12. San José: Ciudad Universitaria "Rodrigo Facio."
Satz, P.; Achenback, K.; and Fennell, E.
1967   Correlations between assessed manual laterality and predicted speech laterality in a normal population. *Neuropsychologia* 5: 295–310.
Satz, P., and Mogel, S.
1962   An abbreviation of the WAIS for clinical use. *Journal of Clinical Psychology* 18: 77–79.
Secretaría de Salubridad Pública y Protección Social
1930   *Ley sobre drogas estupefacientes*. San José, Costa Rica: Imprenta Nacional.
1930   *Campaña contra las drogas estupefacientes*. (Leyes, decretos reglamentarios y anexos.) San José, Costa Rica: Imprenta Nacional.
Serrano y Sanz, Manuel, ed.
1908   *Relaciones históricas y geográficas de América Central. Colección de libros y documentos referentes a la historia de América*. Tomo VIII. Madrid: Librería General de Victoriano Suárez, Oficina tipográfica de Idamor Moreno.
Shafer, Raymond P., et al.
1972   *Marihuana—A signal of misunderstanding. The Official Report of the National Commission on Marihuana and Drug Abuse*. New York: New American Library, Inc.
Shapiro, D.
1974   The ocular manifestations of cannabinols. *Ophthalmologia* 168: 366–368.
Simón, Pedro
1953   *Noticias historiales de las conquistas de Tierra Firme en las Indias Occidentales*. Por F . . . . del orden de San Francisco del Nuevo Reino de Granada. Tomo IV. Tercera Parte. 1927 edición. Ed. dirigida por Manuel José Forero. Bogotá: Editorial Kelly.
Smith, David E., ed.
1970   *The new social drug: Cultural, medical and legal perspectives on marihuana*. Englewood Cliffs, New Jersey: Prentice-Hall, Inc.
Smith, G.
1974   Drugs and personality. NIDA Grant DA 00065, Progress quoted in National Institute on Drug Abuse 1974: 19.
Sotela, Alfredo, and Morales de Flores, Irma
1972   *Problemas de dependencia de alcohol y drogas en Costa Rica*. San José: Comisión sobre Alcoholismo.

Souief, M. I.
1976   Differential association between chronic cannabis use and brain function deficits. In R. L. Dornbush, A. M. Freedman, and M. Fink, eds., *Chronic cannabis use. Annals of the New York Academy of Sciences* 34: 323–343.
1971   The use of cannabis in Egypt: A behavioral study. Bulletin on Narcotics 22 (no. 4): 17–28.
Stefanis, C.; Dornbush, R. L.; and Fink, M.
1977   *Hashish: A study of long-term use.* New York: Raven Press.
Stefanis, C.; Liakos, A.; and Boulougouris, J. C.
1976   Incidence of mental illness in hashish users and controls. In R. L. Dornbush, A. M. Freedman, and M. Fink, eds., *Chronic cannabis use. Annals of the New York Academy of Sciences* 282: 58–63.
Stenchever, M. A., et al.
1974   Chromosome breakage in users of marihuana. *American Journal of Obstetrics and Gynecology.* Pp. 112–113.
Stewart, Watt
1964   *Keith and Costa Rica.* Albuquerque: University of New Mexico Press.
Stone, Samuel
1975   *La dinastía de los conquistadores: La crisis del Poder en la Costa Rica contemporánea.* San José, Costa Rica: Editorial Universitaria Centroamericana.
Tart, C. T., and Crawford, H. J.
1970   Marijuana intoxication: Reported effects on sleep. Abstract. *Psychophysiology* 7: 318.
Tarter, R. G.
1975   Psychological deficit in chronic alcoholics: A review. *International Journal of the Addictions* 10: 327–368.
Tashkin, D. P.; Shapiro, B. J.; Lee, Y. E.; and Harper, C. H.
1976   Subacute effects of heavy marihuana smoking on pulmonary function in healthy men. *New England Journal of Medicine* 294: 125–129.
Thomas, R., and Chester, G.
1973   The pharmacology of marihuana. *Med. J. Austral.* 2: 229–237.
Tinklenberg, J. R., and Darley, C. D.
1975   Psychological and cognitive effects of cannabis. In P. H. Connell and N. Dorn, eds., *Cannabis and man* 3: 45–65.
Valk, L.
1973   Hemp in connection with ophthalmology. *Netherl. Ophthal. Soc.* 167: 413–421.
Vázquez de Espinosa
1948   Compendio y descripción de las Indias Occidentales. Transcrito del manuscrito original por Charles Upson Clark. Vol. 108, Smithsonian Miscellaneous Collections. Washington, D.C.
Vegge, T.; Neufeld, A.; and Sears, M.
1975   Breakdown of blood aqueous barrier of ciliary processes of the rabbit eye after prostaglandin E_2. *Invest. Ophthal.* 14: 33–36.
Wagley, Charles, and Galvão, Eduardo
1949   *The Tenetehara Indians of Brazil.* New York: Columbia University Press.
Walsh, F., and Hoyt, W.
1969   *Clinical neuroophthalmology.* Baltimore: Williams and Wilkins. Pp. 414–465.
Walton, Robert P.
1938   *Marihuana: America's new drug problem.* New York: Lippincott.
Wechsler, D.
1965   A standardized memory scale for clinical use. *Journal of Psychology* 19: 87–95.

1968   *Escalas de inteligencia Wechsler para adultos.* Trans. R. F. Green and J. H. Martínez. New York: Psychological Corporation.
Williams, M.
1968   The measurement of memory in clinical practice. *British Journal of Social and Clinical Psychology* 7: 19–24.
Williams, R. L.; Karacan, I.; and Hursch, C. J.
1974   *The electroencephalogram (EEG) of human sleep: Clinical applications.* New York: John Wiley and Sons.
Zinberg, N. G.
1976   The war over marihuana. *Psychology Today* 10 (no. 7): 44–53.
Zucker-Franklin, O.
1974   Eosinophil function and disorders. *Advances in Internal Medicine* 19: 10–12.

Index

1 2 3 4 5 6 7 8 9 10 11 12 13   89 88 87 86 85 84 83 82 81 80

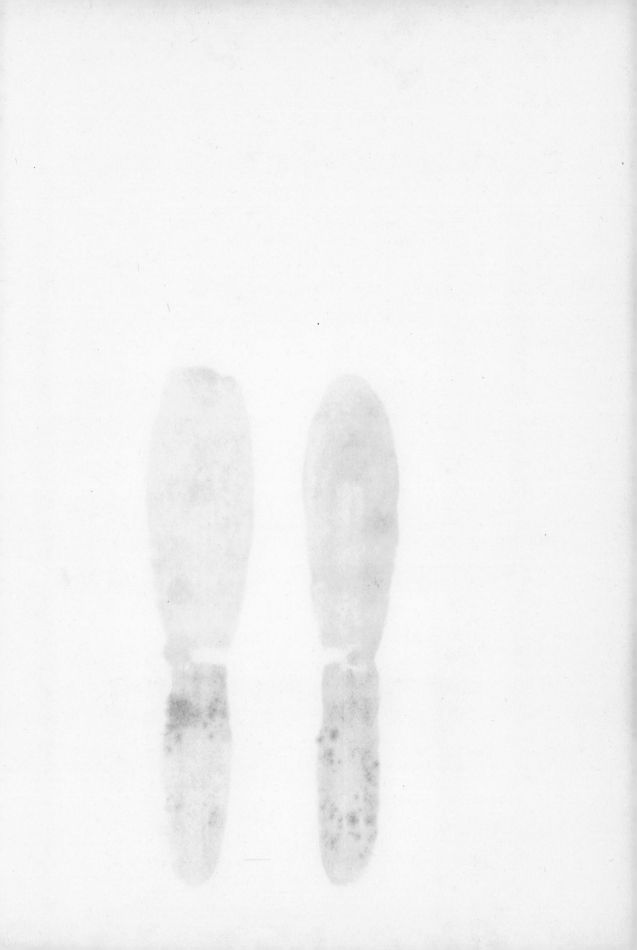